AF760797

Yokohama and the Silk Trade

New Studies in Modern Japan

Series Editors: Doug Slaymaker and William M. Tsutsui

New Studies in Modern Japan is a multidisciplinary series that consists primarily of original studies on a broad spectrum of topics dealing with Japan since the mid-nineteenth century. Additionally, the series aims to bring back into print classic works that shed new light on contemporary Japan. The series speaks to cultural studies (literature, translations, film), history, and social sciences audi-ences. We publish compelling works of scholarship, by both established and rising scholars in the field, on a broad arena of topics, in order to nuance our understandings of Japan and the Japanese.

Advisory Board

Michael Bourdaghs, University of Chicago
Rebecca Copeland, Washington University in St. Louis
Aaron Gerow, Yale University
Yoshikuni Igarashi, Vanderbilt University
Koichi Iwabuchi, Monash University
T. J. Pempel, University of California, Berkeley
Julia Adeney Thomas, University of Notre Dame
Dennis Washburn, Dartmouth College
Merry White, Boston University

Recent Titles in the Series

Japan's Multilayered Democracy, edited by Sigal Ben-Rafael Galanti, Nissim Otmazgin, and Alon Levkowitz

Resilient Borders and Cultural Diversity: Internationalism, Brand Nationalism, and Multiculturalism in Japan, by Koichi Iwabuchi

Traveling Texts and the Work of Afro-Japanese Cultural Production: Two Haiku and a Microphone, edited by William H. Bridges and Nina Cornyetz

Japan Viewed from Interdisciplinary Perspectives: History and Prospects, edited by Yoneyuki Sugita

Single Mothers in Contemporary Japan: Motherhood, Class, and Reproductive Practice, by Aya Ezawa

Creating Japan's Ground Self-Defense Force, 1945–2015: A Sword Well Made, by David Hunter-Chester

Rethinking Japan: The Politics of Contested Nationalism, by Arthur Stockwin and Kweku Ampiah

The Politics and Literature Debate in Postwar Japanese Criticism: 1945–52, edited by Atsuko Ueda, Michael K. Bourdaghs, Richi Sakakibara, and Hirokazu Toeda

Yokohama and the Silk Trade: How Eastern Japan Became the Primary Economic Region of Japan, 1843–1893, by Yasuhiro Makimura

Yokohama and the Silk Trade

How Eastern Japan Became the Primary Economic Region of Japan, 1843–1893

Yasuhiro Makimura

LEXINGTON BOOKS
Lanham • Boulder • New York • London

Published by Lexington Books
An imprint of The Rowman & Littlefield Publishing Group, Inc.
4501 Forbes Boulevard, Suite 200, Lanham, Maryland 20706
www.rowman.com

Unit A, Whitacre Mews, 26-34 Stannary Street, London SE11 4AB

Copyright © 2017 by Lexington Books

Studies of the Weatherhead East Asian Institute, Columbia University
The Studies of the Weatherhead East Asian Institute of Columbia University were inaugurated in 1962 to bring to a wider public the results of significant new research on modern and contemporary East Asia. http://www.columbia.edu/cu/weai/weatherhead-studies.html

All rights reserved. No part of this book may be reproduced in any form or by any electronic or mechanical means, including information storage and retrieval systems, without written permission from the publisher, except by a reviewer who may quote passages in a review.

British Library Cataloguing in Publication Information Available

Library of Congress Cataloging-in-Publication Data

Names: Makimura, Yasuhiro, 1971- author.
Title: Yokohama and the silk trade : how Eastern Japan became the primary economic region of Japan, 1843–1893 / Yasuhiro Makimura.
Description: Lanham, MD : Lexington Books, 2017] | Series: New studies in modern Japan | Includes bibliographical references and index.
Identifiers: LCCN 2017023874 (print) | LCCN 2017007450 (ebook) | ISBN 9781498555609 (electronic) | ISBN 9781498555593 (cloth : alk. paper)
Subjects: LCSH: Japan—Commerce—History—19th century. | Silk industry—Japan—Yokohama-shi—History—19th century. | Japan—Economic conditions—1600–1868. | Japan—Economic conditions—1868–1918.
Classification: LCC HF3826 (print) | LCC HF3826 .M27 2017 (ebook) | DDC 330.952/031—dc23
LC record available at https://lccn.loc.gov/2017023874

∞™ The paper used in this publication meets the minimum requirements of American National Standard for Information Sciences Permanence of Paper for Printed Library Materials, ANSI/NISO Z39.48-1992.

Printed in the United States of America

Contents

Preface

This book is a history of the connections that the silk trade fostered. It explains how and why silk products were sent from the interior of eastern Japan to Yokohama and then shipped from Yokohama to the West in the nineteenth century. For much of the early modern period, the shogun tightly restricted trade with the outside world. However, in the nineteenth century a total of five ports were opened to international trade, and Japanese trade suddenly exploded. Chief among the products traded was raw silk. This book explains the impact this trade had on the Japanese economy.

In this preface, I explain how I came to this topic. I first started the research for this book because I was attracted to the modern, almost futuristic, aspects of Yokohama, Japan. The Minatomirai (future port) district with its tower, skyscrapers, and hotels, the latest stores in its shopping mall, the Yokohama Bay Bridge, and the beautiful view of the city at night were all seductive. Yokohama's international aspect—with Japan's largest Chinatown and the former Western quarters at Yamate—was also alluring. It was easy to choose this modern and exotic city as the focus of my research.

Once I began to learn about the city, Yokohama continued to enthrall me. Unlike many other cities in Japan, it is a new city founded in 1859 with little to remind visitors of Japan's feudal past. It was also one of the five ports that allowed trade between Japan and the outside world in the nineteenth century. It was a city that suffered tremendously in the Great Kantō Earthquake of 1923 and then recovered to become a major industrial city. Yokohama also burned during the fire bombings of World War II but then emerged after the war greater than before. In this postwar era Yokohama continued to transform itself from a port city to an industrial city and then to a suburban city. By 1978 Yokohama surpassed Osaka to become Japan's second most populous city. With its strong Western influences and my personal background as a Japanese person growing up in the United States, writing the social history of this remarkable city seemed to be the obvious thing to do.

However, as I continued to study the history of the city of Yokohama, its economic history became an obsession. Yokohama was the center of the silk trade for Japan. From this city, various silk products were shipped to the West, and this trade helped Japan earn valuable foreign currency. In fact, raw silk was Japan's number one export until the start of World War II, and it was crucial in financing Japan's early industrialization. Slowly the focus of my research changed from the social history of Yokohama to the various aspects of the silk trade in Yokohama. As the research interest changed, new sites and new sources emerged that needed to be examined. Thankfully the Yokohama kaikō shiryōkan (Yokohama Archives of History), the Yokohama Silk Center, and other libraries in Yokohama had plenty of material. Sources on the merchants who helped to gather the silk products at Yokohama and made the port city a thriving center of trade were particularly plentiful and, I must confess, enjoyable to recount.

The stories of these merchants connected the city of Yokohama with its hinterland. Until the end of the nineteenth century, the raw silk shipped from Japan was mostly produced in the hinterlands of eastern Japan, namely Gunma, Yamanashi, and Nagano prefectures. As such I enjoyed my research trips that traced in reverse the flow of raw silk from the former centers of production near the mountains to the port city of Yokohama. Merchants also connected Yokohama with its export destinations in Europe and America. Eventually a few producers sought to directly connect the producers of eastern Japan with the consumers of the West, bypassing the merchants of Yokohama, and their stories are in this book as well. Visiting the places where raw silk was made, the Tomioka Silk Mill, the early factories in Yamanashi and Nagano prefectures, and the fields in which mulberry were grown was an important experience in understanding how these people lived their lives.

Then one day I realized that if I could understand how raw silk was gathered at Yokohama, I might be able to shed light on the wider story of Japan's industrialization as well. One of the weaknesses of the "silk exports helped Japan industrialize" theory was that the silk industry mainly created small-scale factories in the interior of eastern Japan. As an industry, the silk industry did not build factories all over Japan. In other words, silk was Japan's largest export, but it alone could not explain the industrialization of the entire country. Therefore, the silk industry's place in explaining the industrialization of Japan was that it helped finance Japan's overall industrialization and some created some localized industries.

Let us reconsider the gathering of raw silk at Yokohama. If a product flows in one direction, then that means something must be flowing in the opposite direction. In the case of raw silk in the nineteenth century, so much raw silk flowed from the producers to Yokohama that money flowed from

Yokohama to the producers. There simply were not enough goods flowing from Yokohama to the raw silk producers to balance the flow of raw silk. Furthermore, this flow of money must be understood not only within a national framework, but also within an international framework, because the raw silk gathered at Yokohama was exported to Europe and America. Perhaps tracing the flow of raw silk in reverse, from Yokohama to the hinterlands, gave me the realization that the flow of silk was in fact the flow of money in reverse.

Once this flow of money is understood, then one can formulate a new hypothesis that does not depend solely on the silk industry to build factories in the entire country. In other words, instead of focusing on one specific industry, I could trace the flow of money to explain early Japanese industrialization.

Finally, in explaining why raw silk gathered at Yokohama, one must explain why Yokohama was chosen as a treaty port in the first place. Researching this topic has been unexpectedly fruitful. For example, the opening of Yokohama was actually driven by Japanese initiative and not by the Americans. It was also part of a grand plan to reorganize the economic geography of Japan. In this sense, Yokohama surpassing Osaka as the number two city of Japan was something the original masterminds sought.

This research on how and why silk products gathered in Yokohama opened so many new and revealing historical insights that I abandoned my original project on the social history of Yokohama. As a result, this book has become a hybrid that has elements of political history, economic history, microhistory, economic geography, and regional history. There is no one simple word to define this book, but if I had to use a phrase, this book is about the connections that the silk trade fostered. I hope that it is an enjoyable book that opens new ways to think about late-nineteenth-century Japanese economic development.

Acknowledgments

In writing this book I have accumulated too many debts to repay. Here I can only thank the people and institutions that have helped me along the way. In coming to this topic and encouraging me along the way, I owe a very large debt to my former advisor Carol Gluck. I must also thank Henry Smith for pointing me in the right direction and for introducing me to invaluable people for my research at Yokohama. I am also grateful to other Columbia professors such as Anders Stephanson, Gregory Pflugfelder, Wm. Theodore de Bary, and Conrad Schirokauer, who have helped me grow as a scholar and teacher.

Support from the Yokohama Association for International Communications and Exchanges Fellowship, also known as the YOKE Fellowship (a Yokohama city government grant), the Japan Foundation, Columbia University's Heyman Fellowship, the Social Science Research Council Fellowship, and the Japan Society for the Promotion of Science were crucial in funding the research and writing of this book. The staff from each of these organizations were extremely kind, and with their help, I was able to research and write in Japan and New York.

In Yokohama, Katō Yūzō provided me with many hints and advice on this project and helped me to expand my vision after I arrived. Through him I was introduced to many researchers and institutions in Japan that were invaluable in producing this work. The Yokohama kaikō shiryōkan, with its many researchers such as Nishikawa Takeomi, Itō Izumi, and Saitō Takio, made me realize that I should focus more on economic history. At Osaka, professors such as Honda Saburō and Abe Takeshi helped me tremendously in furthering this project.

I also owe a large debt to the librarians in places like the Yokohama kaikō shiryōkan, Yokohama City University Library, the Yokohama City Library, the Tokyo Metropolitan Library, Osaka University of Economics Library, Osaka University Library, libraries in various cities in the Kantō region, the C. V. Starr East Asian Library at Columbia University, and the Iona College Library. Their friendly help and tireless work are appreciated very much.

During the writing phase, which took a long time, I am extremely grateful to my colleagues at Iona College, particularly the successive department chairs Joseph Morgan, James Carroll, and Daniel Thiery, for their patience and understanding. My friends Yan Zelener and Kazunori Tanaka have encouraged me and helped with the writing by reading my earliest drafts. The anonymous readers before publication have also helped me explain where the writing was lacking and in providing useful advice for the organization of this hybrid book. It also gives me pleasure to thank Claudio Zanier, a professor in Italy, for identifying Italian names from the Japanese pronunciations, a task that was impossible for me to accomplish alone.

Thanks are due to people from the Weatherhead East Asian Institute and Lexington Books—Ross Yelsey, Brian Hill, Eric Kuntzman, Bill Tsutsui, and Doug Slaymaker—for helping me through the publication process. I am certain that I have neglected to thank others because this project took a long time to come to fruition. To them, I give my sincerest thanks.

Above all I must thank my family: my parents, Hirotami and Junko, for encouraging me through the years; my brother, Hideo, and his family, Marysol, Reina, and Emi; and my sister, Shiho, for their support. I owe my largest debt and thanks to my wife, Hitomi, and our child, Atsuhiro. Hitomi was extremely patient throughout the years, and I cannot thank her enough. To her, I dedicate this book.

Introduction

From 1859 to 1940 raw silk dominated Japanese exports. In the first eight years, from 1860 to 1868, raw silk accounted for 49 to 86 percent of exports. Until 1900 raw silk was never less than 25 percent of exports, and until 1940 raw silk reigned as the number one export item.[1] During this time, production of raw silk also contributed to Japanese economic development through the industrialization of silk reeling. In this transition from hand-reeled raw silk to machine-reeled raw silk, the critical decade was the 1910s.[2] These two important points have been noted by many eminent scholars in the story of Japanese economic development.[3]

The numbers speak for themselves. In 1870 the total value of Japanese exports was ¥14.5 million. Raw silk was the number one export item at ¥4.4 million. Tea was the second largest export item at ¥3.6 million. Silkworm eggs were the third export item at ¥1.6 million. Coal replaced the silkworm eggs as an export good in the 1880s and the rise of machine-reeled cotton yarn for export at the end of the nineteenth century easily over took tea. However, neither came close to the amount or value of silk exports. By 1900 the total value of exports was ¥200.2 million. Raw silk remained the number one export item at ¥44.7 million, while the number two export item was cotton yarn exports at only ¥20.6 million, and the third export item was silk fabrics at ¥18.6 million. By 1917, cotton fabric exports at ¥127.5 million replaced cotton yarn as the number two export item at ¥108.1 million, making cotton products the second and third largest of the export goods. But these two cotton goods together still did not match a single product, namely raw silk, at ¥351.9 million. Raw silk would hit its export peak in 1925 at ¥877.8 million, and then slowly decline to ¥446 million in 1940. It was only in 1934 that cotton fabrics at ¥492.3 million finally displaced raw silk at ¥286.8 million as Japan's chief export. Even then, in 1939 and in 1940, raw silk replaced cotton fabrics as the number one export item.[4] Thus the history of pre–World War II Japanese exports is intimately tied with raw silk exports.

Befitting this important role, Japan's silk industry has a wealth of studies. In the aftermath of the post–World War I economy, Hayakawa Naose declared sericulture (the rearing of silkworms) and the raw silk reeling industry as the keys to Japanese industrial development and wrote many books to encourage both.[5] Historians followed with studies to understand the changes brought by sericulture and raw silk reeling. These included Marxist historians, such as Yamada Moritarō, who identified sericulture to be an important sector of Japanese capitalism, and Fujita Gorō and Yagi Akio, who emphasized the silk reeling industry.[6] In 1962 Yamaguchi Kazuo broke new ground by analyzing raw silk production through the flow of capital: from the Bank of Japan and the Yokohama Specie Bank to the local Dai jyūkyū ginkō (The Nineteenth Bank) in Nagano prefecture and then to the raw silk wholesalers and the producers.[7] Then in 1972 Ishii Kanji wrote the classic work on the silk industry in Japan, *Nihon sanshigyōshi bunseki*.

Studies on sericulture and raw silk reeling continued to be published, and in the 1990s a series of important monographs were published in Japan. Nishikawa Takeomi examined the silk merchants at Yokohama, Araki Mikio examined sericulture near Kyoto, and Hirano Yasushi examined sericulture and silk reeling in Nagano prefecture, while Yamazaki Masukichi and others examined the silk industry in Gunma prefecture. Igawa Katsuhiko undertook a comparative analysis with the Chinese producers and an analysis of cocoon production, because Ishii Kanji had not focused on the expanding production of silkworm cocoons.[8]

Among English language works, Stephen Vlastos examined sericulture and its impact on the peasants of Shindatsu district of Fukushima prefecture as part of his study of peasant protests in the Tokugawa period. Kären Wigen studied the long-term economic geography of Shimo-Ina valley in southern Nagano prefecture and discussed the adoption of raw silk reeling by the locals in the late nineteenth and early twentieth centuries and how that linked the valley into a modern national economy centered on Tokyo. Giovanni Federico wrote an important global study on the silk industry that covers various aspects of the industry in Japan, United States, Italy, France, China, Germany, and Switzerland.[9] This attention on the silk industry is likely to continue because in 2014 the United Nations Educational, Scientific and Cultural Organization (UNESCO) selected Tomioka *seishijō* (Tomioka Silk Mill) the model factory for early Japanese industrialization as a world heritage site and a tourist destination.[10]

Mysteriously, no previous work offers an in-depth study about the early years of the international development of the Japanese silk trade and its industry. Brief mention of a global silk shortage caused by a silkworm disease called pebrine in Europe and the Taiping Rebellion (1850–1864) in Qing China is usually made in explaining Japan's success in selling raw silk. However, no one explains how the Japanese producers managed to overcome difficulties after pebrine was eradicated in Europe and after the Chinese raw silk exporters returned once the rebellion was over. This book aims to fill that gap, namely the development of a network of merchants and producers to sell the silk products overseas from the 1850s to the 1880s, and to build on previous studies to deepen our understanding of nineteenth-century Japanese history.

In this study two strategies are employed: a regional focus on the development of the economy and a focus on the flow of goods from the producers to the customers.[11] Employing an explicitly regional focus is helpful to understand the development of the Japanese economy. The focus on the flow of goods is useful in understanding the story of Japanese economic development within a global context. Finally, in the process, this book also demonstrates the contingent nature of history and the deeply interconnected nature of politics and economics during this period.

The rest of this introduction describes each chapter in the book.

THE CHAPTERS

The short first chapter reviews Japan's early modern political economy before the start of modern international trade in 1859. It focuses on the three centuries from 1568 to 1859. First it examines how the early modern political economy emerged in the sixteenth century. Then it covers the ecological, demographic, and economic changes that followed in the seventeenth and eighteenth centuries. An important point stressed in this chapter is the need to examine this issue through a regional and local analysis. Too many past analyses were based on a national scope, and that clouded our understanding of the Tokugawa economy. Thus impressions diverged between "stagnant and gloomy" or "developing and bright" for the Tokugawa economy.

The Tokugawa *bakufu*'s (shogunate) analyses and major policy decisions are also covered in this chapter. From its very inception, the early modern economy was a political economy that entangled politics with economics. In the beginning this system yielded tremendous benefits for the shogunate. However, by the end of the early modern period, the shogunate was in a dire financial condition. Coupling this shift with major changes in the balance of power in East Asia helps explain the decisions it made starting in the 1840s.

The second chapter narrates the debates within the Tokugawa *bakufu* about whether to open the country for trade from both political and economic perspectives. From the 1630s until 1854 the shogunate had imposed *sakoku* (closed country policy).[12] Japan was not completely cut off from the outside world, but the shogunate did monopolize the trade with the Chinese and the Dutch, and ordinary Japanese were forbidden to leave the country. Changing this two-hundred-year-old policy was a major issue aptly examined by many.

From a regional perspective, it is important to understand that under the leadership of *rōjū* (senior minister) Hotta Masayoshi, the shogunate decided to commence trade with the vision of linking eastern Japan with the rest of the world. Hotta was seeking to acquire wealth and technology from trade and thus to strengthen the shogunate's regional power base. Traditionally historians have focused on the first contact in 1853 between Commodore Matthew Perry of the United States Navy and the shogunate, lead at the time by *rōjū* Abe Masahiro, but as Michael Auslin points out, the truly pathbreaking treaty was the 1858 Treaty of Amity and Commerce between the United States and Japan.[13] This book also focuses on the 1858 treaty and shows that it was actually a Japanese initiative to open commercial relations between the *bakufu* and other Western countries.

The third chapter analyzes of the actions of Nakaiya Jūbei, arguably the first Yokohama merchant. Nakaiya left a three-month diary before he established his store. A careful examination of his diary demonstrates how the Tokugawa shogunate and the various domains intervened in the opening of Yokohama and the creation of his store. Nakaiya had a meteoric career in Yokohama that lasted less than two years. His rise and fall demonstrates how the late Tokugawa economy functioned for prominent merchants. Nakaiya and Japan's entry into the global silk trade was truly fortuitous. As mentioned earlier, initially there were twin boosts: one from pebrine, a disease that struck silkworms in Europe, and another from the general chaos in southern China. In other words, Japan entered the international silk trade during a time of global silk shortage. European demand encouraged many to sell raw silk, rear silkworms, and try to capitalize on this seemingly insatiable demand. This is the first of the three microhistorical chapters focusing on individual lives.

The fourth chapter is a short chapter that analyzes Yokohama's role in early Japanese trade. Today after waves of decolonization, the global order seems better represented by the economically derived concepts of core, semi-periphery, and periphery of Immanuel Wallerstein's world systems theory. But in the nineteenth-century world, the economic realm and the political order reinforced each other. Being a member of the core economy in world system theory meant being a great power in world politics. A great power like Britain could then use its military to conquer a weaker state and demote that state's political status from that of an independent country to a colony, such as India. Once a country was turned into a colony, its economy could be yoked for the benefit of the core country and turned into an economic periphery. Thus India's "deindustrialization" from a global manufacturer and exporter of cotton cloth, namely Indian calico, to an importer of British textiles and exporter of raw cotton cannot be understood without the active role of British colonial policy. Similarly, one of China's socioeconomic crises in the nineteenth century, namely the addiction to opium, cannot be understood without the political coercion (i.e., the two Opium Wars) by the British. It was British military power that forced open five Chinese treaty ports, including Shanghai, in 1842 and prevented the Chinese from keeping opium out of its borders. The result of its addiction was the outflow of Chinese silver to British coffers despite high volumes of Chinese exports in tea and silk. Politics and economics were intricately connected in the nineteenth century. The city of Yokohama, the last major international treaty port, was created in part to serve the Western international order and was one of only five ports that connected Japan with the rest of the world. Would Yokohama become like Batavia or Calcutta, the center of future Western conquests? Or would Yokohama become like Shanghai, the center of the Western drug trade? Or would Yokohama become something else?

The fifth chapter chronicles two other merchants, Yoshimuraya Kōbei and Kōshūya Chūemon. Yoshimuraya was a prominent merchant, and his activities in the early years of international trade show how working with political authorities was beneficial for both merchants and authorities. Kōshūya did not become a prominent merchant, and his business struggled, buffeted by the capricious raw silk and silkworm egg markets. Reading their letters written during the ten years before the shogunate collapsed and the first years of the new Meiji government, this chapter shows how connections were forged between Yokohama and its hinterland. Thus they represent the two ways in which a regional economic network was forged in the Kantō Plain, one through political connections and the other through commercial connections.

The Kantō Plain, the largest plain of Japan, is surrounded by mountains in the west and north and by sea in the south and east. Near the mountains many peasants engaged in various silk industries, silkworm egg rearing, silkworm cocoon production, raw silk reeling, and silk cloth manufacture. Tokyo Bay cuts into the center of the plain from the south, and Edo (renamed Tokyo in 1868) lies at its heart. Near the coast many engaged in fishing and aquaculture. During the Edo period, Yokohama was a day's journey from Edo by boat. Once steamships and railroads connected Edo/Tokyo and Yokohama, the distance shrank to only a few hours. This relatively flat Kantō Plain had highways that crisscrossed the region and connected Yokohama and Edo with its smaller cities.

Southwest from Yokohama, the Tōkaidō highway connected the port with Nagoya and eventually Kyoto. From Yokohama going northeast, the Tōkaidō highway connected Yokohama with Edo. Going northwest from Yokohama, a minor road called the "silk road" of Japan connected the port with Hachiōji city. This path merged with the Kōshū kaidō highway, which originated from

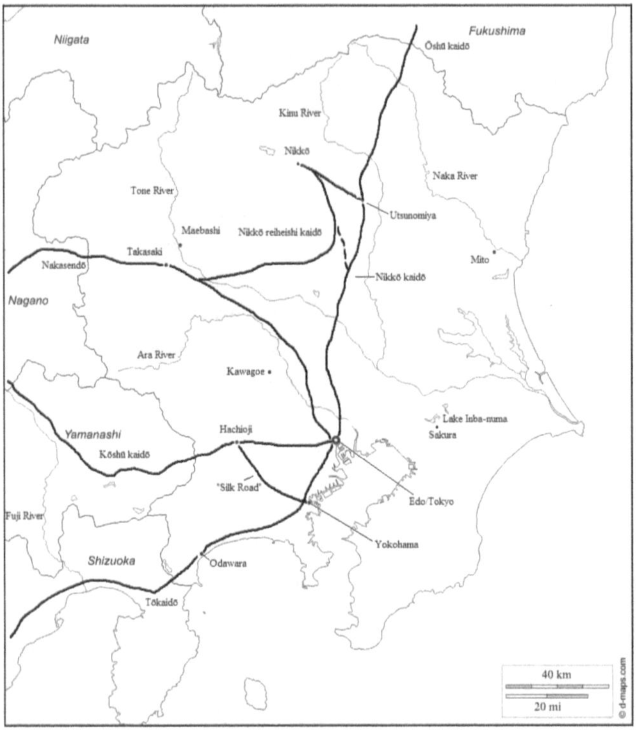

Figure 0.1. Map of Kantō Plain with Highways during the Edo Period *Source*: http://d-maps.com/carte.php?num_car=115415&lang=en. Modified by the author to include highway routes and the names of cities.

Edo, and took travelers into Kōshū or Kai province (today's Yamanashi prefecture) and into Lower Suwa town, Shinshū or Shinano province (today's Nagano prefecture). From Edo travelers could take the Nakasendō highway toward Urawa and Ōmiya (today's Saitama city) to the north and make their way to Takasaki city in Jōshū or Kōzuke province (today's Gunma prefecture) and then head west toward Lower Suwa town where it merged with Kōshū kaidō highway. The Nakasendō continued toward Kyoto. Maebashi city lay to the north of Takasaki off the Nakasendō highway. Travelers could also take the Nikkō highway northeast from Edo and head toward Utsunomiya city in Yashū or Shimotsuke province (today's Tochigi prefecture) and then continue onward to Nikkō, the tomb of Tokugawa Ieyasu. Those who needed to go to northeastern Japan could continue northeast from Utsunomiya on the Ōshū kaidō highway to go to southern Ōshū or Mutsu province (today's Fukushima prefecture). If anyone needed to go from Takasaki to Fukushima, one could always take the Nikkō reiheishi highway, which connected Takasaki with Imaichi near Nikkō, and then head to Utsunomiya. These cities, or "points," on the Kantō Plain were connected by merchants to become a functioning economic zone and Yokohama would connect that zone with the world.

The sixth chapter covers the period when the industry had to adjust to a Europe in which pebrine was eradicated and China returned to peace, in other words, a time when competition suddenly became more intense. Shimamura, a village on the border of Gunma and Saitama prefectures north of Tokyo, attempted to export directly by bringing its goods to the Italian market through a cooperative venture starting in 1879. Its attempt ultimately failed and the villagers suffered a boom and a bust within the span of two decades. The brothers Hoshino from Gunma prefecture exported directly to the American market and succeeded. While one brother stayed at home and produced the raw silk, the other brother went to New York in 1876 to sell their raw silk. The brothers built a basis for a new silk trade that connected Japanese producers with American consumers. The American consumers, enriched from their own industrializing economy, had an insatiable appetite for silk products. The answer to increased competition in Europe and from China was to find a new consumer in America. Despite the contrasting results, these individual stories demonstrate how a regionally based story ultimately connects the local, regional, national, and international developments.

Finally, the concluding chapter restates the argument and reviews some more statistics to propose a new hypothesis on Japanese economic development before the 1890s. Since many scholars have already covered the history of the Japanese silk industry after the 1890s, this book ends here.

NOTES

1. Appendix D.

2. Per Ishii Kanji, the two main producers of raw silk in the early twentieth century were Gunze seishi and Katakura seishi; Kanebō seishi became a major producer after the 1920s. In the 1910s Gunze seishi expanded its factory production greatly while Katakura seishi transitioned from hand-reeled to machine-reeled raw silk. Ishii Kanji, *Nihon sanshigyōshi bunseki* (Tokyo: University of Tokyo Press, 1972), 89–91.

3. William Lockwood, *The Economic Development of Japan: Growth and Structural Change* 1868–1938 (Princeton, NJ: Princeton University Press, 1954), 94, and Takafusa Nakamura, *Economic Growth in Prewar Japan*, trans. Robert A Feldman (New Haven, CT: Yale University Press, 1983), 63 are two important general works that mention the importance of the silk industry.

4. Yokohama-shi (ed.), *Yokohama shishi: Shiryōhen 2 Nihon bōeki tōkei (zōteiban) 1868–1945 Tōkei hen* (Yokohama: Yūrindō, 1980), 2, 6, 16, 18, 19, 26, 33. National statistics can also be obtained online, for example, from Ōkurashō (ed.), *Dainihon gaikoku bōeki nenpyō, Meiji 33* (Tokyo: Ōkurashō, 1990), 17. National Diet Library Kindai dejitaru raiburarī (Modern Digital Library), http://kindai.ndl.go.jp/info:ndljp/pid/804310.

5. Hayakawa Naose was an agronomist and a booster of the silk industry who wrote academic books and popular books. Hayakawa Naose, *Kiito to sono bōeki* (Tokyo: Dōbunkan, 1922), 4–7. Other books by Hayakawa include *Honpō sanshigyō to Beikoku kengyō* (Tokyo:

Meibundō, 1917), *Yōsan rōdō keizairon* (Tokyo: Dōbunkan, 1923), and *Seishi keizaigaku* (Tokyo: Meibundō, 1927). He also wrote books about the American silk industry and on Indian agriculture.

6. Ishii, *Nihon sanshigyōshi bunseki*, 3–8; Yamada Moritarō, *Nihon shihonshugi bunseki* (Tokyo: Iwanami, 1934); Fujita Gorō, *Nihon kindai sangyō no seisei* (Tokyo: Nihon hyōronsha, 1948); Yagi Akio, *Nihon kindai seishigyō no seiritsu* (Tokyo: Ochanomizu shobō, 1960).

7. Yamaguchi Kazuo, "Meiji jidai no seishi kin'yū," *Keizaigaku ronshū* 28, no. 2 (1962): 1–45.

8. Nishikawa Takeomi, *Bakumatsu Meiji no kokusai shijō to Nihon: Kiito bōeki to Yokohama* (Tokyo: Yūzankaku, 1997); Araki Mikio, *Nihon sanshigyō hattatsu to sono kiban: Yōsan nōka keiei* (Kyoto: Mineruva shobō, 1996); Hirano Yasushi, *Kindai yōsangyō no hatten to kumiai seishi* (Tokyo: University of Tokyo Press, 1990); Takasaki keizai daigaku fuzoku sangyō kenkyūjo (ed.), *Kindai Gunma no sanshigyō: Sangyō to seikatsu kara no shōsha* (Tokyo: Nihon Keizai hyōronsha, 1999); Igawa Katsuhiko, *Kindai Nihon seishigyō to mayu seisan* (Tokyo: Tokyo keizai jōhō shuppan, 1998).

9. Stephen Vlastos, *Peasant Protests and Uprisings in Tokugawa Japan* (Berkeley: University of California Press, 1986); Kären Wigen, *The Making of a Japanese Periphery, 1750–1920* (Berkeley: University of California Press, 1995); Giovanni Federico, *An Economic History of the Silk Industry, 1830–1930* (Cambridge: Cambridge University Press, 1997). Federico's work was originally published in Italian in 1994. Books that focus on the workers of this important industry are also plentiful, starting with the autobiographical account of Wada Ei (1857–1929), a landmark study by Hosoi Wakizō on female laborers, namely *Jokō aishi*, to English language works by E. Patricia Tsurumi and recently Janet Hunter. Wada Ei, *Tomioka nikki* (Tokyo: Chikuma shobō, 2014, first published in 1905); Hosoi Wakizō, *Jokō aishi* (Tokyo: Kaizō, 1925); E. Patricia Tsurumi, *Factory Girls: Women in the Thread Mills of Meiji Japan* (Princeton, NJ: Princeton University Press, 1990); Janet Hunter, *Women and the Labour Market in Japan's Industrializing Economy: The Textile Industry before the Pacific War* (London: Routledge, 2003).

10. Tomioka *seishijō* is also known as the Tomioka filature. "UNESCO World Heritage List: Tomioka Silk Mill and Related Sites," http://whc.unesco.org/en/list/1449. For more specifically about Tomioka, see Stephen W. McCallion, "Trial and Error: The Model Filature at Tomioka," ed. William D. Wray, *Managing Industrial Enterprise: Cases from Japan's Prewar Experience* (Cambridge, MA: Council on East Asian Studies, Harvard University, 1989).

11. Two important works inspired this book. One is William Cronon, *Nature's Metropolis: Chicago and the Great West* (New York: W. W. Norton, 1991). This book traces the flow of three products—grain, lumber, and meat—from the American West to Chicago. The other is Tsurumi Yoshiyuki, *Namako no me* (Tokyo: Chikuma shobō, 1993). This book focuses on one product—dried sea cucumbers—and connects Hokkaidō, Japan, China, the Spice Islands of Indonesia, and Australia through its trade. Popular history books that trace the movement of a single product also inspired this book, such as Mark Kurlansky, *Cod: A Biography of a Fish That Changed the World* (New York, Walker, 1997); Usui Ryūichirō, *Kōhī ga mawari, sekai ga mawaru* (Tokyo: Chūōkōronsha, 1992); and Tsunoyama Sakae, *Cha no sekaishi* (Tokyo: Chūōkōronsha, 1980). In fact, these works have inspired me to teach an integrated history of the globe from the fifteenth century to the present by tracing the movement of a dozen trade goods.

12. Many historians have begun to describe the Tokugawa polity as a mini empire modeled after the Chinese civilized barbarian order. This can be seen in an attempt to understand *sakoku* (closed country) policy as a variant of *kaikin* (sea ban) that the Ming, Qing, and Korea employed. Ronald Toby, *State and Diplomacy in Early Modern Japan: Asia in the Development of the Tokugawa Bakufu* (Stanford, CA: Stanford University Press, 1984) reexamines *sakoku* in English.

13. Michael Auslin, *Negotiating with Imperialism: The Unequal Treaties and the Culture of Japanese Diplomacy* (Cambridge, MA: Harvard University Press, 2004), 18.

Chapter One

The Early Modern Japanese Economy

Before entering into a discussion of modern economic history, a discussion of the early modern economic history of Japan, a lively topic, is in order. After the Tokugawa period ended many Japanese intellectuals, most prominently Fukuzawa Yukichi, saw the early modern period as a period of authoritarian rule and a period marked by poverty for the commoners.[1] Japanese scholars trained in Marxist historiography, such as Yamada Moritarō, have also tended to see the Tokugawa period as a long period of oppression and economic stagnation. However, a few Marxist scholars such as Hattori Shisō disagreed, arguing that Japanese economic development in the Meiji period is unthinkable without adequate Tokugawa economic development.[2]

In general, American scholars starting with Thomas Smith and continuing with David Howell, Kären Wigen, Edward Pratt, and others have tended to view early modern Japan as the foundation for modern Japan's economic growth.[3] This divide in opinion about Japan's past between Japanese and Westerners is old. As early as 1904 Basil Hall Chamberlain, the foremost Western scholar of Japan at the time, noted that educated Japanese felt their past was not important, whereas Chamberlain thought Tokugawa Japan was "a community as highly cultured as it was intelligent," moral, and humane.[4] In the late twentieth century, Susan Hanley, after considering the data on the quality of life, such as health and life expectancy, argued that "the standard of living around 1850 was not only appreciatively higher than in the 1700s, but also high in comparison to most of the industrializing West in 1850." Her concluding sentence is: "But if I had to choose where to live in 1850, I would rather live in England, if wealthy, and in Japan if working class."[5]

Starting in the 1960s and 1970s, as Japan grew more prosperous after World War II, Japanese scholars also began to support these arguments. Yasumaru Yoshio argued that the twin development of commercialization and of a people's morality in the Tokugawa period was a necessary precursor to the economic development in the Meiji period.[6] Hayashi Reiko examined the concrete economic changes taking place in early modern Japan and argued convincingly that the Tokugawa period saw major advances in commercialization.[7] By the 1990s their view that the early modern Japanese economy developed significantly and that some people lived decent lives gained a wider audience in Japan.[8]

So, were the early Meiji thinkers and Marxist historians wrong in thinking of early modern Japan as a long period of stagnation and economic oppression? Their understanding is not necessarily wrong when examining the conditions of the countryside in nineteenth-century eastern Japan. Yasumaru based his work on the devastated landscape of eastern Japan. Even Hayashi Reiko admits that the economy crashed in the eighteenth century in eastern Japan for an extended period of time.[9] The famous biography of Ninomiya Sontoku (1787–1856), who travelled the devastated villages of eastern Japan and restored them, is further anecdotal evidence.[10]

One way to make sense of this contradiction is to rethink the question. In other words, instead of assuming that the economy of Japan was more or less the same throughout the entire country, scholars should have examined the issue from a regional perspective. Economic conditions within Japan diverged dramatically depending on location and time. Villages in eastern Japan suffered from harsh economic conditions in the eighteenth century, but in western Japan the economy had developed throughout the entire period. The next section delves deeper into the divide and examines the origins of the two regions of early modern Japan: eastern and western.

THE ORIGIN OF THE TOKUGAWA ECONOMIC SYSTEM'S REGIONAL DIVIDE

Early modern Japan's economic system emerged in the sixteenth century. The key to this system was the castle towns founded toward the end of the Warring States period. Historians credit Oda Nobunaga (1534–1582) with inventing these castle towns. Nobunaga forced his samurai off the land and relocated them to his castle. These samurai now received their income as stipends from the Nobunaga and no longer collected rice directly from their fiefs. Liberated from overseeing their fiefs directly, Nobunaga's samurai could wage war all year round. In turn, lords (*daimyō*) who allowed their samurai to stay on the land were at a severe disadvantage, because Nobunaga could attack during the agricultural busy season or invade before his enemies could muster their samurai. Not surprisingly, many lords copied Nobunaga and ordered their samurai to live near their castles. The merchants and artisans then flocked to the castles to service the samurai, and thus the castle towns were born.

Toyotomi Hideyoshi (1537–1598), Nobunaga's successor, linked these castle towns in one giant network once he unified the country in 1590. Hideyoshi's castle town, namely Osaka in western Japan, became the central marketplace where various goods were gathered for sale and the prices of these goods were determined. The unification of Japan also put an end to the unceasing internecine warfare, and lords began setting up their castle towns at the center of the domain or near a location easily accessible by water. Then domain leaders rationalized the marketplaces, opening one every eight to twelve kilometers (five to seven and a half miles) and closing the rest. These marketplaces were frequented by local peasants who were expected to buy what was necessary and sell what they did not need. These "surplus" goods—the goods the local peasants no longer needed—were sent from these local marketplaces to the castle town. From the castle town, the surplus goods were sent to Osaka to be sold at "the realm's kitchen." The profits gained from the sales in Osaka would fall in the hands of the merchants who had special connections to the domain or to the domain authorities directly if they had moved the goods. With these profits, the authorities bought any product that they needed (such as items they could not produce inside their domain for geographic or technological reasons) and then shipped these products back to their castle town. The castle towns therefore acted as relay cities that controlled the flow of goods between the new economic capital of Osaka and the countryside of various parts of Japan. The lords and the merchants who assisted them benefitted from controlling these key cities.[11] At this point, the early modern economic system was unified.

However, Tokugawa Ieyasu (1542–1616), ally and rival of Toyotomi Hideyoshi, became the first Tokugawa shogun to rule Japan after Hideyoshi's death in 1598. And Ieyasu's castle town and power base was Edo, in eastern Japan.[12] Moreover, Edo was too new and too small to serve as the central marketplace of the country. At the time of the unification, Hideyoshi had ordered Ieyasu to relocate his castle town to Edo when it was still a minor fishing town. This explains why, when Ieyasu became the de facto ruler in 1600 and then the shogun in 1603, the new castle town of Edo could not hope to act as the economic center of the country. Consequently, the Tokugawa shogunate designated three cities as important metropolises: Edo, Osaka, and Kyoto.

The shogun's city, Edo, was the political center and eventually grew to be one of the largest cities in the world. Starting from a fishing village, Edo quickly became a city with approximately 150,000 people in 1609 and then a megacity of more than a million by the early 1700s.[13] It expanded in size because the various lords had to attend the shogun on alternate years. Thus Edo concentrated roughly half of all the feudal lords in Japan at any given time. When these lords came to Edo, they brought with them their samurai, their weapons (though guns were carefully regulated), their money, and their food for emergencies, mostly rice. Every lord also built a mansion or multiple mansions to house their families and their samurai. Even when the lords left, these mansions had to be maintained by samurai staff, since the lord's family had to remain in Edo as hostages. This meant Edo probably maintained a high population of at least a million people until 1862, when the system of alternate attendance ended. This can only be estimated because the population of the samurai was considered a military secret and thus not part of the census. Of course, once alternate attendance ended, the population immediately decreased as samurai from other domains returned home. The Meiji state then conducted its early surveys on the population of Edo, with the results being 503,703 in 1869.[14]

Edo typically had enough rice to withstand a siege (by consuming the emergency rice to feed the samurai and the populace), but few daily products and even fewer luxuries. Salt was deemed a strategic item, and Ieyasu gave monopoly rights to salt manufacturers in Gyōtoku, just south of Edo, for sale in his city. Most other goods, such as wood for construction, textiles for clothing, *sake*, soy sauce, and dried goods for food, had to be imported into Edo. Fortunately for Edo residents, these imported goods could be paid with the tax the lords collected from their domains and brought to the city. As a result, even in 1724 after more than a century as the center of shogunal power, Edo continued to import from Osaka massive quantities of goods such as silk cloth, cotton cloth, oil, *sake*, and soy sauce. Even salt had to be imported from the salt producing regions in the Inland Sea west of Osaka despite the existence of monopoly salt producers in Gyōtoku. The monopoly salt manufacturers failed to supply enough salt for the million residents of Edo. This flooding of Edo with imports from Osaka prevented the regional economy surrounding Edo from producing its own manufactured goods.[15] In other words, the people near Edo found it difficult to compete with this flood of manufactured goods from Osaka.

Osaka, "the realm's kitchen," remained the economic center and supplied Edo. Osaka's central role could not be challenged in 1603 and remained unchallenged for years. However, this meant that as long as Toyotomi Hideyoshi's son controlled Osaka, the Tokugawa clan would never have full control over the economy of Japan. Thus in 1614 Ieyasu sent the Toyotomi clan an ultimatum: either relocate or be destroyed. When the Toyotomi clan refused, Ieyasu destroyed the clan in summer 1615. This war reduced the city's population but it recovered quickly. With the Toyotomi gone, Osaka became a city directly controlled by the Tokugawa clan and remained the economic center of the country. By 1730 the population of Osaka matched Kyoto, the imperial capital and the largest city in Japan until that point, at around 370,000. Osaka hit its peak in the 1760s at more than 420,000 people.

From thence Osaka's population slowly declined to around 281,000 by the end of the Tokugawa period, hitting its nadir in 1873 at 271,992.[16]

The third city was Kyoto, the ancient capital and the home of the emperor. This city's political power was neutralized when Ieyasu enacted a law in 1615 that forbade the emperor of Japan and the imperial court from interfering in politics. For most of the Tokugawa period's history, Kyoto remained a politically powerless, high skilled manufacturing city directly controlled by the shogun. According to one calculation, Yamashiro province (where Kyoto is located) produced 437 of the 1,807 specialty items (24 percent) in the seventeenth century. Of these 1,807 items, 70 percent of the handcrafted manufactured items were produced in Kinai.[17] Thomas Smith estimated the combined urban population of Osaka, Kyoto, and other minor cities to be at least 400,000 in 1590.[18] Others have estimated that Kyoto itself had around 400,000 people, with Hamano citing a 1634 survey that recorded 410,000 townsfolk.[19] In 1750, the combined population of Osaka and Kyoto numbered around 780,000 people.[20] Intriguingly recent research suggests that Kyoto—unlike Edo—steadily lost population from approximately 400,000 in the seventeenth century to around 318,000 in 1766 and then fell to a low point of 237,647 in 1871.[21] Kyoto was thus an important city, but for the Tokugawa economic system, it did not have the importance of Edo or Osaka and suffered gradual decline.

In short, Ieyasu modified Hideyoshi's economic system by adding Edo to the existing economic network centered on Osaka. Edo (the capital of the shogun) sat on top of a distribution network by consuming "surplus" goods; Osaka (the distribution center) remained at the center of the distribution network by collecting the goods from across Japan and then shipping the surplus to Edo; while Kyoto (the center of high-end manufacturing) produced the luxury goods. This divide between east and west was further accentuated because eastern Japan centered on Edo used gold as the means of exchange, while western Japan centered on Osaka used silver as the means of exchange.[22] The exchange merchants (*ryōgaeshō*) symbolized this divide, for

Table 1.1. Chart of estimated population of Edo, Osaka, and Kyoto in thousands of people

	1609	*1634*	*1730*	*1750*	*1766*	*1820*	*1868–69*	*1871–73*
Edo	150		1,000+	1,000+	1,000+	1,000+	504	
Osaka			370	410	422	379	281	272
Kyoto		410	373	370	318			238

Source: Information compiled from Tokyo-to (ed.), 416–20, 675–87; Ōishi, *Edo jidai*, 113–17; Sekiyama, 228; Kitō, 188, 196, 201; Osaka-shi (ed.), *Osaka shishi*, vol. 5, 639; Saitō Seiji, "Edo jidai no toshi jinkō,"48–63; Hamano, 28, 36, 38.

they converted the gold coins used in Edo with the weighted pieces of silver used in Osaka. Politically the country remained unified but economically it was now divided.

For a century, this politically ordered economy worked well and served the samurai of Edo. Despite the divide between the regions using gold and those using silver, developments in transport interconnected the two. *Higaki kaisen* ships and *taru kaisen* ships directly connected Osaka with Edo starting in 1619. Half a century later, in 1671 Kawamura Zuiken pioneered a safe sea route linking the Pacific Ocean side of northeastern Japan with Edo. And in 1673, Kawamura pioneered a safe sea route linking the Japan Sea side of northeastern Japan with Osaka. These three coastal routes furthered commercialization by linking all parts of coastal Japan.[23] With Edo becoming the largest city in Japan, Osaka had an outlet that was willing to consume all the surplus goods that it could send and a seaborne route to do so in bulk. Moreover, after Ieyasu destroyed the Toyotomi clan in 1615, warfare among the lords ceased for almost 240 years in Japan.[24] This *Pax Tokugawa* brought

Figure 1.1. Map of Japan with Major Cities and the Gold and Silver Zones
***Source*: http://d-maps.com/carte.php?num_car=29463&lang=en. Modified by the author to include the dividing line and the names of cities.**

a massive peace dividend in the form of newly opened agricultural fields, increased population, and further commercialization.

THE NEED FOR A REGIONAL AND LOCAL ANALYSIS OF TOKUGAWA AGRICULTURE AND DEMOGRAPHICS

The first part of this section is a short history of this rise and stagnation in agricultural production from a national perspective and how that influenced economic understanding. The second part of this section is a discussion of the demographics of Tokugawa Japan from a regional perspective.

Of the three peace dividends from the *Pax Tokugawa*—opening agricultural fields, increased population, and further commercialization—the opening of agricultural fields hit its limits first. After a rapid increase in areas under cultivation, the expansion suddenly slowed. Estimates of area under cultivation vary because the Tokugawa shogunate and the lords focused on *koku* rather than the area under cultivation.[25] A *koku* of rice was approximately 150 kilograms by weight and is considered enough rice to feed one male adult per year. Thus during the Tokugawa period, the authorities converted the productive capacity of the land, even if the land grew wheat, into rice equivalents and used *koku* to denote this. This was in effect the gross domestic product (GDP) of the land expressed in rice. As such the historical records are richer in terms of *koku* than in terms of acreage.

The expansion of the productive capacity of Japan as a whole was dramatic. Most historians agree that there was a huge boom in the sixteenth century from around 18.5 million *koku* in 1598 to 24.6 million koku in 1645 to around 25.9 million *koku* in 1697. Production continued to increase, ending up at around 30.6 million *koku* in 1834. When one compares the growth in the first half of the seventeenth century (an increase of 6.1 million *koku* between 1598 and 1645) with the growth over the next two centuries (an increase of 6 million *koku* between 1645 and 1834), one can see the truly rapid pace in the early years of the *Pax Tokugawa*.[26]

Signs of problems with this rapid expansion came first in Kansai. In the mid-seventeenth century, floods began to strike and rivers became filled with silt, particularly the Yodo River near Osaka. The shogunate quickly recognized that excessive tree cutting for construction materials and the cultivation of marginal lands led to soil erosion and flash floods. In 1666 the shogunate banned the rooting out of plants and trees in Kansai and instead encouraged the planting of trees on the banks of rivers upstream where there were no more trees. The shogunate also banned the creation of new fields that encroached upon existing riverbanks and banned slash-and-burn agriculture in the mountains.[27] Thus the age of rapid economic expansion based on opening new agricultural fields came to an end in the late seventeenth century. Tokugawa Japan had hit its ecological limits.[28]

Population growth mirrored agricultural field expansion. Historical demographers such as Hayami Akira have noted the rapid expansion of population in the seventeenth century (similar to the expansion of agricultural fields) and then its stagnation in the later part of the Tokugawa period. Hayami estimated that the population of Japan as whole was around 12 million in 1600, which then ballooned to around 30 million in 1721. This number remained stable until the early Meiji period. In 1873, the new Meiji government conducted its first census yielding a population of 33.3 million.[29] Thus this population dynamic mirroring the agricultural story initially was seen as proof supporting the theory that the Tokugawa economy stagnated and could not raise the living standards of the people.

However, this apparently stable national population actually masked a stark regional divide. Hayami and others have demonstrated that the population of Japan took severe hits during times of famine but that in western Japan, the population was able to recover and increased, whereas in eastern Japan, the population was not able to recover and decreased. From 1721 to 1846 eighteen provinces in western Japan increased their population by more than 20 percent. Meanwhile three provinces in eastern Japan, Kōzuke (present-day Gunma prefecture), Shimotsuke (present-day Tochigi prefecture), and Hitachi (present-day Ibaraki prefecture) recorded a population decline of more than 20 percent.[30] The overall stability of the Japanese national population was the result of a declining population in the east and a rising population in the west.

Even more interestingly, despite the rising population in western Japan, the population of Kinai at the heart of western Japan declined more (11.2 percent decline) during this period from 1721 to 1846 than the population of southern Kantō at the heart of eastern Japan (5.2 percent decline).[31] So the large urban centers in both western Japan and eastern Japan declined. Hayami's elegant explanation for this loss of population in the major cities is

Table 1.2. Chart of Estimated Production in *Koku* and Estimated Overall Population

	1598–1600	*1645*	*1697*	*1721*	*1834*	*1873*
Rice, *koku*	18,500,000	24,600,000	25,900,000		30,600,000	
Population	12,000,000			30,000,000		33,300,000

Source: Information compiled from Kimura, *Kinsei no mura*, 25–26; Hayami, *Rekishi jinkōgaku de mita Nihon*, 57, 66–70; Kitō, *Jinkō kara yomu Nihon no rekishi*, 16–17, 81–86, 95.

called the "city as antlion trap theory." According to this theory, as commercialization expanded, peasants no longer saw the need to migrate to cities in search for work. Instead, the peasants remained on the farm and additionally produced commercial goods to be sold on the market. Thus when peasants surrounding Osaka and Kyoto stopped immigrating to Osaka and Kyoto, these two cities began to shrink. They shrank because premodern cities required the constant influx of immigrants to maintain their population. Premodern cities, unlike cities with modern medicine and hygiene, were death traps that killed more people than it bore. This is the "Toshi arijigokusetsu" or "city as antlion trap theory."[32]

To understand the Tokugawa period's agriculture and population, scholars started with agriculture and initially thought there was a story of rise and then of stability/stagnation. But with a more careful analysis of the national, regional, and local pictures, historical demographers have demonstrated that the seeming national population stability masks a dynamic demographic shift, both at the regional level (western rise and eastern fall) and at the local level (decline of Osaka and Kyoto). This history of early modern agriculture and demography further highlights the need to understand the Tokugawa economy from a regional perspective and not just a national perspective. A recent work by Fabian Drixler precisely addresses this issue and explains the decline and fall of the population of eastern Japan.[33]

REGIONAL RESPONSES TO COMMERCIALIZATION

If the expansion of agricultural fields and overall population growth slowed dramatically after the eighteenth century, commercialization continued relentlessly. During the seventeenth century, commerce connected all of Japan via sea routes. During the eighteenth century, merchants sold more specialty products in greater quantities than ever before. As long as a vast consuming market in Edo existed, someone would emerge to supply the demand. And those able to supply this demand became wealthy. So who supplied the demand? In general it was the people and domains in western Japan that responded to this demand by diversifying and producing specialty goods.

For example, domains sought to create products that they could monopolize: Satsuma domain in southern Kyushu produced sugar, Saga domain in northern Kyushu produced porcelain, Chōshū domain in western Chūgoku produced paper, Akō domain in eastern Chūgoku produced sea salt, and Tokushima domain in Shikoku produced indigo. Ordinary farmers and artisans also specialized: the Nada district near Kobe produced sake, the farms surrounding Osaka produced cotton and vegetable oil, while in the city of Kyoto artisans produced Nishijin silk and the farms surrounding Kyoto produced tea. Also in what is geographically eastern Japan but within the "silver zone" of the Osaka-centered economy, Yamagata domain in the Japan Sea side of the northeast produced safflower (*benibana*), while others produced dried seafood (*tawaramono*). Even if many of these goods were known before the eighteenth century, the increased production, the wide distribution, and mass consumption inside Japan were new developments.

This surge in various specialty goods production also owes much to two shogunal policies. One policy curbed international trade. In 1715 Arai Hakuseki, a shogunal adviser, limited the amount of international trade and also forbade the export of gold and silver to pay for cotton cloth and silk cloth imports. Therefore, Japan after 1715 had to undergo import substitution for cotton and silk, and discovered dried seafood as the main replacement for the export of gold and silver.[34] The other policy spurred peasants to work harder. Under the *jōmenhō* (predetermined tax), the peasants paid a predetermined amount in taxes to the authorities each year, regardless of the harvest, bountiful or lackluster.[35] Initially adopted in various parts of western Japan, in 1723 the shogunate also adopted this policy under the eighth shogun Yoshimune. By promising not to collect the extra harvest during bountiful years as tax, the *jōmenhō* encouraged peasants to produce as much as they could, as they could keep the difference. If they were making commercial products, any extra cash income would remain theirs. Unfortunately in many parts of eastern Japan, many domains did not adopt this tax policy and instead relied on the more traditional *kemihō* (assessment tax), wherein officials examined the harvest and collected as much taxes as they could.

If western Japan responded to commercialization by producing more specialty products in the eighteenth century, eastern Japan responded by producing more rice. Faced with a flood of products from Osaka, the peasants and domains in the east made an understandable decision. After all, rice was the yardstick of wealth. Producing more rice meant being able to sell that extra rice in Osaka or in Edo. However, with the technology available at the time, rice production in northeastern Japan was barely within its ecological limits and thus a very dangerous choice. A cold summer easily destroyed much of the rice crop.[36] And when that happened, the domains in eastern Japan were in a poor position to respond. If their rice crop failed, they did not have the food or the potential income to buy food elsewhere. The production of specialty products in eastern Japan,[37] such as soy sauce in Chōshi (present-day Chiba prefecture), silk in Kiryū (present-day Gunma prefecture), cotton in Shimodate (present-day Ibaraki prefecture), and tobacco in Hadano (present-day Kanagawa prefecture), lagged behind western Japan significantly.

Thus the regional variation in population growth and decline, as seen in the previous section, was actually the result of divergent regional responses to commercialization. In general, western Japan (or more precisely, the silver zone) rode the wave of commercialization through specialization, and its domains and peoples benefitted from it. This change was not an easy change, but it did lead to an "industrious revolution," a phrase coined by Hayami Akira, in which the people learned the benefits of working hard and willingly put in more hours for a better life.[38] These peasants stayed in the countryside, engaged in by-employment, and did not go to the urban centers, the antlion traps. The domains in turn did their best to protect their people's livelihoods despite struggling with debt or famine (even if they failed, their people were better off than their counterparts in eastern Japan). For example, one of the major famines of the Tokugawa period, the Kyōhō famine (1732–1733), struck western Japan particularly hard but the region recovered.[39] The population increase in many parts of western Japan was not an accident.

Eastern Japan (or more precisely, the gold zone) responded to the wave of commercialization by making more rice to sell on the Osaka or Edo markets and to buy goods from western Japan. When crops failed, many domains in the east initially responded by squeezing the peasants for more rice. The Hōreki famine (1753–1757) and the Tenmei famine (1783–1786) devastated eastern Japan, killing hundreds of thousands. This led to starving peasants flooding into Edo looking for food or work. Therefore, the large population decline in eastern Japan was also not an accident but rather a response to failed domain policy in the face of commercialization and famines. The cases of Sakuramachi, Sōma domain, and of most domains in present-day Gunma prefecture are illustrative of this failure in government policy.[40] The fact that the population of south Kantō did not decline as much compared to Kinai (as mentioned in the previous section) actually reflects the failure of the domains in eastern Japan to protect the livelihood of their peasants and is indicative of the influx of destitute peasants to Edo. However, when the Tempō famine (1837–1838) struck eastern Japan again, many officials had learned their lessons and prevented deaths by lowering or exempting taxes and providing emergency aid to the starving poor. For these domains, the nineteenth century proved to be a time of resurgence.

REGIONALISM AND THE FIRST THREE MAJOR SHOGUNAL RESPONSES TO COMMERCIALIZATION

The *bakufu* made four major policy responses to commercialization: (1) the series of laws passed by Ogiwara Shigehide and Arai Hakuseki, (2) shogun Yoshimune's Kyōhō Reforms, (3) Tanuma Okitsugu's policies, and (4) the Tempō Reforms by Mizuno Tadakuni. This section covers the first three.

During the late seventeenth and early eighteenth centuries, Ogiwara Shigehide and Arai Hakuseki led the first response. These two men shared a similar foreign trade policy of limiting trade to prevent the outflow of silver and gold. This agreement was important because it shows how shogunal policy makers began to see Japan as an economic unit. They may not have been fully mercantilist, of encouraging the flow of gold and silver into the country, but the policy makers agreed upon a close variant, preventing the outflow of gold and silver, and consciously adopted a policy of import substitution.[41]

However, despite this agreement, they had opposite monetary policies. Ogiwara astutely realized that increased commercialization meant the need for more currency and in 1695 initiated a mild inflationary policy by debasing the currency and increasing the money supply. In fact, Ogiwara recognized the viability of a fiat currency by declaring that currency is created by the state and that even pottery shards can be used as money.[42] Arai believed that currency was backed by the content of precious metals and argued against this policy of debasement. Ultimately Arai prevailed and reminted the coins issued under Ogiwara to restore the old gold and silver content of the money in 1714.[43] Unfortunately because Japan's gold and silver mineral resources were depleted, in increasing the gold and silver content of the money, the amount of coins in circulation had to decrease. By shrinking the available money supply, Arai caused a major deflation.

The eighth shogun Tokugawa Yoshimune undertook the second major economic policy response, called the Kyōhō Reforms (1716–1745). These reforms were necessary because the rice price compared to the price of other goods was now lower, most likely from increased rice production in eastern Japan and the relative scarcity of specialty goods from western Japan. In other words, for the samurai who collected rice as tax, the low rice price meant a lowering of their income if other goods were more expensive. Typically a samurai received the majority of his income as rice and sold the excess that he and his family could not eat. This cash income was used to purchase the other goods.[44]

Under the Kyōhō Reforms, the shogun first raised taxes to collect more rice.[45] Raising taxes was the intent behind the adoption of the *jōmenhō* mentioned earlier: getting the peasants to work harder was a byproduct. By collecting more rice, the shogunal coffer could offset the lower price by selling more rice, but this did not solve the problem of high prices of other goods in Edo. Second, Yoshimune tried to lower the price of various goods by encouraging merchants to form guilds. These were not monopoly guilds, but the shogunate wanted to monitor the flow of goods and thus organized the merchants. When merchants parked their wares outside of Edo to wait for higher prices, shogunal officials could order the merchants to ship the goods into Edo. Unfortunately for the shogunate, this monitoring had a negligible effect on prices. In another attempt to lower the price of non-rice goods, the shogunate encouraged the production of specialty goods. It hoped that a larger supply would lead to lower prices.

In the end, the treasury officials changed the silver and gold content of coins by devaluing the silver currency in Osaka more relative to the gold currency in Edo. Although Yoshimune was initially opposed to this policy, with a stronger gold-based currency in Edo, cheap goods flowed from Osaka once again.[46] Thus during this second major economic policy response, the shogunate once again recognized its regional and class interests by prioritizing the lives of the samurai living in Edo. The shogunate had to carefully balance the national economic interests with its regional economic interests.

In the third major economic policy response under Tanuma Okitsugu, the shogunate tapped into the commercial economy that had grown significantly and tried to resolve the regional divide. Starting in the late 1750s, the government granted monopoly rights to various commercial guilds in exchange for a yearly tax and greatly increased its revenue. In other words, the shogunate now taxed the merchants. Tanuma also tried to unify the currency by issuing gold coins denominated in the silver currency of *monme* and silver coins denominated in the gold currency of *shu*. His boldest plan was to directly administer Ezochi (present-day Hokkaido) and seek to conduct trade with Russia. During the Tenmei famine, he sought to move food from the surplus regions to starving regions, but this plan failed due to *daimyō* resistance. Tanuma Okitsugu had a national vision for the role of the Tokugawa shogunate. However, these economic policies were almost all reversed by his political opponent, Matsudaira Sadanobu, in the Kansei Reforms (1787–1793).[47]

Matsudaira Sadanobu focused on decreasing the spending of the shogunate instead of increasing its income. To do this, he imposed his grandfather Yoshimune's personal policy of frugality. Unfortunately, he imposed it on everyone including the commoners. Perhaps his most important reform was to order each domain to stockpile emergency food and for Edo landlords to stockpile emergency cash in cases of famine.[48] He also urged moral reforms to restore order, such as the ban on heterodox Confucianism. His economic policies tended to ignore economic reality, such as annulling all debts accrued by shogunal retainers before 1784 or ordering the peasant migrants in Edo to return to their home villages. Of Tanuma's policies mentioned above, only the monopoly guilds survived. Unsurprisingly, reforms that ignored reality proved unpopular, and in 1793 Matsudaira Sadanobu fell from power.[49]

As can be seen from the shogunal responses to commercialization, the shogunate exhibited a dual role: a role to protect and regulate the national economy and a role to protect and defend the interests of Edo and its samurai residents. In the first response the shogunate articulated a quasi-mercantilist policy to protect the country as a whole. In the second response, the shogunate intervened to protect the samurai of Edo. In the third response, the shogunate tried to unite the two currencies with an eye on the national picture. In repealing most of third response, the shogunate not only reverted to protecting its narrow interests, but also informed domains that ultimately they were on their own in cases of famine. Both a national approach and a regional approach are indispensable to understanding the history of early modern Japan.

THE LAST MAJOR SHOGUNAL RESPONSE TO COMMERCIALIZATION

While the shogunate was combating low rice prices and its ballooning expenses, a new structural problem emerged to threaten the Tokugawa economic system. If the early Tokugawa economic system relied on three cities—Edo, Osaka, and Kyoto—the relentless commercialization eroded the position of all three. In other words, before the shogunate figured out whether it was a truly national government or a more regional government, the economy began to change under its feet.

By the mid-eighteenth century, Kyoto began to lose its manufacturing edge. The carefully guarded secrets, such as the techniques for making *chirimen* (crepe) of Nishijin silk and the dyeing of threads and fabrics, eventually seeped out to various locations throughout the country. Merchants now began to buy the raw materials near the local production centers and peasants made the specialty goods locally without sending them to the artisans of Kyoto. The development of silk markets at Kiryū and Takasaki in Gunma prefecture is one such example.[50] These specialty goods in turn were sold directly to consumers without sending them to castle towns or to Osaka. Even in the deep interior of mountainous Japan, the Shimoina valley, Kären Wigen notes this same phenomenon of merchants connecting the producers directly with the consumers.[51]

By the late eighteenth century, just as Kyoto lost its manufacturing role, Osaka began to lose its role as the central distribution city. This was problematic for the shogunate because by gathering all goods at Osaka, the shogunate artificially created a hypercompetitive market at Osaka. This competition artificially lowered prices of many goods, and these goods then travelled to Edo. This was how the residents of Edo reaped the benefits of the early modern economic system. However, if goods no longer gathered at Osaka then two things happened: First, without a hypercompetitive market, the prices of various goods would rise in Osaka and Edo. Second, without the products gathering in Osaka, there would be fewer jobs. Without the demand for jobs in Kyoto and Osaka, the peasants in western Japan stopped migrating to these cities. Consequently Osaka's population declined starting in the second half of the eighteenth century as described by Hayami's city as antlion trap theory.

In eastern Japan, relentless commercialization coupled with domain mismanagement resulted in demographic disaster. Numerous peasants unable to feed themselves began flooding into Edo. And thus Edo began to see an influx of destitute migrants. This alone was a major problem, but when peasants made specialty products locally and some places began to see a recovery after domain mismanagement ended, new buyers of various products emerged in the countryside. Thus, by the early nineteenth century Edo also began to lose its role as the preeminent consuming city. The famous cultural flowering of the Kasei period (1804–1829) included the rural countryside and was not limited to the cities for a reason.

In other words, increasing commercialization robbed the special privileges of the three key cities in the Tokugawa economic system, and no amount of moralizing from the Kansei Reforms (1787–1793) could protect them. Moreover, greedy guild merchants demonstrated how famine conditions could be made even worse under the existing system and the need for further response to economic change. At the peak of the Tempō famine in 1837, Atobe Yoshisuke, the governor of Osaka, prioritized the residents of Edo and ordered rice to be shipped from Osaka to Edo. As rice became scarce, the wealthy rice merchants of Osaka cornered the remaining rice and raised prices, making a figurative killing in profit and a literal killing of the starving poor. Seeing this, Ōshio Heihachirō, a former shogunal police official, planned to revolt in Osaka, calling for the people to burn the corrupt Osaka governor's office and destroy the homes of the heartless rice merchants. Unsurprisingly, many people at the time thought the governor was conspiring with the wealthy rice merchants. Since Ōshio's colleagues leaked the plan, his rebellion was crushed before it could start, but it was a worrying sign that the system designed to benefit Edo, Osaka, and Kyoto was failing.

During the Tempō Reforms (1841–1843), a governor of Osaka, Abe Shōzō, explained the key factor. According to his memorandum dated Tempō 13, third month (April 1842), the emergence of "brands" was the culprit of this change. After two hundred years of Tokugawa peace, commercialization and technological know-how had spread to all parts of Japan. More importantly, the governor recognized that "branding" allowed for goods to bypass Osaka. Commercialization had created certain favorites among the consumers (particularly of Edo) and those brand-name products could command high prices regardless of whether it was shipped via Osaka.

Previously, "shipped from Osaka" acted as a type of brand for all types of goods. High-quality items produced in Kyoto were sent to Osaka to be sold in Edo, and other high-quality goods produced elsewhere were also sent to Osaka to be sold in Edo. Meanwhile, goods produced near Edo were of such low quality that those products not shipped from Osaka were dismissed by the customers in Edo. These low-quality goods were called *kudaranai*—goods that were not shipped "downstream" (i.e., from Osaka and Kyoto to Edo).

However, once brand names for each product emerged, "shipped from Osaka" was no longer necessary as a guarantor of quality. Thus even if the product was made near Edo, as long as the product had brand recognition as a quality product, it could now be sold anywhere in Japan. With many individual brand goods being produced locally then shipped and sold directly to the customers, the role of Osaka diminished. In other words, a new distribution system was threatening Osaka because of "branding."[52]

Daimyō domains, especially those in western Japan, made the problem worse. They created domain monopolies, such as Saga domain's porcelain and Tokushima domain's indigo dye, and sold their products directly to consumers through branding. Moreover, according to the governor, more people were willing to speculate and earn as much as possible as commercialization spread.[53] In other words, merchants hoarded goods until the prices rose and then finally sold the items. Japan was no longer a country that required a central marketplace to determine the prices of various goods. Japan was now a unified market that collectively determined prices. And Japan was increasingly a country dominated by mercantile values and not by samurai or Confucian values.

Another development also lowered Osaka's role as the central marketplace in determining prices and diminished Edo's role as the ultimate consuming city. According to governor Abe, recent shogunal attempts to dictate the flow of goods by strengthening the monopoly guilds had encouraged the creation of "black market" routes that bypassed Osaka and Edo. This was another reason why Osaka no longer accumulated as many goods as in the past,[54] contributing to the decline of its population.[55] And with goods being sent directly to the consumers, the forced hyper-competition of all goods concentrated at Osaka came to an end. As explained earlier, that in turn meant the consumer of Edo could no longer reap the benefit of low prices coming from Osaka.

The governor's solution to this daunting problem was therefore simple but wrong. Ban the new interregional traders, such as the *utsumibune*, which shipped goods directly from the producers to the consumers to destroy the "black market" routes, and restore the system that worked to supply cheap goods to Osaka and Edo.[56] Governor Abe may have understood the problem, but he clearly did not see a new way to actually solve the problem created by branding and commercialization.

The health of Edo, Osaka, and Kyoto was of vital concern to the shogunate. But the most important was always the city of Edo, the shogun's city. This explains why Atobe, the shogunal official who sent rice from Osaka to Edo during a massive famine, was not punished but rather rewarded with higher office. Thus in 1841 after the famine and the death of the previous shogun, the chief *rōjū* Mizuno Tadakuni[57] launched the Tempō Reforms, the last of the four major economic policy responses. In the face of persistently high prices of various goods in Edo, the reform abolished the monopoly guilds and experimented with free trade. The governor of Osaka never sent his memorandum of 1842, perhaps for the better, since Mizuno tried to solve the problem through traditional plans and two bold new plans.

The traditional plans were to increase rice production through the opening of new fields, a call to frugality, and returning the migrants in Edo to their villages. Mizuno's bold new plans attempted to (1) abolish the monopoly guilds and (2) consolidate lands in twenty-five mile radius around Edo and Osaka. Mizuno Tadakuni concluded that the monopoly guilds had raised the price of goods and decided to believe in the new commercial economy. Mizuno hoped that open competition would lower prices by allowing entrepreneurs to enter the economy.[58] After two centuries of deliberate shogunal policy to import cheap goods from the Kansai region and suffering from various natural and manmade disasters, the Kantō regional economy was finally producing goods that could compete with goods from Osaka. But this reform did not lower the price of goods in Edo. Although there may have been cases of price gouging by the monopoly guilds, the main problem was that goods were now bypassing Osaka and Edo and were being sold on the national market as the governor of Osaka indicated.

In confiscating land near Edo and Osaka from the lords and bannermen (*hatamoto*) and consolidating them as direct shogunal territory, the goal was to strengthen shogunal control over these cities and to increase the government's revenues. Mizuno thought that this was a necessary precaution after news of Qing China's military defeats in the Opium War (1839–1842) arrived. However, most of the lords and bannermen probably did not know of the Opium War and protested loudly against the consolidation of territory. Even if they were compensated with other lands, they knew that the lands near Edo and Osaka were worth more than lands nominally equivalent in *koku* in the countryside.

Faced with an uproar by the lords against the consolidation plan, the failure to lower the prices of various goods in Edo, and the loss of taxes from disbanding the monopoly guilds, the Tempō Reforms failed. Mizuno stepped down in 1843 and the consolidation plan was scrapped. Later in 1851 the shogunate allowed the guilds to reconstitute. The shogunate and the treasury officials had no ideological commitment to free trade. They felt only the responsibility to keep prices low in Edo to safeguard the lives of the vassals living there.

Thus after the failure of the Tempō Reforms, the shogunate under the leadership of *rōjū* Abe Masahiro tried to mollify the angered lords residing near Edo and Osaka and sought to restore some control over the economy by allowing the guilds to reform. However, Mizuno's plan to rely on the local economy surrounding Edo did not die. Abe did not give monopoly rights to the reconstituted guilds. These guilds no longer paid yearly taxes, but they lost their monopoly rights and could no longer prevent new merchants from entering their businesses. This ten-year experiment to disband the monopoly guilds signified that the economy surrounding Edo had finally matured and that the shogunate wanted to keep the economy open to entrepreneurial novices (*shirōto*).

The failure of the fourth and last major response to commercialization proved that the shogunate could no longer enhance its powers as the central government in the face of concerted *daimyō* opposition. Considering that many of the top officials in the shogunate, such as the *rōjū*, were also *daimyō*, this is not surprising. The regional divide of the economy (between eastern and western Japan) and the dual nature of the Tokugawa shogunate (as a national government and as a regional government) remained when American Commodore Matthew Perry came to Japan in 1853. In negotiating with foreigners the Tokugawa shogunate had to act as a national government while collecting taxes from only its territories.[59]

CONCLUSION

In examining the development of the international silk industry in Japan, one of the methods used is a regional perspective. This regional perspective can also be used to examine the history of Japan more broadly. The origin of Tokugawa economic system in the seventeenth century explained the divide between the silver-using zone centered on Osaka, namely western Japan, and the gold-using zone centered on Edo, namely eastern Japan. Detailed examinations of the demographic dynamics reveal a rising population in western Japan and a declining population in eastern Japan after the eighteenth century. This difference in population dynamics reflected relatively successful economic policies in western Japan and their failures in eastern Japan.

The political structure overseeing these two regional economies also had a strong regional element. The nominally central government, namely the shogunate, oversaw foreign trade and tried to integrate the entire economy. In the end the shogunate proved to be more of a regional government that did little to interfere in domain policies. Instead it concentrated on its own territories, particularly Edo, and would focus on strengthening its own navy and army by the time of its demise.

And yet by the nineteenth century commercialization connected the economy of early modern Japan into a national market where brand-name producers could sell their goods anywhere in Japan. This national market began to shake the foundations of the economic system put in place in the early seventeenth century. This united yet divided system should not be strange. After all, today humanity lives within a single global capitalist economic system with global brand-name products while using various currencies in countries with widely differing living standards.

In the next chapter this book examines how the shogunal government attempted to organize a new foreign trade for its own benefit. In other words, we trace shogunal policies after the failure of the Tempō Reforms and both a national perspective and a regional perspective are employed. Also how important were the Americans? Chapter 2 reexamines the diplomatic issues from a Japanese domestic policy perspective as well.

NOTES

1. Fukuzawa Yukichi, *Bunmeiron no gairyaku* (1875), vol. 5, ch. 9. Available online and accessed on 23 December 2014, www.geocities.jp/hgonzaemon/bunmeironnogairyaku.html/.

2. Yamada Moritarō, *Nihon shihonshugi bunseki* (Tokyo: Iwanami, 1934); Hattori Shisō, "Ishinshi hōhōjō no shomondai," *Rekishi kagaku* 2, no. 3 (1933). The Marxist historians of Japan fought a famous intellectual battle called the "Nihon shihonshugi ronsō" (debate on Japanese capitalism). Yamada Moritarō and Hattori Shisō were the main participants. This debate was affected by the changing directives from the Communist International in Moscow and the contemporary political debate over whether Japan required one revolution (a socialist revolution) or two revolutions (a capitalist revolution and a socialist revolution). Regardless of the political background, the historical research undertaken by both sides remains valuable.

3. Thomas Smith, *Agrarian Origins of Modern Japan* (Stanford, CA: Stanford University Press, 1959); Thomas Smith, *Native Sources of Japanese Industrialization, 1750–1920* (Berkeley: University of California Press, 1988); David Howell, *Capitalism from Within: Economy, Society, and the State in a Japanese Fishery* (Berkeley: University of California Press, 1995); Kären Wigen, *The Making of a Japanese Periphery, 1750–1920* (Berkeley: University of California Press, 1995); Edward Pratt, *Japan's Protoindustrial Elite: The Economic Foundations of the Gono* (Cambridge, MA: Harvard University Press, 1999).

4. Basil Hall Chamberlain, *Japanese Things: Being Notes on Various Subjects Connected with Japan* (Rutland, VT: Charles E. Tuttle, 1971), 3, 239. Of course, there were exceptions on both sides, such as E. H. Norman or Okakura Tenshin.

5. Susan Hanley, "A High Standard of Living in Nineteenth-Century Japan: Fact or Fantasy?" *Journal of Economic History* 43 (March 1983): 183–92.

6. Yasumaru Yoshio, *Nihon no kindaika to minshū shisō* (Tokyo: Heibonsha, 1999). Originally published in 1974.

7. Hayashi Reiko, *Edo tonya nakama no kenkyū* (Tokyo: Ochanomizu shobō, 1967). During the early Tokugawa period, the distribution network was based on points (cities) and lines (*shoshiki donya*, wholesale merchants dealing in various goods). Later in the eighteenth century it expanded into a network of nodes (rural markets covered by *nakagaishō*, specialized business-to-business merchants who in turn were overseen by specialty *tonya*). Finally, toward the end of the Tokugawa period, a planar distribution wherein small retail merchants directly bought from producers and sold to consumers emerged. Hayashi Reiko and Ōishi Shinzaburō, *Ryūtsū rettō no tanjō* (Tokyo: Kōdansha, 1995).

8. The series *Shinsho: Edo jidai* published from Kōdansha is one attempt at popularizing this new idea. Ōishi Shinzaburō, *Shogun to sobayōnin no seiji* (Tokyo: Kōdansha, 1995); Satō Tsuneo and Ōishi Shinzaburō, *Hinnō shikan wo minaosu* (Tokyo: Kōdansha, 1995); Hayashi and Ōishi, *Ryūtsū rettō no tanjō*. Their view is available in English in Chie Nakane and Shinzaburō Ōishi (eds.), *Tokugawa Japan: The Social and Economic Antecedents of Modern Japan*, trans. Conrad Totman (Tokyo: University of Tokyo Press, 1990).

9. Hayashi and Ōishi, *Ryūtsū rettō no tanjō*, 164.

10. Tadasu Yoshimoto, *A Peasant Sage of Japan: The Life and Work of Sontoku Ninomiya* (New York: Longmans, 1912). This is a translation of Tomita Kōkei's *Hōtokuki*. Yasumaru also rates Ninomiya Sontoku highly as a propagator of a new austere morality. Yasumaru, *Nihon no kindaika to minshū shisō*, 35–39.

11. This setup can be examined in further detail in the case of Mito domain in Itō Yoshiichi, *Kinsei zaikataichi no kōzō* (Tokyo: Rinjinsha, 1967), 26. The case of Ueda domain is described in Ōishi Shinzaburō, *Edo jidai* (Tokyo: Chūōkōronsha, 1977), 81, 88–91.

12. On 3 September 1868, the Meiji government renamed Edo as Tokyo.

13. Edo's commoner population in 1630s was around 150,000. By the 1730s it was 540,000, and it fluctuated between 550,000 and 660,000 until the end of the period. Total population—including the samurai population—remains only an estimate, because samurai population was considered a military secret. However, most scholars agree that there were a significant number of samurai present in Edo, thus making it a city of roughly one million. Ōishi, *Edo jidai*, 113–17. Sekiyama Naotarō estimates 1.1 million. Sekiyama Naotarō, *Kinsei Nihon no jinkō kōzō* (Tokyo: Yoshikawa kōbunkan, 1958), 228. Kitō Hiroshi adopts the estimate of roughly 1.3 million by the 1730s. Kitō Hiroshi, *Jinkō kara yomu Nihon no rekishi* (Tokyo: Kōdansha, 2000), 188, 196. See also Hamano Kiyoshi for a historiography of early modern urban demography. Hamano Kiyoshi, *Kinsei Kyoto no rekishi jinkōgaku teki kenkyū* (Tokyo: Keio University Press, 2007), 23–33.

14. Tokyo-to (ed.), *Tokyo shishikō: Shigaihen* vol. 50 (Tokyo: Tokyo-to, 1961), 416–20, 675–87.

15. Hayashi, *Edo tonya nakama no kenkyū*, 77–78; Hayashi and Ōishi, *Ryūtsū rettō no tanjō*, 88–90. For a more detailed discussion on salt, see Saitō Yoshiyuki, *Utsumibune to bakuhansei shijō no kaitai* (Tokyo: Kashiwa shobō, 1994), 108–46.

16. Kitō, *Jinkō kara yomu Nihon no rekishi,* 201. Kitō references Osaka-shi (ed.), *Osaka shishi* (Osaka: Seibundō, 1979), vols. 1 and 2. Also see Osaka-shi (ed.), *Osaka shishi* (Osaka: Seibundō, 1979), vol. 5, 639.

17. Kojima Keizō used Matsue Shigeyori's (1602–1680) *Kefukigusa*, a primer on poetry published in 1645. Kojima Keizō, *Edo no sangyō runessansu* (Tokyo: Chūkō shinsho, 1989), 102. Okazaki Tetsuji also analyzed Matsue's *Kefukigusa* and counted 1,807 items, of which 334 were aquatic products, 276 were agricultural products, 269 were household items, 171 were forestry products, 167 were clothing items, 164 were arts and crafts goods, 115 were ore and animal products, 113 were medicinal goods, 57 were military items, 55 were production goods, 33 were fuels, and 53 were others. Of this list, Kinai dominated the clothing items and arts and crafts goods. Kinai refers to the provinces centered on Kyoto. In today's prefecture they are Kyoto, Osaka, and Nara. Kansai also refers to the prefectures centered on Kyoto but is slightly wider in scope. In today's prefectures they are Kyoto, Osaka, Nara, Hyōgo, Shiga, and Wakayama. Okazaki Tetsuji, *Edo no shijōkeizai* (Tokyo: Kōdansha, 1999), 45–48.

18. Smith, *The Agrarian Origins of Modern Japan*, 4, 67.

19. Hamano, *Kinsei Kyoto no rekishi jinkōgaku teki kenkyū*, 36.

20. The estimated population of Osaka in 1750 was 410,000. The estimated population of Kyoto in 1750 was 370,000. Saitō Seiji, "Edo jidai no toshi jinkō," *Chiiki kaihatsu* 240 (September 1984): 48–63.

21. Hamano, *Kinsei Kyoto no rekishi jinkōgaku teki kenkyū*, 38.

22. The commoners used copper coins and did not use silver money or gold coins in their daily transactions. It was for large transactions that merchants, samurai, and rich peasants used silver and gold. Furthermore, the economic region centered on Osaka, and using silver also included the Japan Sea side of the country as well and was larger than the economic region centered on Edo. Edo's economic region was mainly confined to the Kantō and Tōkai regions with the Pacific Ocean side of northeastern Japan. This book uses the terms western Japan and eastern Japan as shorthand for these two regions defined by their respective use of silver and gold. A map of these two regions can found at Ōishi, *Shogun to sobayōnin no seiji*, 97.

23. A discussion on the decline of the two great shipping guilds is available in Saitō, *Utsumibune to bakuhansei shijō no kaitai*, 51–60. This book is on the rise of regional shippers, in particular the *utsumibune* from Owari domain.

24. The Shimabara Rebellion of 1637–1638 was a peasant Christian rebellion and an exception to the general peace. Chōshū domain's assault on the imperial palace in 1864, Hamaguri gomon no hen, became the first open conflict among the lords since the fall of Osaka castle in 1615.

25. Area under cultivation is further complicated because the land can be divided into rice paddies and dry fields. Kimura Motoi argues that the acreage under cultivation rose from an estimated 2 million hectares in 1600 to 2.97 million hectares in 1720 and then to 4.13 million hectares in 1873. Kimura Motoi, *Kinsei no mura* (Tokyo: Kyōikusha, 1980), 26. Ōishi Shinzaburō argues that the acreage under cultivation rose slowly from 0.86 million hectares in 930 to 0.95 million hectares in 1450 and then dramatically increased to 1.64 million hectares in 1600. With the peace dividend, the acreage doubled further to 2.97 million hectares in 1720 and then remained stable until 1874, with 3.05 million hectares. Ōishi, *Edo jidai*, 37.

26. Kimura, *Kinsei no mura*, 25–26. Kitō, *Jinkō kara yomu Nihon no rekishi*, 95. Kojima Keizō and Miyamoto Matao estimated rice production to be higher, 31 million *koku* by 1700 and 41 million *koku* by 1850. Kojima, *Edo no sangyō runessansu*, 59. For more on this topic in English, see Hayami Akira, "A Great Transformation: Social and Economic Change in Sixteenth and Seventeenth Century Japan," *Bonner Zeitschrift für Japanologie* 8 (1986); Kozo Yamamura, "Returns on Unification: Economic Growth in Japan, 1550–1650," in *Japan before Tokugawa: Political Consolidation and Economic Growth, 1500–1650*, ed. John W. Hall, Nagahara Keiji, Kozo Yamamura (Princeton, NJ: Princeton University Press, 1981), 334.

27. This is the famous *Shokoku sansen okite* of 1666. Satō and Ōishi, *Hinnō shikan wo minaosu*, 13–15, 39–40; Ōishi, *Edo jidai*, 55–62. A translation is available in Conrad Totman, *Early Modern Japan* (Berkeley: University of California Press, 1993), 230.

28. Totman also incorporates an environmental approach to understand Tokugawa economic history but continues to treat Japan as one unit and does not examine the regional variations. Totman, *Early Modern Japan*, 249–59.

29. Hayami Akira, *Rekishi jinkōgaku de mita Nihon* (Tokyo: Bungei shunjū, 2001), 57, 69–70. Kitō has a more precise number of 31,278,500 persons in 1721. Kitō, *Jinkō kara yomu Nihon no rekishi*, 16–17, 83–86.

30. Kitō adds the Hōreki famine (1753–1757) to the three that Hayami lists: the Kyōhō famine (1732–1733), the Tenmei famine (1783–1786), the Tempō famine (1837–1838). Kitō, *Jinkō kara yomu Nihon no rekishi*, 96–100; Hayami, *Rekishi jinkōgaku de mita Nihon*, 60–64.

31. Kitō, *Jinkō kara yomu Nihon no rekishi*, 99.

32. Hayami, *Rekishi jinkōgaku de mita Nihon*, 64–66. This theory is also argued by Thomas Smith in *Native Sources of Japanese Industrialization, 1750–1920*, 35.

33. Drixler argues that population of eastern Japan began to recover starting in 1850. Fabian Drixler, *Mabiki: Infanticide and Population Growth in Eastern Japan, 1660–1950* (Berkeley: University of California Press, 2012), 2.

34. Ōishi credits shoguns Tsunayoshi and Yoshimune with limiting international trade and encouraging the production of specialty products, respectively. Tsunayoshi's treasury magistrate Ogiwara Shigehide began limiting trade by replacing the export of silver with the export of copper in 1697. Arai Hakuseki's policy reinforced existing policy by banning outright the export of silver. Ōishi, *Shogun to sobayōnin no seiji*, 118–20, 185–86. Murai Atsushi thinks Ogiwara was more important because the shogunate came to directly control foreign trade under him. This control prevented smuggling and lowered prices while profiting the shogunal coffers. Murai Atsushi, *Kanjō bugyō Ogiwara Shigehide no shōgai* (Tokyo: Shūeisha, 2007), 140–58. Kate Wildman Nakai sees Arai Hakuseki's policy of limiting foreign trade more positively as this policy successfully stood the test of time. Kate Wildman Nakai, *Shogunal Politics: Arai Hakuseki and the Premises of Tokugawa Rule* (Cambridge, MA: Harvard University Press, 1988). Itakura Kiyonobu argues Yoshimune did not encourage the production of new specialty products but rather froze the existing economic framework. Itakura Kiyonobu, *Nihonshi saihakken: rikei no shiten kara* (Tokyo: Asahi shimbunsha, 1993), 188–93. This is an exaggeration as it is well known that under Yoshimune, the shogunate imported of Dutch scientific books, encouraged the production of sweet potatoes to prepare for famines, succeeded in cultivating a domestic supply of ginseng (an important medicine), and other novel endeavors.

35. In famine years, the authorities typically relented and did not collect the same amount as tax. Kimura, *Kinsei no mura*, 60–63.

36. Kitō argues that the Little Ice Age came to Japan from 1750 to 1850 and hurt eastern Japan more than western Japan. Kitō, *Jinkō kara yomu Nihon no rekishi*, 101–2.

37. In western Japan, where they did produce specialty products, the people could always sell their products and use the cash to buy rice grown elsewhere during times of rice crop failure.

38. Hayami made this argument in 1976. Hayami, *Rekishi jinkōgaku de mita Nihon*, 98. Yasumaru Yoshio makes a similar argument about how this commercialization created the people's morality of Japan in eastern Japan. Yasumaru argues that it was the possibility of falling into poverty that caused people to adopt a new morality in the east. Yasumaru, *Nihon no kindaika to minshū shisō*, 25–43. Considering that Ninomiya Sontoku admonished villagers for being lazy and for the need "to work hard and live frugally" to become prosperous in eastern Japan, both are correct. Yoshimoto, *A Peasant Sage of Japan*, 107, 127. For more in English see Smith, *Native Sources of Japanese Industrialization, 1750–1920*, 211–20.

39. An infestation of *unka* (small winged insects) destroyed the rice harvest of western Japan in the Kyōhō famine. Kitō, *Jinkō kara yomu Nihon no rekishi*, 96–102.

40. The decline of Sakuramachi in Tochigi prefecture can be seen in Yoshimoto, *A Peasant Sage of Japan*, 30, 37–38, 45, 94. The cases of Sōma domain and of domains in Gunma are addressed in the next chapter.

41. Arai Hakuseki estimated that in one hundred years of trade, approximately one quarter of Japan's gold and three quarters of its silver had been exported. In response, he urged that Japan adopt domestic medicine, use domestic cotton, tobacco, and silk, and seek foreign seeds for plants that were imported. Arai Hakuseki, *Oritaku shiba no ki* (Tokyo: Iwanami, 1999), 281–84.

42. Murai, *Kanjō bugyō Ogiwara Shigehide no shōgai*, 117, 120–25. Ōishi, *Shogun to sobayōnin no seiji*, 94.

43. Arai Hakuseki's hatred for Ogiwara Shigehide was intense, calling him a man without talent or virtue who spread poison throughout the land. Arai, *Oritaku shiba no ki*, 259–73.

44. For more on the daily life of samurai, the following are illustrative: Komatsu Shigeo, *Hatamoto no keizaigaku: Oniwaban Kawamura Nagatomi no todomeshū* (Tokyo: Shinchōsha, 1991) and Isoda Michifumi, *Bushi no kakeibo: "Kagahan gosanyōmono" no bakumatsu ishin* (Tokyo: Shinchōsha, 2003).

45. The raising of taxes coincided with a rise in the number of peasant protests (*ikki*) to lower tax rates. Ōishi, *Edo jidai*, 185–88. Combined with these peasant protests, the rise in rural commercial production meant living standards in villages rose during the second half of the Tokugawa period. This is because the shogunate did not conduct a large scale land survey after the Genroku land survey (ca 1700). Murai, *Kanjō bugyō Ogiwara Shigehide no shōgai*, 65. As long as the shogunate maintained the *jōmenhō* and collected the same amount of taxes, actual tax rates declined because income increased. Satō and Ōishi, *Hinnō shikan wo minaosu*, 114–19; Smith, *Native Sources of Japanese Industrialization, 1750–1920*, 69–70.

46. Both the gold and silver contents were devalued in 1736. This devaluation also worked because the gold coins issued since 1714 had caused deflation and this devaluation increased the amount of currency in circulation to restore a balance between the increased economic activity and the amount of money in the economy. Ōishi, *Shogun to sobayōnin no seiji*, 172–74. For more on monetary policy, see Hayashi Reiko, "Provisioning Edo in the Early Eighteenth Century: The Pricing Policies of the Shogunate and the Crisis of 1733," in *Edo and Paris: Urban Life and the State in the Early Modern Era*, ed. James McClain, John Merriman, and Ugawa Kaoru (Ithaca, NY: Cornell University Press, 1994), 211–33 and Ohkura Takehiko and Shimbo Hiroshi, "Tokugawa Monetary Policy in the Eighteenth and Nineteenth Centuries," *Explorations in Economic History* 15, no. 1 (January 1978):101–24. The same essay is also available in *Japanese Economic History 1600–1960: The Japanese Economy in the Tokugawa Era, 1600–1868*, ed. Michael Smitka (New York: Routledge, 1998), 241–65.

47. According to Ōishi, Tanuma Okitsugu became influential in 1758, critical for policy in 1767, and fell from power in 1786. Ōishi, *Shogun to sobayōnin no seiji*, 198–200, 213–23, 237–38. One English language work on Tanuma is John Whitney Hall, *Tanuma Okitsugu, 1719–1788: Forerunner of Modern Japan* (Cambridge, MA: Harvard University Press, 1955).

48. Matsudaira Sadanobu as lord of Shirakawa domain secured the lives of all his peasants during the Tenmei famine, but he did so by ignoring Tanuma Okitsugu's orders and importing extra rice from Osaka and Aizu. Perhaps he understood better than anyone that lords would not

be willing to let food out of their domains during famines. Ōishi, *Shogun to sobayōnin no seiji*, 207.

49. An English language work on Matsudaira Sadanobu is Herman Ooms, *Charismatic Bureaucrat: A Political Biography of Matsudaira Sadanobu, 1758–1829* (Chicago: University of Chicago Press, 1975).

50. Gunma kenshi hensan iinkai (eds.), *Gunma kenshi: Shiryōhen* IX, *Kinsei* I (Maebashi: Gunma ken, 1970s), no. 283.

51. Wigen, *The Making of a Japanese Periphery*, 66–67.

52. Saitō, *Utsumibune to bakuhansei shijō no kaitai*, 152–54, 159–60.

53. For many western domains, taking advantage of the commercial economy was necessary, for they could only make their ends meet through engaging in commerce. Saitō, *Utsumibune to bakuhansei shijō no kaitai*, 160–62.

54. In just twenty years between 1820 and 1840, there was a serious decline in the volume of goods shipped to Osaka. In 1840 only 72 percent of the rice arriving in 1820 came to Osaka; for raw cotton, 67 percent, paper 64 percent, wax 60 percent, iron 42 percent, ceramics 30 percent, and so forth. This clearly shows that goods were now bypassing Osaka and going straight to the customers. Saitō, *Utsumibune to bakuhansei shijō no kaitai*, 157–58.

55. Osaka's population declined from 413,000 in 1769 to 379,000 in 1820 and then to 281,000 in 1868. Osaka-shi (ed.), *Osaka shishi*, vol. 5, 639. Also see table 1.1.

56. Saitō, *Utsumibune to bakuhansei shijō no kaitai*, 147–50.

57. Atobe Yoshisuke was the biological younger brother of Mizuno Tadakuni (*rōjū* from 1834 to 1843 and 1844 to 1845), another likely reason why Atobe was not punished but promoted for sending rice from Osaka to Edo in 1837.

58. Hayashi and Ōishi, *Ryūtsū rettō no tanjō*, 155.

59. By the nineteenth century, the total productive capacity of Japan was nominally at 30.6 million *koku*, while the shogunate directly controlled land worth 4 to 4.5 million *koku*, and another 4 million *koku* was controlled by its *hatamoto* (banner men). Added to this are the income from its gold, silver, and copper mines, the income from foreign trade at Nagasaki, and (until 1841) the income from taxes on monopoly guilds. In short, it had to take on the role of a national government with the income of roughly one quarter of Japan.

Chapter Two

The Failure of the Tempō Reforms and the Opening of Yokohama

The opening of Japan is normally told from the perspective of the West. American Commodore Matthew C. Perry sailed into Edo Bay with his "Black Ships," forcing the shogunal officials to sign the first modern treaty between Japan and the West in 1854. Then, in 1858, the only Western diplomat in Shimoda, Townsend Harris, successfully cajoled the Japanese to sign the first modern commercial treaty, despite the unenthusiastic response of the shogunal government.

With these two stories, historians project the image that the West pushed Japan to open and that Japan did not want to open itself to the outside world. This image is both correct and wrong at the same time. It is correct because the United States did want to open contact with Japan and initiate trade. And the Japanese signers of the Perry treaty and the Harris treaty, namely Abe Masahiro and Ii Naosuke, were reluctant to open the country. It is wrong because there were people inside Japan who wanted to open the country to trade. This chapter is about those in the shogunal government who wanted to open Japan. Their story can be seen clearly by adopting an economic perspective, a vantage point that is usually overlooked in diplomatic history.

In this economic story one individual stands out, namely Hotta Masayoshi. Serving as the leader of the shogunate between Abe and Ii, Hotta wanted to open Japan and gain revenue for the shogunate through tariffs. Moreover, he and Iwase Tadanari sought to reorder the economic geography of Japan. Their goal was to make the area surrounding Edo the preeminent economic region of the country through international trade. In other words, these two men of the shogunate proposed to open Japan, with Yokohama as the main foreign trade port. Once Yokohama was put on the table, there was no going back. Even after Hotta fell from power and the conservative Ii Naosuke took over, the opening of Yokohama could not be reversed. Therefore, the first sentence of this chapter should more properly be: American Commodore Matthew C. Perry opened Japan's diplomatic relations, but Hotta Masayoshi opened Japan to trade. In order to understand this decisive moment led by Hotta, this chapter starts by examining the failure of the Tempō Reforms (1841–1843) and not with the arrival of Commodore Perry in 1853.

REPERCUSSIONS FROM THE FAILURE OF THE TEMPŌ REFORMS

On the thirteenth day of the intercalary ninth month of Tempō 14 (1843),[1] the shogun fired Mizuno Tadakuni as chief *rōjū* (minister). Mizuno's Tempō Reforms had come to an end. Two days prior, Abe Masahiro, the lord of Fukuyama domain (100,000 *koku*), was appointed *rōjū*. The twelfth shogun, Tokugawa Ieyoshi, had selected Abe because he was seen as a man of good judgment who could resolve interpersonal disputes without unduly harming the reputation of important people. This was most likely the result of Abe's temperament, but also because he had a traditional Confucian education and tried to act as a Confucian gentleman. Even after he was selected as *rōjū*, Abe continued to invite Confucian scholars to his mansion three times a month to further his studies and cement his image as a sincere Confucian.[2] In short, the shogun tasked Abe Masahiro and others to quietly resolve the disaster that was the Tempō Reforms.

The Tempō Reforms were put in place to solve three perennial issues facing the shogunate: a shortage of shogunal revenue, national defense, and the lack of cheap non-rice goods for the samurai in Edo. Mizuno sought to solve these issues by restraining spending, raising taxes, consolidating land near Edo and Osaka for defense, and dismantling the monopoly guilds.[3]

Restraining spending was simple. The previous eleventh shogun had spent too much on his harem, and thus Mizuno ordered a drastic reduction of spending for the harem. Moreover, he issued sumptuary edicts to end what he considered extravagant spending by the shogun's vassals and even the ordinary citizens of Edo. Naturally the women of the harem and ordinary citizens hated Mizuno for these acts.

Mizuno then proposed to raise taxes by developing new fields and increasing taxable land. His most famous civil engineering project tackled the marshy Lake Inba-numa.[4] This project was not only a plan to increase cultivatable land and to prevent floods, it was also part of his national defense plan. Mizuno wanted to open new fields and to create a new waterway connecting Chōshi city on the Pacific coast with Edo. The key to this waterway would be a new canal dug between Lake Inba-numa and Kemigawa River. This new alternate waterborne route for foods and supplies coming into Edo would not only improve things economically, it was also designed to be a backup route in case of a war. Thus even if Uraga channel, the main entrance to Edo, was blockaded by foreign ships, the shogun's city would not starve.[5] Considering that the Qing surrendered because the British cut the supply of rice flowing into Beijing, Mizuno's ambitious plan had merit.

To lower the prices of goods in Edo, Mizuno disbanded the monopoly guilds. These guilds used to pay the shogunate taxes for their monopoly rights. By disbanding the monopoly guilds, Mizuno hoped competition would lower the price of goods in Edo. Mizuno had also stopped the minting of debased coins in 1842 and issued orders to assess the possibility of reminting higher quality coins to end the inflation. When the gold guild reported that an estimated twenty million *ryō* (gold coins) would be necessary to restore the quality of the gold coins, Mizuno halted the restoration plan.[6] The shogunate simply had no extra gold to collect the debased Tempō coins and replace them with higher quality coins. But by stopping the debasement of currency, he could at least end the ongoing inflation, and by encouraging competition, he hoped prices would decrease.

As one might expect, these three reforms were highly unpopular. The women of the harem, ordinary citizens, the lords who paid for the canal's construction, and the monopoly merchants all complained. But Mizuno did not stop there. He ordered the *agechirei* edict of 1843, the most controversial of his reforms. The *agechirei* was a plan to consolidate an area twenty-five miles in radius surrounding the cities of Edo and Osaka. The plan was for the shogun to take all vassal-held land in this area and compensate them with land elsewhere. This plan was intended to increase shogunal revenues from the economically valuable suburban land.

The *agechirei* was also a plan to strengthen the defense of Edo and Osaka in case of a foreign attack. The news from China that Britain had decisively defeated Qing China in the Opium War (1839–1842) was momentous. Consequently in 1842, Mizuno repealed the 1825 edict to fire on all foreign ships approaching Japanese shores. Instead he ordered lords to rescue and provide foreign shipwrecked vessels with water, food, and fuel. This eliminated possible pretexts for war. The *agechirei* of 1843 complemented this order by consolidating the land near Edo and Osaka and thereby increased the shogunate's ability to defend the two coastal cities in case of a war.

In this way Mizuno Tadakuni took responsible action when confronted with the changing balance of power in East Asia and the triple problem facing the *bakufu*. However, news of a distant war did not gather the attention of most vassals. In fact many were more concerned with their own finances, about losing valuable land near Edo and Osaka. As opposition to the Tempō Reforms increased, Mizuno's political ally and fellow *rōjū* Hotta Masayoshi remonstrated with him. When Hotta realized that Mizuno would ignore his advice, Hotta resigned, ending his first stint as minister after twenty months on the job.[7] Eventually other high-ranking shogunal officials and Mizuno's own brother opposed the *agechirei*, and in a storm of protest Mizuno's days as chief minister came to an end. The Tempō Reforms ended with a major rift between the shogun and his vassals.

The shogun selected Abe Masahiro to end this controversy and heal the divide between the shogun and his vassals. As such, the first thing that Abe and the other ministers did was to revoke the *agechirei*. However, scrapping this edict meant that they needed to solve the problems that the *agechirei* was supposed to resolve. In other words, they still needed to increase revenue and defend the country. And they still needed to worry about the lack of cheap goods in Edo, the third problem facing the shogunate. Among the three problems, the lack of revenue became the most serious problem because a fire burned down Edo castle in 1844. On top of the existing problems, the shogun now had to rebuild his home.

When Abe and others repealed the *agechirei*, they could have also repealed Mizuno's ban on monopoly guilds. Allow monopoly guilds to re-form and collect taxes from them to raise the revenue. Or they could continue to push on with the development of Lake Inba-numa to increase future taxes. However, Abe and others chose to continue with Mizuno's experiment with free trade and abandon the costly Lake Inba-numa project. Unlike the *agechirei*, the disbanding of monopoly guilds had already gone into effect starting in 1841, and Abe chose not to cause further economic disruption by repealing a law that had already been in effect for two years. The revenue that was raised from the taxes on monopoly guilds was not small, at roughly 10,200 *ryō* when Mizuno Tadakuni abolished them,[8] but compared to the shogunate's main source of income, taxes on rice production or the potential from the debasement of currency, this sum was insignificant.[9] As for the Lake Inba-numa project, it was deemed too costly and thus abandoned.

The solution Abe and other *rōjū* adopted was to resume the minting of debased coins and gain the difference, namely seigniorage. They saw no other choice: rebuilding the burned-down Edo castle was of paramount importance. In 1844, seigniorage brought in roughly 840,000 *ryō* as profit and paid for the cost of rebuilding the castle: a princely sum of 206,255 *ryō* for the lumber and 483,933 *ryō* for construction.[10] Unfortunately, issuing the debased coins resulted in inflation. Quite simply, there were more coins in the economy chasing the same amount of goods, so the price of various goods rose accordingly. Considering that the bulk of the shogun's vassals never had a pay raise, the continued inflation made them feel poorer.

MIZUNO TADAKUNI'S REINSTATEMENT AND FALL

Of the three problems identified at the time of the Tempō Reforms—lack of revenue, national defense, and the lack of cheap goods—the revenue problem was resolved through currency debasement. The third problem, namely the lack of cheap goods, worsened because of it, while the second issue, national defense, was ignored. But national defense could not be ignored.

Since the eighteenth century, the shogunate planned to defend Edo by keeping hostile ships out of Edo bay. Thus Uraga channel, the narrow strait between Miura peninsula's Kannonzaki and Bōsō peninsula's Futtsu, was the strategic line of defense, and Uraga became a key port that inspected ships entering and leaving Edo bay.[11] However, Abe and others were too busy resolving the *agechirei* controversy and the lack of revenue, so nothing had been done on the issue of strengthening national defense.

This is probably why the shogun decided to reappoint Mizuno Tadakuni as *rōjū* on 1844/6/21 (4 August 1844), less than ten months after Mizuno was fired. No new defensive preparations were made when the shogunate learned from the Dutch in Nagasaki that William II, king of the Netherlands, had sent a formal letter and gifts to the shogun, due to arrive sometime later in the year. In other words, although Mizuno was unpopular among the lords, he still retained the shogun's confidence; the shogun probably hoped that Mizuno could help resolve foreign policy and defense issues.[12] Naturally, Abe Masahiro was opposed to this appointment, but the shogun's will was firm and Mizuno returned to power. Abe in protest claimed to be ill and stayed at his mansion until the shogun ordered him to report to work.[13]

This decision to reinstate Mizuno in 1844 would lead to a political alliance between Abe and Tokugawa Nariaki, Mizuno's critic. Nariaki was a xenophobe who had previously criticized Mizuno's foreign policy as being too dovish. As mentioned earlier, in 1842 as part of the Tempō Reforms, Mizuno had repealed the 1825 edict to fire upon any foreign vessels encroaching Japanese waters and instead ordered shipwrecked foreign ships to be supplied with water, food, and fuel. This conciliatory edict of 1842 came in direct response to learning about Qing China's military defeats in the Opium War and thus the same order of 1842 also exhorted the lords to increase their coastal defense capabilities. This decision to reexamine foreign policy in the wake of the Opium War angered Tokugawa Nariaki, a diehard isolationist.[14]

Tokugawa Nariaki was the champion of the Mito school, a popular school of thought formed in Mito domain that advocated isolationism. Aizawa Seishisai, Mito school's foremost theorist, had reimagined Japan as the "divine realm" or the "middle kingdom": the one place where civilization, as understood in Confucian terms, reigned. Thus Nariaki, Aizawa, and many others saw the spread of Christianity, as evidenced by the global reach of Western colonial empires, as a direct threat to their civilization. For these men, reforming and strengthening the shogunate, the multitude of domains, the hierarchical social system, and the policy of isolation became not only a matter of self-interest but also of defending the one true civilization.[15] Because

Nariaki's domain academy, called Kōdōkan, published Mito school's thoughts widely, xenophobia became a common sentiment among politically aware samurai.[16]

Tokugawa Nariaki was also the lord of Mito domain, one of the "three honorable houses" (*gosanke*). The three honorable houses were collateral domains of the shogun because they were direct descendants of Tokugawa Ieyasu's younger sons. According to tradition, these three collateral domains were to supply the next shogun if the shogunal family had no male sons. For this, Nariaki held very high status among the lords and Nariaki used his influence to convince the other lords that Japan should maintain isolationism, by force if necessary.

Finally, Nariaki had overseen Confucian-based reforms within Mito domain, which were successful in resolving the domain's financial issues, increasing the military preparedness of Mito domain, and promoting talented reformers such as Fujita Tōko. For these reasons—espousing the protection of Japan as a divine and Confucian realm, being a member of the collateral house, and effectively reforming his domain—Tokugawa Nariaki became an influential voice among the lords and the samurai. As a critic of Mizuno during the Tempō Reforms over its foreign policy, Nariaki must have been furious when he found out that Mizuno Tadakuni was returning to power.

However, Nariaki was powerless to stop the shogun. According to the same tradition that honored the collateral domains, the "three honorable houses" were not supposed to interfere in the decision-making process of the shogun's government. In theory, decisions were to be made by the shogun in consultation with his vassals. And the vassals that could engage in shogunal politics were the direct vassals of the shogun called *hatamoto* (bannermen) or *gokenin* (honorable housemen) and the *fudai daimyō* (vassal lords). These three were descendants of men who served the Tokugawa family before Ieyasu ruled Japan. The *hatamoto* and *gokenin* became the rank-and-file bureaucrats, while the *fudai daimyō* supplied the uppermost ranks in the shogunal government. The *rōjū* (ministers), for example, were appointed from the ranks of major *fudai daimyō* and no lords from the collateral domains were formally part of the decision-making process before the 1850s. Perhaps in response to criticizing the Tempō Reforms vociferously and continually criticizing shogunal policy during this period—something that Nariaki should not have done as a lord of a collateral house—Nariaki was ordered in 1844 to place himself under house arrest and to retire from his position as lord of Mito in favor of his son.[17]

Neither Abe Masahiro nor Tokugawa Nariaki could stop the shogun from reappointing Mizuno as *rōjū*. Reappointed as *rōjū*, Mizuno in 1844 was optimistic that he would return as chief *rōjū* and restore his influence within the shogunal government. After all, with Nariaki under house arrest and Abe as a recent appointee, they could do nothing about Mizuno becoming the chief minister.

Unfortunately for Mizuno, after Abe's "illness" was over, Abe was able to become the treasury minister and limited his influence. Since the chief minister was normally the treasury minister as well, Abe becoming the treasury minister meant the shogun's confidence in Mizuno was limited. Also, because many of the officials who had helped Mizuno during the Tempō Reforms were fired or purged following the failure of the reforms, Mizuno could not influence policy as much as before. Those who saw him sitting idly in Edo castle secretly compared him to a *deku* (a wooden doll, meaning he was seen as a useless person). Unhappy that he did not have the same powers as before and realizing that even his opinions were being ignored, Mizuno stopped coming to work after six months citing illness and then resigned in early 1845.[18]

The shogun's decision to reappoint Mizuno created a lasting political alliance between Abe and Nariaki. After Mizuno's resignation, Abe Masahiro became the new chief *rōjū* and remained a major political figure until his death in 1857. Tokugawa Nariaki, who was ordered to place himself under house arrest in 1844, recovered his influence with Abe's help. Between 1845 and 1853, Abe sent Nariaki information on the internal discussions within the shogun's government.[19] By the end of 1845, Tokugawa Nariaki was released from house arrest. By 1849 Nariaki could once again openly intervene in Mito domain politics. In 1853 Nariaki formally entered shogunal politics as a special adviser to the shogun on maritime defense, a new post created by Abe after Commodore Perry's arrival (this obviated the need for letters between Abe and Nariaki). By 1853 a man who should not have had a political voice in the formal structure of the shogunate, a man who was forced into retirement, entered the center of shogunal politics alongside Abe Masahiro, the Confucian chief minister.

Now that Mizuno was gone, how did Abe respond to the letter from William II, king of the Netherlands? Even if Nariaki wanted to return to the older policy of firing on all foreign ships approaching Japanese waters and terminating trade between Japan and the Netherlands and between Japan and Qing China,[20] Abe decided to maintain cordial relations while holding firm on the policy of isolation.

In replying to the letter from the Dutch king, Abe carefully addressed the reply to the aristocrats of the Netherlands and to the Dutch leader in Nagasaki. The response letter was not addressed to William II. He explained that a formal reply to the king would initiate diplomatic exchange (*tsūshin*), and because the shogunate's ancestral laws prohibited diplomatic exchange between the two countries, they could not reply to the king. The relationship with the Dutch would remain a purely commercial one (*tsūshō*). However, he also informed them that the shogunate now had a new policy of supplying water, food, and fuel to foreign ships in need.[21] In this way, the Dutch initiative to open diplomatic relations with Japan was rebuffed by Abe Masahiro. But Abe also informed them that they would not initiate hostilities by firing on foreign ships approaching Japanese waters.

The Tempō Reforms opened a serious rift between the shogunate and the lords. The shogun chose Abe Masahiro to resolve the issues quietly and cooperatively, something that Abe was inclined to do temperamentally. As such he addressed two of the three issues—the lack of revenue, national defense, and the lack of cheap goods in Edo—in just such a manner. On revenue he ended the controversial *agechirei*, cancelled the costly Lake Inbanuma project, and continued the debasement of currency. He placated the angry lords and raised revenue without angering them. On defense Abe informed the Dutch of a new conciliatory policy and formed an alliance with Tokugawa Nariaki. Thus he continued Mizuno's foreign policy while mollifying diehard isolationists within Japan. The major problem with Abe's approach was the continuing inflation and the lack of cheap goods in Edo.

ABE MASAHIRO RECOGNIZES THE NEED FOR COOPERATION IN NATIONAL DEFENSE

Abe Masahiro may have agreed with Tokugawa Nariaki about keeping Japan isolated, by force if necessary. However, as finance minister and chief minister, Abe actually led the shogun's government, and in the process he must have recognized the structural problems behind the shogun's government and its limits. As explained in the introduction, the economies of eastern Japan and western Japan were not united. Edo was still reliant on goods coming in from Osaka. The shogun's revenue was too low. This was partly because the shogun only controlled roughly one quarter of Japan, though he was in charge of defending the entire country. Moreover, as more news from Qing China came, it seemed less and less possible for the shogunate to defend Japan if the British attacked in full force.

Thus despite Nariaki's desire to fire on foreign ships, Abe realized that this belligerent isolationism was also not possible. First, as Mizuno made clear in his 1842 order, it was ultimately the local lord who defended the immediate coastline in most of Japan. Second, neither the shogun nor the lords had large vessels necessary to fight a war with the West. Third, the shogunate did not have the requisite funds for building new ships and defending the coast. For a man who was selected to heal the divide stemming from the controversial *agechirei*, Abe could conceive of only one solution to this problem of national defense: intensifying the cooperation between the shogun and the lords. And Abe came to this realization early in his tenure as chief *rōjū*.

It turns out that while Abe was busy with the Dutch letter in 1844, French and British ships began to arrive at Ryukyu Kingdom. In 1846 the French had even stationed a missionary in the kingdom. But distance delayed this news, a matter of critical importance to Abe.

The Ryukyu Kingdom used to be an independent kingdom that sent tributary missions to Ming China. In 1609 under Tokugawa Ieyasu's order, Satsuma domain conquered Ryukyu Kingdom, and since then Ryukyu Kingdom was a kingdom in name only. After the Satsuma conquest, the kingdom continued to send tribute missions to Ming China and then after 1644 to Qing China in order to conduct trade with China. However, because the kingdom was now under Satsuma control, the kingdom also sent tribute missions to the shogun in Edo. In other words, formally the Ryukyu Kingdom became a vassal to two lords, the emperor of China and the shogun of Japan. In reality, however, the kingdom was under the control of Satsuma domain.

Thus when these Western ships arrived at Naha, the kingdom's capital, and demanded to open relations, the Ryukyu officials reported the news immediately to Satsuma domain. Satsuma domain officials understood that they could do nothing even as the Western ships proceeded to survey the coast and forwarded the news to Edo.

In 1846 Shimazu Nariakira, the heir to Satsuma domain, and his father, the lord of Satsuma, received these troubling reports and in turn informed the shogunate. By the time the two delivered their report, the British and French ships had set sail and the events had already passed by. Therefore there was nothing for Abe to do except to listen to what Shimazu Nariakira and his father had to say. At the meeting, the two explained that the foreigners had three demands: trade, diplomatic exchange, and the proselytization of Christianity. Satsuma domain did not want to initiate hostilities with the French or British, even if provoked, because they were not ready. Thus in order to prevent hostilities, Shimazu Nariakira proposed that one out of the three demands of the foreigners be met, namely trade. The other two had to be refused. If the foreigners were not satisfied and attacked, then Satsuma would fight. And if Satsuma domain could not handle French or British forces alone, then Satsuma hoped to receive help from the shogunate. After listening to this explanation, Abe agreed and ultimately granted Satsuma domain full control over the foreign relations of Ryukyu Kingdom. What else could Abe Masahiro do? Satsuma domain was far in the south, Ryukyu Kingdom was even further south, the events in question had already passed, and the Opium War demonstrated the military superiority of Western ships. As Shimazu Nariakira made clear, first the lords must acquire Western ships and cannons before fighting against them.[22]

When Abe reported this conversation to Tokugawa Nariaki, Nariaki became furious and demanded that not a single foreign demand should be met. Abe replied in turn that Ryukyu Kingdom is a small island in the southern sea that's difficult to defend and whose inhabitants are not ready for war. Moreover, the shogunate did not have the ability to build the ships to repel the foreigners if they came into Edo Bay or other parts of Japan, and only after Satsuma domain and the shogunate had built their ships could they fight a war.[23] In other words, Abe repeated Shimazu Nariakira's argument that allowing trade at Ryukyu was a means to buy enough time to get the lords ready to fight wars after enjoying two hundred years of peace. Tokugawa Nariaki could not understand this logic. After all, the point was to keep the foreigners out; trading with the foreigners to get their weapons to fight against the foreigners made no sense. At least consistent, Nariaki had in the past suggested that Mito domain be assigned a massive fief in Ezochi to defend the country and argued that large ships be built domestically to defend the country and keep it closed.[24] These proposals by Nariaki, however, were structurally dangerous for the shogunate and thus rejected. If any lord became too strong—even Nariaki's Mito domain, one of the three collateral domains of the Tokugawa shogun—the shogun's rule over the country would be threatened. The shogunal government was ultimately based on the fact that the shogun had overwhelming power compared to each domain, and it was not about to strengthen a vassal's army substantially more than the shogun's personal army.

Abe Masahiro in a was conflicted position about national defense. Emotionally he agreed with Tokugawa Nariaki.[25] As a fellow Confucian he wanted to maintain Japan's isolationism, and the Dutch letter is testimony to his sentiment. In fact, for the Confucian Abe, a trading relationship was less offensive than a formal diplomatic relationship with a Western power or the spread of Christianity. Realistically, however, he understood that diehard isolationism was not possible and did not want to start a war. The news from Qing China was enough to shock his predecessor to change course, and the news from Satsuma and Ryukyu indicated that currently the shogunate or the lords would likely lose. This news reinforced Abe's belief that the only course of action was to cooperate with the major lords such as the Shimazu clan to defend Japan under the shogun's leadership.

It was this line of thinking that led Abe to open discussion among the lords when Perry arrived in 1853. In short, for Abe Masahiro, the most important lesson from the failure of the Tempō Reforms was the need to avoid another major dissension among the feudal elite. This lesson, along with the need to cooperate with major domains such as Tokugawa Nariaki of Mito domain and Shimazu Nariakira of Satsuma domain made Abe take the historic step of asking the various lords what the shogunate should do when Perry arrived with his fleet. Instead of holding a closed discussion among a handful of *fudai daimyō* (vassal lords), Abe would try to form a united front of all the major lords to determine the future of the *bakufu*.

ABE MASAHIRO RECOGNIZES THE NEED FOR GUILDS IN THE EDO ECONOMY

Abe Masahiro restarted the policy of debasing gold and silver coins. This solved the problem of the lack of revenue but made inflation in Edo worse. At the time of Mizuno Tadakuni's Tempō Reforms, two governors of Edo, Yabe Sadanori and Torii Yōzō, the shogun's attendant, Hori Chikashige, a leader of the gold guild, Gotō Mitsuakira, and even Tokugawa Nariaki of Mito domain proposed to end the debasement of currency. They recognized the link between the debasement of currency and the increase in the prices of various goods. Unfortunately their advice was ignored because debasing the currency brought the shogunate enormous profits, money that was desperately needed.[26]

Was there another way to end the inflation and hopefully to lower the price of goods in Edo? Mizuno Tadakuni thought that disbanding the monopoly guilds and increasing competition would lower the prices of goods. As a staunch Confucian, Tokugawa Nariaki also proposed that the great merchants be stripped of their monopoly rights to relieve the burden on commoners.[27] Abe Masahiro, also a Confucian, probably also agreed with this anti-merchant position. Thus the disbanding of guilds that had gone into effect starting in 1841 continued, and guilds were not allowed to re-form.

Abe in effect pursued a contradictory economic policy. He hoped that competition would lower prices, although he issued debased currency, which was guaranteed to increase prices. Even after becoming finance minister and chief minister in 1845, Abe continued this contradictory policy for six more years. Unsurprisingly it did not work. In fact the situation became worse. Not only did prices continue to increase, but goods became scarcer. And in 1850, prices of various goods in Edo spiked upward as fewer goods entered Edo.[28] In other words, something went wrong with the economy.

Why did prices not decline and why did goods become more scarce during this period of free trade in Edo? The lack of low prices can be explained by the debasement of the currency. But why would goods become more scarce and cause a sudden rise in prices? The governor of Edo, Tōyama Kagemoto (aka Tōyama Kinshirō of the eponymous Japanese TV series) explained that the guilds performed an important function by facilitating borrowing among the merchants. After these guilds were disbanded, borrowing and lending slowed, and thus commerce in general slowed down. Since Edo relied on imports to supply its consumers, without robust commerce, goods become scarcer. In short, banning the monopoly guilds had hurt the overall economy. As a result the governor feared that eventually the commoners would all become poorer. Thus he argued that the guilds be allowed to re-form.

Okazaki Tetsuji examined the available data during this period with modern econometrics and substantiated the sense that the people at the time had. In other words, after the disbanding of the guilds, the economy not only felt like it was in a decline as those at the time attested, but the flow of goods and the market mechanism of the economy also suffered.[29]

Ironically the market mechanism failed because the guilds were disbanded. Okazaki argues that aside from their role as guarantors of debts, the guilds acted as adjudicators of disputes. In other words, the guilds punished rule breakers. Because the shogunate frequently ignored commercial suits and told merchants to resolve disputes among themselves, the guilds played a more important role than the government realized.

For example, consider some of the rules established by the guilds. If a rice merchant agreed to buy rice from a seller and paid for it but did not receive the rice, then this rice merchant could complain to his rice merchant guild. As punishment, all members of this rice merchant guild would refuse all future business with that seller. In the case of a charcoal guild, if a buyer did not pay even after the charcoal had been delivered, then all the charcoal guild members would no longer sell to that buyer. These are clear cases of fraud, and collective punishment is meted out to the offending seller or buyer. In dealing with cheaters, guilds were just as harsh. One salt guild stipulated that if a buyer sent only a partial payment, the salt merchant should not accept it, and all guild members should take collective action by not selling salt to that buyer in the future. A firewood guild had a similar rule, meting out collective punishment to buyers who would not pay on schedule or who continually complain about the quantity of firewood being delivered. According to Okazaki, the collective actions against possible fraudsters and cheaters ensured the smooth transaction of business during Edo period Japan by keeping people honest. In an environment without adequate judicial oversight, the guilds played an important role in policing the buyers and sellers. The sudden disbanding of guilds robbed merchants of this guarantee and led to fewer transactions. Without guilds, one could no longer conduct trade with an unknown person, because if that person cheated you, the only recourse was the shogunal courts or the local *daimyō*'s courts. And there was no guarantee that these courts would take up a commercial suit.[30]

Moreover, because many producers had also formed guilds, which performed a similar function as outlined above, the sudden disbanding of guilds not only led to fewer transactions, but also to lower production. By the nineteenth century, in the case of Kiryū silk, at each stage of production, there was a guild: the silk buyers guild, the weaving guild, the dyeing guild, the silk cloth guild, and more. The silk cloth guild at Kiryū stipulated that if a particular silk yarn producer or a weaver did not produce as many products as reasonable from the amount of material the silk cloth guild supplied or if there was a case of stealing the supplies and selling on the side, the silk cloth guild would terminate all future transactions with such producers. In this way, the silk cloth guild could punish cheaters in the production of silk cloths and expand by including new producers.

However, when all guilds were disbanded, the silk cloth producers took fewer risks. Therefore the sudden termination of all guilds not only led to a slowdown in commercial transactions, but also to a slowdown in production as well.[31] In short, the disbanding of guilds had the opposite effect of what Mizuno and Abe had hoped. Instead of invigorating the economy and encouraging competition, it made both merchants and producers more cautious of fraudsters and cheaters in the absence of a reliable court system, thus leading to a slowdown of the economy.

The lack of goods in Edo and the attendant price spike in 1850 forced Abe Masahiro to recognize that this policy failed. In 1851 chief minister and treasury minister Abe reversed course and finally accepted the repeated requests of the governor of Edo, Tōyama. The former monopoly guild merchants could re-form into new organizations. However, Abe made clear that the new organizations would not have monopoly rights and that they were forbidden to prevent newcomers from entering their trades. Lacking monopoly rights, these merchants were not required to pay taxes to the shogunate.[32] Lacking monopoly rights, these entities were not guilds; rather they were more akin to mercantile associations (not *kabu nakama* but *ton'ya nakama*). In this way Abe hoped to keep competition alive, which should push down prices.

In theory, by allowing the reorganization of guild merchants but not allowing them to have monopoly power, commercial activity and production should rise, fostering competition and lower prices. According to the long-term data, the Tokugawa economy expanded near the end.[33] Thus the economy contracted during this ten-year experiment with free trade and then recovered. Even prices went down in 1851 after the sudden spike in 1850. However, long-term inflation continued. This was most likely because of the monetary inflation caused by the debasement of the currency. According to Ootsuka Hideki, the estimated number of gold coins in Japan in 1818 was roughly 19,114,000 *ryō*, the number in 1833 was roughly 23,699,000 *ryō*, and by 1858 the number was roughly 28,315,000 *ryō*.[34] This continual expansion of the number of gold coins with ever-lower gold content per coin was the background for the long-term inflation during nineteenth-century Edo. According to Kitagawa Morisada, who lived during this period and wrote the Morisada encyclopedia, prices of various goods roughly doubled in the sixty years before the start of modern international trade in 1859.[35]

From this economic perspective, one can see that the shogunate was in a bind. It had long wanted to lower the price of goods in Edo, but this goal was hampered by its debasement of the currency. Yet they could not stop the debasement of currency, because reminting brought in the needed revenue.

As Mizuno learned earlier, reversing the debasement of the currency would require a massive amount of gold; gold that the *bakufu* simply did not have. Caught in this bind, the shogunate was desperately seeking an alternate source of revenue. It was only a matter of time before someone would realize that trade could raise revenue through tariffs.

THE IMPORTANCE OF MATTHEW PERRY'S ARRIVAL

In the traditional story of the opening of Japan, the first step was taken when Commodore Matthew Perry of the U.S. Navy knocked on Japanese doors in 1853. In 1854 he walked through and signed the Japan–United States Treaty of Peace and Amity, or the Treaty of Kanagawa, the treaty that established relations between the United States and Japan. Within two years, the British, the Russians, and the Dutch asked for and signed similar treaties. None of these treaties granted new trading privileges, but the shogun agreed to open Nagasaki, Hakodate, and Shimoda as ports of refuge for vessels from these four countries.[36]

After signing these treaties, Japan signed more treaties that opened its ports to trade and fully integrated the country within the framework of Western international law. In this sense the arrival of Matthew Perry is normally seen as the dramatic first step that heralded a modern Japan. Although many traditional historians and some recent historians, such as Katō Yūzō, emphasize the Perry treaty for its revolutionary impact, a few scholars, such as Michael Auslin, emphasize the later Harris treaty as being truly pathbreaking. This chapter does not engage too much with the diplomatic and foreign policy aspects of the treaties, but a quick review of recent scholarly work is warranted.

Katō rightfully points out the peaceful, negotiated nature of the treaty-making process. From this start, he reaches the conclusion that in the nineteenth century, international law divided the world into four tiers. The top tier was composed of Western countries such as Britain and France, which were independent and had full sovereignty. The bottom tier was composed of colonies such as India and Indonesia, which had no sovereignty and were at the mercy of the colonizers. The two middle tiers were a small number of non-Western independent states that signed "unequal treaties." These treaties recognized the sovereignty of these states but not fully. These middle-tier states such as Qing China, Siam (Thailand), and Japan had to accept extraterritoriality and did not have tariff autonomy, major restrictions on their sovereignty. The difference within this group was whether a country signed unequal treaties by force, such as Qing China, or through negotiation, such as Siam and Japan. Forced to sign these unequal treaties after a military defeat, China was punished through loss of territory and payments of reparations.

Negotiating these treaties, Japan was not punished and in fact was able to revise them through later negotiations. Only when Japan abolished extraterritoriality and recovered tariff autonomy did Japan became fully sovereign.[37]

Michael Auslin, in contrast, sees the Perry treaty as a "tentative pact between the two countries . . . predicated on chance and impermanence: the chance that U.S. ships would have a need for Japanese ports and supplies, and the transitory nature of such contact."[38] For him, the later treaty negotiated between Townsend Harris and the shogunate is more important, for it formed a permanent trading relationship between Japan and the West and fully incorporated Japan within the Western international order. Like Katō, Auslin emphasizes the fact that Japan negotiated with the West and that it preserved its sovereignty, like Siam, and escaped the fate of China, but the two disagree on which treaty was more important for Japan: the Perry treaty for Katō or the Harris treaty for Auslin.

Instead of focusing on the diplomatic aspect, this chapter focuses on Perry's arrival from a domestic politics and an economic perspective. Seen from these perspectives, Perry's arrival is important for two reasons. Its impact on the *bakufu*'s domestic political decision-making process and its impact on the finances of the *bakufu*.

First, Abe Masahiro chose to ask others what should be done when Perry arrived. Instead of deciding unilaterally and raising a storm of protest (as Mizuno had done with the *agechirei*), Abe wanted to gain a consensus before moving forward. After all, he was the man selected to resolve the rift created by the Tempō Reforms. But asking others, even those who traditionally were not consulted, was a major break from past precedent.

Tokugawa Nariaki, who traditionally had no right to interfere, became the special adviser to the shogun on maritime defense and predictably opposed the opening of Japan. He even argued for war if it was necessary.[39] Most of the people who responded to Abe's "open letter," which included not only the major lords, but also ordinary samurai and even commoners, recognized that Japan was the weaker party. These people urged the shogun to avoid war. A few recognized that a few ships far from home could not fight a long war and realized that the United States was only bluffing and not about to start a war. Regardless of the details of the Japanese reactions, as Katō Yūzō points out, what was important about Abe's actions was this decision to open politics to discussion. Today this action may look democratic and in fact commendable, but at the time it was fatal, for it demonstrated that the *bakufu* was losing its ability to impose its will on the lords.[40] Perry's arrival was truly radical for altering the decision-making process of the shogunate.

So why did Abe Masahiro open discussion? Despite his desire to seek consensus, he must have known that he could not achieve consensus within one year. Abe probably took this action as a calculated gamble. Either it would buttress his position as chief minister or end his career. The shogun who had appointed Abe as *rōjū* in 1843 had full confidence in him. However, this shogun had died shortly after Perry's arrival in 1853. Without the confidence of the new shogun, the thirteenth shogun, Tokugawa Iesada, Abe's position would be weak. Becoming a weak chief minister would be awful, as Mizuno Tadakuni demonstrated after his reinstatement in the wake of the Tempō Reforms' failure. Thus by opening discussion and inviting xenophobes led by Nariaki to attack him, Abe forced the new shogun to choose sides. If the new shogun agreed with Nariaki and other xenophobes, Abe would simply resign. However, if the new shogun retained Abe, he could say to Nariaki that he has the shogun's confidence and that Nariaki's continued opposition would not be welcome. Since many within the shogunate knew of Abe's political alliance with Nariaki and that Abe did not want to sign the treaty at heart, those who opposed him did not have much of a chance. Abe won this political gamble. He received the shogun's confidence, signed the treaty, and would stay on as *rōjū* until his death.[41]

The official pronouncement of the shogunate argued that the primary purpose of these treaties was to save the lives of shipwrecked sailors and to aid battered ships. This purpose was in line with the Confucian principle of benevolence or humaneness (*jin* in Japanese or *ren* in Chinese), and nothing new compared to the earlier edict issued by Mizuno Tadakuni. Therefore this 1854 treaty and other early treaties were acceptable, for they prevented war and maintained national pride.[42] For them these treaties opened formal relations, but they were not the first step toward international trade.

The second reason Perry's arrival was important is because it further strained shogunal finances. Most lords and shogunal officials agreed on strengthening coastal defense in order to defend against a possible attack. Moreover, they agreed that large ships should be built and a navy needed to be formed. After Perry's arrival in 1853, the *bakufu* not only rescinded the ban on the construction of large ships, it also ordered steamships from the Dutch.[43] The construction of coastal defense batteries, the purchase of ships, and eventually the construction of the Nirayama reverberatory furnace, the Yokosuka arsenal, and other facilities, along with training a new, modern Western-style army and navy would strain shogunal finances to the limit.

Under these circumstances, the shogunate had no choice but to continue the debasement of its currency and use the seigniorage. In 1854, it gained 654,700 *ryō* through this currency debasement.[44] This meant, of course, that there was little hope for inflation to end and relieve the pressure on the ordinary samurai of Edo. Ironically this need for more revenue pushed many officials within the *bakufu* to see international trade as a possible answer.

By incorporating the domestic and economic perspectives to the foreign policy issues of the day, one can see how the decision-making process changed and how the revenue problem worsened. In this sense, the arrival of Matthew Perry had a major domestic and financial impact for the shogunate.

Signing treaties with Perry was not a revolutionary change in the foreign relations of Japan, at least according to Abe Masahiro, but it was a dramatic first step in the opening of Japan, leading to the start of international trade.

GRIDLOCK: ABE MASAHIRO VERSUS HOTTA MASAYOSHI

Eleven years after the failure of the Tempō Reforms, three problems still remained: the lack of revenue, national defense, and the lack of cheap goods in Edo. As a good Confucian, Abe probably thought that the problems could be resolved through cooperation. As such he papered over the lack of revenue with currency debasement, even though it made inflation worse. He hoped that the shogun and the lords would cooperate in strengthening national defense. And when the dissolution of guilds proved to be ineffective in lowering prices, in fact causing more problems, he reversed course and allowed the guild merchants to reconstitute themselves. If competition would not lower prices, hopefully cooperation between the merchants and the authorities would somehow lower prices. But his policy was reaching its limits. Inflation continued unchecked. Signing the Perry treaty caused more commotion. More revenue than ever was needed. The Tokugawa *bakufu* had entered its final period, the *bakumatsu* (literally, the end of the *bakufu*) period.

The treasury officials (*kanjō bugyō* and their staff) and Abe Masahiro wanted to maintain the status quo and opposed any further contact with the foreigners. The shogunate was in a bad situation, but they thought they could continue to hold the line. The xenophobes led by Tokugawa Nariaki totally opposed all relations and even wanted to scrap the 1854 treaty in order to forcibly expel the "barbarians." They hoped to restore the past glory of the shogun. A few officials insisted that the shogun initiate trade negotiations before terms were forced upon the country. These men, mostly shogunal governors (*bugyō*[45]) of the port cities of Nagasaki, Hakodate, Uraga, and Shimoda, and inspectors (*metsuke*) argued that being forced to sign treaties after a military defeat, like the Qing dynasty did after its defeat in the Opium War, would deal a severe blow to the shogunate. Moreover, for some of these men, trade represented new opportunities to buttress the government's finances and thereby strengthen the shogunate. They hoped to make the situation better by embracing change.

Abe Masahiro did not want to preside over this type of divided government. After all he was chosen as minister to heal the divide between the shogun and the lords after the Tempō Reforms. He also wanted cooperation among the lords to defend the country. But papering over the political divisions within the shogunate reached its limit after summer 1856. That summer a number of important reports reached Edo castle: the Crimean War had ended; a British fleet determined to sign a trade treaty was on its way to Japan; and a man called Townsend Harris arrived as the U.S. representative to Japan. Unlike the policy of currency debasement, foreign policy debate raged inside Edo castle.

The governor of Nagasaki wrote urgently that Japan must not make the same mistake as Qing China. There was simply no way to maintain the policy of seclusion. Trade must commence. The governors of Hakodate and Uraga sent a joint memorandum also arguing for trade with Britain and other countries. Moreover, they reported that they could not stop any fleet from entering Edo Bay and exposing the shogun as impotent. This would be particularly embarrassing for the man who held the title *Sei-i tai shōgun*, literally "the grand general in charge of suppressing barbarians." The inspectors who were members of the maritime defense council sent a report detailing how the shogunate could benefit from trade. They argued that the government could charge tariffs, encourage coastal trade, and send Japanese trading ships abroad.

The treasury officials in the maritime defense council rebutted these arguments by sending their report arguing that trade would be disastrous. Emphasizing how troublesome trade with the Chinese and the Dutch at Nagasaki had become, they argued that if foreigners came and traded freely, they would drain whatever goods the country was producing. Besides, the shogunate had already signed treaties with the foreigners without opening Japan to trade. They surmised that a similar feat would be possible during a new round of negotiations.

Amid this spate of reports, the emergency session of the maritime defense council of Ansei 3, ninth month, second day (30 September 1856) was gridlock. The council postponed any final policy decision by ordering further study. At this time the maritime defense council consisted of Abe, the maritime defense minister Makino Tadamasa, relevant inspectors and treasury officials, and the governors of Nagasaki, Uraga, Shimoda, and Hakodate. The council simply could not decide whether to initiate trade talks or not. It first declared that in the long run Japan should open trade with the rest of the world and not just with the current treaty signatories. It also noted that the country would not have the capability to conduct overseas trade on Japanese terms for at least five to seven years, even if the most strenuous effort was made. Finally, because there was the potential danger of goods being siphoned from the domestic economy, as the treasury officials feared, more studies were necessary before a decision could be reached.[46]

A month later and after a further spate of reports from both sides, the maritime defense council again postponed taking action at its meeting on 1856/10/8 (5 November 1856). The governors and the inspectors had sent reports rebuffing the treasury officials' earlier economic argument against trade. The governors of Uraga and Hakodate, for instance, argued that trade in Nagasaki was troublesome and failing only because it was official trade. They argued for trade to be placed in private hands so prices could fluctuate. The outflow of copper, one of the treasury officials' main fears, would stop because its price would eventually become prohibitive. The governors suggested exporting manufactured or renewable goods, such as silk cloth, paper, lacquerware, and tea. They cited Peter the Great's economic reforms in Russia and Britain's maritime trade as means toward military might. The inspectors at Nagasaki were more urgent and insisted upon a decision. They reiterated that "first denying the requests of the Americans and Russians and then when all other options were lost, to reverse ourselves and do as they bid was a sure way to lose credibility. It makes us seem as if naked power will affect our policy."[47] Moreover, in unusually strong language, they complained that they could not study the merits of trade if the more fundamental question of initiating trade itself was undecided. They argued instead that a decision to trade or not to trade be made so that they could then study the consequences. In response, the treasury officials changed arguments while still defending their position. Sensing that private trade might indeed solve most of the problems cited earlier, the treasury officials hardened their opposition. According to them, as a principle, a government should not suddenly change positions simply because of changes in relative power. They no longer discussed the possibility of denying trade in new negotiations. Furthermore, they did not refrain from stoking revulsion toward foreigners when they pointed out their meat-eating habits and the foreign officials' requests for women. Though the treasury officials conceded the gravity of the situation and the difficulty of defending the policy of seclusion, they argued for increasing armament and enduring the times that test men's souls (*gashin shōtan*).[48]

Thus by autumn 1856, the treasury officials were losing the argument. One last push was necessary to end this political gridlock; that would come from Hotta Masayoshi, the former political ally and colleague of Mizuno Tadakuni during the Tempō Reforms.

A year earlier, on 1855/10/9 (18 November 1855) Shogun Iesada appointed Hotta Masayoshi as the new treasury minister and chief *rōjū*. Hotta was the *fudai daimyō* (vassal lord) of Sakura, a major domain that produced the equivalent of 110,000 *koku* of rice. His appointment was important for three reasons: First, he had previous experience as minister and knew how the government worked. As such he would prove to be a competent and valuable member of the council of ministers. Second, he was clearly in favor of opening Japan. When Commodore Perry came to Japan, Abe Masahiro asked the opinion of the all the major lords on the proper course of action. Hotta replied that Japan should open its ports, conduct trade, adopt what is necessary, and after ten years of trade and strengthening the military, the government should decide to keep trade open or to close the country again.

Third, after Hotta resigned as *rōjū* thirteen years earlier (right before the Tempō Reforms collapsed), he focused on strengthening his domain by adopting Western methods and became known by Tokugawa Nariaki and others as being "Dutch crazy" (*ranpeki*). Hotta had not only adopted Western medicine and vaccinated his own children and the children of his domain, he even adopted Western military training by reorganizing his domain army into Western-style cavalry, artillery, and infantry with up-to-date guns instead of muskets. During these thirteen years, his financial reforms had also righted the domain economy, allowing him to restore the pay of his samurai,[49] a rarity among eastern domains. Thus, if Tokugawa Nariaki championed strengthening domains by traditional reforms, then Hotta Masayoshi championed strengthening domains by Western reforms.

Abe clearly knew about Hotta's pro-Western opinions and activities, but he primarily wanted help in running the government. Also, since Abe wanted the lords to cooperate, having the "Dutch crazy" Hotta on the council of ministers would help him to form a united front on the issue of foreign policy. Thus Abe suggested to the shogun the reappointment of Hotta as *rōjū*. Since Abe was younger than Hotta Masayoshi, precedent dictated that Hotta become the treasury minister and the chief *rōjū*. Tokugawa Nariaki was shocked by this suggestion and opposed the appointment of Hotta.[50] Regardless, the shogun overrode Nariaki's opposition and appointed Hotta as suggested by Abe.

This appointment did not mean that Abe abandoned his foreign policy goals. Abe still opposed trade and wanted to maintain the status quo. He probably thought that he would be able to contain Hotta's pro-Western stance with the help of Tokugawa Nariaki. The immediate course of events proved Abe correct. Despite Hotta's position as chief minister and his pro-Western attitude, for one year no action was taken on foreign policy. The shogun's confidence probably lay more with Abe Masahiro than Hotta Masayoshi.

However, once Hotta recognized his weaker position, he asked to be the foreign minister and changed his post on 1856/10/17 (14 November 1856). Abe resumed his position as the treasury minister. As chief minister and foreign minister would Hotta be able to resolve the foreign policy gridlock? Or would Hotta be like Mizuno, the former *rōjū* who returned as chief minister but was unable to impact policy? The shogun and Abe both reminded Hotta that "matters of importance must be discussed by the group."[51]

HOTTA MASAYOSHI'S DECISION TO OPEN JAPAN

Hotta Masayoshi was not Mizuno Tadakuni. After witnessing one year of political gridlock and after the events of summer 1856, Hotta managed to get the overall policy clarified on 1856/11/14 (11 December 1856), a month after his appointment as foreign minister. He convinced the *rōjū* as a group to agree to open the country for trade.[52] The inspectors and the governors had already made most of the important points. War was unwinnable. Negotiation was preferable to war because the shogunate could assert its demands. Trade could bring in revenue. Though not mentioned, with this added revenue, currency debasement could end, if not be reversed.

The decision to open Japan to trade was a momentous decision. Until this day, only the maritime defense council had mentioned opening Japan to trade, and it was to be in the distant future. Now the council of *rōjū* agreed, and it was clearly in the near future. The decision to open Japan to trade had been made within the *bakufu* one year before the meeting Townsend Harris.

Yet even after this agreement, Abe still managed to delay the issue. Hotta's first action after the council's decision was limited to ordering another round of study on the issues of trade, albeit this time under the assumption that Japan would enter trading relationships with the rest of the world.[53] Studying the issue again was like flogging a dead horse. The response from the lower levels of government was predictable. Those in favor of trade proposed new initiatives and countered previous arguments by the treasury officials. The treasury officials responded in turn with a new set of arguments against trade. Ultimately, their objections boiled down to the fear that the West would "mollify the people with wealth, disrupt their spirits with the evil cult [of Christianity], and finally take the land by force." They understood "Western societies to base their fundamental principles on profit and design their societies according to the laws of commerce, ultimately leading to the dismantling of the difference between the ruler and the ruled."[54] This was incompatible with Japan, "which favors the lords but also righteousness, and has an unbroken line of rulers of divine descent." Thus at the opening of the *Bansho shirabesho* (Institute for Research on Barbarian Books), which accepted any person regardless of rank or age, they recommended that youths first complete their training in Japanese and Chinese classics before studying at the institute. If the students learned Dutch at an early age without prior "inoculation," they might be overly influenced by the West and fall prey to Christianity.[55] Not surprisingly this round of study led to no action.

For Hotta Masayoshi news of overseas events continued to help him argue his points. News arrived from Nagasaki on 1857/2/24 (19 March 1857) that the British had burned Canton.[56] What would later be called the Arrow War, or the Second Opium War, was afoot in China. At the 1857/3/19 (13 April 1857) maritime defense council meeting, the members agreed that their current policy was outdated. The repeated news of British victories and Chinese defeats changed the minds of his opposition. The fate that befell Canton had to be avoided, therefore foreign demands had to be met and the old laws changed as quickly as possible.[57]

After the meeting, Hotta sent a memorandum outlining the topics to be discussed at the next meeting. These covered policy issues ranging from whether to be friendly toward foreigners, whether to treat each country similarly, to details about what items were to be traded, whether agricultural or manufactured. His personal position is reflected in another note he sent to the committee studying the issue of trade. Trade was inevitable; it would strengthen Japan and the foreigners demanded it. For him the important issues were about implementing trade: Whether to inform the Dutch and the Americans beforehand so that it would not look like the decision was forced upon the country. Whether to inform the populace before trade started. Whether to allow the various lords to trade and accumulate wealth. And among other things, whether to limit trade to official exchange between governments or to include private commerce between merchants.

Hotta also thought that the previous pattern of dealing with foreigners—initially denying their requests but later granting them when the shogunate's position finally became untenable—was senseless. This approach only diminished the shogun's prestige. His suggestion was to align the shogunate's interests in accordance with the ways of the world and then determine the country's interests in that context, for then a reasonable position could be held regardless of pressure from others.[58] In answering these questions, Hotta would formulate a new concrete vision for how the shogun could maintain his rule. It would not be an overtly Confucian worldview like the Mito school, rather it would be one based on power and commerce. In effect, Hotta was thinking like the Westerners as imagined by the Confucian samurai. Hotta's nickname "Dutch crazy" was an apt one in more ways than one.

ABE AND TREASURY OFFICIALS VERSUS HOTTA, GOVERNORS, AND INSPECTORS: PERSPECTIVES ON SHOGUNAL POWER

If Hotta thought that a newfound sense of urgency and his own memoranda might create a stable consensus, he was wrong. The two factions agreed that the mistake Qing China made must not be repeated, but that was the only thing they could agree upon.[59] Fundamentally the conflict stemmed from different perspectives on the source of shogunal power. Both sides saw no real alternative to opening the country for trade in the face of British military might, but Abe and the treasury officials were opposed to altering the status quo.

The reason for their opposition came from their view of the role of the shogun. Informed by the Mito school of thought, Tokugawa Nariaki, Abe Masahiro, and the treasury officials saw the Tokugawa system as an interlocking whole. The Tokugawa *bakufu* created a system in which there was no concrete division between domestic and international spheres. The Japanese *ka-i* (civilized-barbarian) world order was a smaller modified version of the imperial Chinese world order. The Japanese version placed the shogun at the center of all political power and relegated the emperor as a symbolic source of authority from which the shogun's power derived. "Hiding" the emperor and the attendant imperial court, the shogun and his vassals could hold the central position of power and morality. The fiefs of lords traditionally loyal to the shogun surrounded the center, and the fiefs of those who had opposed the Tokugawa clan existed outside this core. Beyond this smaller Japan lay the lands of barbarians who bowed to the power and moral authority of the shogun. As proof, the barbarians sent periodic missions, traversing the country to Edo, to pay their respects to the *taikun*,[60] literally "the great lord," or in other words, the shogun. This was a system based on ritual and morality.

To acknowledge the existence of other states on an equal basis meant contradicting this arrangement. Equal states meant that there was no civilizing center from whence the shogun shined unparalleled power. This new Western international order could ultimately undermine the regime. Signing treaties of friendship to repatriate shipwrecked sailors was one thing. It was an acknowledgment of geopolitical reality, and most of the domestic political repercussions could be controlled. The Koreans provided a precedent. Even though the two countries treated each other on an equal footing, the Korean king's missions to Japan were paraded in public like those of other tributary barbarian missions.[61] Perhaps a similar arrangement could have been maintained with Western states if contact was minimal. After all, when Townsend Harris eventually traveled to Edo to meet the shogun, the *bakufu* persuaded Harris (without much difficulty) to proceed like a feudal lord from his residence in Shimoda to Edo castle.[62] But allowing trade and having more contact with foreigners—including having foreign representatives stay in Edo on an equal basis—was an entirely different matter. There was no ideological place for such arrangements within the civilized-barbarian world order, nor could they be masked as something else.

Hotta, the inspectors, and the governors articulated a different vision and consequently argued for change. They were neither radicals nor visionaries who conceptualized a modern Japan.[63] Rather, they were loyal vassals of the shogun who saw the shogun's personal holdings to be the basis of his power. In other words, the regional origins of Tokugawa power dominated their minds. After all, naked power was what elevated the Tokugawa family to become shogun. With the shogunate in repeated fiscal troubles since the mid-eighteenth century, international trade seemed to them to present a new source of income and strength. By commanding the strongest army in the realm, the shogun could maintain supremacy and keep the political system stable.[64] Moreover, with added revenue, they could finally end the currency debasement and consequently help ordinary samurai hurt by inflation. This "realist" vision of why the shogun held power competed against the Confucian view held by Nariaki and Abe.

Institutional divisions further divided the two groups. The treasury officials tended to think of the Tokugawa government as a coherent system because they had a national reach. The treasury department had two major agencies, legal affairs and finance. The legal affairs agency settled suits in the Kantō region and was thus limited to the area, but the finance agency's rural administration section governed the shogun's vast holdings throughout the archipelago through sheriffs and deputies (*gundai* and *daikan*). More importantly, the finance agency's treasury section controlled spending and the mint. Lords could issue their own paper currency, but the mint was the only source of hard currency acceptable throughout the realm. By the mid-nineteenth century treasury officials had learned that they could affect the overall economy by increasing or decreasing the money supply, enrich government coffers by lowering the gold and silver content of their coins, and address regional economic imbalance by manipulating silver and gold contents. Conversely they also knew how difficult it was for the shogunate to manipulate the economic system. In other words, they knew the extent of but also the limits to the power of the shogun. Competent top-level officials in this massive department, with staff in the judiciary, rural and metropolitan administration, and finance, developed an understanding of how the entire system of shogunal rule worked and thus were vehemently opposed to changing the status quo.

Governors, who held ranks comparable to the treasury magistrates, administered the shogun's cities and special locations such as gold mines. These shogunal vassals kept an eye on affairs in the areas surrounding their posts. As such, governors of cities on the frontiers understood the formidable military threat from the foreigners and spoke out in favor of conducting trade negotiations. The actions of the Western naval captains in and near Japanese waters sometimes spoke all too clearly. Although some were courteous and respectful of the detailed instructions of the shogun's officials, others disregarded them and acted as they saw fit. Gunboat diplomacy in East Asia meant individuals like Captain Osborn of the British Royal Navy, who believed in the reasonableness of their own actions regardless of what the natives may think, had free rein: "The hour had arrived for Japan to yield to reason, or to be prepared to suffer, as the Court of Pekin had done, for its obstinacy."[65] The governors knew from firsthand experience that peaceful negotiations were not easy.

The inspectors, who reported any misconduct by shogunal officials and grand inspectors, who reported the misconduct of lords, represented the long arm of the shogunate. Because their principal function was to maintain the authority of the shogun, it was perhaps the most natural for them to seek out new ways to increase the shogun's power. But neither the governors nor the inspectors experienced how the system as a whole worked. They were representatives of the shogun's authority, the supreme power in the realm, there to enforce his will. Institutionally the structure of Tokugawa government made consensus building among the lords very difficult. And among the shogun's vassals, if the treasury officials were reluctant to change the system, the governors and inspectors were amenable for pragmatic reform.[66]

Ideological conflicts, political disagreements, institutional divisions, and finally personal animosities all contributed to the gridlock that paralyzed the shogunate. For Abe Masahiro, who wanted to maintain the status quo, this was acceptable. However, after the events of summer 1856, Hotta Masayoshi decided to convince the other ministers that Japan needed to open itself to trade. By winter 1856 and 1857, they were convinced that they had to change the ancestral laws. The only problem was that Hotta continued to have strong opposition from Abe Masahiro and Tokugawa Nariaki.

ABE MASAHIRO'S DEATH AND HOTTA MASAYOSHI'S PUSH TO OPEN JAPAN

In the traditional story of the opening of Japan, Townsend Harris is second only to Matthew Perry in importance. The American representative arrived in 1856 with only Henry Heusken, his translator, to help him. Once in Japan, Harris began to demand his right and duty to present his credentials to the shogun in Edo. During negotiations over his rights to an audience with the shogun, which would last for fourteen months, Harris insisted on following Western diplomatic protocol and demanded that Japan open an embassy in the capital, that Japan open ports to trade, and that this trade ought to be free trade. In other words, "opening Japan" meant not just signing a piece of paper, but also conducting free trade and joining the Western system of international relations with its diplomatic traditions. Amazingly Harris accomplished all this through diplomacy alone with no U.S. military help. The details of his travails and his negotiations can be read in Oliver Statler's *Shimoda Story*.[67]

What this chapter emphasizes, however, is that this decision to open Japan to trade was already made in December 1856, one year before Harris met Hotta in Edo in December 1857.[68] This fact then raises a simple question: Why did it take so long for Hotta to invite Harris to Edo and meet the shogun? The main answer is because Abe resisted trade and because Abe still had Tokugawa Nariaki's support and the shogun's confidence. Even if Hotta had convinced the council of ministers that opening trade was inevitable, Hotta did not want to take any chances and have his decision overturned by the shogun. Thus, the sudden death of Abe Masahiro on 1857/6/17 (6 August 1857) at the young age of thirty-nine began to change events rapidly.

During the next month Hotta, as chief minister and with no one to oppose him, submitted a report in which he advised the shogun to call the American representative to Edo castle for an audience and begin negotiations for a new treaty. This was his trial balloon and in that report he concluded that the time was not yet appropriate. But with Abe dead and Nariaki back at his home domain in Mito, there was no obvious opposition. Consequently, Hotta ordered the treasury officials and inspectors to begin preparations to receive Harris, to study how trade would be conducted, and to submit candidates for a new trading port. By the end of the seventh month Hotta had issued new official directives to invite the American representative to Edo. Then on 1857/9/11 (28 October 1857) Hotta arranged for the shogun to grant Tokugawa Nariaki parting gifts for Nariaki's services as the special adviser to the shogun. Hotta had fired Nariaki, the late Abe's ally, and his last remaining political opponent. In short, Hotta now had the shogun's confidence and became the *bakufu*'s effective leader.

During these few months Hotta consolidated his position by installing a new treasury magistrate, packing the treasury staff with his appointees, and sacking a few antitrade diehards. Clearing the stage for the start of trade negotiations, Hotta was determined to sign an American treaty negotiated under Japanese terms as a precedent for any future negotiations with other Western states.[69]

The main opposition to Hotta at this juncture came from other lords, men he could not remove and some who traditionally were not part of the official policy-making process. The day after dismissing Nariaki, Hotta circulated a letter among the shogun's relatives and the lords eligible to become *rōjū*. In the letter, he explained that it was the world's custom for national representatives to be received by the shogun and that as the world was changing rapidly around them, it was "time to change the manner we deal with foreign countries that had continued since the Kan'ei period [1630s]."[70] The early replies Hotta received were not encouraging. Immediately, Nariaki's son, the lord of Mito, expressed disapproval. This was expected. Then the lord of Owari concurred with the lord of Mito's position. And finally the lords of Takamatsu, Hikone, Aizu, Oshi, Matsuyama, and Kuwana all agreed that this American representative should not come to Edo. But it was too late. Hotta had already made up his mind. Townsend Harris was invited and en route to Edo. By the time the relatives of the shogunal family had sent their letter 1857/10/23 (9 December 1857) expressing their hope that Harris would be confined to Shimoda, Harris was in Edo. In the end, the great lords could only protest by sending a letter on 1857/11/3 (18 December 1857) asking that in the future they be informed before a major decision such as the arrival of a foreign representative to Edo.[71] For Hotta, the fact that he had to ask the lords for their assent must have been an annoying legacy of Abe, a legacy that would eventually lead him to make a fatal error for the shogunate.

Townsend Harris and his (mostly hired Japanese) retinue arrived at Edo on 30 November 1857. A week later, on 7 December 1857, Harris had his short audience with the shogun and on 12 December 1857 Harris met with the chief *rōjū*, Hotta. After some pleasantries Harris delivered a six-hour-long speech to Hotta about how the United States was a friend of Japan and wished to help economically. Although some of his remarks were clearly lies (such as the claim that the U.S. had never expanded its territory by war, since Hotta knew of the recent Mexican-American War), the impressive speech focused on what Hotta had already determined himself, namely that trade was beneficial. Harris emphasized the evil intentions of the British by repeatedly referring to their plans to sell opium and seize territories in East Asia. Other European countries such as France were not praised in Harris's speech, either, though in all fairness, Western exploitative intentions were easy to believe. The treasury officials did not forget later to remind Hotta of the fact that American merchants were second only to British merchants in selling opium to the Chinese.[72] Nevertheless, the main result of Harris's speech was to solidify Hotta's convictions about the benefits of trade. The economy of both countries would prosper, the world would be as one, and the treaty would be a precedent that could be used in later negotiations. If only Harris had known that he was already preaching to the converted, the laborious process of translating from English to Dutch then to Japanese and then back could have been shortened.[73]

After Harris's speech, Hotta wrote a memorandum to his subordinates stating his views. He rejected the treasury officials' policy of delaying action as long as possible. Hotta also rejected the suggestion of Nariaki and other extremists to attack foreigners on sight. If the first policy was irresolute, the second would be downright dangerous, incurring "the wrath of every country on Earth." He agreed with everyone concerned that the primary objective was national strength. But as he saw it, only a "rich country" could field a "strong army," and a "rich country" was based on trade. Hence it was imperative that Japan change its old policy and trade with the rest of the world. The country had to learn the strengths of the foreigners and strengthen itself. Eventually the world would respect Japan's virtue and the country would become "the leader of the world." "Even if Japan was a small country, the land was rich and populous, and the people were just, brave, and decisive." He ended his memorandum with an exhortation to work hard in unison to overcome this time of crisis.[74]

IWASE TADANARI'S PROPOSAL TO OPEN YOKOHAMA

Now that the decision to open Japan had been agreed upon, the question was where the main port should be. Iwase Tadanari answered this question by selecting Yokohama, and Hotta approved of this selection by appointing Iwase as one of the two negotiators to negotiate a trade deal with Harris. The other negotiator was Inoue Kiyonao. The two appointments were based on a number of reasons. Inoue was the governor of Shimoda and already knew Harris. It was also customary for the local governor who oversaw the foreign representative's port city to be involved in negotiations with that representative. Iwase was selected because he had also negotiated with Harris earlier, but more importantly because he had more experience in trade negotiations. In fact Iwase had concluded a Dutch trade agreement during summer 1857, the first time Japanese negotiators drafted international treaties in the nineteenth century. Also Iwase's knowledge and ability were admired among the officials and he was well liked as a leader among the inspectors. Most importantly Hotta and Iwase agreed politically, and thus Hotta expected Iwase to be the main negotiator.[75] It is worth repeating that Hotta had already decided that Japan needed to be opened in December 1856, and then after meeting Harris in December of 1857, Iwase suggested Yokohama as the port near Edo for trade. In short, Harris was successful because the *bakufu* wanted to open Japan to trade.

Iwase was a brilliant official. The grandson of Hayashi Jussai, the head of the shogun's academy called the Shōheikō, Iwase originally studied the Confucian classics and himself became a professor at the Shōheikō at age thirty-three. Two years later Commodore Perry came to Japan in 1853, and Abe Masahiro selected Iwase and other scholars who graduated from the academy to help him deal with the political turmoil. Perhaps because of his formal education, Iwase was initially antiforeign, but his work experience transformed him. As inspector he first participated in the construction of forts defending Edo Bay, then he inspected the two-masted, Western-style warship, the *Hōōmaru* (the Phoenix) that the shogunate had just created. Perhaps the event that changed him most dramatically came in 1855. In that year Iwase helped establish the Institute for Research on Barbarian Books (*Bansho shirabesho*), but more importantly he went to Shimoda to negotiate with the Russian representative to Japan, Yevfimy Putiatin. The negotiations were a failure, but Putiatin had been directing local Japanese shipbuilders to build a new ship. This new ship was a replacement for Putiatin's old ship, the *Diana*, which sunk when a tsunami hit Shimoda. After returning to Edo and reporting their failure in negotiations, Iwase headed to Shimoda once more. There he and the Japanese shipbuilders built ten Western-style schooners modeled after Putiatin's new ship. These schooners shortened the trip between Edo and Shimoda to one day by sail, instead of the customary five days by palanquin, and deeply impressed Iwase. Since Iwase was making many trips between Edo and Shimoda to deal with Townsend Harris, anything that could shorten travel time to a fifth was a godsend. These experiences changed Iwase. By the end of 1855 Iwase no longer supported the closed country policy. He was for opening the country. Iwase was originally Abe's man because of his pedigree and education, but after his work experience, Iwase had become Hotta Masayoshi's man.[76]

As Hotta Masayoshi's man, he had gone to Nagasaki in summer 1857 with Mizuno Tadanori[77] to discuss new trade regulations with the Dutch representative and to act as negotiators in case the British arrived in Nagasaki. After receiving news that the British burned Canton, they needed to be prepared.[78] In other words, Hotta had sent to Nagasaki two men to negotiate a possible trade deal with the Dutch before the British arrived and before the Americans. Leaving Edo before the sudden death of Abe Masahiro, Hotta may have hoped that in Nagasaki the two could open Japan to trade with the Dutch.

Mizuno Tadanori, however, was not ready to open Japan to trade. Mizuno was a stubborn, capable, and loyal servant of the shogun. He was not a xenophobe and knew that opening the country was the one practical option open to the shogunate. Abe Masahiro selected him as an inspector and then appointed him governor of Nagasaki, where he negotiated with the Dutch to buy Western-style ships in order to found the shogun's navy in 1854. In 1855 he became one of the treasury magistrates and through his work as a treasury official became a conservative reformer. In short, Mizuno was Abe Masahiro's man and remained Abe's man.[79]

At Nagasaki, Mizuno and Iwase waited for British ships that never came. The two men later discovered that a rebellion in India had intervened. They would also learn that Abe Masahiro had died. The two who graduated with top honors from the shogun's academy quarreled at first, such as when Iwase petitioned to visit Hong Kong. But Iwase, the inspector, and Mizuno, the treasury official, eventually agreed to cooperate. They started and completed negotiations with the Dutch and later the Russians. Initially proposed by the Dutch official in charge, Donker Curtius, the new trade agreement expanded on the "private" trade conducted by the Dutch personnel in the Dejima and maintained the "official" trade between the now-defunct Dutch East India Company and the shogun's agents. In effect this treaty sanctioned a form of smuggling between representatives of the treaty signatories and Japanese merchants. Mizuno in particular rushed to sign it to use it as precedent for future negotiations with the British and to forestall Hotta from signing a more expansive trade treaty.[80]

Mizuno and Iwase's cooperation elicited a positive reaction from Hotta back in Edo. Hotta had wanted to open the country to trade after all. Plus, the Dutch treaty seemed to demonstrate that the divided bureaucracy could cooperate. However, the response of the shogunal officials was divided. Some feared that the British, Americans, and Russians (in Edo they did not know that the Russians had already signed a treaty similar to the Dutch one) would demand similar treatment and did not like the new treaties. Others, particularly treasury officials, hoped that the Westerners would be satisfied with similar terms because the sanctioned smuggling would primarily benefit the Western merchants and that the Dutch and Russian treaties would prevent a full opening of Japan to trade.[81]

Finished with their task, Mizuno Tadanori and Iwase Tadanari were on their way back to Edo from Nagasaki. It was on this return journey that Iwase learned of Harris's audience with the shogun and the chief minister. Upon receiving this news, Iwase must have realized that Hotta was planning to fully open Japan to trade and not simply to allow smuggling by merchants affiliated with Western diplomats. In response, Iwase wrote two letters to Edo, one to his colleagues and another to his superiors. In these letters dated Ansei 4/11/6 (21 December 1857), Iwase argued that Yokohama should be opened to strengthen Edo's economic position. He wrote that on his return trip he had seen firsthand how Osaka merchants reaped the benefits of the Nagasaki trade. He also anticipated that the foreigners would ultimately insist on opening Osaka as the center of trade with Japan. If the shogunate persisted in denying the foreigners a port near Edo but capitulated in opening a port near Osaka, Osaka's position as the preeminent mercantile city would be enhanced while Edo's relative economic position would decline. This was detrimental to the shogun because the ultimate source of his power was Edo.

Furthermore, since Osaka was only a day's trip from Kyoto but far from the center of the shogun's power, it also presented a security threat to the shogunate. If they opened Yokohama, a port near Edo, then the port would generate trade, enticing people to bring local goods to Yokohama in order to exchange them with foreign goods. In addition, advanced foreign technology would first appear at Yokohama and be distributed near Edo before spreading to the rest of the country.[82] This was an unabashedly Edo-centric view, preoccupied with buttressing shogunal power in its base in the east, relative to the other major region in Japan, the Kansai.

Iwase's former colleague, Mizuno Tadanori wrote a long memorandum in response to Hotta's and Iwase's letters. Mizuno must have realized that his efforts to limit trade was failing and argued against stationing foreign representatives in Edo and vehemently rejected Kanagawa and Yokohama as too close to Edo. If the foreigners wanted to open Osaka, they could have an isolated port in Kii or Shima province. According to Mizuno, if the foreigners insisted on ports closer to Edo and Osaka, then Uraga and Toba could be opened but nothing closer. Reminding Hotta and the ministers that the shogunate had recently tried to lower the population of Edo because vagrants filled the city, Mizuno declared that there was no need to be concerned about the decline of Edo.[83] As a treasury official, Mizuno was opposed to altering the roles of Osaka and Edo and preferred to limit foreign influence so that the system, as it was established by Tokugawa Ieyasu in the seventeenth century, could continue. This memorandum turned out to be Mizuno's last before

Hotta reassigned him. Hotta promoted Mizuno from treasury magistrate to the counselor of a prestigious but powerless lord.[84]

Iwase's rebuttal to Mizuno's memorandum laid out the position of the shogunate before entering into negotiations with Harris.

> We have been given the responsibility of defending the imperial lands, temple grounds, and other lords' domains. Since all the responsibilities under heaven are ours, we must maintain justice. But only by bringing the wealth of the country to our doorsteps can we police the country and provide benefit for eternity. A rich country and a strong army (*fukoku kyōhei*) must be the basis of our policy. Regardless of the foreigners' intent, whether for real or not and whether it is a minor injustice taking advantage of us or not, we must bring order and stability. Following that, we can be just.[85]

Through a new treaty the shogun would strengthen his domain first and then restore order to the realm.[86] Hotta's idea that trade should strengthen the *bakufu* took concrete shape with Iwase's proposal to open Yokohama.

During winter 1856–1857 Hotta Masayoshi convinced the other *rōjū* that Japan needed to open trade. During summer 1857 Abe Masahiro died and Hotta's man Iwase opened trade between Japan and the Netherlands and between Japan and Russia. During autumn 1857 Hotta sacked Tokugawa Nariaki to eliminate opposition within the *bakufu*. By winter 1857–1858, Hotta was as ready as he could be. He consolidated his position as the chief minister. He initiated a new campaign convincing the other lords that proceeding with trade negotiations would benefit the country. He even exhorted officials to work together after the (un)timely death of Abe and the signing of a new Dutch treaty.[87] He invited Harris to Edo only after making sure that he could open Japan to trade. This is why the invitation of Harris to Edo was delayed for so long.

After the December 1857 meetings between Harris and Hotta, Iwase had suggested Yokohama as the new trading port to benefit Edo and eastern Japan. Hotta then appointed Iwase as chief negotiator. Hotta's political maneuvering and Abe's death had resolved the gridlock within the shogunate. Moreover, Hotta articulated a new holistic vision that could resolve the three problems hounding the shogunate: One, raise revenue through trade and tariffs. Two, buttress the shogun's military and economic power by rerouting international trade through eastern Japan, not western Japan. Three, use the added revenue to stop the currency debasement and thus help the ordinary samurai of Edo. But this vision could not be implemented the way that the late Abe Masahiro preferred, of resolving conflicts quietly. Hotta's style was similar to Mizuno Tadakuni's forceful style and likely to invite backlash.

IWASE TADANARI AND TOWNSEND HARRIS'S NEGOTIATIONS

Hotta wanted to open trade with the West even before meeting Harris. Under these favorable circumstances, it is not surprising that Iwase and Harris negotiated a treaty relatively quickly. At the Ansei 4/12/2 (16 January 1858) meeting the three men, Hotta, Iwase, and Harris, agreed on the basic outline of the treaty.[88] The Americans could station a minister in Edo, trade between the two countries would commence, and a new port would replace Shimoda. Further details were left to the negotiators but Hotta and Iwase knew that they wanted to open Yokohama. The month-long negotiation tested the patience of the two negotiators. Harris, baffled by Japanese intransigence on what seemed to him minor matters, exploded a number of times.[89] Iwase, infuriated by Harris's wily diplomatic maneuvering, also became visibly upset often.[90] But when negotiations came to a close, both Harris and Iwase were proud of their achievement. In an interview with Fukuchi Gen'ichirō, Harris recalled how surprised he had been when Iwase premised the negotiation on trust.

> I [Iwase] do not know what a trade treaty is, nor does anyone else in the government. You [Harris] explained to minister Hotta that you came to Japan on orders from your government, and to negotiate with us on the basis of friendship. You also claimed that a treaty trade would be beneficial for Japan. I shall trust your fairness to provide us with a draft treaty. Write a draft that incorporates Japanese interests and publicly demonstrate that your words are true.[91]

Iwase was not telling the truth, because he had negotiated other trade treaties, but Iwase himself confirmed Harris's recollection. Harris wrote a draft and the two studied the treaty in minute detail to ensure mutual benefit. With pride, Iwase believed that no one else could have negotiated a better treaty for Japan, unless Japan had been a greater power.[92] Although six more months passed before the shogun signed the treaty, Britain, France, the Netherlands, and Russia shortly followed the United States. In the mid-nineteenth century, this treaty became the model for future trade treaties with Japan.

By the end of the century these agreements were known far and wide as "unequal treaties" and seen as symbols of Japanese capitulation. The treaty that Harris and Iwase were so proud of contained two elements that were later considered particularly unjust. The treaty granted extraterritoriality to Americans in Japan and denied tariff autonomy to Japan. In other words, U.S. consular officials, and not Japanese courts, tried Americans accused of crimes in Japan, and the treaty denied Japan's right to unilaterally change the predetermined tariff rates stipulated in the agreement.[93] What made the situation even more irritating was that this treaty and others based on it had no termination date and included a most-favored-nation clause. The most-favored-nation clause guaranteed that benefits granted to another country would automatically apply to the signatory. Thus if the British managed to sign a treaty that contained lower tariffs for their products, which indeed happened, similar American products would also obtain the lower rate. The lack of a termination date meant that these treaties were permanent unless both parties agreed to a revision or one party unilaterally denounced the treaty. Combined, the treaties effectively denied protective tariffs for Japanese goods, reduced possible government revenues, granted foreigners immunity from Japanese law, and imposed all of these terms indefinitely. But to be realistic, Iwase was probably right; Japan could not have fared better at that point in its history. This was the standard type of treaty that Asian and African countries signed with the Western powers in the mid-nineteenth century. In addition to the unequal clauses, other aspects were also standard. Merchants, not governments, were to conduct trade. In the settlements there was to be religious freedom, although it was understood that the *bakufu* could ban Christianity for its own people in its domestic laws. Foreign representatives could be stationed in the capital. Indeed, most of the issues that Abe and his supporters had opposed appeared in the treaty. But it also contained elements that might have heartened them. Foreigners could reside only in the five open ports and the two open cities. Except for diplomats on official business, the shogunate forbade foreigners, including missionaries, to travel in the countryside. Also, as part of Harris's longstanding objection to opium and as part of Japanese policy, the treaty expressly banned the opium trade.[94]

By signing the treaty Japan had entered a global system structured by the power and principles of Western international law. Japan would have to dismantle its own international order on the fringe of Asia and cooperate and compete in a framework created by Western states. Questions about Japan's borders with respect to the shogunate's borders remained to be sorted out later. The tariff rates that Iwase and Harris agreed upon (20 percent) would be lowered to 5 percent as part of indemnities for the antiforeign activities of the southwestern lords. Nevertheless, the shogunate as the official government of Japan never waged war against a Western state and thus never had to pay a crippling indemnity or lose territory. Furthermore a negotiated treaty held the promise of further negotiations to revise the treaties.

HOTTA MASAYOSHI'S NEGOTIATIONS WITH THE IMPERIAL COURT

Although Hotta Masayoshi escaped the treaty negotiations that tested the patience of Iwase and Harris, he found himself among obstinate lords (*daimyō*) and court nobles (*kuge*) at the imperial court in Kyoto. If Abe Masahiro had not opened the political process in 1853 when Perry arrived,

Hotta probably would not have needed to do this. However, the genie was out of the bottle. Hotta had to gain not only the confidence of the shogun, but also some sort of tacit understand among the lords. The problem was these lords.

Earlier the lords had expressed their disapproval of inviting Townsend Harris to Edo. Would they now be in favor of opening Japan for trade? It was unlikely, but Hotta had to try. He sent them a copy of Harris's six-hour speech at Hotta's mansion and another copy of the conversations between Harris and shogunal officials on Ansei 4/12/21 (4 February 1858).[95] This time the results were more encouraging. The opposition of xenophobes was expected. For example, Nariaki flew into a rage, threatened to behead Harris and urged that Hotta commit ritual suicide.[96] But others were cautiously supportive and almost everyone agreed on the need for some kind of reform. When Hotta called Iwase to explain the situation to some of the lords, many more understood the situation and decided to support Hotta's policy. One even suggested opening Shinagawa instead of Kanagawa. This was encouraging but still far from a consensus. As Inoue Kiyonao explained to Harris, "out of the eighteen great lords, only four supported trade, and out of the three hundred vassal lords, only ninety supported opening the country."[97] Although these numbers were exaggerated, the opposition was real. In the end, an official who reported on the general consensus of the lords suggested that the shogun consult the imperial court and obtain the emperor's approval.[98]

Hotta probably agreed that gaining imperial assent would make his task easier in forging a consensus. And Hotta probably thought that gaining imperial assent would be easy. After all, the imperial court was expressly forbidden to intervene in politics since the founding of the Tokugawa shogunate and was expected to rubberstamp shogunal decisions. But by accepting this suggestion, Hotta made a mistake for which the *bakufu* would ultimately pay a high price. If the emperor did not approve, the damage to the shogun's prestige would be massive. We must recall that for many samurai, and in particular for the Mito school samurai, the emperor was the source of the shogun's authority. The Tokugawa system had effectively neutralized the imperial court's influence over the years by not relying on it to help govern. But by relying on the help of the imperial court, Hotta took the risk of reminding the samurai that the shogun was appointed by the emperor. If the other lords and samurai were duty bound to obey the shogun because the shogun ruled on behalf of the emperor, then what would happen if the emperor and the shogun disagreed?

With the negotiations between Iwase Tadanari and Townsend Harris proceeding, Hotta dispatched two relatively low-ranking officials to Kyoto to get the emperor's approval. But this time the imperial court refused to answer. Since no answer was forthcoming, on 1858/1/8 (21 February 1858)

Hotta decided to go to Kyoto himself. On this trip he brought with him Iwase Tadanari, who had mostly finished his negotiations with Townsend Harris, and Kawaji Toshiakira, a treasury magistrate who strongly advocated getting imperial support.[99]

As these three travelled to Kyoto, the two officials who were dispatched earlier finally received an answer from an imperial envoy. Sensing that many lords were unhappy with the decision to open trade with the United States, being fundamentally conservative, and possibly supplied with some backbone from Tokugawa Nariaki and Mito school ideologues, the emperor's envoys replied that the court would give the shogunate its assent when the lords had come to a consensus.[100] When Hotta arrived in Kyoto on 1858/2/5 (19 March 1858) and learned of this reply, he must have been frustrated. He needed the emperor's assent to create a consensus, but the assent would not be given without a consensus.

To break this impasse Hotta thought that reason and dialogue would be enough. After all when Iwase spoke and explained the situation in detail, a number of important lords changed their minds. Thus he would do his utmost to convince the emperor and the court nobles to sign the trade treaty through open dialogue. Iwase and Kawaji would support him in explaining why the treaty was necessary.[101] Unfortunately for Hotta, this plan would prove to be inadequate. In Edo, the feudal lords could listen to Hotta and Iwase and many were convinced. In Kyoto, the court nobles did not listen to Hotta or Iwase.

If xenophobia was strong among the samurai, it utterly dominated Kyoto. Antiforeign *shishi* (activists, literally "men of high purpose"), including Mito domain samurai, had congregated in Kyoto advocating the violent expulsion of foreigners. The emperor and most of the court nobles agreed with this xenophobia, and those who advocated trade were branded as traitors. Among the major court nobles, only the previous regent was for trade and allowing the shogunate to act as it saw fit.[102] The rest was against the opening of trade, in particular the opening of any city near Kyoto. Moreover, the emperor and the court nobles were simply too ignorant of world affairs to understand the arguments made by Hotta and Iwase. Though one can be sympathetic to Hotta and Iwase on this issue, the ignorance stemmed from the fact that the imperial court was not involved in politics since the beginning of the Tokugawa shogunate. To suddenly ask the court to deliberate on foreign policy after they were forbidden to debate politics for more than two hundred years was a bit hypocritical and likely beyond the capabilities of the court.

First, Hotta Masayoshi presented gifts from the shogun to the emperor, former regent, the current regent, and other nobles. In total he gave a small amount of 50 *ryō* to the imperial court and some silver to the nobles. Then he gave a speech to a few court nobles explaining that opening the country to trade was necessary and that xenophobia would be harmful. Once the court nobles explained that their position was to keep the country closed, Hotta provided the nobles with his formal letter and records of conversations and meetings between shogunal officials and Harris to explain his position further.[103] Here he clearly hoped that his appearance and speech could be overcome with the written word.

Hotta Masayoshi was not a smooth talker. Portly and dark, Hotta had a face that did not immediately inspire confidence. In fact, he did not look like a smart man.[104] This was unfortunate for Hotta, since the appearance of elegance and courtliness was valued above all at the imperial court, and Hotta lacked that appearance. In the end, Hotta was ineffective at convincing the court nobles. He thus tried to turn to his negotiator, Iwase. Iwase was the best official the shogunate had in convincing others that trade was necessary. Unfortunately, Iwase's court rank was lower fifth grade, junior. This rank was the maximum court rank attainable for a shogunal official. But for a person to enter the same room with high-ranking court nobles of third grade or above, that person needed a minimum rank of fourth grade.[105] Hotta was a lord and as such he had a rank of lower fourth grade, junior. But Iwase at fifth grade was barred from entering the same room and speaking his mind. Hotta had underestimated the custom and tradition that prevented lower ranked people from meeting with court nobles.[106] Thus Iwase, the man who was in charge of negotiations, the man who changed the opinion of the *daimyō*, could not even be in the same room as the court nobles.

Hotta's plan to convince the imperial court of the necessity of trade through reason and logic clearly failed. A Confucian scholar at Kyoto who knew of Iwase's vassal suggested a different plan, namely bribery.[107] This was based on Hotta and Kawaji Toshiakira's success in entertaining the court nobles and getting some of them to change their opinions. The small amount of silver was effective in combination with Kawaji, an old treasury official who was known for his wit and amiable personality.[108] However, the xenophobic *shishi* countered this by launching a rumor campaign. One rumor claimed that Kawaji planned on giving 10,000 *ryō* each to the emperor, the former regent, and the current regent. Another rumor claimed that if the three succeeded, Hotta would receive an extra 10,000 *koku* and that Iwase and Kawaji would also receive enough land to become lords (with a fief of at least 10,000 *koku*).[109] These rumors used envy to sabotage Hotta, Iwase, and Kawaji's efforts. Many court nobles preferred to ensure that others fail if they were to receive a pittance while others received an outsize reward. Considering that even the highest ranking court nobles had only 3,000 *koku* as their income and many lower ranking nobles had less than 100 *koku*, the rumored 10,000 *koku* reward could easily have fanned the flames of jealousy. Hotta's biographer believes that the bribing strategy would have worked because the court nobles were expecting bribes from Hotta. The fact that they did not receive any bribes angered them. So if Hotta had not relied on reason but instead relied on bribing the court nobles outright, he would have probably succeeded.[110]

In the end, the imperial court and the religious authorities opposed further opening of the country.[111] The response of the imperial court came on 1858/3/20 (3 May 1858). It rejected the *bakufu*'s proposal and asked for further consultations with the lords. Determined that this trip not be for naught, Hotta petitioned twice for permission to act unilaterally if circumstances became dangerous. The final reply came on 1858/3/26 (9 May 1858), before Hotta left Kyoto to return to Edo; it was still not satisfactory, but the court had grudgingly assented that in emergency situations, appropriate measures could be taken.[112] Hotta had come to the realization that the court nobles in Kyoto were "not sane" and that there was no other course of action left for him to take. The next day, he wrote a letter explaining that the shogun would have to sign the treaty without the assent of the imperial court. Once the *bakufu* received the emperor's reply and Hotta's letter explaining the situation, the shogunal officials also came to the same realization.[113]

THE DISMISSAL OF HOTTA MASAYOSHI

Hotta Masayoshi would not be the man to sign the new treaty. On 1858/4/23 (4 June 1858), three days after Hotta's return to Edo and two days after his audience with the shogun, Ii Naosuke became *tairō*, the regent of the shogun. As regent, Ii superseded Hotta's authority. Political machinations surrounding the childless shogun had come to a boiling point while Hotta was away. An heir needed to be designated and there were only two possible candidates: the young lord of Kii domain or the lord of Hitotsubashi, the biological son of Nariaki. In this battle the lords separated into two groups. The traditionalists reckoned that Kii, being closer in blood, should be the heir. The reformists argued that during this period of crisis, a mature heir clearly seen to be effective was necessary. Of course this was tantamount to calling the current shogun incompetent. Furthermore, the shogun's mother was absolutely opposed to the biological son of Nariaki and pretended to commit suicide over this issue.[114] The shogun's wife was a relative of the lord of Satsuma, a leader among the reformers, and argued for the lord of Hitotsubashi. Caught between the two factions and with his own family divided, the shogun chose to honor his mother. The young lord of Kii became his heir. The leader of this faction, Ii Naosuke, lord of Hikone, was then appointed as regent and replaced Hotta as the most important man among the lords.

Ii, the traditionalist, may have wanted to close Japan again as his letter to Hotta in 1857 suggested. But the diplomatic momentum could not be ignored. The Japanese negotiators had already promised to sign the treaties; they just needed to buy some time to mollify the xenophobic court nobles and lords. When Harris delivered the news of the impending arrival of a British fleet in 1858, Ii was backed into a corner. Ii understood the threat Britain posed and had, like Hotta, contemplated making the American treaty a precedent and signing it before a fleet of British ships arrived. Coupled with his first priority of restoring shogunal power, Ii went ahead and signed the new treaty on Ansei 5/6/19 (29 July 1858) without imperial approval. This turn of events surprised many people who thought Ii was one of the lords who opposed inviting Harris to Edo. However, in his joint letter to the council of ministers, he displayed surprising pragmatism; he saw no other alternative and even suggested sending missions to other countries.[115]

Ii was an interesting man who believed that building coastal forts were generally a waste of money and preferred to build a navy to defend the country. His goal was ultimately to defend the shogun and the feudal order as set out by Tokugawa Ieyasu. If he was for adopting Western technology, it was for the defense of the Tokugawa order.[116] Thus it was the reality of Western pressures, the tactical advantage in negotiating a treaty first, and the possibility of strengthening shogunal power that pushed Ii to accept open trade with the West. If the gentlemanly Abe had a Confucian view, the "Dutch crazy" Hotta had a realpolitik vision, then the regent Ii Naosuke had pragmatism.

On Ansei 5/6/23 (2 August 1858), four days after signing the Harris treaty, Ii had the shogun fire Hotta Masayoshi.[117] After this dismissal Hotta retired from politics and his son became the new lord of Sakura domain. Ii continued to purge his enemies, particularly those who were active in foreign policy and advocated the selection of Hitotsubashi instead of Kii as the next shogun. Kawaji Toshiakira, the treasury official who helped Hotta in Kyoto was "promoted" to an honorable but powerless position. Tokugawa Nariaki, his son Tokugawa Yoshiatsu (lord of Mito domain), and Tokugawa Yoshikumi (lord of Owari domain, one of the "three honorable houses"), three men who had intervened in the succession issue, were also punished. The lords of Mito and Owari were ordered to retire and Ii placed Tokugawa Nariaki under house arrest. On 1858/9/5 (11 October 1858), two days after Iwase finished negotiations with France, the last of the five major Western countries to sign the early treaties, Ii transferred Iwase and made him the construction magistrate.[118]

CONCLUSION

This chapter examined the opening of Japan from an economic perspective. Starting with the failed Tempō Reforms, the chapter traced how the *bakufu* desperately sought revenue, how it addressed national defense, and how it tried to tackle the problem of the lack of cheap goods in Edo. These three issues intertwined in complex ways to bedevil the leaders of the shogunate. Among these leaders, this chapter focused on Hotta Masayoshi. The dual foci on the economy and on Hotta are not by accident. The economic story sheds light on the long-term problem facing the shogunate and how it led Hotta to decide that opening the country to trade was necessary in December 1856, one year before he met Harris. In other words, the opening of Japan was as much a Japanese story based on economics, defense policy, and diplomacy as it was an American or Western story.[119]

The rest of this book continues to address many of the economic issues raised in this chapter. The most important issue is the reordering of the economic geography of Japan. Iwase Tadanari proposed the opening of Yokohama to effectively redraw the trade routes and make Edo the center of the Japanese economy. In the long run, his vision came true, and today Tokyo is the unquestioned center of the Japanese economy. However, after Iwase's and Hotta's dismissals, this plan ceased to be the *bakufu*'s plan. Thus chapters 3 and 4 follow the merchants who tied the new port of Yokohama with Edo's hinterland without the backing of the *bakufu*. Chapter 5 traces the people who then linked eastern Japan with Europe and those who linked eastern Japan to the United States. These three chapters show how the economic geography of Japan came to be redrawn and provide hints in understanding modern Japan's economic growth.

Another major economic issue in chapter 2 was the problem of shogunal finances and currency debasements. This issue became linked with the international monetary system, and its resolution as described in chapter 3 resulted in intense inflation. The role of guilds, specifically the role they played to prevent fraud and cheating, and the role of voluntary associations are also examined in the next three chapters. If fraud and cheating were problems within Japan, they became even bigger problems when Japan entered international trade. Every person involved in business had to deal with these problems in some way or another.

The story of Hotta Masayoshi ends with this chapter. Ii, after dismissing Hotta and virtually the entire foreign policy team under him, had almost no one competent to open Yokohama. At this point Mizuno Tadanori, who had been promoted but relegated to the sidelines by Hotta, returned as foreign magistrate and took charge of preparing for Yokohama's grand opening. Recall that Mizuno wanted to keep foreign influence to a minimum in his last major memorandum. Thus the political drama resulted in Yokohama's dual character. Hotta and Iwase envisioned Yokohama as an international port to strengthen shogunal power and enrich eastern Japan (at the expense of western Japan). Ii and Mizuno remolded Yokohama as strategic port to confine the barbarians away from the shogun.

Ii's attempts to strengthen shogunal authority eventually led to a crackdown known as *Ansei no taigoku* (or the Ansei Purge, literally the "great jailing of Ansei"). Anger against Ii erupted on Ansei 7/3/3 (24 March 1860), a day of light snow. A former Mito domain samurai assassinated Ii Naosuke. Inexplicably Hotta Masayoshi, who was in retirement since 1859, was blamed for helping Ii and placed under house arrest on Bunkyū 2/11/20 (9 January 1863). On 1864/3/21 (26 April 1864), Hotta died at fifty-four years of age.[120] The end of the *bakufu* was near.

In the next chapter, we see how Nakaiya Jūbei, the first merchant of Yokohama, helped turn Hotta and Iwase's vision of rerouting the economic geography of Japan into reality.

NOTES

1. The Japanese calendar at the time was a lunisolar calendar. Each month was twenty-nine or thirty days long depending on the cycle of the moon; the first was always a new moon and the fifteenth was a full moon. Twelve months equaled a year. Since twelve of these "short" months meant that a lunisolar year was usually eleven days short of a solar calendar, every three years or so an intercalary month, a "leap month," would be inserted to synchronize the length of the year to the solar cycle of the earth revolving around the sun. For this book, Japanese dates are shortened as follows: year/month/day. Anno Domini or the Japanese year will be used to denote the year. Thus the day Mizuno was fired would be 1843/int 9/13 or Tempō 14/int 9/13. Western dates are shortened as follows: day/month/year. The same day would be 4 November 1843 in the Gregorian calendar.

2. At the age of twenty-two, as temple magistrate, Abe quietly but firmly handled the case of two monks entering the shogun's harem illicitly and conducting affairs. The shogun recognized Abe's ability to solve disputes judiciously. Three years later, in 1843 as Mizuno Tadakuni's ambitious reforms failed, the shogun promoted Abe to *rōjū*. Tokutomi Iichiro, *Kinsei Nihon kokuminshi*, vol. 29 *Bakufu jitsuryoku shittsui jidai* (Tokyo: Minyūsha, 1928), 29–41. Henceforth abbreviated as KNK.

3. For a historiographical discussion on the importance of the reforms, see Fujita Satoru, *Tempō no kaikaku* (Tokyo: Yoshikawa kōbunkan, 1989), 1–8. For a biography on Mizuno Tadakuni, see Fujita Satoru, *Mizuno Tadakuni: Seijikaikaku ni kaketa kinken rōjū* (Tokyo: Tōyō Keizai shimpōsha, 1994).

4. Plans to develop Lake Inba-numa have been carried out numerous times and have all failed before the twentieth century. Mizuno's plan was to open new fields and open new internal shipping routes in case foreign ships tried to close Edo bay. Like the *agechirei*, he tried to kill two birds with one stone. Unfortunately success in developing Lake Inba-numa had to wait until contemporary times. The first successfully completed project came in 1969. Shiratori Kouji, *Inbanuma monogatari* (*Story of Lake Inba-numa*) (Chiba: Committee for Lake Inbanuma Watershed Management and Chiba prefecture, 2014), 28–30.

5. Fujita, *Tempō no kaikaku*, 216–22; Fujita, *Mizuno Tadakuni*, 176.

6. Fujita, *Tempō no kaikaku*, 145–53; Fujita, *Mizuno Tadakuni*, 156–61.

7. Chiba-ken naimubu, *Hotta Masayoshi* (Tokyo: Shōbundo, 1921), part I, 80–82. Henceforth abbreviated as HM.

8. Okazaki Tetsuji, *Edo no shijō keizai* (Tokyo: Kōdansha, 1999), 101.

9. Since the shogunate directly controlled roughly 4 million *koku* worth of land and taxed it at roughly 30 to 40 percent, it had an annual tax yield of 1.2 million to 1.6 million *koku*. The official rate of exchange was 1 *koku* equals 1 *ryō*. In the eight years that it debased gold coins from 1818 to 1826, the shogunate gained 1.85 million *ryō*. In the fifteen years that it debased silver coins from 1820 and 1835, the shogunate gained 3.84 million *ryō*. One can see how 10,200 *ryō* was not a major factor in Mizuno's or Abe's calculations. Fujita, *Mizuno Tadakuni*, 98–99.

10. Iijima Chiaki, *Edo bakufu zaisei no kenkyū* (Tokyo: Yoshikawa Kōbunkan, 2004), 113, 118, 120.

11. Nishikawa Takeomi, *Edo naiwan no minato to ryūtsū* (Tokyo: Iwata shoten, 1993), 32; Katō Yūzō, *Bakumatsu gaikō to kaikoku* (Tokyo: Chikuma shobō, 2004), 112. As a specific measure, Mizuno ordered Kawagoe domain to defend the Kannonzaki side and Oshi domain to defend the Futtsu side; together they were in charge of the southern part of Edo bay. He then created a new post, the Haneda *bugyō*, so the shogunate directly defended the northern part of Edo bay. Fujita, *Mizuno Tadakuni*, 172.

12. Fujita argues that Mizuno was appointed simply to add gravitas to the cabinet. However, considering that Mizuno appointed Takashima Shūho to spread western artillery widely, asked the Dutch if the shogunate could buy a steam engine and a steamboat from them, and was active on foreign policy before his fall, I think it more likely that the shogun wanted Mizuno to help. Fujita, *Mizuno Tadakuni*, 170, 173, 185, 190–204.

13. KNK, vol. 29 *Bakufu jitsuryoku shittsui jidai*, 53–57.

14. Nariaki saw this conciliatory gesture as cowardly and instead favored a ban on *rangaku* (Dutch learning) and a termination of the Dutch and Chinese trade, and he even asked to receive Ezochi (modern day Hokkaido) as a fief so that he could use it to help defend the country. KNK, vol. 28 *Tempō kaikakuhen* (Tokyo: Minyūsha, 1928), 59–78, 225–26.

15. For more on Mito school, see J. Victor Koschmann, *The Mito Ideology: Discourse, Reform and Insurrection in Late Tokugawa Japan, 1790–1864* (Berkeley: University of California Press, 1987), and in particular on Aizawa Seishisai, see Bob Tadashi Wakabayashi, *Anti-Foreignism and Western Learning in Early-Modern Japan: The* New Theses *of 1825* (London: Harvard University Press, 1991).

16. KNK, vol. 28 *Tempō kaikakuhen*, 32–53, 225. KNK, vol. 29 *Bakufu jitsuryoku shittsui jidai*, 93–101, 130–32.

17. KNK, vol. 30 *Perī raikō izen no keisei* (Tokyo: Minyūsha, 1935), 219.

18. In regard to the letter from the king of the Netherlands, we do not know what Mizuno had in mind; however, it is unlikely that he advocated opening the country at the time. Some claim that Mizuno did advocate the opening of Japan and that was the reason for being sidelined. In the case of Torii Yōzō, Mizuno's right-hand man during the Tempō Reforms, Torii felt guilty for betraying Mizuno by opposing the *agechirei* and resigned shortly after Mizuno's reinstatement. In the end both Mizuno and Torii were put under house arrest. KNK, vol. 29 *Bakufu jitsuryoku shittsui jidai*, 57–64, 145–53; Fujita, *Mizuno Tadakuni*, 197, 204–9.

19. The letters between Tokugawa Nariaki and Abe Masahiro are compiled as *Shinisemonogatari*. Katō Yūzō, *Kurofune zengo no sekai* (Tokyo: Chikuma shobō, 1994), 333.

20. KNK, vol. 28 *Tempō kaikakuhen*, 74.

21. Nariaki, after reading the reply to the Dutch aristocrats, predictably wrote a letter to Abe advocating the return to the 1825 edict of firing upon any foreign vessels encroaching Japanese waters and to consider the possibility of ending the Dutch trade. KNK, vol. 29 *Bakufu jitsuryoku shittsui jidai*, 81–87, 97–101.

22. KNK, vol. 29 *Bakufu jitsuryoku shittsui jidai*, 119–25.

23. KNK, vol. 29 *Bakufu jitsuryoku shittsui jidai*, 131–33.

24. KNK, vol. 28 *Tempō kaikakuhen*, 59–78, 225–26.

25. Katō Yūzō, *Kurofune zengo no sekai*, 335.

26. Fujita, *Mizuno Tadakuni*, 157–59; Fujita, *Tempō no kaikaku*, 80; Okazaki, *Edo no shijō keizai*, 100.

27. Fujita, *Tempō no kaikaku*, 145–46; Okazaki, *Edo no shijō keizai*, 99.

28. Prices rose steadily from the late 1830s and then spiked upward between 1849 and 1850. Okazaki, *Edo no shijō keizai*, 35.

29. Okazaki, *Edo no shijō keizai*, 102, 106–29, 141–43.

30. Okazaki, *Edo no shijō keizai*, 138–43. Okazaki argues that this situation is analogous to the Jewish Maghribi traders of the Mediterranean in the eleventh century who straddled many jurisdictions and lived in states with weak powers that could not enforce contracts. Avner Greif, "Contract Enforceability and Economic Institutions in Early Trade: The Maghribi Traders' Coalition," *American Economic Review* 83, no. 3 (June 1993): 525–48.

31. Okazaki, *Edo no shijō keizai*, 144–53.

32. KNK, vol. 34 *Kōmei tennō shoki sesōhen* (Tokyo: Minyūsha, 1935), 297–300.
33. Okazaki, *Edo no shijō keizai*, 34–35.
34. Ootsuka Hideki, "Edo jidai ni okeru kaichū no rekishi to sono hyōka," Nihon ginkō kin'yū kenkyūjo, *Kin'yū kenkyū* 18, no. 4 (September 1999): 81.
35. Ono Takeo (ed.), *Edo bukka jiten* (Tokyo: Tenbōsha, 1998), 67. From the *Morisada mankō*.
36. For British activities, see W. G. Beasley, *Great Britain and the Opening of Japan, 1834–1858* (Sandgate, Folkestone, Kent: Japan Library, 1951), 87–144. The Dutch were the only exception among the four states. The longstanding trade relationship going back to the seventeenth century continued to be honored. After the U.S.-Japan treaty was signed on 31 March 1854, the Anglo-Japanese treaty was signed on 14 October 1854, the Russo-Japanese treaty was signed on 7 February 1855, and the Dutch-Japanese treaty was signed on 30 January 1856.
37. Katō Yūzō, *Bakumatsu gaikō to kaikoku* (Tokyo: Chikuma shobō, 2004), 238–42.
38. Michael Auslin, *Negotiating with Imperialism: The Unequal Treaties and the Culture of Japanese Diplomacy* (Cambridge, MA: Harvard University Press, 2006), 18.
39. KNK, vol. 31 *Perī raikō oyobi sono tōji* (Tokyo: Minyūsha, 1935), 236.
40. Katō, *Kurofune zengo no sekai*, 386–90; *Katō, Bakumatsu gaikō to kaikoku*, 97–104.
41. KNK, vol. 32 *Kanagawa jōyaku teiketsu hen* (Tokyo: Minyūsha, 1935), 388–90, 398–99, 403–4; Fukuchi Gen'ichirō, *Bakumatsu seijika* (Tokyo: Heibonsha, 1989), 24–31, 167.
42. Katō, *Kurofune zengo no sekai*, 428.
43. Katō, *Bakumatsu gaikō to kaikoku*, 107–9.
44. Iijima, 141.
45. Many shogunal offices during the Edo period were called *bugyō*. For the sake of readability, this book differentiates the *kanjō bugyō* as treasury officials, *bugyō* of cities as governors (this includes the Edo *bugyō* and the other *ongoku bugyō*), and the *jisha bugyō* as temple magistrate.
46. Tokyo daigaku shiryō hensanjo (ed.), *Dainihon komonjo: Bakumatsu gaikoku kankei monjo* (Tokyo: Tokyo University Press, 1930), vol. 14, no. 160, 193, 201, 188, 213. Henceforth abbreviated as BGKM, XIV, 160 (Nagasaki), 193 (Hakodate, Uraga), 201 (inspectors), 188 (treasury), 213 (council).
47. BGKM, XIV, 289.
48. BGKM, XV, 11 (council), 3 (Hakodate); XIV, 250 (Hakodate, Uraga), 289 (inspectors), 278 (treasury).
49. HM, part II, 5, 15; part I, 90, 102, 105, 99.
50. Fukuchi, *Bakumatsu seijika*, 44.
51. BGKM, XV, 74 (Hotta appointment as foreign minister); HM, part II, 44.
52. BGKM, XV, 75 (*rōjū* policy directive on trade).
53. BGKM, XV, 80 (*rōjū* to Hotta and *wakadoshiyori* [junior minister] Honda, study trade), 81 (Hotta to inspector Atobe, study trade).
54. This is the best simple definition of capitalism as a general concept that I have stumbled upon. Capitalism, or "money-ism," is the idea that one ought to dedicate one's life to making money. A capitalist society is a society in which the pursuit of profit is not only normal, but in fact encouraged. In that sense, Japan during the Edo period was not a capitalist society, while Meiji Japan became a capitalist society.
55. BGKM, XV, 158 (treasury report), 132 (opening of institute).
56. This probably refers to the chain of actions starting with the destruction of Chinese forts near Canton and the British bombardment of the offices of the governor of Guangzhou (Canton) on 23 October 1856. Stanley Lane-Poole, *Life of Sir Harry Parkes, vol. 1—Consul in China* (London: MacMillan, 1894), 230–31.
57. BGKM, XV, 216.
58. BGKM, XV, 256, 262.
59. Unable to file a single reply to Hotta's memorandums, the council wrote three reports. The joint report asserted that the country must reform quickly so that a Japanese city does not suffer Canton's fate. The treasury officials and inspectors then wrote two separate reports. On one hand, the treasury argued for opening Nagasaki alone and limiting trade to official trade. If

British demands had to be met, minimizing them was the best course. On the other hand, the inspectors argued that this was an opportunity to return to the period before the Kan'ei edicts closed Japan. And as such, they proposed sending representatives and students overseas, accepting foreign representatives at Edo, opening more ports such as Osaka and sending ships abroad for trade, and ultimately making tariff revenue the basis for the treasury. In short, an overhaul of government and an all-out engagement with the rest of the world. BGKM, XV, 263 (treasury), 264 (joint), 265 (inspectors). Perhaps sensing the irreconcilable split and the resulting futility of a meeting, Hotta never called for the council to meet.

60. The Japanese word *taikun* became "tycoon" in English.

61. On this system, see Ronald Toby, *State and Diplomacy in Early Modern Japan: Asia in the Development of the Tokugawa Bakufu* (Stanford, CA: Stanford University Press, 1984), 38, 64–76, 97–109.

62. As Harris himself put it, he rested in a "rest house for persons of the highest rank, such as the princes," and Harris's procession also shouted, "stay low, stay low," as they travelled, standard practice for a feudal lord. Oliver Statler, *Shimoda Story* (Honolulu: University of Hawaii Press, 1969), 513–14, 520, 525.

63. The flag of modern Japan (with the red sun in the center of a field of white) to represent all Japanese vessels was invented during this period. This flag was necessary to differentiate it from the shogunal flag (the three-leaf *aoi*, the hollyhock). Other symbols of modern Japan also emerged, but symbol making was not yet part of a nationalist program. BGKM, XVI, 23.

64. BGKM, XVIII, 121 (Iwase's letter encapsulates their position).

65. Beasley, *Great Britain and the Opening of Japan*, 187.

66. For details on the operation of the shogun's government, see the retrospective oral records left by former shogunate officials in Shinji Yoshimoto (ed.), *Kyūji shimonroku: Edo bakufu yakunin no shōgen*, 2 vols. (Tokyo: Iwanami, 1986).

67. Statler, *Shimoda Story*. Also see Henry Heusken, *Japan Journal, 1855–1861*, trans. Jeannete C. van der Corput and Robert A. Wilson (New Brunswick, NJ: Rutgers University Press, 1964). Michael Auslin also covers this in his *Negotiating with Imperialism*, 34–49.

68. Statler and Auslin argue that Harris meeting Hotta was the turning point. Statler, *Shimoda Story*, 535–36. Auslin, *Negotiating with Imperialism*, 35.

69. BGKM, XVI, 133 (Hotta's memorial to the shogun); XVII, 11, (Harris to be granted audience), 13 (Nariaki granted gifts and then sacked), 24 (a new appointee as treasury official and maritime defense council member), 38 (spear magistrate assigned task at treasury department), 96 (grand inspector temporarily assigned task at treasury department); XVIII, 170 (sacking Mizuno, the leader of the treasury officials).

70. BGKM, XVII, 20.

71. BGKM, XVII, 34 (Mito), 177 (Owari), 178, 192, 224 (replies from other *daimyō*).

72. BGKM, XVIII, 87.

73. William Elliot Griffis, *Townsend Harris: First American Envoy in Japan* (Boston: Houghton, Mifflin, 1895), 182–240. BGKM, XVIII, 17, 19, 20, 21, 35, 36, 61, 62, 88, 158.

74. BGKM, XVIII, 159.

75. BGKM, XVIII, 171.

76. Matsuoka Hideo, *Iwase Tadanari* (Tokyo: Chūkō shinsho, 1981), 15, 23, 29–35, 39–47, 73–79.

77. Not to be confused with the *rōjū* Mizuno Tadakuni. Mizuno Tadanori was a *hatamoto*.

78. BGKM, XVI, 36.

79. Fukuchi, *Bakumatsu seijika*, 248–70.

80. BGKM, XVI, 128 (Mizuno inspects Nagasaki), 139 (Iwase petitions to go to Hong Kong), 207 and 210 (the two starting treaty negotiation based on Dutch proposal); XVII, 122, 185, 196 (Mizuno's letters to his colleagues); XVII, 197 (Iwase's letter to his colleagues). Auslin argues that Iwase convinced the more cautious Mizuno. The letters indicate that Mizuno wanted to sign the treaties but they do not make clear whether he was convinced by Iwase. Auslin, *Negotiating with Imperialism*, 37.

81. BGKM, XVII, 139, 140, 142, 144, 145, 147 (reactions to Mizuno and Iwase's actions in Nagasaki).

82. BGKM, XVIII, 89, 90.

83. BGKM, XVIII, 117.
84. BGKM, XVIII, 170.
85. BGKM, XVIII, 121.
86. Auslin takes the position that Yokohama was primarily chosen to isolate the foreigners in a symbolic area where Perry had signed the 1854 treaty. The isolated nature and the symbolism would be used to persuade Ii Naosuke later, but at this time, I believe the economic argument of redrawing the economic geography of Japan and bringing in revenue was at the core of Hotta and Iwase's vision. Auslin, *Negotiating with Imperialism*, 37–39.
87. BGKM, XVIII, 159.
88. BGKM, XVIII, 167; Griffis, *Townsend Harris*, 249; HM, part II, 397–404.
89. For instance, he could not understand why a single treaty might cause such an uproar. BGKM, XVIII, 178. More subdued but simmering comments from his perspective: "In this journal I shall confine myself to the leading facts of actual transactions, omitting the interminable discourses of the Japanese, where the same proposition may be repeated a dozen times; nor shall I note their positive refusal of points they subsequently grant, and meant to grant all the while; . . . They do not know the value of a straightforward and truthful policy; at least they do not practice it. They never hesitate at uttering a falsehood, even where the truth would serve the same purpose." Griffis, *Townsend Harris*, 256–57.
90. Negotiations from the shogunate's perspective: BGKM XVIII, XIX, articles titled "Conversations at the Institute of Barbarian Books." From Harris's perspective: Griffis, *Townsend Harris*, 253–307.
91. Fukuchi, *Bakumatsu seijika*, 257.
92. Perhaps it was a necessary diplomatic ploy to get Harris to trust Iwase. Fukuchi, *Bakumatsu seijika*, 261–62 (Iwase's words from an interview with Inoue Kiyonao).
93. American courts tried Japanese accused of crimes in America, and of course the U.S. government could unilaterally set tariffs on Japanese goods. Extraterritoriality and the loss of tariff autonomy were not mutual, making them "unequal."
94. BGKM, XX, 194. Clive Parry (ed.), "Treaty of Amity and Commerce between Japan and the United States," *The Consolidated Treaty Series*, vol. 119 (London: Oceana, 1969).
95. BGKM, XVIII, 103.
96. HM, part II, 525.
97. HM, part II, 530–37, 551.
98. BGKM, XVIII, 105 (Nariaki), 181 (report on *daimyō* reaction). There were six opposed to trade, twenty-two who were either actively for trade or would follow the shogun's decision, and one undecided.
99. HM, part II, 577–79.
100. HM, part II, 571–72.
101. Fukuchi writes that Hotta had another plan, to bribe the court nobles and gain their assent. Hotta's biographer chronicles that this plan was debated by the three but ultimately rejected. They gave only 50 *ryō* to the court and some silver to a few court nobles. Fukuchi, *Bakumatsu seijika*, 74. HM, part II, 599–602, 672–76.
102. HM, part II, 621.
103. HM, part II, 600–20, 675.
104. HM, part III, 2.
105. Fukuchi, *Bakumatsu seijika*, 259.
106. The tea ceremony can be understood as one way to break this stifling custom. At the tea ceremony, there is no consideration of rank; only the host and guest(s) exist. Perhaps if Hotta had hosted a tea ceremony it may have been possible to have Iwase in the same room as the court nobles.
107. HM, part II, 673–76.
108. Fukuchi, *Bakumatsu seijika*, 74–75.
109. HM, part II, 622–23.
110. HM, part II, 684.
111. BGKM, XIX, 166, 324 (Hotta's speeches and pleas), 173, 207, 229, 230 258, 259, 260 (letters from court aristocrats), 270 (letter from an imperial prince), 272 (and a letter from a temple).

112. BGKM, XIX, 318 (imperial court's first response), 323, 329 (Hotta's petitions), 330 (court's final reply).

113. HM, part II, 713–14, 720–24.

114. HM, part II, 774. Women of the Ōoku probably hated Nariaki for his general anti-Buddhist attitude, destruction of Buddhist statues, and the melting of bronze bells to build cannons. These actions obviously elicited strong opposition from the Buddhist clergy in Japan, and many of the top-ranking clergy were widows of the previous shoguns. These cannons, built by melting down religious items, were not even effective in actual combat during Mito domain's civil war. The Western designed cannons were superior to the ones Mito domain built. Yamakawa Kikue, *Oboegaki, Bakumatsu no Mitohan* (Tokyo: Iwanami, reprint edition 1991), 96–99.

115. BGKM, XIX, 144 (Ii's position); XX, 194 (treaty signed).

116. Shimada Saburō, *Kaikoku shimatsu: Bakumatsu ishin shiryō sōsho* (Tokyo: Jinbutsu ōraisha, 1968, reprint of 1888 edition), 32–34, 84–86.

117. HM, part II, 857.

118. Matsuoka, *Iwase Tadanari*, 164, 173–74.

119. Also I must add that I focused on Hotta Masayoshi partly because I felt that he deserves more credit. Sandwiched between the two leaders who signed the Perry and the Harris treaties, namely Abe Masahiro and Ii Naosuke, the "Dutch crazy" Hotta has gotten little attention.

120. HM, part II, 857, 881, 883.

Chapter Three

The First Merchant of Yokohama

The shogunate (*bakufu*) opened Japan to trade on 1 July 1859 or Ansei 6/6/2. Since the raw silk that would dominate early Japanese exports came mostly from eastern Japan, the shogunate could have used this new foreign trade to center the Japanese economy on Edo and Yokohama, as Iwase Tadanari and Hotta Masayoshi had hoped. That was not to be. Instead, officials who were skeptical about foreign trade controlled Yokohama. Thus for the next ten years, as the shogunate staggered to its demise, the shogunate simply watched as the merchants of Yokohama created a new trade network. This network connected the interior of Japan with the rest of the world without aiding shogunal power.

Since Yokohama was nothing but a fishing village when it first opened, the vast majority of merchants were immigrants from other parts of the country. These merchants had to rely on three types of connections to create a new trade network inside Japan. One was a connection with shogunal officials. After all, without a shogunal license to trade, Japanese merchants could not buy or sell in Yokohama. In this, the House of Mitsui—the merchant house that traditionally served the shogunate—potentially had the advantage. Fortunately for others, Mitsui was not particularly interested in foreign trade at this time. Moreover, the international treaties ruled out a shogunal monopoly over foreign trade, so the field was wide open. Another connection the merchants could exploit was with the domains. Considering that there were more than 250 domains at the time, any merchant prominent enough in his home domain had the potential to enrich himself at Yokohama. Here the advantages lay with merchants from eastern Japan. Domains in western Japan tended to rely on Nagasaki (also opened to foreign trade on 1 July 1859) and later Kobe (opened to foreign trade on 1 January 1868), so merchants from western Japan did not find many openings in Yokohama.

The last type of connection was the local private connection, primarily of family and friends. Once the main trade goods became clear, anyone who knew people who made those goods or wanted those goods could enter the market. For these merchants, if they were complete novices, the big hurdle was getting the license to trade.

This chapter follows the career of Nakaiya Jūbei, a man who used all three types of connections to the full and then fell to ruin. He became the first merchant of Yokohama, nicknamed the "Lord Bishop of 'Hama."[1] He was one of the earliest merchants to open shop in Yokohama, and he became the richest among them. Nakaiya Jūbei left a diary that details the ninety days before he opened his shop in Yokohama titled *Shōhei nichiroku.* He and other merchants together would forge the economic ties that would bind Japan with the outside world. By examining this merchant's rise and fall, we shall see how international trade first impacted Japan under the shoguns.[2]

NAKAIYA JŪBEI: THE EARLY YEARS

In the eighth month of Ansei 6 (September 1859), two months after the opening of the port, Nakaiya Jūbei celebrated the completion of his mansion in Yokohama. Built with rare and expensive materials, most notably brilliant red copper roof tiles, it was the first major store in Yokohama.

> On the fourth stretch of Motomachi, there is a store called Nakai. The store itself is a curiosity. Foreigners appreciate the layout of the store, particularly the courtyard in which birds roam free, a courtyard covered only by a thin metal wire ceiling. Fashionable glass covers the inside of the walls and goldfish swim in an artificial pond. In the middle of this courtyard is a large four-legged music box, measuring two feet by twenty inches with a height of six or seven inches, playing high and beautiful notes.[3]

Soon other Japanese merchants finished building their stores and warehouses near him, enticing the American merchant and physician, Dr. George Hall, to establish the first Western store (Walsh & Co.)[4] in Yokohama as well.[5] In a report dated Ansei 6/8/13 (9 September 1859), a shogunal official described the Japanese stores along the five blocks of Motomachi, the area facing the main avenue, as 90 percent completed with most of the structures well built and 60 percent of the stores in the back alley as complete. In a secondary stretch, Kaigan dōri, 20 percent of the shops were completed. The tariff office and the residences for the shogunal officials were completed as well. The foreigners, on the other hand, had only demarcated with shallow trenches where each nation would lease land and had not yet built much.[6]

Western merchants had only constructed a few buildings of their own in Yokohama because there was a minor diplomatic dispute between the West

Figure 3.1. A Map of Yokohama in 1859. Notice that only the port and the Japanese side of the city have been prepared. The foreign quarters are still undeveloped and consequently ignored by the painter. As can be seen, the natural shape of the terrain was a peninsula, with many rice paddies built on lands recently reclaimed from the nearby marshes. *Source*: A segment from a map in Takashima Keishi, *Yokohama onkaichi meisai no zu* (Ōtoridō, 1859).

and the shogunate. The misunderstanding began when Townsend Harris and Iwase Tadanari negotiated the opening of a trading port and agreed upon Kanagawa in January 1858. Iwase had said "Kanagawa" referring to the area around Kanagawa and specifically Yokohama. Harris had assumed "Kanagawa" to refer the existing port city on the Tōkaidō highway. The British representative to Japan objected to Yokohama, calling it the new Dejima, the artificial island in Nagasaki on which the Dutch merchants were isolated for more than two hundred years.[7] The Western diplomats suspected that the shogunate was trying to isolate the Westerners again, and they were correct. Although Iwase and his superior, Hotta Masayoshi, did not want to isolate the Western merchants, by October 1858 they were dismissed. The *bakufu* was now led by Ii Naosuke, who had appointed Mizuno Tadanori as the new foreign magistrate. These two men wanted to keep foreign influence to a minimum.

As such, Western merchants were divided between opening shop at Kanagawa (the port city according to the treaties) and Yokohama, the new port city across the bay. In the end, Yokohama became the de facto treaty port for at least two reasons. First, Yokohama had a deepwater port that allowed the larger Western vessels to dock and Kanagawa did not. Second, the *bakufu* had effectively created a new trading city with all the necessary services for trade in Yokohama, but it did not for Kanagawa. Faced with these realities, the foreigners settled in Yokohama as well. Attempts by Western diplomats and some merchants to conduct business in Kanagawa failed, settling the diplomatic squabble.[8]

Among these early stores, Nakaiya Jūbei's mansion was not only the first major store, it remained the grandest building until it burned down. So who was this man? Like almost everyone else, he was an immigrant to Yokohama and a man who had cultivated ties with interesting people.

Traditionally Nakaiya Jūbei's family produced the village headmen of Nakai village, a village in Kōzuke province (today's Gunma prefecture) near the border with Shinano province (today's Nagano prefecture). This village sat on a road that connected a major pilgrimage destination, the Zenkōji temple, with the famous Kusatsu hot springs. His father, aside from being a headman, dabbled in business and once ran an inn in the village. He was also a prominent painter, listed in an 1859 directory of cultured men (*Bunga jinmeiroku*). Perhaps it was his painting that drove Jūbei's father to travel often and extensively, eventually securing a patron in Inaba Masakuni, lord of Yodo domain (102,000 *koku*).[9]

Jūbei's mother was the daughter of a Confucian scholar of Maebashi/Kawagoe domain.[10] A wealthy peasant of Kōzuke province related to the Confucian scholar adopted her as his daughter at the age of sixteen. Jūbei's father and mother met when the two families went to the Kusatsu hot springs. However, the marriage between the two was a short one. After the marriage with Nakaiya's father failed, she most likely went to Edo to stay with her mother (Jūbei's maternal grandmother). Jūbei's maternal grandmother had also divorced and remarried an Edo publisher and bookstore owner named Izumiya. Maebashi/Kawagoe domain commissioned Izumiya to republish Rai Sanyō's *Nihon gaishi* (*Unofficial History of Japan*) recently edited by the domain's Confucian scholar (perhaps this was the same Confucian scholar who was Jūbei's maternal grandfather). In the end his mother remarried into the family that had adopted her at sixteen and lived with her new family.

The point of this short but complicated family history is that Nakaiya Jūbei grew up in an interesting family with a mix of tradition, arts, scholarship, and wide personal latitude. It was a family in which no one could stop him from pursuing his interests because everyone else had done so. It was also a family that had ties with many different groups of people, peasants, merchants, artists, a lord, intellectuals, and townsfolk. Growing up, he helped the family farm and learned how to read and write and do arithmetic. On occasion, his father's travels forced him to act as the village headman from a young age. He also studied the chemistry of gunpowder as a hobby. Like his father, Jūbei was not content to stay at home as the village headman, and in 1838, when he was nineteen years old, he left for Edo to stay with his mother and grandmother at Izumiya.[11]

At Edo, Jūbei continued his study of chemistry. Through these studies, he interacted with *rangaku* (Dutch learning) scholars.[12] Through Izumiya, the publisher of *Nihon gaishi*, he probably interacted with Mito school radicals as well. Rai Sanyō's *Nihon gaishi* was a bestseller, avidly read by Mito school radicals who believed in the uniqueness of Japan and the need to protect its culture and institutions from Western encroachment.[13]

By 1849, at the age of thirty, Nakaiya Jūbei had become an arms dealer. It is unknown how successful he was at this point in his life, but he had established himself enough that he could intercede on behalf of his villagers when Sakakibara Uzume, a shogunal bannerman (*hatamoto*), tried to impose forced loans upon his village back home. Despite being a new arms dealer, Nakaiya's advantage most likely came from his studies of the chemistry of gunpowder and the connections he cultivated in Edo through his teachers. He even wrote a treatise on mass-producing dependable gunpowder.[14] This is speculative, but by this point he probably believed in defending the country as a whole. After all, he was aware of the increasing frequency of foreign ship sightings, and in his 1853 letter, he noted not only the fluctuations of prices of goods, but also the reasons for them. He believed that the appearance of foreign ships off the coasts of Uraga and Izu, and the shogunate's responses, namely the construction of forts along Edo Bay and the forging of cannons, caused shortages of various goods and thus price spikes in Edo. Thus *rangaku* had provided him with Western scientific knowledge and Mito school thought provided him with the political framework to understand why the West was encroaching upon Japan and China. He probably saw himself as a patriot and not just as an arms dealer making weapons for the shogunate.

By 1859, after ten years in business, Nakaiya Jūbei had become quite successful in his chosen field. He was able to produce 3,000 percussion caps (for igniting gunpowder) ordered by the shogunate in three days (1/13, 1/16)[15] and then fulfill another request for 5,000 caps and 10 *kan* (37.5 kilograms or more than 82.7 pounds) of gunpowder ordered by another shogunal official in ten days (1/15, 1/25).[16] Moreover, he successfully cultivated many contacts in the shogunate and among the domains.

NAKAIYA JŪBEI: HOW TO ESTABLISH A STORE IN YOKOHAMA

Yokohama opened for business in 1859. And Nakaiya Jūbei had begun preparation to start another business in the new port city as well. Preparing since the previous summer, when the *bakufu* announced that it would open Kanagawa for foreign trade, he probably thought that it was an opportunity not to be missed. As such he also helped his relatives and other villagers who wanted to open an inn or store at Yokohama by forwarding their petitions to the proper authorities.[17] His reasons for his career change is not fully known, but for the ninety days starting on New Year's Day of Ansei 6 (1859) and ending on the first day of the fourth month, he kept a diary called *Shōhei nichiroku*, describing his activities in detail, which enables us to see how an arms dealer transformed himself into a foreign trade merchant.[18]

In this diary, Nakaiya first mentions Kanagawa on the eighth day of the first month of Ansei 6 (1859/1/8). Since the first seven days of the New Year were traditionally treated as holidays, this meant Nakaiya's first business of the year was related to the new port. On that day he sent a map of Kanagawa to Matsudaira Katamori, lord of Aizu domain (a *fudai daimyō* in northeastern Japan, 230,000 *koku*). The next day, he asked Nakano Hirauchi, Aizu domain's samurai commissioner for domain products, what goods they could export. By the tenth, Nakaiya, Nakano, Kawachiya Hanbei, Yorozuya,[19] and Nakaiya's father (who was staying at his patron's mansion in Edo) conferred to discuss the matter in detail. On 1/23 Nakaiya, Kawachiya, Yorozuya, and another merchant nicknamed Nakagen met at Yorozuya's place. According to the diary it was a cloudy day and a stormy night. Perhaps the weather compounded their worry and their impatience over the long wait. Finally after more than a month, on a cold, sunny day Nakano Hirauchi came to visit Nakaiya on 2/17. Presumably he brought good news since Nakaiya entertained him with sake and three days later the official letter arrived. On 2/20 Aizu domain authorities granted Nakaiya the commission to handle domain goods. Later that day, Nakano brought merchants, presumably from Aizu domain, to introduce them to Nakaiya.

Among many things, this episode illustrates, the continued involvement of his painter father. Keeping his father, who knew Inaba Masakuni (a future rōjū) and many others throughout Japan, informed could only help. His father's contacts would help Nakaiya later in attaining contracts. Another is the issue of fraud and cheating, which was discussed in chapter 1. Without the legal frameworks to enforce contracts consistently, trust was essential, especially in new enterprises. Thus maintaining personal relationships was crucial and Nakano (Aizu domain's commissioner) and Nakaiya became close enough to visit each other's homes, presumably before his diary began, and they continued to meet even after Nakaiya gained the commission (2/28, 3/5, 3/17, 3/22). As part of this issue of trustworthiness, Nakaiya's connection with the shogunate was leveraged to make him reputable to domains close to the shogun. Nakaiya was a respected arms merchant serving the shogun and had close relations with one of the shogun's bankers, Kawachiya. For Aizu domain, a domain that was created for the illegitimate son of the second shogun, this connection to the shogunate enhanced his credibility. Finally, this episode illustrates that Nakaiya's preparation for opening a new store in Yokohama must have started well before 1859. Presumably, he began negotiations with Aizu domain in the previous year, otherwise sending a map makes no sense (although who initiated the contact is unknown).

How did he know about this new trade? Officially the shogunate had announced that foreign trade would commence at Kanagawa in summer 1858 after the signing of the treaty on Ansei 5/6/19 (29 July 1858). Most likely Nakaiya had access to privileged information, so he probably knew even before the official announcement. His father's connection with Lord Inaba, a patron of the arts and also an up-and-coming *fudai daimyō*, might have helped but it is also possible that he received information from shogunal officials. His business led to many meetings with shogunal officials: sometimes explicitly for the arms business, at other times not.[20]

Before Nakaiya could open a store in the treaty port, he needed to accomplish two things. First, he needed to determine what to buy and sell. He became Aizu domain's mercantile representative on 1859/2/20, but without knowing what products would earn a profit, he needed to diversify as much as possible; only later could he specialize. Second, he needed to get a permit from the shogunate to open a store.

Aside from Aizu domain, Nakaiya became the representative for at least two more domains, Kii and Ueda. Kii was one of the three collateral domains (555,000 *koku*) of the shogunal family located in the southern regions of Kinai, and its family had produced the fourteenth and current shogun. Ueda was a medium-sized *fudai* domain (53,000 *koku*) in central Shinano province in the mountainous region of central Japan. Fortunately, his diary seems to record the transactions of these two negotiations from the beginning. Ueda also happened to be near his hometown, on the road between the Kusatsu hot springs and Zenkōji temple. Among other things, it was famous for its raw silk sent to Kyoto and its unruly silkworm egg merchants. Both the raw silk and the eggs were profitable products within Japan, and thus by the Tempō era, the domain regulated both items.[21]

Beyond Aizu, Kii, and Ueda domains, during the three months recorded in the diary, Nakaiya would negotiate with at least four more domains: Tanakura, Akita, Nanbu, and Yonezawa. The interest in foreign trade was mutual. At least two of the seven domains approached Nakaiya first to handle their goods.

The negotiations with Kii began with his father. On 1/11[22] his father visited a certain Nagashima, a samurai of the Kii domain. Seven days later,

Nagashima visited Nakaiya and expressed interest in appointing him as the domain representative for foreign trade. In the case of the Ueda domain, they approached him first. On 1/21, the chief merchant of the Ueda domain products associations, the elderly Horiichi, visited him to ask about trade. The lord of Ueda, Matsudaira Tadakata, was a former minister (*rōjū*), political ally of Hotta Masayoshi, and an advocate of foreign trade.

On the same day, 1/21, Nakaiya invited Nagashima to his store and entertained both Horiichi and Nagashima. By evening two other merchants, Tōdaya and Shirakoya, joined them and had moved the venue to Shirakoya's place for dinner. The next day Nakaiya with Nagashima went to see Ida Yōemon, the sixty-eight-year-old samurai commissioner of Kii domain products, and had a pleasant dinner. In effect, a group to discuss the sale of domain products overseas was formed between Kii domain's commissioner and Ueda domain's chief merchant with Nakaiya, Tōdaya, and Shirakoya.

During this period in late 1859/1 and early 1859/2, Nakaiya had established contacts among a group of men who were eager to trade with foreigners and consulted with them extensively. These men were either local Edo merchants or merchants and nonmerchants from eastern Japan, specifically modern-day Gunma, Nagano, Shizuoka, and Kanagawa prefectures. Thus while Nakaiya had his formal audience at the lord of Kii's mansion on 1/26 and was informed by Ida to officially submit a letter requesting permission to handle Kii domain goods the following day, his colleagues sent out applications to handle other domains' goods. Nakaiya records the case of at least two men, a certain Nagoya and Suzuki Toramatsu from Yōga village, each of whom petitioned two domains. The records do not seem to indicate cutthroat competition but rather an effort to work together to succeed together.

After the submitting his petition, negotiations with Kii domain languished, perhaps because of the appointment of another samurai commissioner for domain products, requiring further exchanges and banquets. However, negotiations with Ueda domain proceeded smoothly. After all, they had approached Nakaiya Jūbei first. On 2/7 when Nakaiya met Ueda domain's treasury magistrate at the domain office and later had an extravagant dinner (paid for by the domain) with him and other domain officials, the domain's elder counselor appeared at the dinner and informed him that he had received the commission. It was his first.[23] On his return home from the banquet, he stopped by the house of the foreign magistrate, Muragaki, and his father, perhaps to inform the former and celebrate with the latter. Negotiations with Kii continued into the middle of 1859/2. In the meantime he kept himself busy with further negotiations, such as with Tanakura domain (in modern-day Fukushima prefecture), when its representative arrived to discuss matters. It is not known what happened with Tanakura in the long run. On 3/1 Ida Yōemon finally informed Nakaiya that he had received the commission at the domain products office of the Kii domain mansion.

The next thing Nakaiya Jūbei needed to do was to secure a permit for foreign trade from the shogunate. Shortly after contacting Aizu and Kii domain authorities, Nakaiya asked Kawachiya Hanbei, the shogun's official money exchange merchant, to send in his petition to trade. On 1/16 Kawachiya visited him and informed Nakaiya that he had submitted Nakaiya's petition the day before but feared that it might be rejected. The foreign magistrate had told Kawachiya that the treasury magistrate had requested a reference. Presumably Nakaiya's contacts with shogunal officials in supplying gunpowder was not enough. The next day, 1/17, foreign office functionaries visited him. Although the content of the meeting is unknown, perhaps they complained about a turf war inside the shogunate, making the difficult job of attracting merchants to foreign trade more difficult due to confusion and red tape. Since 1858/12, the foreign magistrate's office and the Edo magistrate's office had been fighting over who should grant permission to the merchants to open shop in the new port.[24] More likely, the functionaries advised him of what the foreign merchants might like to purchase, and they may have suggested that he acquire a domain commission and bolster his petition with potential buyers and sellers.[25] In any case, a minor shogunal official, the elderly Yoshida Jūsuke, seems to have become the unofficial liaison with Nakaiya. After visiting Nakaiya's store and being entertained with sake on 1/20, they would meet and drink often thereafter (1/29, 2/16, 2/17, 3/16, 3/30). Yoshida would inform Nakaiya that the magistrate rejected his petition to trade on 1/29.

In getting the license to trade, Nakaiya's father's connection to Lord Inaba turned out to be the key. The day before the rejection, on 1/28, Muragaki Norimasa, Iwase Tadanari, and Lord Inaba Masakuni of Yodo domain visited Nakaiya Jūbei. As mentioned previously, Lord Inaba Masakuni was his father's arts patron and a future minister. As discussed in chapter 1, Iwase Tadanari was the man who envisioned linking the Edo regional economy to the world (in order to move the center of the Japanese economy around Edo and thus strengthen the shogunate). Muragaki Norimasa was the foreign magistrate who had been appointed after Iwase was "promoted" as construction magistrate. Muragaki was no lightweight. He would later travel to the United States as the shogun's vice-envoy in the 1860 trip to ratify the commercial treaty negotiated by Iwase and Harris. Incidentally this was the first official Japanese trip to circumnavigate the globe.[26]

When these four men met, Iwase Tadanari may have been the construction magistrate, a man who had been officially relieved of duty from the front lines of foreign affairs. However, he wanted to see his vision come to fruition, and thus he came with his successor Muragaki to ensure that a strong trade relationship could be established at Yokohama. How did Iwase know of Nakaiya? Here the link probably lies with his father's patron, Lord Inaba. Lord Inaba most likely knew Iwase, and Lord Inaba may have suggested his artist's son as the man to fulfill Iwase's vision. This explains the arrival of all three at Nakaiya's house. Or perhaps Iwase (or Muragaki) already knew about Nakaiya through their jobs as foreign magistrate and arms dealer, since the shogunate was constructing a coastal defense system at this time and the three came to visit him. Or perhaps something in Nakaiya's petition caught Muragaki's eye, and the new magistrate referred him to Iwase and Inaba. However, the fact that the three visited Nakaiya's store together seems to imply that it was Nakaiya's father's connection that helped Nakaiya meet with senior shogunal officials. Nakaiya's diary can be frustrating in that he only records the to and fro of people and letters and the occurrence of certain events.[27] Regardless, his connection with Iwase would not to be a casual one, and most likely was not connected to Iwase's official business as construction magistrate.

As Kawachiya Hanbei feared, the elderly Yoshida Jūsuke informed Nakaiya on 1/29 that his petition would be rejected by Yoshida's superiors because it lacked sufficient references. But he probably knew what needed to be done from his conversation with Muragaki, Iwase, and Inaba on 1/28, if not from the earlier meeting with foreign magistrate functionaries on 1/17. When Nakaiya received Ueda domain's commission at the dinner banquet on 2/7, he immediately informed foreign magistrate Muragaki by visiting the magistrate's residence and then went to his father's home, even though it was raining and rather late. He managed to get home around 10 pm.[28] Two days later, on 2/9, Nakaiya sent his petition to trade to Inoue Kiyonao, Muragaki's colleague and Iwase's former partner in the negotiations with Townsend Harris. In the early morning of the eleventh, Nakaiya went to see Muragaki, but he was away on business at Kanagawa. Nakaiya left word that he understood that his original petition lacked references but that he hoped they would reconsider his petition to trade. After all, he now had a commission to trade from a domain. Later, on the same day, Nakaiya visited Kawachiya to convince him to write a letter of reference. The next day, on 2/12, he submitted a reference written by Kawachiya Hanbei to the foreign magistrate, Muragaki. Nakaiya Jūbei must have understood that this was a chicken-and-egg problem: How can a merchant sell his service to conduct a domain's foreign trade when the merchant does not have the license to trade? But then how can a merchant get the license if he has no domain to back him up? If foreign trade was an established business, he could have joined the foreign trade guild, and the guild could have backed him to break the impasse, but there was no such guild. Under the circumstances, Nakaiya understood that the only way to get over this hurdle was to demonstrate his sincerity and trustworthiness. And for that, his fellow merchants, the wining and dining of officials, and his father's contacts proved invaluable.

On 2/20 Aizu domain officially designated Nakaiya as its agent, and its samurai commissioner visited him. The very next day Nakaiya went to see his father and then visited Iwase. Two days later, when Tsuruta, a man who lived just north of Kanagawa, visited Nakaiya to inform him of the geography of the port city, Nakaiya Jūbei dutifully sent a letter to his father and to Iwase, probably to inform them of what he learned. Keeping close contact with officials was one way to prove his sincerity about engaging in trade. On two further occasions before the end of the diary, on 2/29 and on 3/17, he visited Iwase. How much of Iwase's vision rubbed off on Nakaiya is unknown, but Nakaiya's giant mansion, which was completed two months after the opening of Yokohama, may have had something to do with Iwase's vision.

Unfortunately for Nakaiya, the foreign magistrate's office was a conflicted office. The foreign office was staffed with former inspectors and former treasury officials. The former inspectors like Iwase were generally enthusiastic about foreign trade. However, of the former treasury officials, many were indifferent or worse, hostile to foreign trade. After all, these men believed in maintaining the economic system the shogunate had carefully crafted during the last 250 years. Foreign trade could only complicate this system. Thus petitions to trade were subject to very different scrutiny from within the same office. This fact that the office was divided would have complicated Nakaiya's petition to trade by itself. But Nakaiya tried to hedge his bets by gaining a government contract to supply the Kanagawa magistrate's office as well. He must have reasoned that if his trading venture failed, supplying the shogunal officials would guarantee his survival in the new port city. Thus on 2/5, before he received Ueda domain's commission, he sent his petition to supply the Kanagawa magistrate to the Edo magistrate's office.

In other words, in the first thirty-four days of Ansei 6 (1859), Nakaiya had (1) opened negotiations to act as the merchant to sell domain products for at least seven domains, (2) sent a petition to the foreign magistrate to become a merchant in Yokohama, initially without a domain sponsor but later with domain sponsors, and (3) sent another petition to the Edo magistrate to supply the shogunal office in Yokohama. In principle these three activities should complement each other. And on 3/6, permission to supply the Kanagawa office was granted. However, the next day, the Kanagawa magistrate, a branch of the foreign magistrate, ordered him to appear at an official questioning at its Edo office. On 3/8 Nakaiya Jūbei went to the office at 9 am to see Mizuno Tadanori, the man who opposed Iwase and was now reappointed by the regent Ii to be the foreign magistrate and also to act as the Kanagawa magistrate. There at the office he was questioned by Gōhara Isaburō, a shogunal official, and he had to write another letter. While he was held up, a heavy downpour of rain came and went. In the end, he was held at the office for roughly twelve hours, until 9 pm that day, and was released only after being informed to return on 3/10.

On 3/10 in the second round of questioning, Mizuno asked not only about supplying the Kanagawa office, but also about his commissions, particularly the one with Kii domain. Mizuno was a former treasury official and probably had no contact with Nakaiya (there is no previous mention of him in the diary). And these two petitions put side by side must have seemed suspicious to Mizuno. Here was an arms merchant who used to supply the shogunate but now claimed that he wanted to become a foreign trade merchant on a petition to the foreign magistrate and that he wanted to supply the Kanagawa office on a petition to the Edo magistrate. Was Nakaiya interested in foreign trade or was he more interested in expanding his business with the shogunate? And if Nakaiya was interested in foreign trade, Mizuno probably wanted to know who his main supplier would be: Ueda, the commission won earliest on 2/7, but a small domain at only 53,000 *koku*; Aizu, won on 2/17, a large domain at 230,000 *koku*; or Kii, won on 3/1, and not only the largest domain of the three at 555,000 *koku*, but also the current shogun's former home. Unable to answer some of the sharp questioning, Nakaiya left the office complaining of a stomach ache and promised to return the next day.

In his attempt to become the mercantile representative for foreign trade of three domains and the supplier of the Kanagawa office, something had gone wrong. Kii domain, with intimate connections with the shogunate, had proved to be the weak point in his testimony. After leaving the office, he hired a palanquin and rushed home, then hired another palanquin to see Ida Yōemon, the former commissioner of Kii domain products. The next morning he went to see his father. His father immediately left for Kanagawa. He then visited other merchant colleagues including Kawachiya[29] and Yoshioka Motohira, a shogunal official, formerly an inspector. Because Yoshioka was absent, he was forced to stay overnight at Asakusa with Kawachiya. On the following day, 3/12, after seeing Yoshioka in the morning, the two of them went to the mansions of Ueda, Aizu, and Kii. Finally after seeing another official, he returned home at dusk. That evening he and his neighborhood association went to the foreign magistrate's office and asked for an extension until the fifteeenth to explain his situation. In the morning of the fourteenth, however, Mizuno called him to the office. On this day of heavy rain, after another twelve hours at the office where other merchants were petitioning to trade, Mizuno granted Nakaiya Jūbei's petition to trade in the new port. However, he also ordered Jūbei to submit a testimonial.[30] Mizuno had a conservative temperament, preferring slow and steady progress to radical change, but he too recognized that the shogunate needed merchants to trade in Yokohama.[31] Isolating the foreigners did not mean jailing them. Nakaiya finally managed to return home at around midnight that rainy day.

Winning the shogunal license to trade was not the end; it was the start. Nakaiya continued to cultivate his contacts and meet people. On the very next day (3/15) he started his rounds again and sent his friend to Kanagawa.

Interestingly, a former treasury magistrate, Tamura Iyo-no-kami,[32] who also became an elder for the Tayasu family like Mizuno Tadanori, came to take him out for a "walk." It is not explained why Tamura came, but perhaps he came to apologize or at least explain why his former colleague Mizuno detained Nakaiya for so long on 3/8 and on 3/10. In any case this "walk" lasted long enough that he returned home at night. On the sixteenth, Yoshida Jūsuke—the old man who warned him earlier that his petition to trade would fail—and other merchants called on him. These men were entertained with sake. On the seventeenth, after Yoshioka Mitohira—the shogunal official Nakaiya went to see with Kawachiya on 3/11—visited him, he went to see the lord of Ueda, then Muragaki, and finally Iwase. When he returned home, Nakano of Aizu domain and later Kawachiya came to see him.

Nakaiya's energetic activities paid off. Not only did he become the mercantile representative for these three domains and receive permission to trade in Yokohama, he became the supplier for the Kanagawa magistrate's office. Moreover, these successes brought more opportunities. Yoshioka, the shogunal official, asked Nanbu domain representatives about making Nakaiya their representative (3/19). Later, the lord of Kii and Nakano met with Nanbu authorities on his behalf as well (3/22). Two days later, foreign magistrate officials introduced him to Yonezawa domain's treasury officials (3/24). Once he had the license to trade, officials spread word that he was a merchant that could be trusted to handle foreign trade. Reflecting his high visibility, other merchants flocked to him asking for help in gaining permits for foreign trade (on 3/19 two more merchants from his home province came to see him and on 3/27 three merchants from Ueda visited him, presumably to discuss foreign trade, since one of the merchants dealt in wax, an item Nakaiya would try to export).

By 4/1, the last entry in his diary, opening day for Yokohama (6/2) was fast approaching. Considering that everything had to be built anew in Yokohama, in 1859/4 he sent this letter to the shogunate asking for the land to build his store:

> I, Sennosuke [Nakaiya Jūbei's earlier name], a house owner at Shiba kanasugikata block, humbly request the following. Now that trade with foreign countries has been permitted, and having permission to traffic in the following items from the domains of Kii, Aizu, and Ueda in the paper attached [paper is lost], I would like to open a shop in Kanagawa to export and import goods. Therefore I humbly request permission to export and import these goods. If this request is granted, I ask for a plot of land 30 *ken* by 40 *ken*, 1200 *tsubo*, for my shop.
>
> Ansei 6, Fourth Month
> Shiba kanasugikata block
> House owner, Sennosuke[33]

The officials granted Nakaiya's request. He received his license to trade on Ansei 6/4/18 (20 May 1859) and would open a large store, 17 *ken* by 28 *ken*, or more than 17,000 square feet, in Yokohama.[34] Unlike other reluctant merchants, such as the House of Mitsui, which was forced to open shop in Yokohama as part of the shogunal plan to create a fait accompli, Nakaiya was eager to start a new business and it showed in the mansion that he built.

NAKAIYA JŪBEI: RUNNING A BUSINESS IN YOKOHAMA

At the mansion Nakaiya sold the following items.

From Kii: lacquerware, cotton goods, umbrellas, hemp palm broom, hemp palm bark, tangerines, bergamot (an orange-like citrus fruit), unprocessed wax, dried seaweed, kudzu (or arrowroot), porcelain, and tea.

From Aizu: lacquerware, ginseng, hemp and hemp cloth, raw silk, silk cloth, and silk floss, tobacco, swords and accessories, and moxa (to stimulate the acupressure points).

From Ueda: white silk and silk cloth, cotton, silk floss, hemp, lacquer, paper, wax, umbrellas, coal oil, pine oil, ginseng, flour, lead, metal saws and sheet metal, and tobacco.[35]

The three domains provided him with a variety of products to sell, including textiles and lacquerware, products that shogunal officials and foreign representatives speculated might sell during their negotiations over the commercial treaties.

Why did Nakaiya enter foreign trade? Many merchants who faced the same opportunity initially reacted with skepticism.[36] Was he one of those who saw a business opportunity and merely pursued it to the logical conclusion? Or was he convinced by Iwase, and had other motives, such as strengthening the economy of eastern Japan? Six of the seven *daimyō* he negotiated with were in eastern Japan (Kii, a collateral house of the shogun, was the exception). A most logical trading partner to pursue would have been Lord Inaba of Yodo domain, his father's patron, but that seems never to have been contemplated. This bias toward eastern Japan probably owes more to his family's origins in Kōzuke (Gunma), the existing economic network in eastern Japan, and from his previous contacts as an arms merchant supplying the shogunate. It is probably too hasty to conclude that Iwase had a direct influence on Nakaiya. Perhaps his influence was more indirect, such as the time when the foreign magistrate officials mediated between Nakaiya and Yonezawa domain in the northeast, a mediation that the officials seemed more eager to conduct than Nakaiya himself. Nakaiya for his part exploited to the fullest extent his connections with shogunal officials, domain authorities, and family and friends.

As the first major store to open in Yokohama and with a variety of goods on display for sale, Nakaiya's business immediately took off. It was a store that allowed foreigners to enter with their shoes on[37] and to examine the goods freely while walking on tatami mats. The open courtyard with songbirds flying freely attracted attention of both foreigners and Japanese visitors. And he paid magicians and other showmen from Edo to entertain people at his store. Because he was kind to the Chinese visitors, the Chinese came in large numbers. But the gleaming red copper tiles caught the attention of shogunal authorities. The Kanagawa magistrate, Akamatsu Noritada, threw him in jail and ordered that Nakaiya remove the copper tiles and replace them with ceramic tiles. Nakaiya had overstepped the bounds of a merchant. Supposedly he was also ordered to cease mercantile activity for five days as well. However, according to *Nakaiya sonnō kyōiki*, Nakaiya Jūbei explained that he was secretly ordered by regent Ii to build an outstanding merchant house, at least on the outside, so that foreigners would accept Yokohama as the main port and prevent them from opening shop in Kanagawa. Therefore he complained that five days' suspension was too heavy a punishment. Since the magistrate did not enforce the five days of suspension, Nakaiya had effectively won this part of the case. Considering that he had multiple meetings with Iwase and long discussions with Mizuno and his colleague Tamura, Nakaiya's claim that he was ordered to make his mansion lavish is a distinct possibility. Moreover, oral history from that time claims that Nakaiya Jūbei was not even jailed, for he hired an imposter who spent time in jail. In the end, Jūbei replaced the gleaming copper roof tiles with a black asphalt roof by Ansei 6/9/28.[38] The gleaming red copper tiles were gone in less than two months, but business boomed.

Of the products that Nakaiya was selling, the big seller turned out to be raw silk. And fortunately for him, he could get even more raw silk from eastern Japan. Kai and Shinano provinces, today known as Yamanashi and Nagano prefectures respectively, and the northern Kantō region had become a major producer of raw silk by this time. In a letter from Mitsui's store in Yokohama to its main branch in Kyoto dated Ansei 6/10/8 (2 November 1859), Nakaiya Jūbei was the biggest seller of silk at around 17,000 to 18,000 *kin*.[39] Since the next largest seller of silk was Takasuya Seibei at 5,000 to 6,000 *kin*, Nakaiya was far and away the largest seller of silk. By 1860 Nakaiya's primary business had become the export of raw silk. According to his biographer, Hagiwara Susumu, Nakaiya Jūbei had personally gone to towns near Ueda domain in southern Nagano and visited towns along the way in Kai province and then to the city of Hachiōji. Since he was dealing with domains in eastern Japan and Kii domain, his business reach extended from northeastern Japan to central Japan.

By collecting vast amounts of raw silk for export, Nakaiya had become the wealthiest merchant of Yokohama, nicknamed the "Lord Bishop of 'Hama."[40] According to an old man who recalled Nakaiya's life in a newspaper interview, Jūbei bought only 100 *monme* (375 grams) of raw silk at 1 *ryō* (gold coin) in Kōzuke and Shinano when the going rate was around 150 *monme* (562.5 grams) of raw silk for 1 *ryō*.[41] According to the old man, Nakaiya did this because he had advance knowledge that the foreigners would buy raw silk at high prices. I find much of this old man's story about Jūbei's life to be outlandish and incorrect, but if the prices he recalled are correct, then Nakaiya stood to gain a huge amount because the Westerners bought silk at 64 *monme* (240 grams) for 1 *ryō* in Yokohama.[42] In other words, if Nakaiya had spent 27,200 *ryō* to buy 2,720,000 *monme* of raw silk (17,000 *kin* x 160 *monme/kin*, the amount the House of Mitsui estimated Nakaiya sold), he could get 42,500 *ryō* when selling the same 2,720,00 *monme* of raw silk to the Western merchants: a profit of 15,300 *ryō* (minus transportation costs). If Nakaiya had paid the going rate in the interior of Japan, he would have made even more money.

By the end of 1859, Nakaiya had become the richest merchant in Yokohama.[43] Other merchants from his home province recognized his success and rushed into the raw silk exporting business themselves, driving up the price of raw silk in Japan. He became so successful that one of his former employees, Kobayashi Shichirōji, recalled in 1913 the details of a trip when Nakaiya Jūbei returned to his home village in 1860. He had travelled the entire way by palanquin, spent 7.5 *ryō* for his stay at an inn at Usui,[44] dedicated a stone lantern worth 75 *ryō* to the Bodhisattva Kannon at a temple nearby, and then spent 1,500 *ryō* at the Kusatsu hot springs over the course of three days by giving money to the poor and partying.[45]

NAKAIYA JŪBEI: A MERCHANT IN THE TOKUGAWA ECONOMIC SYSTEM

If Nakaiya Jūbei was so successful, why did he fail? This important question forces us to look at the political dimensions of the Tokugawa economic system. As explained in the introduction, the shogunate was designed to protect the interests of the samurai, particularly the samurai residents of Edo. This was the reason why the government was obsessed with the rise in prices of various goods vis-à-vis the price of rice in Edo. Since the samurai were mainly paid in rice, they sold the excess rice that they could not eat and received cash payment. Then they used this money to buy other goods. If the price of rice relative to other goods was high, they could lead a rich life. But if the price of rice fell relative to other goods, then the samurai effectively became poorer. Remember that the shogunate had a dual role: as the government of the entire country and as a government of the largest *daimyō* of Japan, the Tokugawa clan.

Nakaiya Jūbei happened to live through a tumultuous period when shogunal policy shifted dramatically to deal with the aforementioned economic issues. Just after he started his studies in Edo, the Tempō Reforms started, which disbanded the monopoly guilds and welcomed entrepreneurs. The intent of the reforms was to increase competition from the entrepreneurs in order to lower the prices of various goods. As one such entrepreneur, Nakaiya became successful in the gunpowder business and profited from the reforms. Then Abe Masahiro, the man who sought cooperation among the major lords after the failure of the Tempō Reforms, eventually allowed the former monopoly guilds to re-form into mercantile associations (associations without monopoly rights). Abe did this to supply the city of Edo with necessary goods, but he was also concerned with the stability of the entire Tokugawa economic system as well. As a successful businessman, Nakaiya could have simply continued in the gunpowder trade. However, he risked everything when Hotta Masayoshi and Iwase Tadanari changed shogunal priorities. Hotta and Iwase shifted shogunal policy from cooperation among all the major lords and maintenance of the system as a whole to strengthening the Tokugawa clan through foreign trade. Nakaiya thought that this was his chance to cooperate with the government to engage in foreign trade. But then Hotta and Iwase were replaced by Ii Naosuke, the new regent to the shogun, before the opening of Yokohama. Ii, working with treasury officials such as Mizuno Tadanori, sought to maintain the traditional system and keep foreign trade to a minimum.

In other words, Nakaiya was trying to run a business when the government was designed to defend the interests of the samurai in whatever way they defined it. Their definition of samurai or shogunal interest could change dramatically and quickly. Merchants such as Nakaiya had to react to changing circumstances. Thus Nakaiya's early success was in line with Hotta's and Iwase's hopes to strengthen the Tokugawa clan. However, under Ii and Mizuno, the same success was seen as harming the interests of the Tokugawa shogunate. For Ii and Mizuno, successful foreign trade. For Ii and Mizuno, successful foreign trade at Yokohama disrupted the overall economic system that linked Osaka, Edo, and the rest of Japan, the very system over which the Tokugawa shogunate presided.

As seen in the debates in chapter 2, the treasury officials who traditionally oversaw economic policy feared that foreign trade might complicate their efforts to lower prices for the consumers of Edo even before the start of trade. If valuable commodities were exported outside of Japan in large quantities, then the price of those goods had to rise. This clashed with their overriding mission: to keep prices low in Edo. Hotta Masayoshi overrode their concerns, noting that foreign trade would instead strengthen the shogunate by bringing in tariff revenue, and Iwase argued that the Japanese economy needed to be recentered around Edo. If domains in eastern Japan could benefit from the trade, that was an added bonus. If the dismantling of monopoly guilds was a major economic experiment that had led to failure and required treasury officials to rectify, now Hotta and Iwase wanted to engage in foreign trade, an even bigger experiment that would inevitably make life for treasury officials even more difficult.

Initially, the fears of the treasury officials came true. Once Yokohama opened, foreigners drained Japan of its gold because the price of gold inside Japan was too low compared to the price of silver outside Japan. Roughly speaking, all parties (Japanese officials, Western officials, Japanese merchants, and foreign merchants) agreed that the value of any currency lay in the weight of pure gold or pure silver contained in the various coins. When international trade started, the international exchange rate was 1:15 (in other words, 1 ounce of gold was worth 15 ounces of silver). But in Japan the exchange rate was 1:5 (1 ounce of gold was worth 5 ounces of silver). Therefore any foreigner could make an enormous sum just through currency exchange. For example, a visiting foreigner brings with him 50 ounces of silver to Yokohama. He exchanges the 50 ounces of silver with 10 ounces of gold at a Japanese money exchanger (since the ratio is 1:5 inside Japan). Then he takes that 10 ounces of gold from Yokohama and travels to Shanghai (or San Francisco or London). Because the international rate is 1:15, in Shanghai the 10 ounces of gold can be exchanged for 150 ounces of silver. Thus, just by exchanging currencies legally, the foreign visitor could triple his silver (from 50 ounces in Yokohama to 150 ounces in Shanghai).

Mizuno Tadanori and the treasury officials quickly saw that this was a problem and first tried to raise the silver content of Japanese coins. But there simply was not enough silver inside Japan to do this.[46] As seen in chapter 1, the shogunate had in fact been debasing currency to deal with its lack of revenue. Thus on 11 February 1860, seven months after the opening of Yokohama, treasury officials reluctantly declared that a new gold coin that had only a third of the gold content as before would be minted. This reset the gold-silver ratio inside Japan at 1:15 and prevented the further outflow of gold. But it also meant that any Japanese person who had the old gold coins could exchange one of his old gold coins with three new gold coins. In the end, the shogunate did not mint enough new gold coins (with one-third the gold content as before) and instead started to mint a large quantity of half coins on 29 May 1860, which had gold content lower than one sixth, further debasing the currency. This debasing of the gold coins meant the sudden increase of currency in circulation, as numerous people went to the money exchangers in Japan to exchange one of their old gold coins for three new ones (or six half coins).[47]

Naturally inflation surged after this. One of the problems facing the shogunate since the Tempō Reforms became worse: the lack of cheap non-rice goods in Edo. As mentioned in chapter 2, if the estimated number of gold coins in Japan in 1858 was 28,315,000 *ryō*, by 1869 the number was 74,321,000 *ryō*.[48] This was a massive increase considering that the increase between 1833 and 1858 was less than 5 million *ryō*. Even the quality of silver coins more than doubled. Overall total currency in circulation rose nearly two-and-a-half times in just eleven years. For the average person in Edo, the price of various goods doubled immediately after Yokohama opened for business; thereafter prices tripled, quadrupled, and sometimes even quintupled by 1865.[49] However, this debasement alleviated the other long-term problem, namely the lack of revenue, and the increased revenue allowed the shogunate to tackle its second long-term problem: national defense. In this environment of massive inflation, the Tokugawa *bakufu* continued its modernization projects until the moment it fell in 1867.

Aside from foreigners buying up Japanese gold, the other major problem encountered by the treasury officials after the opening of Yokohama was the sudden rise of raw silk prices. This also happened because the foreign merchants bought the raw silk in large quantities. This became clear when a Kanagawa magistrate official happened to inspect the Dutch Warehouse #7 in Yokohama early in 1860 and discovered to his horror a vast amount of raw silk piled up.[50] He feared that raw silk could be cornered by the foreigners, and when he informed his superiors of this, the response was swift. A few days later the Kanagawa magistrate decreed that raw silk exports should not total more than 500 *kin*[51] per day, a seemingly large number. But Nakaiya Jūbei ignored this decree, selling more than was allowed, and as a consequence was jailed.[52] He was probably not alone because foreign demand was extremely strong.

As mentioned earlier, during the first few months after Yokohama was opened in 1859, Nakaiya alone sold 17,000 to 18,000 *kin* and likely wanted to sell more. The large foreign demand drew many merchants to Yokohama to sell raw silk. Combined with the effects of inflation from debasing gold coins entering circulation, the price of raw silk skyrocketed. The price of raw silk doubled in 1861, quadrupled by 1866, and in 1867 reached six times the price before the opening of Yokohama in 1859. This price rise was not sustainable and eventually it settled between triple and quadruple the price before the opening of Yokohama.[53] From the perspective of the shogunal officials, this sudden rise in raw silk prices was an extreme manifestation of the inflation that they wanted to avoid; after all, the goal of successive shogunal ministers was to keep prices low for the residents of Edo.

This was the underlying cause for Nakaiya's downfall. The foreign magistrate (and its branch, the Kanagawa magistrate) was a battleground between two factions within the shogunate. But with Ii Naosuke's ouster of Hotta

Masayoshi, the more traditional treasury faction effectively won over the pro-trade inspectors and governors. Iwase Tadanari was out and Mizuno Tadanori was in. The shogunate was always committed to defending the samurai of Edo. Except that by replacing Hotta with Ii, it changed from promoting trade to cracking down on trade. As a consequence, the largest raw silk merchant came into its sights.

NAKAIYA JŪBEI: THE FALL

Nakaiya Jūbei's fall began a week after Ii Naosuke's assassination. On Ansei 7/3/3 (24 March 1860) outside the Sakuradamon gate, the regent to the shogun was assassinated. This event may have given Nakaiya the wrong idea that the treasury officials and the traditionalists would be ousted and that men like Hotta Masayoshi and Iwase Tadanari would return to office and once more encourage foreign trade. Or perhaps Nakaiya Jūbei may have simply been greedy; regardless he defied the Kanagawa magistrate's order to limit the sale of raw silk to less than 500 *kin* (300 kilograms) per day.

Unfortunately for Nakaiya, Hotta and Iwase did not return to power. Instead, the Kanagawa magistrate was still staffed by those sympathetic to the treasury officials. If he sold more raw silk than the limit because he thought the political scene would change once more, he had miscalculated. Moreover, Nakaiya had no one to protect him. Earlier when he was in trouble with the Kanagawa magistrate about the red copper roof tiles, Nakaiya Jūbei could claim that he had secret orders from the regent, Ii Naosuke, and from the former inspectors. But now Ii was dead and the former inspectors were out. From the perspective of the Kanagawa magistrate and treasury officials, Nakaiya not only ignored the order, but he was also sabotaging their plans to try and keep the price of raw silk low and thus maintain the living standards of the residents of Edo. Naturally, the magistrate jailed Nakaiya Jūbei for breaking the edict.

But Nakaiya was not done yet. Once out of jail, he continued to gather raw silk from Kōzuke, Shinano, and Kai provinces for export. Unfortunately for him, the shogunate issued a new law on 9 May 1860 to combat the price rise, mandating that five goods must pass through Edo before being sent to Yokohama. These five goods were millet (or more broadly non-rice grains), wax, silk cloth, clear rapeseed oil, and raw silk. Moreover, merchants in Yokohama could not receive more than forty boxes of raw silk per day from Edo, and the amount they could sell to foreigners was limited to no more than 1,000 *kin* (600 kilograms) per day. The *bakufu* had doubled the amount the merchants could sell, but this law was still highly unpopular among the merchants and the foreign community. F. Howard Vyse, the British consul at Yokohama, in a meeting with British merchants at Yokohama on 19 February 1861, declared that the shogunate's limit on the sale of goods, namely oil, silk, tea, and vegetable wax, was a major problem that needed to be addressed. However, he also claimed that little could be done as "The ruling classes believe the country is being ruined, as it is, by too large and unrestricted foreign trade. The ministers tell Her Majesty's Envoy [Rutherford Alcock] this nearly every time he sees them."[54]

Nakaiya Jūbei saw these restrictions as boneheaded. Instead of breaking the law, he circumvented it and protested against it. He circumvented the law by lodging thirty to fifty Japanese merchants at his store and then helping them to sell their raw silk by introducing them to Western merchants. Nakaiya Jūbei probably made money by charging these merchants a small fee.[55] He protested by writing a letter to the Kanagawa magistrate, Takemoto Masatsune. In the letter, Nakaiya argued that Japan should not rely on imports, since it would drain the country of gold and silver. Instead the country should encourage the export of raw silk to pay for the imports because silk could be produced year after year. And because silk could be produced year after year, fearing its depletion was wrong.[56]

For continually defying the Kanagawa magistrate's office, he earned their enmity. After all, the treasury and the Kanagawa magistrates were staffed by people who sincerely believed, as explained in chapter 1, that Japan was a country that "favors the lords but also righteousness, and has an unbroken line of rulers of divine descent." Thus anyone who prevented them from doing their work—of favoring the samurai—was suspect. In fact, adopting the Western way of putting profit first could be seen as a possible sign of treason. They thought that the West might entice a few merchants to get rich first and then convert them to become the first collaborators in a future invasion of Japan.[57]

Nakaiya Jūbei clearly did not think this way. In fact, Nakaiya might have been an early nationalist, a man who thought of Japan as a single nation and thus recognized the need for a new government that would look out for all Japanese. His educational background and his family's affiliations with the Confucian scholars associated with the Mito school strongly encourage this view.[58] The critical difference between him and the treasury officials was probably the fact that he did not think that the role of the government was mainly to serve the samurai living in Edo. He was thinking in terms of enriching the entire country.

According to his daughter, Nakaiya was the sort of merchant highly interested in politics and who donated generously to the cause of Mito school radicals. A former employee, Kobayashi Shichirōji, also claims that Nakaiya Jūbei knew of the plot to assassinate Ii Naosuke, the regent.[59] If shogunal authorities had knowledge of Nakaiya's involvement in politics—that he not only opposed the limit of exports but was also supporting Mito school radicals—there would be no reason for them to go easy on Nakaiya Jūbei, and their suspicions of him as a traitor to the *bakufu* would only deepen.

The final blow came sometime in early 1861. According to the recollections of Fujie Akifusa, an early Yokohama resident, Nakaiya's house was normally filled with thirty to fifty raw silk merchants on the second floor. As stated earlier, Nakaiya had tried to overcome the 1,000 *kin* (600 kilogram) per-person limit on the sale of raw silk by acting as the agent on behalf of these men. He was trying to follow the letter of the law. But one day a foreign merchant begged him to sell copper, an item the shogunate had banned for export. When the shogunate discovered that he had indeed sold 100 *kin* of copper to a foreign merchant, the Kanagawa magistrate threw the book at him, arresting him and closing his shop. If the magistrate had recalled Nakaiya's earlier letter about not selling gold or silver and instead selling silk because it could be grown year after year, the hypocrisy might have upset the magistrate as well. The raw silk merchants at his house were surprised by this turn of events, and they all left Nakaiya's store and fled to Tezuka Seigorō's shop next door.[60]

The income stream that Nakaiya Jūbei lost was substantial. Tezuka Seigorō alone could not handle the business of all the raw silk merchants that left Nakaiya, so he and another merchant handled the wares of the merchants that fled Nakaiya's store. In just five to six months, Tezuka claimed to have made 700 *ryō* from charging a 1 percent commission. If Nakaiya Jūbei had handled all the merchants, he potentially could have made 1,400 *ryō* in five to six months, or roughly 2,800 *ryō* in ten to twelve months by charging the same 1 percent commission. Moreover, the closure of the shop dealt a huge blow to Nakaiya. Considering that he earned tens of thousands, if not hundreds of thousands, of *ryō* from selling raw silk in 1859 and 1860, even a temporary closure of his shop truly hurt his business. The fact that other merchants left him and did not help was the icing on a bitter cake.

By summer 1861 Nakaiya's influence was gone. Francis Hall, an American reporter for the *New York Tribune* and a resident merchant in Yokohama, describes Nakaiya's last days in Yokohama in a long journal entry on 11 June 1861:

> A *merchant's residence*. In Yokohama lives a merchant Nakai [Nakaiya], whose residence is one of the curiosities of the place. It is situated on the principal business street and consists of one large main fireproof building used as a shop and residence and several outbuildings, fire proof warehouses, etc. The building is conspicuous to one passing in the street by its dark heavy tiles, roof timbers, and its massive perpendicular sign over the main entrance. Curtains of dark blue cotton emblazoned with the merchant's name and marks depend from the eaves in front till they sweep the earth and enclose the narrow sidewalk. Occupying two thirds of the front is a fish pond of masonry four or five feet wide and full of gold fish. This is fenced by pickets from the street.

> The entrance is into a large room open to the street covered with mats, where a few clerks and boys in waiting remain. A quiet still spot is this unindicative of traffic, and just now Nakai, whose fortunes are on the wane, has little traffic.
>
> My visit was with Dr. S[immons], who had the master of the house as a patient. . . . We found the master of the house lying on thick quilted mattresses under silk coverlets spread on the mats in the center of the room. Three attendants were with him, a man, his own concubine, a woman of pleasant exterior, and a little servant girl. The room was an elegant one, for Japan a luxurious one, and for any country a comfortable, pleasant, and remarkably tidy one. Some foreign comforts had been engrafted upon the Japanese simplicity of house adornment. Glass windows occupying one side of the room opened into a little court of trees and flowers, birds hung in handsome cages within the recessed windows, curtains of gay shiffs festooned them and on the broad bench of the window were ornamental articles both native and imported. The mats were of a remarkably fine texture and bound with white after the style of the imperial palace at Yedo. This visit was made in the spring and at the time pots of flowering cherry trees adorned the room, among them some artificial trees so accurate that it needed the touch to detect their fabrication of paper. The projecting timbers and uprights always visible in a Japanese house were handsomely lackered in black and the plastered walls were covered with a neat hanging of paper representing the blossoming cherry trees. In one recess were some articles of antique design and a Japanese landscape painting. Three sides of the room were hung with French colored engravings of scenes in the Crimea campaigns and allegorical pictures of the old mythology whose half nude gods and goddesses were attractive to Japanese taste in art. A nude Pandora opening the fatal box was conspicuous. . . .
>
> At our desire to see more of his house the little maid threw back the screens that separated an adjoining apartment which was the chief room of the house. It was bare of furniture but was covered with mats of a size I had never seen before. The walls were covered with hangings of silk exactly fitted on which were painted the birds of Japan. The gold and silver pheasants, the snowy herons, etc., in proportional drawing and colored to life. The ceiling was covered with fan shaped devices—on a white ground—of flowers, landscapes, historical characters, divinities in a not unpleasing though strange mixture. Those too were beautifully colored. This room opened upon the aviary before mentioned and its tapestries were in harmony therewith. . . .
>
> Few merchants live in so royal a style and I am told men of rank and wealth seldom surround themselves with such luxuries as did this merchant. He said he would not be allowed to do it in Yedo. A parting cup of tea and some more bits of sugar and we left the merchant sick on his mats wretched amid all his elegant surroundings.[61]

The opulence of Nakaiya's store is in stark contrast to its lack of customers. Presumably they avoided a store under suspicion. Perhaps Nakaiya Jūbei was ill because of his jail time. There is no way to know at this point. But his store, normally full of people, was empty when Francis Hall and Dr. Duane Simmons visited. Other historians have recorded that after his arrest, his wealth was confiscated and his store burned down when his manager was careless.[62] This version of Nakaiya's end seems to have condensed events.[63] His daughter claimed that when shogunal authorities came for him at their home (once again), he got on a small boat and escaped Yokohama. From there he fled to modern-day Chiba prefecture and then snuck back into Edo. There he is said to have died of measles. The illness he was suffering when Hall and Dr. Simmons visited him had fatally weakened him. His mother records that in Bunkyū 1, eighth month (September 1861) Nakaiya Jūbei died in Kagurazaka, Edo.[64] Since Nakaiya had fled Yokohama, it would not be surprising for the authorities to confiscate his wealth. Later that year on 12 November 1861, Francis Hall records that a devastating fire at 2 am destroyed half the Japanese business quarters of Yokohama "involving the loss of a great amount of property. Several blocks in length and five streets in breadth were consumed."[65]

In less than six months, Nakaiya Jūbei went from being a new foreign trade merchant given special dispensation to build a luxurious store to the richest man in Yokohama. During the following year, Nakaiya would clash with shogunal authorities over the limit on the sale of raw silk and became a marked man. Despite the clashes, in 1860 he was still an extremely wealthy man spending enormous sums travelling, buying and selling raw silk, inviting other raw silk merchants to his store to sell their raw silk to Westerners, and donating to charity, temples, and political causes. But in early 1861 he would sell contraband copper and be jailed. Before the summer was over, he had to flee Yokohama. He may have planned a comeback, but he fell to disease.

His meteoritic rise demonstrates how fostering a strong connection with shogunal officials and domain authorities could benefit a merchant. His contact with local merchants kept him at the top of the merchant world, and he became known as *Hama no monzeki-sama*. His swift fall also illustrates the nature of the Tokugawa economic system: merchants were tolerated as long as they served the interests of the Tokugawa shogun and the samurai. The shogunate crushed merchants who harmed their interests, and other merchants knew that they could not help him once he was targeted. This is the story of Nakaiya Jūbei, the first merchant of Yokohama.

CONCLUSION

The story of Nakaiya Jūbei, the first merchant of Yokohama, is illustrative of the close relationship between politics and economics. It is also illustrative of the contingent nature of history.

In terms of political economy, Nakaiya demonstrated through his success that close ties with high-level shogunal officials and domains could lead to enormous profits. Nakaiya also demonstrated through his downfall that defying the shogunal official's wishes would lead to ruin. His downfall also illuminated how *bakufu* power worked. No government can enforce its laws and edicts on everybody at all times. The question is how to get ordinary people to follow the law, to gain the consent of the governed. In the case of Tokugawa, the "carrot" was to show mercy and benevolence, and the "stick" was punishment of high-profile people to serve as a warning for others. By repeatedly defying the Kanagawa magistrate's office, Nakaiya had to pay the price: jail time and the closure of his business. When this happened, the many merchants who were indebted to him fled without helping him.

In terms of historical contingency, the clash between the pro-trade Hotta Masayoshi and Iwase Tadanari and the antitrade Ii Naosuke and Mizuno Tadanori yielded interesting results. Hotta and Iwase, through the help of merchants like Nakaiya, did succeed in reorienting Japanese foreign trade, and eventually this would lead to the transformation of eastern Japan as the economic region to surpass western Japan. However, this success did not help at all in saving the shogunate. The expected income from tariffs was dwarfed by the income gained from debasing currency. Currency debasement helped in the short run, but it ultimately destabilized the Tokugawa economy. The 5 percent tariffs were not a large enough source of income for both the Tokugawa shogunate and the Meiji government, and both governments had to rely on the land tax. Of course, debasing currency was itself another unforeseen event for the *bakufu*. Iwase had hoped that by making Yokohama the center of foreign trade, the shogun might be the first to acquire foreign technology and gain its benefits. However, the fact that Nagasaki remained open to foreign trade meant that *daimyō* in the west could also buy up-to-date weapons, just like the shogun. The opening of Yokohama yielded no benefits in terms of superior military technology as Iwase hoped.

Ii and Mizuno failed to contain foreign trade, despite all the roadblocks they placed. However, Ii and Mizuno did succeed in preventing the foreigners from settling in Kanagawa. They also physically cordoned off the foreigners at Yokohama by digging a canal through the peninsula, turning it into an island like Nagasaki's Dejima. After 1860 bridges linked the island city of Yokohama to the outside world and each of these bridges was guarded by shogunal officials. It was only in 1867 that ordinary foreign residents could reside on top of the bluff on the opposite side of the canal. For men such as Ii and Mizuno, however, these minor victories probably paled in comparison to their failure in controlling or limiting foreign trade. Reminting gold coins to prevent the outflow of precious metals signified that the Japanese economy was now fully linked to global trade. The failure to limit the sale of raw silk also proved that the Japanese economy was now fully linked to global trade. The treasury officials were no longer operating in a closed economic system.

The most interesting historical contingency, then, is the trade itself. The next short chapter discusses this issue.

NOTES

1. I rendered the nickname *Hama no monzeki-sama* as Lord Bishop of 'Hama because *monzeki* is a title reserved for the leader of a Buddhist temple who is also of aristocratic or imperial descent. 'Hama is short for Yokohama.

2. This chapter owes much to the diary *Shōhei nichiroku* reprinted in Yokohama kyōdo kenkyūkai (ed.), *Kurofune raikō to Yokohama: Yokoreki sōsho vol. 12* (Yokohama: Yokohama kyōdo kenkyūkai, 1993) and Hagiwara Susumu, the biographer of Nakaiya. Hagiwara Susumu, *Hono'o no kiitoshō: Nakaiya Jūbei* (Yokohama: Yūrindō, 1988).

3. Hashimoto Gountei Gyokuransai Sadahide, *Yokohama kaikō kenbunshi* (Tokyo: Meicho kankōkai, 1967), 33.

4. Francis Hall was not related to Dr. George Hall, but later Francis Hall would join the Walsh brothers when Dr. George Hall left Japan and form Walsh, Hall & Company in 1861. The British merchant William Keswick established the second Western shop in Yokohama.

5. Francis Hall, *Japan through American Eyes: The Journal of Francis Hall Kanagawa and Yokohama 1859–1866*, ed. F. G. Notehelfer (Princeton, NJ: Princeton University Press, 1992), 102–3 footnote section.

6. "Yokohama fūbun torishimarisho," in *Mikan Yokohama kaikō shiryō*, ed. Kanagawa-ken toshokankyōkai kyōdoshiryō shūsei hensan iinkai (Yokohama: Kanagawa-ken toshokankyōkai, 1960), 221–23.

7. Rutherford Alcock, *Capital of the Tycoon*, vol. 1 (New York: Harper, 1863), 141.

8. On 16 January 1860, Townsend Harris addressed the American merchants in Yokohama and asked them to move to Kanagawa since that was the original location stipulated in the treaty and because Kanagawa, located on the main highway, would be conducive to further contacts with Japanese merchants. American merchants opposed this proposal, citing the shallow waters off Kanagawa and the need for deepwater ports. The British representative Rutherford Alcock gave up early when he came in July 1859 and saw that "We were in fact, to all appearance, insisting upon a right in behalf of our merchants which they themselves, the chief parties interested, repudiated as much as the Japanese Government!" Thus Western consuls initially set up their offices in Kanagawa and in official documents Yokohama became known as Kanagawa: Kanagawa magistrate, Kanagawa consulate, etcetera. Hall, *Japan through American Eyes*, 102, and Alcock, *Capital of the Tycoon*, vol. 1, 141.

9. Lord Inaba would later become a member of the *rōjū* (minister) twice, first from 1864 to 1865 and again from 1866 to 1868.

10. The lord of Kawagoe domain in modern-day Saitama prefecture was actually supposed to be in Maebashi, Gunma prefecture. However, when repeated floods destroyed Maebashi castle in 1767, the lord moved his headquarters to Kawagoe castle. Thus from 1767 to 1867 Maebashi domain would be known as Kawagoe domain, with roughly half the land near Kawagoe, Saitama and the other half near Maebashi, Gunma. This is why a Confucian scholar in Kawagoe had relatives in Gunma.

11. Hagiwara, *Hono'o no kiitoshō*, 8–28.

12. Hagiwara Susumu argues that Nakaiya Jūbei had studied under Sakuma Shōzan, for he claims that Nakaiya had close ties to *rangaku* specialists surrounding Sanada Yukitsura, *daimyō* of Matsushiro (100,000 *koku*). The fact that Takashima Shūhan, the foremost expert on gunnery, wrote an introduction to a book Nakaiya wrote proves that he did have contact with prominent *rangaku* scholars.

13. Mito school's popularity was not confined to the samurai and had wider appeal as many of its ideas began to merge with Kokugaku (national studies) and began to form a basis for nationalism. For more on the emergence of this mentality, see H. D. Harootunian, *Toward Restoration: The Growth of Political Consciousness in Tokugawa Japan* (Berkeley: University of California Press, 1991). Shimazaki Tōson, *Yoakemae*, 4 vols. (Tokyo: Shinchōsha, 1932,

1935) is a historical novel that depicts how peasants from the mountains became interested in national politics.

14. Hagiwara, *Hono'o no kiitoshō*, 68–90.

15. For the rest of this chapter, I use a modified shorthand for dates, without including both Japanese and Western dates. The year is converted from the Japanese system to anno Domini, but the months and days continue to be in the Japanese system. Thus, Ansei 6, first month, thirteenth day, is written as 1859/1/13.

16. Nakaiya Jūbei, *Shōhei nichiroku*, in Yokohama kyōdo kenkyūkai (ed.), *Yokoreki sōsho* vol. 12: *Kurofune raikō to Yokohama* (Yokohama: Yokohama kyōdo kenkyūkai, 1993), 60–63.

17. Hagiwara, *Hono'o no kiitoshō*, 30–60, 110–11.

18. Nakaiya, *Shōhei nichiroku*, 53–82. Since each journal entry is short, I use dates as well as page numbers to cite the events.

19. Kawachiya was the *bakufu*'s official exchange merchant, converting gold coins used in Kanto with silver coins used in Kinai, a banker, and a merchant who minted coins for the *bakufu*. Gold coins were organized along the following pattern: 1 *ryō* = 4 *bu* = 16 *shu*. Yorozuya was most likely a retail merchant.

20. In the first month alone he met with shogunal officials seven times: 1/13, 1/15, 1/16, 1/17, 1/24, 1/25, 1/28. Nakaiya, *Shōhei nichiroku*, 60–63.

21. Ueda-shi (ed.), *Ueda shishi* (Tokyo: Shinano mainichi shimbunsha, 1975), vol. 1, 1070–74, 1098–1102. Henceforth cited as US.

22. This is the day after Nakaiya and his father conferred with the Aizu domain commissioner and two other merchants about the possibilities of foreign trade. Nakaiya, *Shōhei nichiroku*, 59.

23. Aizu's grant followed two weeks later on 2/20. Nakaiya, *Shōhei nichiroku*, 66.

24. Tokyo daigaku shiryō hensanjo (ed.), *Dainihon komonjo: Bakumatsu gaikoku kankei monjo* (Tokyo: Tokyo University Press, 1930), vol. 21, 398, 418. Hereafter cited as BGKM.

25. The *bakufu* had some idea about what could be sold through its various conversations with foreign representatives as it debated opening the country for trade. Harris claimed from an early interview that the salted Japanese chicken eggs he had in Siam and Japanese tea had a pleasing taste and thus were exported and exportable. Later in his letter to Hotta Masayoshi, 1857/11/10 he argued that Japan could export lacquerware, silk, tea, and copper. Muragaki, who was the Hakodate magistrate at the time, hoped to sell cloth (including silk), paper, lacquerware, tea, and everyday items to help the producers. Iwase learned from his conversation with a Dutch merchant at Shimoda that copper and camphor (*shōnō*) would be the primary exports, followed by tea, lacquerware, and porcelain. BGKM XIV: 178, 250; BGKM XV: 4.

26. Tsudayū, Gihei, Sahei, and Tajūrō, four crew members of a merchant ship, became the first Japanese to travel around the world after being shipwrecked off the Aleutians in 1793. They rode along with the first Russian vessel to circumnavigate the globe and returned to Japan after twelve years. Their story is recorded in Ōtsuki Gentaku, Shimura Kyōkō, *Kankai ibun* (manuscript is available in the Kyūshū University digital archives).

27. The fact that he did not keep his diary for a more extensive time period is another source of frustration.

28. Considering that shogunal officials went to work before dawn (so that they could start their work at dawn), visiting someone at 9 pm was late.

29. This Kawachiya is recorded as Kawachiya Matsunosuke. It is not known if this is the same Kawachiya or not, but I am assuming that he is the same person as Kawachiya Hanbei, since the name Hanbei does not appear after this date. It was common for people to change their names in Edo-period Japan. Another possibility is that Matsunosuke could be Hanbei's son or, of course, that he is someone altogether different.

30. It is unknown what exactly this testimonial was. Perhaps he had to write in detail what he planned to buy and sell. Kōshūya Chūemon writes in his letter that when he went to see Mizuno, he had to submit a list of items he planned to sell and buy. Ishii Takashi (ed.), *Yokohama urikomishō Kōshūya monjo* (Yokohama, Yūrindō, 1984), 2, #4.

31. Fukuchi Gen'ichirō, *Bakumatsu seijika* (Tokyo: Heibonsha, 1989), 265. Fukuchi Ōchi (Gen'ichirō's other name) was Mizuno's secretary and translator. Among the biographers of Mizuno, he knew Mizuno's personality best.

32. This is probably Tamura Akiakira, who was the treasury magistrate from 1853 to 1855.

33. His earlier name was Kuroiwa Sennosuke. Nakaiya Jūbei was born Kuroiwa Takenosuke, then changed his name to Kuroiwa Sennosuke, and then finally to Nakai(ya) Jūbei; sometimes with the "-ya," sometimes not. Hagiwara, *Hono'o no kiitoshō*, 15–16, 109.

34. A *ken* is approximately 6 feet, making 1 square *ken* or 1 *tsubo* approximately 36 square feet. Most of Yokohama's early shops were less than 100 *tsubo* (3,600 square feet); even the larger ones were less than 300 *tsubo* (10,800 square feet). For example, Mitsui had a shop only 208 *tsubo*, Kōshūya was 102 *tsubo*, Yoshimuraya was 270 *tsubo*, and Nakaiya's friend Kawachiya Hanbei had a shop only 35 *tsubo* (1,260 square feet). Compared to those and other shops listed, such as a barbershop (5 by 30 feet), Nakaiya's 476 *tsubo* (17,136 square feet) was enormous. Yokohama kyōdo kenkyūkai (ed.), *Yokoreki sōsho*, vol. 12: *Kurofune raikō to Yokohama* (Yokohama: Yokohama kyōdo kenkyūkai, 1993), 136 (for Nakaiya), 104–5 (for Mitsui), 97–99 (for Kōshūya), 138 (for Yoshimuraya), 115 (for Kawachiya), 89 (for Rokujirō's barbershop).

35. Hagiwara, *Hono'o no kiitoshō*, 130. This list mostly agrees with the listed products for sale in the 1859-1862 directory of Yokohama merchants. In the directory "lacquer" is clarified to be lacquerware. "Yokohama shōninroku" in *Kurofune raikō to Yokohama*, 136–37. Also in US, 1101–2.

36. Yokohama-shi (ed.), *Yokohama shishi*, vol. 2 (Yokohama: Yūrindō, 1959), 206–7.

37. One is supposed to take off the shoes when entering Japanese buildings, particularly homes.

38. The imposter's name was Kichiemon. Hagiwara, *Hono'o no kiitoshō*, 168–72.

39. 1 *kin* = 600 grams; 1 *monme* = 3.75 grams; 1 *kin* = 160 *monme*.

40. *Hama no monzeki-sama*. Hagiwara, *Hono'o no kiitoshō*, 168–72.

41. This was the price of raw silk in 1858 in Maebashi, Gunma prefecture. In 1859 the going rate was 120 *monme* per 1 *ryō*. If the old man's story is true, Nakaiya paid a premium to collect raw silk whether he bought it in 1858 or in 1859. It is impossible to convert 1 *ryō* or 1 gold coin to today's currencies, but a decent rule of thumb is to think of 1 *ryō* as being about $1,000 during the early Edo period, about $600 during the middle Edo period, and then approximately $400 during the late Edo period; this is the period when it was roughly 1 *ryō* = 1 *koku*. After 1861, an induced inflation in gold coins (the shogunate reduced the amount of gold in 1 *ryō*), so the price of 1 *ryō* falls rapidly to under $100 depending on the goods and services bought. The Bank of Japan Financial Research Center Currency Museum website contains more detailed information on this topic.

42. The price of raw silk in Yokohama was very high compared to Japanese prices in the early years. We discuss this further in the next section, but the prices recalled by the old man are in accordance with historical records and believable.

43. Ishii Mitsutarō and Tōkairin Shizuo (eds.), *Yokohama dontaku*, vol. 1 (Yokohama: Yūrindō, 1973), 318–21. This book is a republication of *Yokohama bōeki shimpō*'s (Yokohama Trade Newspaper) fifty-year retrospective column titled "Kaikō sokumenshi" (Side Stories of the Open Port).

44. Instead of using the rough 1 *ryō* = $400 estimate, which gives us 7.5 *ryō* = $3,000, another way to think about how much he spent is to think about the cost of a stay at an inn. A stay at an inn in late Edo period was normally around 200 *mon* per person. Legally, 4,000 *mon* equaled 1 *ryō*, but the rate fluctuated so that by late Edo period it was closer to 6,500 *mon* per 1 *ryō*. Calculating by the the going rate, Nakaiya spent 48,750 *mon* (7.5 *ryō* x 6,500 *mon*/*ryō*)! Since he travelled with seven or eight servants, an ordinary party would have spent only 1,600 to 1,800 *mon*. So instead of spending between 1,600 and 1,800 *mon* a night for a party of eight or nine, he spent 48,750 *mon* that night.

45. Nakaiya spent $600,000 during three days at the Kusatsu hot springs. Hagiwara, *Hono'o no kiitoshō*, 154.

46. Fukuchi, *Bakumatsu seijika*, 267.

47. For more about this topic in English, see Peter Frost, *The Bakumatsu Currency Crisis* (Cambridge, MA: Harvard University Press, 1970), 27. Takizawa Takeo, *Nihon no kahei no rekishi* (Tokyo: Yoshikawa kōbunkan, 1996) has a full history of money in Japan, Ishii Takashi

wrote the authoritative book on Japanese economic history after the opening of Yokohama.Ishii Takashi, *Bakumatsu kaikōki keizaishi kenkyū* (Yokohama: Yūrindō, 1987), 69–122.

48. Ootsuka Hideki, "Edo jidai ni okeru kaichū no rekishi to sono hyōka," Nihon ginko kin'yū kenkyūjo, *Kin'yū kenkyū* 18, no. 4 (September 1999): 81.

49. Compared to prices during the Kaei years (1848–1853). Ono Takeo, *Edo bukka jiten* (Tokyo: Tenbōsha, 1998), 67.

50. The Dutch merchant was doing business with Nakaiya. Ishii and Tōkairin, *Yokohama dontaku* vol. 1, 321.

51. One *kin* is equal to 600 grams or 1.32 pounds, so 500 *kin* is 300 kilograms or 660 pounds. Although 300 kilograms seems like a large amount of raw silk, this limit was easily surpassed when taking into consideration the number of merchants involved in the raw silk trade.

52. This story is taken from *Yokohama kaikō gojūnenshi,* which seems to be based on the story told by the old man in Ishii and Tōkairin, *Yokohama dontaku,* vol. 1, 321–25. Hagiwara, *Hono'o no kiitoshō,* 179–80.

53. The amount of raw silk one could buy in Maebashi with 1 *ryō* was 120 *monme* in 1859. By 1861, one could buy only 55 *monme* with 1 *ryō*. By 1867 one could buy only 21.5 *monme* with 1 *ryō*. In other words, the price of raw silk skyrocketed during this period, even when considering the effect of inflation (which should have pushed prices to around triple the original price before the devaluation). In 1871 when the yen was introduced as new currency, the price of raw silk was 30 *monme* for 1 *ryō* (quadruple the price in 1859). Hagiwara, *Hono'o no kiitoshō*, 172.

54. Appendix B in Rutherford Alcock, *Capital of the Tycoon*, vol. 2 (New York: Harper, 1863), 377.

55. Ishii and Tōkairin, *Yokohama dontaku*, vol. 1, 169.

56. Hagiwara, *Hono'o no kiitoshō*, 172–74, 180. The old man recalls the same story, but he recalls that it happened in 1864, three years after Nakaiya's death. Ishii and Tōkairin, *Yokohama dontaku,* vol. 1, 324.

57. BGKM, XV: 158.

58. Nakaiya was an admirer of Kusunoki Masashige, a hero revered by the Mito school as a paragon of loyalty to the imperial family. Hagiwara writes that in early summer 1861 Nakaiya Jūbei visited Kyoto and Kobe and that the temple in Minatogawa, where Kusunoki Masashige is entombed, has a record that states "in the sixth month of 1861 [July 1861], Jūbei a merchant from the east came to the temple were lord Kusunoki was buried, cleaned his tomb, offered incense and flowers, and donated money." Therefore he must have gone to Kyoto and Minatogawa in summer 1861. However, this is probably not the same person, as Francis Hall visits Nakaiya on 11 June 1861 at his mansion in Yokohama when he is ill. It could have been the man who would become his heir and adopt the name "Nakaiya Jūbei." Hagiwara, *Hono'o no kiitoshō*, 186–87.

59. Hagiwara, *Hono'o no kiitoshō*, 185–92.

60. Ishii and Tōkairin, *Yokohama dontaku*, vol. 1, 169. Nakaiya's former employee, Kobayashi Shichirōji, also confirms that the magistrate came after him for selling contraband copper, although he recollected that this happened earlier and that Nakaiya avoided jail. Hagiwara, *Hono'o no kiitoshō*, 153–54.

61. Hall, *Japan through American Eyes*, 344–45.

62. Hagiwara, *Hono'o no kiitoshō*, 190–91. Tokutomi Sohō and the editors of *Kinsei Nihon kokuminshi* cite this version.

63. Another version, relayed by the old man recalling Nakaiya's life, claims that the Kanagawa magistrate's office poisoned him while Nakaiya was in jail in 1864. Ishii and Tōkairin, *Yokohama dontaku*, vol. 1, 325.

64. Hagiwara, *Hono'o no kiitoshō*, 192–93.

65. The fire on 12 November 1861 likely destroyed his mansion, but if it did not destroy Nakaiya's store, then the fire on 8 May 1862 would have. "That portion of the native town which escaped the late conflagration was this time the sufferer and almost wholly consumed. One side of the Ichome [first block] street is all that is left of the business town that has not

within a short time been consumed." Nakaiya's store was on the fourth block (*yonchōme*). Hall, *Japan through American Eyes*, 382, 423.

Chapter Four

Bakumatsu Japan's Trade and Yokohama's Place in That Trade

Today the image of Yokohama is of a prosperous, open, technologically advanced international port city. As such, historians tend to project this image onto the past, showcasing the bright and colorful Yokohama paintings, the foreign quarters, and the newly built city rising out of a former fishing village.[1] However, in the first few years after its opening in 1859, its prosperity was not guaranteed and it was not necessarily safe for foreigners. The shogunate wanted an open city, but a city under its control. When Nakaiya Jūbei tried to defy its terms of limiting the early trade, the officials went after him and his business. Also during these early years, there were nineteen incidents specifically targeting foreigners in Japan and two battles fought by domains against Westerners (Satsuma 1863 and Chōshū 1864). In the Edo-Yokohama region alone, *jōi* (antiforeign) activists killed eleven people, including one Japanese translator working for the British.[2]

Aside from this reality of Yokohama as a violent place, Yokohama was also a town filled with hustlers. Fraud was rampant. Higuchi Tadasuke, who worked for a French merchant by the name of Paruman,[3] recalled that Japanese merchants added lime to the raw silk and tried to increase its weight because Paruman would not bother to check.[4] Francis Hall wrote of his friend Dr. Duane Simmons's experience in early Yokohama. Apparently Dr. Simmons purchased a golden statuette from a Japanese merchant, only to discover later that it was bronze.[5] Hall also noted a case where a Japanese merchant disappeared after owing $8,000 and $3,000 to two Western merchants.[6]

Western cheaters also filled the port. Kōshūya Chūemon complained in a letter to his son, dated Ansei 6/8/12 (8 September 1859), that a British merchant, J. Barber, refused to pay and that he had to go to court to settle the dispute. Even in Hall's journal, two Japanese merchants walked up to Hall and "K" and demanded that "K" pay them. "K" first ignored them, then beat them in the middle of the street.[7] And, of course, sometimes unscrupulous individuals worked together regardless of race or ethnicity. Fujie Akifusa recalled that a British merchant Barber and a Japanese sake dealer Izumiya Toku[8] colluded to steal 3,000 *ryō* (gold coins) worth of raw silk from Tezuka Seigorō.[9]

Rutherford Alcock, the British representative to Japan, called the Western merchants in China and Japan the "scum of Europe."[10] Protected by extraterritoriality, Western merchants could commit wrongs against the local population with impunity. Japanese merchants, for their part, could always escape beyond the reach of the Western merchants by simply leaving Yokohama. Thus in this new port where xenophobic violence stalked in the shadows, merchants from both sides cheated each other. In a world in which there was no functional courts, guilds or mercantile associations were absolutely necessary. The shogunate had discovered this when Abe Masahiro reversed the Tempō Reforms' decree disbanding guilds. The rampant fraud during the *bakumatsu* (late Edo, 1853–1868) period also proved this point. Knowing this, it was a surprise that Yokohama would succeed.

So why did commerce take off? Yokohama was dangerous and many people, both Japanese and Western, were lying and cheating. The answers are desperation and greed. The European silk industry was suffering from the collapse of its raw silk supply. The silkworm disease called pebrine had almost wiped out European silkworms in the mid-nineteenth century. Europe was desperate to import raw silk for the survival of its silk industry.

BAKUMATSU JAPAN'S TRADE IN A GLOBAL CONTEXT

In the fourteenth and fifteenth centuries, Italian city-states and Lyon, France, began producing European silk to substitute for expensive silk imported from China and the Levant. By the seventeenth century, Europe was producing silk cloth from domestic supplies of raw silk and imported raw silk. Raw silk imports chiefly came from Persia. By the eighteenth century Persia had been replaced by Bengal, India.[11] In fact, Bengal became a great supplier of all types of Asian goods from cotton cloth to raw silk for Europe. Thus it was not exactly a surprise that the British East India Company conquered Bengal after 1757. By the early nineteenth century Bengal had been transformed by the British East India Company and lost its ability to supply enough raw silk to Europe.[12] Instead, under company rule, Bengal after 1773 became the chief producer of opium for export to China. And from China, the British would import their raw silk along with their tea. As the Industrial Revolution began in Britain, the British East India Company began to export factory-made cotton cloth to India, thereby creating an Asian triangular trade.[13] Thus by the early nineteenth century, Europeans had only two main suppliers of raw silk: one was the domestic silk industry in Italy and France, and the other was the silk industry in China.

Incredibly, even as pebrine was destroying the European silk industry, the British and French attacked their main foreign raw silk supplier and fought a second war against Qing China from 1856 to 1860 to sell more opium. In effect they had cut themselves off from their only raw silk supplier to sell more drugs. To make matters worse, a Christian-inspired rebellion called the Taiping Rebellion (1851–1864) took hold in opium-ravaged southern China and devastated the silk-producing regions in China during this period. So even if the British and French did not start the Arrow War, there was less raw silk to be exported in the first place.

This explains why, in the mid-nineteenth century, the European silk industry was in a serious crisis. The Middle Eastern suppliers had stopped producing raw silk for export to Europe, the British East India Company effectively destroyed the Bengali silk industry in India, and the British and French cut themselves off from the Chinese silk supply in order to sell more opium to China. With pebrine virtually wiping out the domestic raw silk industry in Europe and with no foreign supplier of raw silk (at least until the Chinese people recovered from the destruction of war and rebellion), European merchants had no choice but to get raw silk from newly opened Japan. That is why, despite the danger, fraud, and cheating, Western merchants bought raw silk from Japanese merchants in huge quantities after Japan opened for trade in 1859. Desperation drove Western merchants to buy the raw silk at much higher prices than Japanese domestic silk weavers, raising the price of raw silk at Yokohama. Greed motivated Japanese merchants to break limitations the shogunate tried to impose on them. After understanding this desperation and greed, the success in Yokohama seems unsurprising. And so the question turns to how.

As a historical possibility, the Japan trade could have been part of the Asian triangular trade (1770s–1910s) forged by the British during the late eighteenth century. In this system, Britain sold its cotton manufactures to India, then colonial India's opium to China, and finally bought Chinese tea and silk for consumption in Britain.

This triangle trade proved to be an enormously profitable enterprise in which the Indian colonial government remitted enough money to Britain to underwrite many of its government services. The system emerged after attempts to sell British textile manufactures to China failed, while British imports of tea and raw silk continued unabated. In fact, for many, opium was seen as an evil but necessary first step to opening the Chinese market to foreign goods. Ultimately, the British hoped that the proper export product, textiles, would supplant opium once the Chinese were used to buying foreign products. Western diplomats and merchants therefore expected Japanese merchants to sell silk, tea, and some copper and in return to purchase textile manufactures or opium.[14]

As a side note, this Asian triangular trade ended the more famous Atlantic triangular trade (1520s–1830s). The Atlantic triangular trade shipped European goods such as guns and Indian cotton cloths (calico) to Africa, then African slaves to the Americas, and finally sugar and silver from the Americas to Europe. As Andre G. Frank and Prasannan Parthasarathi point out, the bulk of this silver was used to buy Asian goods such as Indian calico and Chinese tea and silk.[15] In the eighteenth century, the British East India Company used silver to buy Indian calico from India, then the Royal African Company and private British merchants reexported that calico to buy African slaves and finally sold the slaves in the Spanish colonies of the Americas for the Spanish American silver. The American silver was then used to buy Indian calico to restart the cycle and to buy Chinese tea and silk for consumption. Mercantilist Britain was not happy about this silver drain and encouraged the import substitution of cotton cloth and silk. This leads us to the familiar story of the industrial revolution in Britain.

However, this story of the Atlantic triangular trade and the industrial revolution should not end here. This story should connect to the Asian triangular trade. In other words, once we recognize that the need for American silver (to buy Asian goods) was the systemic reason for conducting the Atlantic triangular trade, then the industrial revolution and the opium trade obviates the structural need for the American silver.

Today the industrial revolution is more famous for its steam engine, but we must not forget that the industrial revolution was also about manufacturing cotton cloth in Britain. This factory-made cotton cloth was supposed to prevent the flow of Indian calico into Britain and prevent the drain of silver to India. For this to succeed, the British conquest of India, starting with Bengal in 1757, was absolutely essential. Conquered India had no choice but to accept low tariffs for imported British factory-made cotton cloth, while suffering a total ban on calico entering Britain in the eighteenth century and an internal tariff of 15 percent.[16] By the nineteenth century, the British cotton cloth industry dominated not only India, but also the globe.

The opium trade was also dependent on the conquest of India. In conquered Bengal, the British East India Company created an opium monopoly and controlled the production of opium in India. This opium from Bengal was used to buy Chinese goods through the "country traders," and the aforementioned Asian triangular trade emerged. Finally, Britain no longer needed American silver. Indian calico was replaced by British cotton cloth, and Chinese goods could be bought with opium. This is the structural reason why the anti–slave trade movement suddenly became powerful in early-nineteenth-century Britain. Britain, formerly the largest slave trader, became the suppressor of the Atlantic slave trade because it no longer needed American silver coming from selling slaves to the Spanish colonies. Ironically, now that Britain was committed to banning the slave trade and outlawed slavery itself in 1833, when the Qing dynasty demanded to end the import of opium to China in 1839, Britain had no choice but to fight the Opium War to ensure the flow of opium. The flow of trade goods tells a global history that connects East Asia, South Asia, Africa, Europe, and the Americas.[17]

Two things transpired to make *bakumatsu* Japan's trade between 1859 and 1868 different from the Asian triangular trade. First, the opium trade was banned thanks to Townsend Harris and Iwase Tadanari's efforts. The illegality did not stop some unscrupulous merchants from attempting to smuggle opium into Japan, as the Hartley case among others shows.[18] Compared to China, though, Western governments and merchants perceived Japan as such a minor market that efforts to force Japan to accept opium never gained ground. Second, the Japanese bought textiles, though in much smaller amounts than its silk and tea exports. Because the absolute size of the Japanese market was small, no major concerns were aroused by the trade imbalance at the time. In short, the Japan trade in its early years was what the China trade was supposed to look like: an arrangement European in orientation involving the exchange of raw consumer goods, namely raw silk and tea, for mass-produced textiles and other manufactured goods.

The results from the first few years of trade confirmed these expectations with a few interesting details that reflected the global economic situation. Records from 1859 are partial (the port opened on 1 July 1859) but the records from 1860 to 1867 in *Yokohama shishi* (*History of the City of Yokohama*), compiled from the British foreign service records, appear in tables 4.1 and 4.2.

Note the dominance of raw silk as a trade item during these years. As a ratio of exports, raw silk alone was worth two thirds of the total exports during the first two years, then in 1862, 1863, and 1865 it increased to more than 80 percent. Even at its lowest ratio, raw silk was worth more than half of the exports in 1867. Aside from raw silk, the other major export items were tea, copper, silkworm cocoons, and eggs. Overall, the items exported from Japan were primary or semi-manufactured goods, whereas imports to Japan were mainly manufactured goods. This is a pattern seen in developing countries today. At first glance the trade seems to be in favor of exports, for the balance of trade is consistently in favor of Japan until 1867. However, there is reason to believe that the situation may not have been quite as export dominated. As British consul F. Howard Vyse suspected, arms sales hidden from the import transactions were substantial.[19] The steep increase in the import of metals and the purchase of ships and guns point to the shogunate and domains readying themselves for war. The sudden increase in the imports of daily items, foods, and medicine from $776,837 (20.99 percent of total) in 1863 to $4,295,448 (28.81 percent) in 1867 might suggest a flourishing foreign settlement that could now afford to import items for daily use but is more likely the result of classifying weapons sold to anti-shogunal forces under the "miscellaneous" category.[20]

The Japanese silk industry was "lucky." The Japanese silk industry entered the global market at a time when there was an acute global shortage of raw silk. Thus the exports of these primary products covered the costs of imported manufactured items and weapons. But this was not all luck. Because Japan succeeded in import substitution of silk in the eighteenth century, as explained in the introduction and chapter 1, Japan could produce raw silk and supply the West. The fact that the Yokohama raw silk market traded at between 40 and 70 percent of the Lyon or London market prices also proved irresistible to merchants, both domestic and foreign.[21] Raw silk flowed from Yokohama to Europe.

POLITICAL AND ECONOMIC RESPONSES TO *BAKUMATSU* JAPAN'S TRADE

The consequences of raw silk flowing out of Japan were multifaceted. Traditional treasury officials of the shogunate were alarmed at this outflow. *Jōi* radicals were opposed to foreign trade itself and attacked the foreigners in the early years of trade. And foreigners responded to the violence with violence.

An internal shogunal report records that domestic silk consumption decreased despite an increase in production. This eventually led to the shogunate in 1864 specifically targeting raw silk and limiting its export in order to protect the domestic silk cloth industry. As seen in chapter 3, Nakaiya Jūbei was ruined, and temporarily the sale of raw silk declined and the price of raw silk skyrocketed in Yokohama. To further add to the contingency, the success resulted partly because of the xenophobic attacks—attacks that the *bakufu* wanted to avoid. Digging a canal to turn Yokohama into an artificial island not only isolated the foreigners, but also protected them from possible attacks.

In 1861 and 1862 samurai and *rōnin* killed Henry Heusken, an American translator, attacked the British legation twice, and killed a British subject, Charles Richardson, for riding into the lord of Satsuma's father's entourage. These attacks raised fears of foreigners retaliating from the sea, which came true later at Satsuma and Chōshū. When the xenophobic imperial court ordered the shogunate to close the port of Yokohama by 1863/5/10 (25 June 1863), fears that antiforeign samurai would attack Yokohama arose.

Table 4.1. Exports in Mexican Dollars

	Total	*Raw Silk*	*Cocoon*	*Silkworm Eggs*	*Tea*	*Copper*	*Raw Cotton*	*Misc.*
1860	3,954,299	2,594,563			308,452	209,248		842,036
1861	2,682,952	1,831,935			448,437	95,815		306,765
1862	6,305,128	5,422,372			567,080	77,588		238,088
1863	10,554,022	8,824,050			541,176		933,940	254,856
1864	8,997,484	6,162,240	24,100	200,000	465,324		1,792,000	353,820
1865	17,467,728	14,611,500	178,160	660,160	1,777,440		58,180	182,288
1866		7,035,750			1,502,100			
1867	9,708,907	5,214,750		2,214,468	1,618,230			661,459

Source: Yokohama-shi (ed.), *Yokohama shishi*: vol. 2 (Yokohama: Yūrindō, 1959), 370, 371, 372, 375, 505, 512, 516, 519. Henceforth abbreviated as YS, II. *Yokohama shishi: Shiryōhen*, vol. 2 is abbreviated as YS:S, II.

Table 4.2. Imports in Mexican Dollars

	Total	*Cottons*	*Woolens*	*Metals*	*Ships*	*Small Arms*	*Cotton Yarn*	*Misc.*
1860	945,714	499,376	373,641	11,472				61,225
1861	1,494,315	687,930	399,605	128,508	16,000		73,396	188,876
1862	3,074,231	595,142	548,671	1,190,880	497,300		128,609	113,629
1863	3,701,089	586,123	1,046,803	796,936	456,500	37,890		776,837
1864	5,553,594	1,714,429	1,621,789	530,504	110,000	120,475	756,120	700,277
1865	13,153,024	4,706,773	5,758,678	403,883	240,000	852,645	861,750	329,295
1866								
1867	14,908,785	3,771,667	3,490,877	134,679	400,000	1,473,669	1,342,445	4,295,448

Source: YS, II, 388, 391, 392, 393, 527, 530, 534, 537.

Caught between sea and land, Yokohama residents began to panic once they learned that Edward St. John Neale, the British acting representative (Rutherford Alcock was back in Britain), was also issuing ultimatums to the shogunate. He was demanding reparations for the attacks on the legation and for the death of Richardson. Francis Hall's journal shows how fear can quickly turn into panic and then quickly subside. On 6 April 1863 Neale issued his ultimatum, but there was no tension among the foreign community regarding it. The Japanese residents were unaware at first. On 26 April 1863 there was hope that a settlement would be reached, with residents euphoric. But once hope was dashed, the resurgent fear quickly morphed into a panic. By 1 May 1863, many Japanese residents were preparing to leave, and by 3 May, the flight had begun. Westerners could not flee and had to stay in Yokohama. Those who chose not to pay the workers for past wages (before the workers could flee) were attacked by their workers. By the morning of 6 May 1863 there was full-scale panic, with merchants selling whatever was left over at rock-bottom prices and laborers fleeing Yokohama. In the afternoon of the same day, the governor of Kanagawa intervened. He simply posted a notice that everyone should return to their jobs, and suddenly the panic subsided. By 11 May 1863 many Japanese began to return to their homes in Yokohama, but the atmosphere remained tense. It was clear that the shogunate had to decide. It could risk a foreign war and honor the imperial court's demands to close the port of Yokohama by 25 June 1863. Or the shogunate could ignore the imperial court, pay the reparations, and avert a foreign war, but in turn risk an internal uprising by xenophobic extremists.[22] Business could hardly go on as usual under these circumstances. Thus when the shogunate tried to

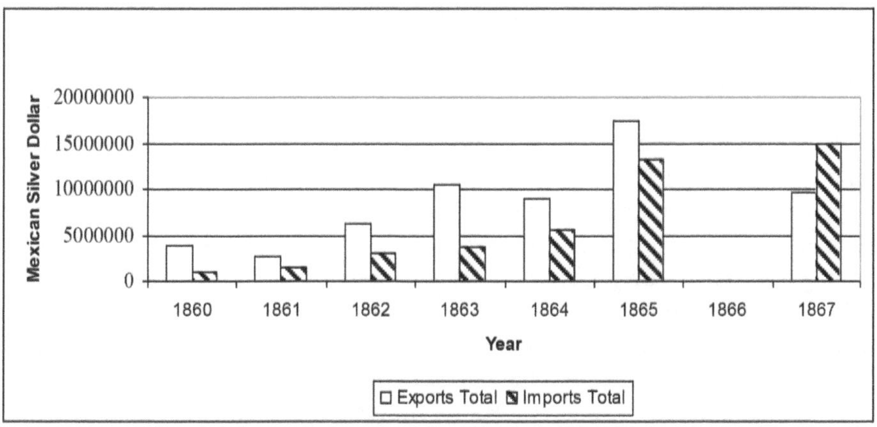

Figure 4.1. Total Imports and Exports Compiled from the data in tables 4.1 and 4.2. Data from 1866 was omitted since it was partial.

Table 4.3. Shogunal Report on Domestic Raw Silk Consumption and Exports

	Domestic Consumption	*Export*
1861	141,737 *ryō*	1,189,685 *ryō*
1862	96,480 *ryō*	3,523,500 *ryō*
1863	28,560 *ryō*	3,420,820 *ryō*

Source: YS, II, 396.

clamp down on the raw silk trade, it was not particularly difficult, and exports declined from 1863 to 1864.

As the clampdown on trade continued, a few merchants tried to circumvent the limit. Some smuggled raw silk in tea crates. Others hid raw silk in bales of cotton or hay. During 1863 and 1864 the merchants who stayed through the panic and managed to bring in raw silk to sell made enormous profits since the demand never went away. But it could also be dangerous. Xenophobic extremists targeted merchants, particularly raw silk merchants who sold to foreigners. They were extorted and sometimes even killed.[23] Eventually the raw silk merchants of Yokohama banded together and formed a mercantile association, which some call the precursor to the Yokohama *kiito kumiai* (raw silk union). These merchants then selected six men to be their leaders: Itoya Kansuke, Kobashiya Den'emon, Yoshimuraya Kōbei, Nakaiya Jūbei,[24] Yamatoya Sanzō, and Tokuemon (shop name unknown).[25] As seen in chapter 1, these merchants recognized the need for mercantile associations and formed them voluntarily. These Yokohama merchants fought back against extortions and against the limits of the sale of raw silk.

Simultaneously Western governments also began to protest against the trade limits. Most important, Western governments had international treaties on their side. After the shogunate began to route the five goods through Edo before sending them to Yokohama and to restrict Japanese merchants from selling more than 1,000 *kin* of raw silk in 1860, Western merchants immediately complained. Western representatives duly remonstrated with the shogunal government, but for a while other incidents took precedence.

Shogunal interference in foreign trade was an important issue, but it became secondary when the diplomats themselves were being attacked. Resolving the series of antiforeign attacks near Yokohama took until late 1863.[26] The shogunate after some delay agreed to pay reparations for the death of Richardson and the second attack on the British legation on 24 June 1863. Wisely the shogunate chose to ignore the imperial court and avert a war. They could now do so because the shogunate and Aizu domain with the help of Satsuma domain had finally eliminated the influence the xenophobic court nobles and Chōshū domain exerted over the imperial court. As Mito domain could not resolve the dispute between those who supported the shogun and those who supported the emperor, Chōshū domain became the champion of xenophobia and of keeping the country closed. In summer 1863 Chōshū domain closed the Shimonoseki Straits to foreign vessels. Thus when Chōshū attacked Western ships,[27] Western diplomats had another conflict to resolve on their hands. Meanwhile Satsuma domain complicated the situation. Although Satsuma supported the shogunate in ousting the anti-Western Chōshū, Satsuma refused to hand over the culprit who killed Richardson or pay reparations to the British.

Only after combat in Kagoshima Bay in August 1863 did Satsuma and Britain agree on terms. On 15 November 1863 the British accepted that Satsuma's leaders did not know where Richardson's killer was, and Satsuma agreed to pay reparations with money borrowed from the shogunate.[28] This ended, at least temporarily, the series of major diplomatic issues regarding antiforeign attacks near Yokohama. Thus in early 1864 the British acting representative, Edward St. John Neale, could now tackle the issue of restricted trade. He bluntly warned the shogunate that the obstruction of trade had to end.

> A long discussion took place, and at length Colonel Neale warned them that they were playing a dangerous game; for, he said "if you stop our trade, we will stop yours. If you stop our supplies we will stop yours." "By stopping our trade do you mean our import trade with foreigners?" was the quick enquiry. And they were politely given to understand, that this was far from the meaning. That what was intended to be stopped was their own internal commerce, and the transit from place to place of those commodities which were necessary for the people.[29]

Rutherford Alcock backed up Neale when he returned from Britain. Convincing other Western countries to join was easy as well. In spring 1864, the shogunate conceded the point to Alcock. Trade would resume without interference.

If the shogunate received a verbal warning, Chōshū received cannonballs for its actions in summer 1863. Seventeen ships from four navies—British (nine ships), Dutch (four ships), French (three ships), and American (one ship)—utterly destroyed the Chōshū forts in September 1864, and Chōshū domain had to concede as well. Ships sailed the Shimonoseki Straits without interference and trade resumed without interference later that year.[30] A wider war between Japan and the West instigated by xenophobic elements was narrowly avoided in 1863 and 1864. The rumors of war that restricted trade in Francis Hall's journal were not baseless.

Meanwhile in domestic politics, major changes had taken place. After Chōshū domain fired on foreign ships in summer 1863 and began its *jōi* activities in earnest, Aizu domain and Satsuma domain expelled Chōshū and their sympathizers from Kyoto. This was the moment when Abe Masahiro's grand vision of major lords united to protect the country came true. Often called *kōbu gattai*, or the unification of imperial and shogunal authorities, this plan was revived after Ii Naosuke's assassination and came to fruition. The shogun had married the emperor's sister, and the lord of Hitotsubashi (Tokugawa Yoshinobu, the son of Tokugawa Nariaki of Mito domain),[31] the leaders of Satsuma domain, Aizu domain, Tosa domain, and other major domains came together to form a committee to lead the country. However, this unity did not last one year. By spring 1864 the committee had disbanded.

When Chōshū domain tried to overturn its desperate situation by storming the imperial palace in summer 1864 and abducting the emperor, shogunal forces with help from Aizu and Satsuma domains repelled Chōshū. This was perhaps the last chance to restore that unity. But during winter 1864 and 1865, shogunal forces marched on Chōshū domain (after it had been bombarded by the four Western navies) and made its leaders at Hagi submit. Confident of its power, the shogunate completely shut out the outer lords, including Satsuma, from national politics, and Abe Masahiro's policy of working together with the major lords collapsed. The shogunate once again asserted the primacy of the Tokugawa clan. Unfortunately for Hotta Masayoshi, he had died in spring 1864 and did not live to see his old policy being revived by Tokugawa Yoshinobu, the son of his political enemy Nariaki.

Returning to the topic of trade, raw silk exports for 1865 became a record year, essentially adding the unexported amount from the previous year. Tea exports were unencumbered by shogunal meddling, so its wax in 1865 and then wane in 1866 and 1867 buttress the theory that Japanese raw silk and tea were substitutes for Chinese raw silk and tea. Once the Taiping Rebellion was over and calm returned to the Chinese coast, Chinese tea exports resumed and Japanese tea exports consequently declined. In the case of raw silk, as long as pebrine wreaked havoc on the European industry, there was room for Japanese exporters even after Chinese exports of raw silk resumed.

If Japanese exports of raw silk and tea owed to these international factors, what about other products? Two other products are worth mentioning. One is copper, the metal the shogunate used to coin its cash. Even before the opening of Yokohama, the shogunate had concerns about copper's excessive export to the Dutch. Fortunately for the government, the rise in copper prices inside Japan slowed its export, and Japan was successful in banning its export. The other product is cotton. The effects of the Civil War in the United States, particularly the North's embargo of Southern raw cotton, reverberated as far as Japan. In 1863 cotton prices skyrocketed and maintained this level in 1864, leading to a massive export of cotton. It was one of the more dramatic examples of Japan's integration into the global economy. Of course, to the dismay of many speculators and producers in Japan, the end of the Civil War also brought an end to the high price of raw cotton, dealing another lesson: a larger market did not eliminate volatility.

Thus in the 1860s, a string of historically contingent events—the Taiping Rebellion (and the Arrow War), the pebrine crisis in Europe, and the U.S. Civil War—raised the prices of Japanese export goods. This was extremely beneficial for Japan, since the long-term global trend in the prices of raw materials was then and continues to be down. Silk, despite its fluctuations, was no exception, with prices falling roughly by a half between the mid-nineteenth century and the early twentieth century.[32] As mentioned earlier, Japan was lucky in entering international trade at this time.

During the last ten years of the shogunate, exports outpaced the cost for the increasing imports of cotton goods and woolen manufactures. These products continued to be imported because they were either cheaper than domestic cotton products or because, in the case of woolens especially, they were a previously unknown novelty item. Eventually even the relatively small amount of cotton imports (as compared to the silk export) destroyed the native cotton growing industry in Japan, forcing the growers to produce something else. But the cotton textile industry survived and became the dominant industry in western Japan in the late nineteenth century.

Woolens probably owe its rise as fabric to Western-style uniforms. Japanese merchants in 1859 were intrigued but they were not inclined to buy woolens as it was too costly. They saw no civilian use for the product. As Francis Hall writes: "Woolen cloths I learned on inquiry they like, but they are unwilling to pay the price for them. They appreciate the comfort, but do not like to purchase it. I do not wonder at it, for their wadded and quilted gowns, which they wear in winter, are very comfortable, the material is cheap."[33] However, governments were not as sensitive to price. Moreover, they saw wool as a military necessity. In 1862 the shogunate began military reforms and created a new Western-style army and navy. Both organizations required wool uniforms and there was no domestic supply of wool. The sudden increase in the imports of wool, from $548,671 in 1862 to $1,046,803 in 1863 (almost double from the year before), probably reflects this turn of events. The continued increase to $5,758,678 in 1865 and $3,490,877 in 1867 probably reflects the fact that other domains such as Chōshū began to form Western-style units garbed in Western-style uniforms in the 1860s.

The civil war that lasted from 1868 to 1869 illustrated the transitioning military of Japan. Not only were the weapons in transition, from muskets to rifles and from muzzle loaders to breech loaders, but the clothing of the participants clearly shows that Japan was in flux. Often the soldiers wore Western-style clothes for ease of movement, but many still carried samurai swords. Westernized Tokugawa units wore a French-style uniform and thus share a look, but the various domain units usually did not have uniforms. Many of these men wore Western-style jackets and frockcoats; a few even wore Western-style trousers. But others wore Japanese military clothes with it and of course carried samurai swords. The tailors in Yokohama and Nagasaki were probably unwilling to make large numbers of intricate uniforms with piping and decorative buttons and thus sold simpler designs of "generic" Western clothes as uniforms to the samurai and the domains.

This story of high export prices, a large trade surplus, cotton and woolen imports, the import of military goods, and changing political policies shows how economics and politics were fused during this period. The shogunate's attempt to limit trade and the *jōi* activists' attempts to terminate trade may seem compatible, but because *jōi* activists, chiefly the Chōshū domain, also demanded a new political realignment with the imperial court at the center of politics, this was impossible. When the shogun—with the help of his relatives—suddenly excluded powerful outer domains, namely Satsuma domain, from national politics, a civil war became highly likely between those at the center of power (Tokugawa clan) and those who were excluded (Chōshū and Satsuma). On top of this internal political dynamics, the desires of Japanese merchants, Western merchants, and Western governments were united in demanding more trade. Japanese merchants resisted the limits the *bakufu* placed on trade. Western merchants demanded items that could not be had in China at the time. And Western governments insisted that Japan follow Western international norms in both trade and diplomacy.

REROUTING JAPANESE FOREIGN TRADE THROUGH YOKOHAMA

Since the previous section covered *bakumatsu* Japan's trade, at this point, we should return to the topic of Yokohama's place in this trade. For more than two hundred years, from the 1630s to the 1850s, Nagasaki was the center of Japanese foreign trade. Then suddenly Nakaiya Jūbei and the merchants of Yokohama managed to reroute Japanese foreign trade so that it passed through Yokohama primarily. This did not eliminate Nagasaki's role, but clearly Yokohama would take center stage in the new trade between Japan and the West.

Yokohama, Nagasaki, and Hakodate were the only three ports open to trade in the first ten years (Kobe and Niigata were delayed for political and infrastructural reasons). Of the three, Hakodate was too remote in the far north of Japan to be economically viable, although it did serve its expected function as a way station for refueling ships and harboring shipwrecked whalers and sailors. Nagasaki maintained its supremacy in its trade with China and other parts of Asia. But because the export of silk and tea to Europe dominated in the early years, Yokohama emerged as the clear winner in capturing the largest share of foreign trade.

Japanese merchants flocked to Yokohama once they realized these products sold at high prices. Even Iida, in the Shimoina valley, which was traditionally a supplier of raw silk to Kyoto, began to switch to selling silk in Yokohama.[34] This change in orientation from a domestic buyer to a foreign buyer probably accounts for the early success in selling Japanese raw silk. Of course, this change worried the treasury officials, for they were more concerned with domestic producers of silk cloth, who faced shortages in their supply of raw silk, and less concerned with the raw silk exporters. For Western merchants, Yokohama offered the availability of raw silk and tea, protection provided by British and French troops, and the services of their country's diplomats, since the port was the locale of foreign diplomatic missions called legations.

More than 90 percent of raw silk and silkworm eggs and more than 70 percent of tea were exported from Yokohama. Consequently, as silk and tea further dominated the export market, Yokohama's share of overall trade increased. Only in the imports of guns, ships, and raw cotton did Nagasaki rival or surpass Yokohama. Thus domains in western Japan were able to build a military that would eventually topple the Tokugawa shogunate, but they did not have the connections to sell their goods.[35]

As mentioned in the previous section, Japan's early international trade became embedded in the Asian triangular trade connecting Britain, India, and China. Japan, like China, exported raw materials to Britain and imported textiles from Britain and gradually raw cotton from India. This pattern, created in the last years of Tokugawa rule, lasted until the late 1870s. As late as 1877, France and Britain imported the bulk of Japan's raw silk (¥4,640,000 and ¥4,031,000 out of total of ¥9,626,931). Despite the emergence of Kobe and other cities as rival ports, Yokohama's position as the primary port for Japan remained undisputed. In 1877 Japanese exports amounted to ¥23,348,521, out of which ¥15,916,368 left from Yokohama, and Japanese imports came to ¥27,420,902, of which ¥21,028,788 entered via Yokohama.

Nevertheless, the Japan trade was distinctive in several important ways. It achieved what the British free traders had thought was the ideal solution for the British-Chinese trade, trading silk and tea for cotton and woolen manufactures. Japan, viewed as an unimportant market by the West, was able to keep opium out and import instead what the British wanted to export. In this twenty-year period, raw silk was the primary connection between Japan and the global economy. In 1877 raw silk exports alone amounted to ¥9,626,956 (¥9,626,931 from Yokohama), a still-extraordinary 41 percent of total exports.[36] Silk linked Yokohama and the Kantō hinterland with London, Lyon, and the rest of Europe.[37]

Table 4.4. Exports and Imports by Percentage Share of the Three Ports

		Yokohama	*Nagasaki*	*Hakodate*	*Total*
1860	Exports	83.89	12.73	3.38	100
	Imports	57.01	42.20	0.79	100
	Total trade	76.89	20.40	2.71	100
1861	Exports	70.85	26.42	2.73	100
	Imports	63.19	35.11	1.69	100
	Total trade	67.91	29.76	2.33	100
1862	Exports	79.63	18.19	2.19	100
	Imports	72.93	26.79	0.27	100
	Total trade	77.31	21.17	1.52	100
1863	Exports	86.45	11.37	2.18	100
	Imports	59.70	39.81	0.49	100
	Total trade	77.44	20.95	1.61	100
1864	Exports	85.10	10.97	3.92	100
	Imports	68.54	29.75	1.71	100
	Total trade	77.92	19.12	2.96	100
1865	Exports	94.47	3.03	2.50	100
	Imports	86.85	12.26	0.88	100
	Total trade	91.04	7.19	1.77	100
1866	Exports	84.85	12.01	3.14	100
	Imports	74.41	25.39	0.20	100
	Total trade	79.77	18.53	1.7	100
1867	Exports	80.08	14.65	5.27	100
	Imports	68.79	30.20	1.01	100
	Total trade	72.84	24.62	2.54	100

Source: YS, II, 558.

CONCLUSION

Analyzing Nakaiya Jūbei's career illuminates how the Tokugawa economic system operated in *bakumatsu* (late Edo) Japan. By the mid-nineteenth century, with the end of the monopoly guilds and the rise of the Kantō regional economy, there was room for private entrepreneurs. But to succeed in this economic environment, it was absolutely crucial to receive official patronage from the domains. And to survive, it was necessary to not go against the shogunate's economic goal: to protect the lives of samurai in Edo. In this economic sense, *bakumatsu* Japan was becoming an open economy but still had feudal restrictions.

The early trade also illustrates how the unequal treaties that the shogunate signed generated both intended and unintended consequences. In terms of intended consequences, Yokohama became the number one port for foreign trade as Iwase hoped. As treasury officials expected, there was confusion and adjustments in the early years of trade, and they mostly managed to resolve them. In terms of unintended consequences, forcing foreigners to stay near Yokohama gave room for Japanese merchants to develop links between various domains and locales in eastern Japan with foreign traders. And although no one realized how dominant raw silk would become for exports from Yokohama, because the product was raw silk, eastern Japan's emerging economic region within the Tokugawa economic system turned out to be able to supply the demand from a global economy.

We now turn to other merchants with a lower profile than Nakaiya Jūbei to understand how merchants who were not scrutinized by shogunal officials could help create a regional economic network in eastern Japan. They also form mercantile associations or suffer when faced with fraud and cheating. Their success helps Yokohama achieve its central position in the Japanese export industry; after all, Nakaiya had fallen from his place by 1861, so others had to carry on his business. Their combined achievement would in turn ensure that the hinterland supplying Yokohama would prosper. We examine the formation of this self-reinforcing feedback loop through the records of two merchants.

NOTES

1. The institution with the most material for the study of Yokohama is the Yokohama kaikō shiryōkan, or the Yokohama Archives of History. Not only does it have an excellent archive, but it has also published books that range from popular titles such as Yokohama kaikō shiryōkan (ed.), *Yokohama gaikokujin kyoryūchi, zusetsu* (Yokohama: Yūrindō, 1998) to more scholarly works such as Yokohama kaikō shiryōkan: Yokohama kyoryūchi kenkyūkai (ed.), *Yokohama kyoryūchi to ibunka kōryū: 19seiki kōhan no kokusai toshi wo yomu* (Tokyo: Yamakawa, 1996). In English, there are few books that treaty Yokohama specifically, but one classic is John R. Black, *Young Japan: Yokohama and Yedo*, 2 vols. (London: Trubner: 1881). A more recent scholarly work on treaty ports is James E. Hoare, *Japan's Treaty Ports and Foreign Settlements: The Uninvited Guests, 1859–1899* (Folkestone, Kent: Japan Library, 1994).

2. For more on *jōi* terrorism during the *bakumatsu* era (1859–1868), see Miyanaga Takashi, *Bakumatsu ijin sasshōroku* (Tokyo: Kadokawa, 1996).

3. Others recall his name as Baruman, so it could be Perman or Berman.

4. Suzuki Rinshō recalls that some added extra paper and white sand to increase the weight. Ishii Mitsutarō and Tōkairin Shizuo (eds.), *Yokohama dontaku*, vol. 1 (Yokohama Yūrindō, 1983), 179, 225–26.

5. Francis Hall, *Japan through American Eyes: The Journal of Francis Hall Kanagawa and Yokohama 1859–1866*, ed. F. G. Notehelfer (Princeton, NJ: Princeton University Press, 1992), 72.

6. Hall, *Japan through American Eyes*, 283.

7. The editor, F. G. Notehelfer, thinks K may have been William Keswick. It is unknown what happened after the beating. Hall, *Japan through American Eyes*, 343.

8. Rendered as Baruberu in Japanese, this was probably J. Barber, the same Baruberu in Kōshūya Chūemon's account. Izumiya Toku was probably Izumiya Jin'emon (according to the *Yokohama shōninroku*, the only sake dealer on 1 chōme (first block) was Izumiya Jin'emon). J. Barber was a "young Jardine's clerk" in Yokohama; in fall 1859 Jardine Matheson sent him back to China "where there would be more senior men on hand to supervise him." John McMaster, "Alcock and Harris: Foreign Diplomacy in Bakumatsu Japan," *Monumenta Nipponica* 22, no. 3 (1967), 328–29; n. 8.

9. Ishii and Tōkairin, *Yokohama dontaku*, vol. 1, 170.

10. Thomas Hansard, *Parliamentary Debates*, Third Series, vol. CLXXII, from 1 July 1863 to 28 July 1863 (London: Cornelius Buck, 1863), quoted by Earl Grey on 10 July 1863, 532. Alcock earned the enduring enmity of the foreign community in Yokohama for this comment. Who was worse: Japanese merchants or foreign merchants? Those who believed in *jōi*, naturally thought the Westerners could not be trusted and this distrust probably infected the Japanese merchants as well. The British and the Americans certainly thought the Japanese were worse. Ernest Satow, Alcock's secretary at the time and later the British representative to Japan and a Japanophile, wrote that "the balance of wrong-doing was greatly against the native, and the conviction that Japanese was a synonym for dishonest trader became so firmly seated in the minds of foreigners that it was impossible for any friendly feeling to exist." Ernest M. Satow, *A Diplomat in Japan* (Philadelphia, PA: J. B. Lippincott, 1921), 22–23.

11. Abdul Amir Amin, *British Interests in the Persian Gulf* (Leiden: E. J. Brill, 1967), 118–37.

12. Abhay Kumar Singh, *Modern World-System and Indian Proto-Industrialization: Bengal 1650–1800*, vol. 1 (New Delhi: Northern Book Centre, 2006), 507–90.

13. Katō Yūzō, *Igirisu to ajia: Kindaishi no genga* (Tokyo: Iwanami, 1980).

14. Katō, *Igirisu to ajia*, 106–58.

15. Andre G. Frank, *ReOrient: Global Economy in the Asian Age* (Berkeley: University of California Press, 1998), 126–30; Prasannan Parthasarathi, *Why Europe Grew Rich and Asia Did Not: Global Economic Divergence, 1600–1850* (Cambridge: Cambridge University Press, 2011), 22, 46–50.

16. Parthasarathi explains that the calico destined for reexportation could be imported to Britain. Unlike the conventional narrative of free-trade Britain, the actual story of cotton cloth manufacturing in Britain is a mercantilist one, heavily protected by the state. Parthasarathi, *Why Europe Grew Rich and Asia Did Not*, 99–114, 127–31, 252–53.

17. I came to this understanding after teaching world history, Western history, Japanese history, and Chinese history for ten years. As such I am grateful to Iona College and in particular to my students for giving me the opportunity to connect the dots and for pushing me to teach a coherent narrative that explains global history. Writing a coherent global history through the movement of trade goods is my next project.

18. The Hartley case began when a British merchant tried to smuggle opium into Japan and was stopped. This case eventually went in front of the British consular court of Yokohama, and the court ruled in favor of Japan, banning the opium trade as stipulated in the treaties. Richard T. Chang, *Justice of the Western Consular Courts in Nineteenth-Century Japan* (Westport, CT: Greenwood Press, 1984), 39–80.

19. YS, II, 393.

20. Although the British report does not note the hemorrhaging of gold, if that phenomenon is included, the primary Japanese export may have been gold in the early years.

21. YS, II, 380.

22. Both Japanese and foreign residents of Yokohama recognized this. Ishii and Tōkairin, *Yokohama dontaku*, vol. 1, 104–7; Hall, *Japan through American Eyes*, 470–77.

23. Ishii and Tōkairin, *Yokohama dontaku*, vol. 1, 222–23; vol. 2, 98–101. Two from Francis Hall's journal entries are 18 September 1863 and 23 September 1864. Hall, *Japan through American Eyes*, 506, 567.

24. Since the Nakaiya Jūbei that we know of, Kuroiwa Sennosuke, had died in 1861, this Nakaiya Jūbei seems to be an heir named Kakunosuke who inherited the business. Yokohama

kaikō shiryōkan (ed.), *Yokohama jinbutsuden: Rekishi of irodotta 50 nin* (Yokohama: Kanagawa shimbun, 1995), 130.

25. Hagiwara, *Hono'o no kiitoshō: Nakaiya Jūbei* (Yokohama: Yūrindō, 1988), 181; Yokohama kaikō shiryōkan (ed.), *Yoshimuraya K ō bei kankei shokan* (Yokohama: Yokohama kaikō shiryō fukyū kyōkai, 1989), 3.

26. In 1862 a samurai who was on duty to guard the British legation in Edo attacked them and killed two British soldiers. The European representatives had enough. They moved their offices from Edo to Yokohama. The British legation would stay in Yokohama until 1866. The fact that on 31 January 1863samurai from Chōshū domain burned down the British legation being built anew in Edo also prevented them from returning to Edo sooner. The American legation moved out of Edo in May 1863 during the war scare. At the 12 May 1863 meeting between the American residents of Yokohama and the American representative during this tense time, Robert Pruyn said that he was staying in Edo "till within an hour of the opening of the English guns on the city." This likely calmed the nerves of the American residents. In the end, an accidental fire, according to Pruyn, on 24 May 1863 forced the American diplomats to leave Edo and go to Yokohama. Hall claims that this was an intentional fire. The American legation stayed in Yokohama until 1874. Hall, *Japan through American Eyes*, 476–78.

27. This was in accordance with the imperial edict to expel the foreigners. Initially Chōshū leaders were sincere in their xenophobia and in their reverence for the emperor.

28. This money was never repaid.

29. John R. Black, *Young Japan: Yokohama and Yedo 1858–79*, vol. 1 (Tokyo: Oxford University Press, 1968; reprint of 1883 edition), 283.

30. Satow, *A Diplomat in Japan*, 184; Hall, *Japan through American Eyes*, 575.

31. Tokugawa Nariaki, lord of Mito domain, had many sons, and one of them became the adopted son of the Hitotsubashi family, a family that was eligible to produce a shogun after Shogun Yoshimune's reforms. Later Hitotsubashi Yoshinobu, Nariaki's son, became the last Tokugawa shogun and chiefly relied on Aizu domain and Kuwana domain to assert the shogun's power. Both Aizu and Kuwana domains were *shimpan*, relatives of the Tokugawa clan. Aizu was founded by the second shogun's bastard son, and the lord of Kuwana could trace his official lineage back to the eight shogun, Tokugawa Yoshimune. Biologically the lords of Aizu and Kuwana were brothers, their grandfather was a son of the sixth lord of Mito domain, making them second cousins of Tokugawa Yoshinobu.

32. Giovanni Federico, *An Economic History of the Silk Industry, 1830–1930* (Cambridge: Cambridge University Press, 1997), 33.

33. Hall, *Japan through American Eyes*, 94.

34. Iida's main products were paper crafts, and raw silk was only a minor product at the time. But the change in orientation is important. Kären Wigen, *The Making of a Japanese Periphery, 1750–1920* (Berkeley: University of California Press, 1995), 82–84, 140–46.

35. YS, II, 557–64.

36. Silkworm egg, ¥346, 998; cocoons, ¥260,395; silk noshi, silk floss, etc., ¥433,647. Silk products in total amounted to ¥10,667,996, comprising 46 percent of exports in value.

37. YS: S II, 6–7, 74–75.

Chapter Five

Yokohama and Its Hinterland

How did Japanese merchants take the opportunity to create a network inside Japan to sell more raw silk to Western merchants? This question is the central theme of chapter 5. Answering *how* gives full weight to answering *why* Japan was able to sell to Europe and temporarily fulfill China's role. To answer this question, this chapter follows the flow of raw silk being shipped inside Japan. Yoshimuraya Kōbei exemplified the merchants who worked with the domains and shipped large amounts of raw silk by corralling the producers. Kōshūya Chūemon is representative of merchants who worked without help from political authorities and built a raw silk exporting business from the ground up. All merchants combined both these elements, but some merchants could rely on the political authorities more than others.

YOSHIMURAYA KŌBEI: STARTING A BUSINESS IN THE SILK TRADE

In 1836 Yoshida Kōbei[1] was born the eldest son of a wealthy peasant and pawnshop owner of Ōmama town on the eastern edge of today's Gunma prefecture. At the time this town was part of Maebashi domain. His grandfather was the neighboring village's headman who also operated a pawnshop and a brewery, but because his father was the second son, he had had to leave the village and start his own pawnshop. In his late teens Kōbei started to buy and sell silkworm cocoons, probably using some of his family's wealth as seed money. By 1855 family records indicate that he bought silkworm cocoons from merchants in nearby Numata and Kiryū then sold them to local peasants who turned the cocoons into raw silk. This raw silk would in turn be shipped to Ashikaga, across the Gunma border in today's Tochigi prefecture, or shipped back to Kiryū and then woven into silk cloth. As part of his father's business, Kōbei would also venture into Edo to sell rice and charcoal.

Kōbei had no way of knowing this, but his upbringing had prepared him well for the upcoming opening of Japan. On Ansei 6/9/28 (23 October 1859), Kōbei went to Yokohama to sell raw silk for the first time. The twenty-three year old arrived in Yokohama only four months after its opening. It must have been exciting and profitable, for the young man immediately began to engage in this trade on the order of hundreds of *ryō*.

Initially he bought raw silk from producers near his home and sold to Japanese merchants in Yokohama (such as Nakaiya Jūbei) who in turn would sell the raw silk to foreigners. By 1860 Kōbei and his friends went further east to modern-day Fukushima prefecture to buy even more raw silk. According to a letter sent from Harimichi, today's Nihonmatsu, Fukushima, his partners begged for at least 600 *ryō* to purchase the raw silk there.[2]

This was risky business because to get that 600 *ryō*, Kōbei had to borrow 500 *ryō* from his friends, neighbors, and relatives.[3] But Kōbei also had his father as a very important backer. In 1860 and 1861, he and his father spent 1,831 *ryō* on silk, while his father's pawnshop, technically the main business, lent out only 570 *ryō* during the same period. From 1862 to 1864, Kōbei and his father spent another 1,664 *ryō* to buy raw silk. Because of the large price differential between Yokohama and the silk-producing regions of eastern Japan at this time, this risky investment paid off handsomely. In 1862 Kōbei's father received massive returns[4] and began to lend larger sums than ever before: 1,845 *ryō* in 1862, 3,225 *ryō* in 1863, and more than 5,097 *ryō* in 1864.[5]

By 1862 Yoshida Kōbei bought the rights to a store in Yokohama called Yoshimuraya (on the fourth block of Bentendōri's north side) behind Nakaiya Jūbei's store (on the fourth block of Ōdōri's south side)[6] and became Yoshimuraya Kōbei. Kōbei no longer required hundreds of *ryō* from his father, reducing aid from his father to 35 *ryō* in 1862, 15 *ryō* in 1863, and 45 *ryō* in 1864, thereafter borrowing nothing.[7] Thus Yoshimuraya gained his early position though the help of his friends, former neighbors in Gunma, relatives, and his father. The shared investment early on gave him access to abundant capital and an abundant return.

MAEBASHI DOMAIN: SETTING UP A DOMAIN MONOPOLY

In the meantime, Maebashi domain authorities also realized that raw silk was one of the major export goods. After grappling with a long history of failures, the domain was not about to fail again. Maebashi domain[8] was a prosperous domain in the seventeenth century. The Sakai clan governed this domain of 150,000 *koku* during this prosperous century. But faced with repeated floods of the Tone River and compounded with domain mismanagement, the domain became bankrupt. Instead of restoring the domain, the Sakai clan petitioned the shogun to move to Himeji, in western Japan. When the clan departed in 1749, Lord Matsudaira Tomonori, a descendant of Ieyasu's second son, entered Maebashi domain as the new *daimyō*. He tried to fix the problems, but the main castle was too damaged from the floods, and he decided to move his headquarters to Kawagoe in 1767. This split his domain between the 75,000 *koku* Maebashi part and the 75,000 *koku* Kawagoe part, and it was the start of a series of disasters and failures for the Maebashi part.

The departure of Lord Matsudaira Tomonori and his samurai meant that the former castle town of Maebashi lost its best customers and the town declined. The town had failed to make a transition to a rural marketplace, unlike the silk market of Fujioka in Maebashi domain, and lost any chance to stop its decline. Nearby Mount Asama erupted in 1783, leading to crop failures and the disastrous Tenmei famine of 1784. By 1817, the castle town, which once had 4,700 households, had dwindled to 800 households. The Tempō famine of the 1830s, caused by unusually cold weather, further hammered the rural population. Thus from 1721 to 1846 in northern Kantō (modern-day Gunma, Tochigi, and Ibaraki prefectures), population declined by 27.9 percent, a major decline.[9] A domain report in 1838 documented that more than twelve hundred people—a quarter of the urban population—left the city of Maebashi and more than nineteen thousand people deserted the countryside since 1767. By 1841 Maebashi city's population reached its nadir of 3,581 townspeople.

Thus when Matsudaira Naritsune, grandson of Tomonori, became the lord in 1816, he resolved to turn the situation around. First, the domain authorities borrowed more money to start a fund to aid the poor in 1820. By 1828 they collected 3,131 *ryō*: more than 2,000 *ryō* came from wealthy peasants—some giving willingly and other not—the rest came from the domain treasury. The interest the fund collected was spent on the poor, helping those fleeing from other domains even worse off, aid for childbirth, a five-year stipend for raising children, and also helping people with major expenditures such as housing, roofing, transportation, fertilizer, and wedding costs. By 1831 a new plan to control the Tone River's floods and to prepare for famines was enacted. The Tempō famine of the 1830s devastated the domain again and bankrupted the fund started in 1820, but this time, the famine killed far less than in the Tenmei famine.

By the 1840s, various policies finally began to bear fruit and the population began to rise. It was in this atmosphere of recovery that Naritsune ordered Yasuoka Reinan, the domain's Confucian scholar (and Nakaiya Jūbei's maternal grandfather), to edit *Nihon gaishi* written by Rai Sanyō. In 1848 through a small tax on raw silk, the domain began another fund to stop infanticide and help child rearing. By the time Lord Matsudaira Naritsune died in 1850, things were finally turning around.[10]

The domain's attitude toward the opening of Yokohama and Yoshimuraya Kōbei's success must be understood from this long-term perspective of failures and nascent success. The domain authorities now knew that it was vitally important to harness this wealth and prevent another period of long economic decline.

Therefore the domain decided to intervene actively in the export business. After the *bakufu* declared that five goods (non-rice grains, wax, silk cloth, clear rapeseed oil, and raw silk) must pass through Edo on 1860/Intercalary 3/19 (9 May 1860), the domain immediately issued orders to comply.[11] Then in 1860/12 it issued an edict to merchants and producers within the domain to send all silk to the domain warehouse in Edo. This is the moment when the domain authorities decided to establish a domain monopoly on raw silk. At the domain warehouse in Edo, raw silk would be sorted between domestic use and for export at Yokohama. However, many merchants ignored the decree, so the domain tried to enlist the wealthy merchants to voluntarily help collect the raw silk in Maebashi before sending to Edo 1861/1. When this was ignored, in 1861/5 the domain decreed that all raw silk must be sent to the domain warehouse in Maebashi first. From there, it shipped the raw silk to Yokohama.[12]

By 1862/5/3 (31 May 1862), the domain authorized Yoshimuraya and five other merchants (Yoshimuraya, Enshūya Mosuke, Nozawaya Sōbei, Ōhashiya Sanjirō, and Nagayoshiya Tomenosuke in May; Umiya Kujihira was added in November[13]), to be domain representatives with monopoly rights to sell raw silks produced in Maebashi domain at Yokohama. The authorities chose these merchants because they were perceived to have the expertise necessary in dealing with foreign merchants and they were large enough to offer lower fees for shipping the silk from Maebashi to Yokohama. With this edict, Yoshimuraya and the other merchants controlled more than several hundred thousand *kin* (1 *kin* is equal to 600 grams or 1.32 lbs.) of Maebashi domain's raw silk.[14] Hence from 1862 to 1869 Yoshimuraya Kōbei maintained his position by becoming Maebashi domain's mercantile representative in Yokohama and earned a stable income from handling fees rather than through the purchase and sale of raw silk.[15] This was the secret behind Kōbei's independence from his father.

The shogunal policy of routing five goods through Edo and limiting the volume of sale would collapse by 1864. Japanese merchants and Western merchants disliked the restrictions on the volume of sale and responded by smuggling. Western diplomats resented the idea that the shogun would interfere so bluntly in "free trade" by limiting the volume of silk sales, and in the face of Western demands, such as by British acting representative Edward St. John Neale, the shogunate had to stop its interference.

However, far inland in Maebashi, the unequal treaties signed between the *bakufu* and the Western powers benefitted the domain authorities. According to the treaty provisions, ordinary Westerners could not venture beyond twenty-five miles (forty kilometers) of the treaty ports, and because Western diplomats were busy dealing with political affairs, Westerners could not know that some domains were beginning to intervene in the raw silk trade to benefit themselves. Moreover, this control the Maebashi domain authorities imposed on raw silk exported from its territory proved to be beneficial for the producers of raw silk in the domain. The domain encouraged many to produce more raw silk and ensured that the quality of the raw silk exported from Maebashi would not be compromised by unethical behavior.[16] Domain monopoly did limit other merchants from becoming raw silk merchants in Maebashi, but in a time when fraud was rampant and guilds nonexistent, the monopoly increased the quantity while ensuring the quality of Japanese silk.

YOSHIMURAYA KŌBEI: RUNNING A BUSINESS AS A DOMAIN REPRESENTATIVE

In 1862 Yoshimuraya and five other merchants became the officially recognized purveyors of Maebashi domain raw silk. Until 1869 they transported a massive quantity from Maebashi to Yokohama, on the order of hundreds of thousands of *kin*. This volume of trade could and did fundamentally alter the type of trade Yoshimuraya engaged in. Political connections also created another major opportunity for him through preferential loans.

As stipulated in the domain edict, the domain did not expect Yoshimuraya to buy the raw silk from the producers, but instead to charge a handling fee for the shipment and sale of raw silk to foreigners. The domain tried to reserve the profit from the sale of raw silk to the producers of raw silk. At a time when Western merchants were buying Japanese raw silk at extremely high prices, this arrangement benefitted the peasants and dovetailed with the domain policy of protecting its inhabitants. After the disasters of the Tenmei and Tempō famines, the number one priority of the domain was to protect and increase the peasant population.

For the six merchants engaged in this trade, Nishikawa calculates that together they could amass 15,750 *ryō* from handling fees alone (assuming the production of 300,000 *kin*—180,000 kilograms—of raw silk in Maebashi domain, with each *kin* of silk selling for 3.5 *ryō* [1862 prices], at a 1.5 percent handling fee).[17] A fortune of more than 2,500 *ryō* could fall into the hands of each monopoly merchant every year through handling fees.

Did this mean that Yoshimuraya would now sit idly by and wait to pick up raw silk guaranteed to him? No, the seemingly insatiable foreign demand for silk and competition among the six merchants pushed Yoshimuraya to expand his business. Records from his father's pawnshop demonstrate that his father lent money to peasants in subsequent years so that those who did not cultivate silk before could begin by purchasing the initial materials necessary for raw silk production—silkworm eggs, mulberry leaves, spinning wheel, and so forth—and presumably covering other expenses between the start of production and the sale of raw silk.[18] Competing only against his colleagues, the five other merchants, and with plenty of capital available, Yoshimuraya expanded his business inside Maebashi domain through these loans.

With the high volatility in silk prices, transforming the core of the business into a shipping-and-handling operation promised stability in a highly risky market. Once converted to a commission-based business, only volume limited the merchant's profitability. As such, the more loans the merchant could provide to encourage new peasant producers into cultivating raw silk, the more the merchant stood to gain. Since the peasant producers who accepted these loans were contractually obligated to sell their products to the lending merchants—similar to the putting-out system—the risks to the merchants were relatively small. Whether raw silk prices were high or low, the merchant would gain from the commission in handling the volume. If silk prices were high, the producer could pay off the principal and the interest, providing extra income to the lending merchant while still making a profit. If prices were low, the producer might fall further into debt, almost guaranteeing that he would again need to borrow from the merchant, maintaining the volume of raw silk for the next cycle. By the next cycle, hopefully prices recovered so that the loans could be paid off. Throughout the process, the raw silk producer had a creditor who would keep the money flowing until the next sale.

In Yoshimuraya's case, initially his father's pawnshop acted as a bank lending out sums anywhere from 300 to 1,000 *ryō* to wealthy locals, who in turn bought the silk themselves or further lent out to individual peasant producers.[19] At a time when raw silk prices were high because Western merchants had no choice but to rely on Japanese raw silk, many peasants wanted to jump into the raw silk business. In other words, Yoshimuraya realized that what was limiting his business was actually the money he could lend to the potential producers of raw silk.

Yoshimuraya's collaboration with domain and *bakufu* authorities proved to be fruitful and perhaps essential for his long-term prospects in two respects. First, as stated above, the domain authorities provided Yoshimuraya with a captive market, allowing him to expand within Maebashi domain with little competition. Second, the shogunate eventually provided him with a large amount of money, freeing him from the capital constraints that he and his father faced.

The shogunate, as explained at the end of chapter 2, was initially not keen on the idea of expanding raw silk exports. The *bakufu* first tried to limit the volume of raw silk sales in 1860 to protect the domestic silk industry and to keep prices low for the residents of Edo. To demonstrate its resolve, the shogunate confiscated the property of the first merchant of Yokohama, Nakaiya Jūbei, when he defied it. Regardless, the shogunate's first attempt to control trade proved ineffective. Some merchants bribed officials in order to sell more. Others began to sell silkworm eggs, since eggs were not among the five items that had to be shipped to Edo first. Some domains complained quietly. Lastly, Western governments and merchants loudly protested the law. By 1864 the shogunate realized its failure to control the silk trade by decree.

As the *bakufu*'s grip over the country slipped away and the need for a punitive war against Chōshū domain rose, the lack of revenue continued to be a major problem. This forced the shogunate to examine new sources of revenue. As such, in 1866, the shogunate established the *Kiito sanshu aratame yakusho*, or the Office of Raw Silk and Silkworm Egg Inspection. This office allowed the *bakufu* to collect taxes more effectively. Instead of trying to control the sale by decree, the office now controlled the sale of silk products by regulation and banned all uninspected silk products from distribution. Designed to monitor and tax the flow of silk products, the domains collaborated with this edict (instead of fighting it) to ensure better control over the production of raw silk and silkworm eggs in their own territory. Furthermore, with this edict, the domains could legitimize the surcharges they had been collecting, for the shogunate and the domains agreed to split the inspection fees they would collect (3 percent of value for export items; 1.5 percent for domestic).[20] This meant that any silk products that had previously eluded domain control were now under much tighter regulation and more likely to be sold only to the merchants who represented the domains.

Thus by getting the domains on its side, the shogunate also indirectly got the merchants who were connected to the domains on its side. These merchants welcomed this new regulation as it increased the portion of raw silk that they could now control. Western governments could not complain about this office, as it did not block the volume of trade and its main goal was ostensibly to reduce the fraud that was rampant in the sale of raw silk.

The shogunate, the domains, and the merchants worked together to bring greater benefits to all of them. But the nature of the Tokugawa economy meant that that the interests of the samurai came first. Shogunal changes in policy reflected the needs of the *bakufu* and not the needs of the producers or merchants. In the case of Maebashi domain, the samurai authorities learned that their interests coincided with the interests of the peasantry, so they created a cartel that would work for the domain government and the peasant producers while mercilessly cutting out the other smaller merchants.

Yoshimuraya Kōbei was one of those merchants favored by the authorities, so he would benefit enormously at this time. But what would happen once the domain realized that it did not need the monopoly merchants to control the flow of raw silk? That is a question that is addressed later.

For now, Yoshimuraya Kōbei would continue to cement his position as a favored merchant. Starting in 1867, the House of Mitsui and a consortium of eight other Yokohama merchants, including Yoshimuraya Kōbei, became the representative merchants for the shogunate. As part of this deal, the *bakufu* used the income from the import and export tariffs to loan large sums of money to these merchants. The shogunate collateralized the loans with the raw silk it gathered. In the case of default by any one of them, the consortium (which slowly increased in number) agreed to repay the full amount to the shogunate. With this loan, the *bakufu* could now collect interest and the merchants in turn had a major source of capital, capital that was lent to new peasant producers in order to encourage further production of raw silk. The case of Nozawaya is exemplary.[21] Mogi Sōbei (1827–1894), the largest and perhaps the most famous Yokohama silk merchant, ran Nozawaya after 1861. Initially Mogi borrowed 5,000 *ryō* from the shogunate at the rate of 1.25 percent per month. In two years, Mogi borrowed a total of at least 25,300 *ryō* and used that money to buy as much raw silk as possible. Like Nakaiya, Mogi's meteoric rise to the top of the Yokohama merchants owed heavily to shogunal favor.[22]

As for Yoshimuraya, by 1864 he was already independent of his father's capital. In fact, his father's loans hit their peak in 1865 at more than 8,119 *ryō* but thereafter declined rapidly. In 1866, his father lent him only 3,841 *ryō*,and by 1867 only 354 *ryō*. The last year his father acted as a business lender was in 1868, lending only 173 *ryō*; he returned to focus on the pawnshop business in 1869. This rapid decline of his father's loans seems to indicate that Yoshimuraya Kōbei availed himself of this golden opportunity to borrow from the shogunate instead. In other words, he became a smaller version of Nozawaya's Mogi Sōbei.[23]

Yoshimuraya's career from 1862 to 1869 demonstrates how working with domain and shogunal authorities was a mutually beneficial affair. The shogunate and domains got some control over the trade and a steady revenue stream, which made life as a merchant vastly easier in *bakumatsu* Japan. As long as Kōbei obeyed the authorities, he had only five other merchants to compete against, and later on, he could even borrow funds from the shogunate to expand his business. What of the merchants who were not as lucky? Merchants who did not have as much support from friends, neighbors, relatives, and parents? Merchants who did not strike it rich early and receive special favors from the political powers that be? We follow such a case with Kōshūya Chūemon.

BAKUMATSU ENTREPRENEURS: TEZUKA SEIGORŌ AND KŌSHŪYA CHŪEMON

Whereas Nakaiya, Yoshimuraya, and other domain representatives relied heavily on domain authorities to provide them with raw silk, Tezuka Seigorō, Kōshūya Chūemon, and other smaller scale merchants had to rely on other contacts. This task was not easy, as can be seen from Tezuka's career.

Fujie Akifusa, an old man interviewed in a Yokohama retrospective from 1907 to 1909, recalls a case of enterprising locals, Shibafu village's Tezuka Seigorō, Matsukiya Seiroku, and Hodaya Zenzō, opening shop. These three men pooled their resources and opened a shop called Shibaya Sanpachi, because they were from Shibafu village (Shibaya) and there were three (*san*) of them (Sanpachi). Since these men had no powerful backers, they worked with other "venture speculators"[24] from their area and built a small[25] but nice store with 30 *ryō* after the authorities instructed them to build a store that would not cheapen the image of the country. Because they were all locals without access to large capital, they did not have the luxury of gathering a variety of goods. Thus when Tezuka was in Edo seeking permission to open the store, he asked a wax merchant, who supposedly knew about the trade in Nagasaki, what foreigners liked to buy. The wax merchant answered: first wax, then silk, tea, and lacquerware. Tezuka bet on silk (wisely not on wax).

For someone with no background nor training in mercantile activity, Tezuka proved to be quite enterprising. He went to an Edo silk garment merchant whom he knew and asked for the merchant's help in contacting a dealer. With this dealer, Tezuka now had access to silk, but he did not know how much to charge for handling the goods. He decided to charge 1 percent, the standard surcharge for goods passing through his village. This small entrepreneur lacked cash, and when he could not afford to pay his share of the cost of building the 30 *ryō* store, he was ejected from the company, albeit given a tiny space from which to operate his business in Yokohama and thus eventually pay back his share. Fortunately, his wife was from present-day Yamanashi prefecture, and thus he acquired more raw silk from Yamanashi and Nagano and turned a small profit.

In a twist of fate, when the authorities stormed Nakaiya's store in 1861 to arrest him for "insolence,"[26] Tezuka's shop happened to be across the street. Consequently, he harbored the merchants who fled Nakaiya's store. Many of these raw silk merchants fleeing Nakaiya's store were from Kōzuke, Nakaiya's home province and a center of raw silk production. These fleeing merchants had travelled to Yokohama with their own merchandise, stayed at Nakaiya's mansion, and sold to Nakaiya or foreign merchants directly. Moreover, over the past two years Nakaiya had become one of the dominant silk merchants, at one point handling almost half of all silk product exports.

With all these merchants fleeing into his store and handling raw silk from them, Tezuka allegedly made more than 700 *ryō* during the next five or six months despite charging only 1 percent, according to Fujie, the narrator.[27] At one point, he was one of the largest merchants in Yokohama, but his business collapsed when he overreached. A British merchant, J. S. Barber, and a sake brewer, Izumiya, agreed to buy 100,000 *kin* of silk after receiving 3,000 *ryō* worth of silk as a sample from Tezuka. Though Tezuka knew he could not possibly gather 100,000 *kin* of silk, he thought that he would receive at least the 3,000 *ryō* for his sample. When Tezuka asked for the 3,000 *ryō*, they asked for the 100,000 *kin* of silk. Unable to gain headway, he hired a translator for 100 *ryō* per day and eventually lost the 3,000 *ryō* worth of silk and incurred further expenses. After losing money twice more in this volatile and virtually courtless market of extraterritorial Yokohama, Tezuka folded.[28]

Kōshūya Chūemon may have had a similar background as Tezuka Seigorō, but he was not as reckless, as evidenced from Kōshūya's records. These records are primarily letters Kōshūya Chūemon wrote to his eldest son, who remained in their home village in Kai province (also known as Kōshū, which is present-day Yamanashi prefecture). Many of the letters from his son to Chūemon do not survive, so one must infer the contents of these letters, but the partial record provides enough insight into the operations of his business, which lasted until 1873.

Kōshūya Chūemon came from one of the two families that provided the village headman. In Higashi aburagawa village, Kōshū, where most families (i.e., thirty families out of forty-two) owned less than 10 *koku* worth of land, owning slightly more than 34 *koku* placed his family among the wealthy. Families that owned between 10 and 30 *koku* numbered only five, while those with more than 30 *koku* numbered three, and another four families owned more than 50 *koku* worth of land. The family mainly produced food for itself with the important exception of cotton, which was its only cash crop. Compared to the capital available to Yoshimuraya's father, the pawnbroker, Kōshūya had virtually no capital. In 1859 before his trading venture made its full impact on his family's fortune, his total annual cash income was under 25 *ryō*, of which 13 *ryō* came from the sale of cotton.[29]

Nevertheless, like Tezuka Seigorō, Kōshūya Chūemon went to Edo in 1859/3 to gain permission from the shogunal authorities to open a store. After the officials shuffled him through three magistrates (the Edo, treasury, and foreign), he received a separate plot of land to build his store. This was unexpected. Initially he and other wealthy men from Higashi aburagawa and the neighboring village had hoped to open a 500 *tsubo* store together to sell products from their home to the foreigners and anyone else willing to buy them. Instead on 1859/3/14 (16 April 1859), the foreign magistrate allocated two 300 *tsubo* plots to him and to his main partner, instructing each to build their own individual store.[30] With an additional directive to build a store that would "not shame the country," Kōshūya and his group of eight Yamanashi villagers had to spend more money than expected to start their business.[31]

In the 1862 directory of Yokohama merchants, Chūemon listed his shop as occupying 102 *tsubo*, or approximately 3,700 square feet, on the southern side of the second stretch of Motomachi. He sublet the other 200 *tsubo* to other merchants and a Chinese resident, presumably a translator under his employment. Legally he owned the shop, but his younger son Naotarō operated it, for his official residence remained in Yamanashi. He records the list of products that he handled in detail, perhaps because Chūemon compiled this directory while he worked for the Yokohama merchants' association. When he first opened, his shop handled a variety of specialty products from Yamanashi, seaweed, dried goods, and raw silk. Later he sold silk clothing, tea, confectionaries, dried seafood, as well as imported foreign goods. By early 1860 he was dealing in lacquerware, medicines, and copper ware, by mid-1860 he also sold flour, and by late 1860 he sold charcoal, firewood, and paper. In early 1861 he traded in foreign foods, fresh vegetables, eggs, and salted fish. By mid-1861, he included cocoons and silkworm eggs, and by the year's end dried scallops and sea cucumbers as well. In early 1862 he sold lumber, wooden furniture, clothes (including laundry service and tailoring), and coal. By the time he was compiling this directory in summer 1862, he was dealing in pharmaceuticals, tobacco, paper, tea, dried goods, rough goods, cotton, raw silk, copper, and wax oil. Thus in three years Chūemon had dabbled in importing and exporting a wide variety of products, indirectly proving that he could not find a stable source of raw silk—which he had been selling since the opening of his store—and that he had to rely on any source of revenue.[32]

Surviving those early years to the point when he compiled the directory was an accomplishment in and of itself. After all, Nakaiya Jūbei had perished by 1861. Chūemon had discovered that what he initially planned to sell, local products such as dried grapes (raisins), cotton clothes, and tobacco, would either not sell or be difficult to acquire. In the days following the opening of Yokohama, he had to quell rumors circulating back home that business was bad and search for what might sell.[33] It was plainly obvious that raw silk sold well, but Chūemon chose to diversify and not overspecialize, as can be seen from the products that he handled by the time of the 1862 directory. Without a strong financial backer or a domain connection, many merchants probably found it difficult to obtain a large supply of raw silk. In fact, in examining the merchant directory one can see that diversification was the normal strategy of most shops at the time.[34] Furthermore, he was a novice and business in his first year proved to be grim. From the end of 1859 and the beginning of 1860, he was begging for more remittances from home to keep his business afloat.[35] Ishii Takashi, the editor of Kōshūya's letters, diagnosed the merchant's main problem as lack of capital. Though he may have been from a relatively wealthy peasant household, its annual cash income was not enough to support a capital-intensive business such as buying raw silk in bulk, à la Nakaiya Jūbei, especially after household expenditures were deducted.

KŌSHŪYA CHŪEMON: BECOMING A MERCHANT IN THE SHOGUN'S REALM

Before examining Kōshūya Chūemon's career in detail, we must sort out a number of important details. First, how did a merchant make money in *bakumatsu* Japan? Broadly speaking, there were two ways and Chūemon used both: charging a commission for each good shipped and arbitrage, buying low and selling high. Second, how were contracts enforced in *bakumatsu* Japan? Since the merchants could not rely on the courts and they had not formed a mercantile association until 1866, contracts could not be enforced, and instead people had to relying on other people's honesty. Third, how prevalent was the sericulture industry in Kai province (Kōshū)? Fortunately for him, sericulture in eastern Japan was beginning to emerge as an industry to serve the local markets so that Chūemon could eventually conduct his raw silk trade.

The preferred way Chūemon wanted to earn a living was through charging commissions for selling goods. In other words, he hoped to be the delivery service for various goods between Kōfu, the capital of his landlocked home province, and Yokohama.[36] Unfortunately for him, for this method to work, a merchant needed to move enough goods to live off the delivery commissions. As someone without prior experience as a merchant, his lack of contacts was a factor more limiting than lack of capital in establishing a business based on commissions.

Therefore, Chūemon had to turn to another way to earn a living: speculation. He had to buy a product cheaply at one location and sell it with a markup at another location. This was not his preferred method, as he himself admitted, but it was the only realistic way for him to make a living.[37] For example, during the American Civil War (1861–1865), global raw cotton prices were high because the North blockaded the South, a major exporter of raw cotton. Sensing his opportunity, on Bunkyū 3/10/5 (20 November 1863), Chūemon bought and transported raw cotton from Yamanashi at less than 18 *ryō* and sold it for more than 24 *ryō* in Yokohama. In that one transaction wherein he bought, transported, and sold the same product, he made a profit of more than 6 *ryō* (including transport costs). Unfortunately for him, he sold all his raw cotton at hand, and he wrote further in this letter. "I took all my cash at hand to Ichikawa first block's Matsudaya and begged him so that he would use the 20 *ryō* to arrange for Kōshū Tenjin's Nakajō Jihei to send 10 horse loads of cargo to me by the end of the month. The cost would be roughly 50 *ryō* with interest, but this money could definitely be repaid."[38]

Although relying on this kind of speculation might seem risky, the joining of the Kantō regional economy with the global economy temporarily created numerous opportunities in price differentials in everything from gold to raw silk to raw cotton to coal. Arbitrage between the global market, Yokohama prices, and the various marketplaces in the interior was the most common way that merchants (both Japanese and Western) made money during this period. Moreover, the fluctuating currency rates promised amplified profits (or losses). For novices like Kōshūya, speculation required few contacts and little capital to start. If he could predict the direction the market would go, then he could accumulate capital very quickly. In the meantime, he hoped to gain the contacts necessary to switch to a business where he charged commissions, a more stable business operation.[39]

Kōshūya Chūemon faced the problem of contract enforcement because the Tokugawa shogunate was not a capitalist regime. Although the shogun operated a government based on the rule of law (more or less), it did not commit itself to resolving civil disputes, particularly mercantile ones. As seen in earlier chapters, it was more interested in safeguarding the lives of the samurai residents of Edo. The growth, both in size and in the complexity, of the Tokugawa economy went beyond the *bakufu*'s expectations, and the explosive growth in lawsuits between merchants took a backseat to "more pressing" administrative issues. When civil lawsuits, particularly over debts and money (called *kanakuji* at the time), overwhelmed the courts in the early eighteenth century, the shogunate simply declared that it would not handle such disputes for the next ten years and that debtor and creditor should deal with each other to solve their problem (*aitai sumashirei*). This is why the guilds became important players in enforcing contracts, as explained by Okazaki Tetsuji at the end of chapter 2.

The *bakufu* made similar declarations of extreme laissez-faire over *kanakuji* in the late eighteenth and early nineteenth centuries. Furthermore, with the fragmented political landscape, civil disputes that crossed domain and status boundaries could potentially take years, if ever, to resolve. A merchant residing in shogunal territory—for example, Edo, Osaka, Yokohama, or Kōfu—suing a samurai of a distant domain—for example, Aizu, or Satsuma—could become a nightmare for the merchant. For example, in 1835 there was a samurai who accepted cotton shipments from an unguilded merchant to store the merchandise at his lord's mansion. Clearly this violated the monopoly rights of the cotton guild, and the guild took the samurai to court. But at court, the shogunal officials could only force the merchandise to be sold to a guild merchant. The samurai was not officially reprimanded. The shogunate could not directly intervene in the affairs of a domain, and thus the court could only pressure the samurai to write a letter promising not to do this in the future and not interfere in the affairs of the cotton guild.[40]

Under these circumstances, guilds that could enforce contract obligations (through threats not to do business with contract breakers in the future) were necessary.[41] But the Tempō Reforms had disbanded the guilds with monopoly power and the international raw silk trade was still so young that there were no mercantile associations yet. These circumstances explain the importance of the link Yoshimuraya Kōbei forged with Maebashi domain.

In the case of Kōshūya Chūemon, the possibility of cultivating ties with his local lord did not exist because Kai province (Kōshū) did not have a domain at the time. Kai province was shogunal territory governed by a deputy (*daikan*). This deputy was sent by the treasury department's rural administration section. Unlike a lord (*daimyō*), the deputy had few staff and could not micromanage local affairs. His main job was to collect taxes and maintain the peace. Unable to control events on the ground, there was no way for a deputy to force the peasants to send their silk products to one location inside Kōshū so that a few selected Kōshū merchants could benefit. Moreover, as a complete novice at trade, Chūemon had no special connections to the shogun or to his officials. Without the legal or extralegal infrastructure to support Chūemon and others like him, early trade could be harrowing, particularly if one was new at business.

Two cases are illustrative. In one case, Chūemon agreed to sell 80 *ryō* worth of silk to Barber[42] on behalf of a certain Hanbei and two others but the buyer would not pay. Because of this, Chūemon had to cancel his plans to return home for the Bon festival and petition the Kanagawa magistrate concerning the matter.[43] Though the results are not known from his subsequent letters, one can only imagine the difficulty if the case had gone to court, for Chūemon would have had to pay for the interpreters and navigate his way through an unfamiliar British legal system, and if he had lost, he would have had to go to Hong Kong to appeal.

The other case involved charcoal. By Man'en 1/11/5 (16 December 1860), Chūemon realized that charcoal could become quite a profitable business. In the town of Kawachi, six bales of charcoal cost only 200 *mon*, while in Yokohama, the Japanese residents paid 400 *mon* for three bales and the foreigners were buying at the rate of 700 *mon* per bale. This is because the cost of transport was 200 *mon* per bale from Kawachi to Yokohama, but even so, the foreigners were paying a very high price. It turns out that this was because the exchange rate was causing the effective price to change for the foreigners, thus one could potentially earn a fortune from this trade if the timing was correct in gauging the exchange rate.

Chūemon sent his younger son, Naotarō, to purchase large amounts of charcoal the next day. Moreover, if he was not require to pay immediately, he agreed to pay a higher price than the going rate and to pay interest for the credit. In a letter dated 12/3 to his elder son, Shōjirō, Chūemon expected four hundred to five hundred bales of charcoal to arrive within the year. However, when the charcoal did not arrive, he wondered if he had been tricked, so sent a clerk to investigate the matter.[44] The clerk reported that because he had not paid in time for the charcoal, the sellers had recalled it after it was halfway to Yokohama. Chūemon became incensed at this, for he had borrowed money for the venture at a high interest rate. Yokohama lenders charged an inordinately high interest rate (6 *ryō* per month for a loan of 30 *ryō*). Every day that the charcoal did not reach him, the interest rate away at his profits,[45] and his potential sales went down, because demand would inevitably diminish as winter neared its end. Furthermore, because Kawachi merchants had informed him that he would not need to pay them immediately, he had used the money he borrowed to pay for charcoal from Izu, planning to pay Kawachi with the profits from the sale of the Izu charcoal. As Chūemon himself stated, he tried to move "200 *ryō* worth of goods with 50 *ryō*." In that same report from the clerk, Chūemon was also informed that Naotarō had failed to meet the merchants from Kawachi and had frittered away time and money. With only 5 *ryō* left in Yokohama, he could only beg for a swift remittance of money from back home to prop up his business.[46]

In the end, the plan failed completely. Of course, with the payments completed and Chūemon's letters of apology on behalf of Naotarō sent, goods flowed again. Unfortunately, the charcoal began to arrive in 1861/2, and a total of fifteen hundred bales of charcoal finally arrived by summer, when prices were so low that he considered waiting until 1861/9 to sell them again. Sitting on top of bales and bales of charcoal, Chūemon turned his wrath upon Naotarō and disowned him. Only later in the year did he accept him back with the urging of Shōjirō and other family members and friends.[47]

During this debacle both Chūemon and the charcoal merchants from Kawachi most likely thought that they had been swindled. Chūemon wrote to this effect when the charcoal did not arrive by the end of the year. The Kawachi merchants undoubtedly thought so when they were unable to meet Naotarō and thus recalled their goods. From this failure, Chūemon learned that he needed to prepare Naotarō better the next time. Hopefully, he could still use credit to buy goods and move "200 *ryō* worth of goods with 50 *ryō*." The charcoal merchants of Kawachi, on the other hand, probably drew a grimmer conclusion after succumbing to the lure of high prices and high interest rates for the credit given for the goods: when dealing with small businesses from Yokohama that had no reputation and were likely new, only sell goods for cash and do not accept credit, even at a high price.

This incident actually proves something else. In the absence of a legal or semilegal framework to settle disputes, whether international or domestic, one could not easily trust others. Cash became king and credit was only granted at a high rate of interest. This is how the lack of functional courts led to problems of contract enforcement.

The final major point is about the sericulture industry in eastern Japan. For despite all the obstacles placed in front of Kōshūya Chūemon, by 1864 Kōshūya had finally become a very profitable business. He did this by engaging in silk products. There was no preconceived formula for his success. He had no help from domain authorities like Yoshimuraya nor from the shogunal authorities like Nakaiya. It was not luck, for he worked hard and was quick to seek opportunities for profit. But his success was also possible only because he was primarily dealing in silk products in the mid-nineteenth century in the Kantō region.

Among the various commercial products circulating in Japan at the time—silk, cotton, vegetable oil, wax, soy sauce, salt, and so forth—a few products finally began to be produced in the Kantō region by the end of the eighteenth century. This was because commercialization and technological know-how had slowly spread from western Japan to eastern Japan. Thus despite the terrible conditions in eastern Japan in which many peasant families fled to Edo, some peasant families began to engage in side production to gain cash income. In particular, those near the mountains on the edges of the Kantō plain began sericulture. This may have been in response to artisans with the know-how setting up shop in towns like Kiryū, Isezaki, and Hachiōji. Together the peasant producers of raw silk and the artisan silk weavers made local silk products to be sold in Edo.

By the end of the eighteenth century, numerous marketplaces specializing in silk cloth sprang up spontaneously, and of the forty-seven markets that traded silk cloth, more than twenty-five marketplaces traded more than 10,000 *hiki* per year.[48] Among them Fujioka, Takasaki, and Ōmiya towered over others, trading 50,000, 30,000, and 30,000 *hiki* per year, respectively.[49] These new marketplaces in the late eighteenth century became one of the few bright spots in the devastated landscapes of eastern Japan hit by Mount Asama's eruption in 1783 and the great Tenmei famine (1782–1788), which killed more than one million people in eastern Japan. The commercialization that transformed western Japan finally began to arrive in eastern Japan.

This trend obviously weakened the position of the silk weavers in Nishijin Kyoto, but the great monopoly silk merchants did not care. Agents of the silk clothing guild arrived to buy more and more Kantō-produced cloth in order to sell directly in Edo.[50] The House of Mitsui, for example, first came to Fujioka when the local merchants petitioned for them to open a branch office in 1722. The presence of guild agents encouraged further silk production and the peasants nearby arranged for their silk to be sold in Fujioka. Thus when Mitsui decided to pull out of Fujioka and relocate their branch office to Takasaki thirteen years later (because the local Mitsui agents at Fujioka spent company money on their personal ventures and ignored instructions from the main branch at Edo), this was a direct threat to the livelihood of Fujioka merchants. One hundred and nineteen Fujioka merchants signed a new petition so that Mitsui would remain. They also sent four representatives of the Fujioka merchant community to Mitsui's Edo branch so that they would reconsider pulling out. Despite it all, the House of Mitsui left Fujioka and went to Takasaki in 1735, contributing to Takasaki's lead over Fujioka in the nineteenth century.[51] This reduction of local silk markets into a few key markets would be followed by Mitsui buying from the Kantō weavers directly. By 1771 they began purchasing large quantities of cheap silk clothing from Kiryū.

By the nineteenth century, as revealed by Itō Yoshiichi's detailed study of the Uenohara marketplace, the silk guild merchants of Edo lost their grip on the silk industry. After only one century, any semblance of control over the Kantō silk industry was gone. Initially rural peddlers brought the silk cloth produced by the peasants to the local silk market, for example, at Fujioka. Then local silk market merchants at Fujioka bought the silk from the peddlers and shipped it to Edo, acting as agents of the silk guild merchants of Edo. At this point, the guild merchants at Edo knew the amount and price of silk flowing out of the Kantō countryside concentrating in Edo. From there they also knew who was buying the silk not consumed in Edo. But competition increased among the silk guild merchants of Edo, and the impatient merchants of Edo began to buy cargo brought to them by the rural peddlers. Some of them began to buy directly from the weavers. By the 1820s the local agents at Kiryū began ignoring Mitsui's main branch orders and by the 1830s, there were rural peddlers who ignored Edo entirely and sold to other rural customers, raising prices at Edo.[52]

The House of Mitsui, the preeminent Edo silk clothing merchants, admitted in its report to the shogunate that the weavers at Kiryū had purchasers from thousands of stores outside the silk guild and that they no longer needed guild patronage to survive.[53] In response the silk guild merchants at Edo filed suit to punish the rural peddlers who sold silk without going through them. In the same year, 1840, the local silk market merchants coordinated their actions with the Edo silk guild by forming a guild themselves and cooperating with their counterparts in Edo (presumably so that rural peddlers would first sell to them, reviving the system that was in place a hundred years ago). However, the reorganization and lawsuits came to naught when the shogunate ordered all guilds to disband with the start of the Tempō Reforms in 1841. The subsequent period of guild-free trade ensured that the rural peddlers would continue their activities and seek new alternate routes that directly connected producers with consumers.[54] By the mid-nineteenth century any semblance of guild control over the distribution of silk or silk clothes had disappeared. In the case of the silk industry, the Tempō Reforms merely formalized the direct trade between buyers and sellers in the Kantō region.

Hence the Kantō silk economy in the 1850s was a strange market. The shogunate had effectively said that it would not intervene in this market. Even after guilds were allowed to be re-formed, the guilds lost monopoly rights and anyone who wanted to enter the silk trade could. Consequently peasant raw silk producers and artisan weavers outside the domains sold directly to consumers who wanted their products. However, many domains, such as Maebashi domain, increasingly interfered to ensure quality and profits (profits for the producers, which in turn helped the domain).

In this economic environment, Kōshūya Chūemon could run energetically throughout the Kantō region and buy products that were produced in shogunal territories and then sell those products in Yokohama. But his competitors who had domain patronage had a huge advantage. For Chūemon to survive, he had to stitch together the local Kantō economic region not under domain control with Yokohama's overseas trade. This meant that in the first stage, Chūemon first had to get his family back in Higashi aburagawa village to produce raw silk and encourage their neighbors to do the same. At least the goods they produced would be sold through the Kōshūya store, so no production would go to waste. Next he cultivated contacts, both among the Kai province merchants and the Yokohama merchants. Finally, with the available capital, which slowly grew, he began to engage in ever-larger deals.

This was how he grew his business organically. In the second stage, without abandoning his earlier arrangements, he entered into deals with his contacts, mostly other small merchants, and together they engaged in speculation. The contacts of multiple merchants were fully employed to gather as much silk products from as wide a geographic area as possible. This was necessary because many parts of silk-producing eastern Japan were off-limits to merchants without domain patronage, for example, Maebashi, Takasaki, and Ueda domains. However, enough of eastern Japan was open; the silk-weaving and market towns of Kiryū, Hachiōji, and Ōmiya were all under shogunal control and could not be enclosed by any domain. And with more capital involved, speculation brought more profits (and losses). Finally, when he deemed that he had gathered enough capital, he stopped dealing with other merchants and speculated on his own once more. Now his former colleagues became competitors in gathering the raw silk and eggs. But since each merchant was presumably telling their family, relatives, friends, and acquaintances to produce more, this cycle increased production and hopefully enough profits to keep everyone in business.

KŌSHŪYA CHŪEMON: RUNNING A BUSINESS WITH NO POLITICAL CONNECTIONS

If the above was the overall pattern, then let us now examine what would become the heart of his operation in detail. The early years, from 1859 to 1861, were the toughest for Chūemon and his family. But they were also the crucial years in which he accumulated the much-needed contacts and capital for his future success. Producing raw silk when one used to produce cotton and cultivating contacts when one had none were not easy tasks. To his credit, when his family started to cultivate silk in 1860 (because of the agricultural cycle, his family was probably unable to switch to silk in the middle of 1859), he informed them of the specifics, such as keeping the thread thin and without breaks or knots, making it resemble silk from the Shinano province (present-day Nagano prefecture).[55] Although 1861 was dominated by the charcoal debacle, there is a hint that he and the villagers were expanding their silk production.[56] By 1862 he was selling silk goods produced at Sunahara, Oginakajima, Karakashiwa, Kubo, Fujimaki, Imai, and Kawachi villages on behalf of the producers. Furthermore, production at home began to switch more toward silk, as the family hired labor to till the fields so that they could tend the silkworms.[57]

During these early years Chūemon was also cultivating contacts, but his letters show that he may not have understood the opportunities open to him. He was not good at cultivating contacts. Because he was one of the few Kōshū merchants in the early years, his shop became the center where Kōshū merchants congregated when they came to Yokohama to hawk their products. In fact, he complained that because forty to fifty merchants came with their merchandise every night, he had no place to sleep. It must have been frustrating in the beginning. Merchants came from various places to do business, but he had no money to do business with them. Regardless, rather than treat these men as nuisances, he should have treated them as potential contacts to expand his business in the future.[58]

During these early years, he also traveled through Shimōsa province (northern Chiba prefecture) to buy tea, but he could not sell the gathered tea in time and was forced to direct his family to pawn their clothes to survive the coming month.[59] In the end, what saved him were his tirelessness, energy, and persistence. By the end of 1860, he learned of the Hachiōji raw silk market in shogunal territory and the favorable prices that could be obtained there. By the end of 1861, he had made new contacts with many Kōshū merchants in exchange for sleepless nights, and with his son representing him, Kōshūya became a founding member of the Yokohama merchants association.[60] By 1862 he was dealing in charcoal again, selling not just to foreigners, but also to the magistrate's office. He then started a new business in *tabi* (Japanese socks) and become friends with Mitsui's branch manager in

Yokohama.[61] He was beginning to connect his home village with a much wider world.

At first Chūemon represented only a few villages in Kai province at Yokohama. By 1862 he was connecting villages near his home, such as Sunahara and Oginakajima. Starting in 1863 he began to forge links that bound Yokohama with counties and later regions. In what he called *noriai*, or "riding together," he and other merchants pooled their resources to buy products in bulk and reap a larger profit. As cotton prices began to rise, he and two other merchants, one from Edo and another from Ichikawa, bought twenty horse loads worth of cotton, and together made a profit of 70 *ryō*.[62] In another case three merchants from Edo who wanted to buy raw silk at Maebashi found the prices too expensive and asked Chūemon for an introduction to the Yamanashi market. Together, they were to spend 2,300 *ryō* in one county.[63] In another case, despite Chūemon's skepticism, he and other rich villagers from near his village traversed northeastern Japan searching for raw silk.[64] It is not known how successful he was; after all, he himself predicted that northerners would not sell to Kōshū merchants.

As the money involved became larger, not only did the scale of operations become larger, but the geographic range of imagined business deals also began to grow larger as well. In this way Yokohama's hinterland grew. People came to Yokohama searching for a deal, and Yokohama merchants searched beyond what they were familiar with for a better deal. Kōshūya Chūemon embodied both of these trends.

By summer 1864, his business became large enough that there was talk of his becoming a representative for Nanbu domain in the northeast. It was an opportunity that never came to fruition but one that he sought.[65] After all, as a domain representative he might be able to switch to a commission-based business. In the meantime, as silkworm egg prices began to rise, he began trading in eggs. At one point, he promised to sell 5,000 cards of eggs, and his agents traveled to Shinano, bragging that they bought the eggs before local merchants could. He even wrote an open letter to the producers of Kai explaining the variation in prices for different levels of quality, comparative prices with Kōzuke eggs, and other concerns.[66] It is not clear whether the egg part of his business was financed through *noriai*, but after a collapse of egg prices, he instructed his son to stop joining *noriai*. He made an exception for people particularly close to the family, but in the failed business ventures, he probably saw that the problems stemmed from an informal agreement to share profits and, in particular, losses.[67]

By the time of the Meiji Restoration, Chūemon had created a network of producers spanning approximately ten miles located in the southeast of Kōfu upon whom he could rely to provide him with eggs to sell.[68] On top of that he had connections to buy a range of products from Edo, the provinces of Kai,

Suruga, Shinano, Kōzuke, Sagami, and parts of Ōshū (northeastern Japan),[69] enabling him to become more or less independent from *noriai.*

His tendency to diversify, countered by his network of silkworm egg producers as his new core business, did not abate, leading him to deal in raw silk, silk fabrics, cocoons, tea, and even capital, among other things, and to import cotton cloth and sugar. Eventually he would start a foreign currency exchange service and open a successful inn at Yokohama.[70]

For someone without domain backing, it was crucial that he mobilize the local connections that he had and aggressively enter markets that the domains could not close. Thus for him, the discovery of the Hachiōji raw silk market was critical, for it was a market that could not be closed by any domain authority, as would be done for Maebashi or Takasaki city markets. Collecting the produce from peasants on lands unfettered by domain monopolies was enough to maintain his business. Although the shogunal edict to "inspect" all silk products became a hassle after the implementation of the *Kiito sanshu aratame yakusho* (Office of Raw Silk and Silkworm Egg Inspection) in 1866,[71] there is no evidence that the edict constrained his efforts to collect goods. Chūemon's life proved that even if territorially coherent domains could impose a monopoly inside their lands, an enterprising merchant could still be successful in collecting goods produced by residents of shogunal lands and bannermen territory.

The first phase of Japan's international trade did not connect the global economy to a unitary Japanese economy. It connected a predominantly European market to a highly fragmented regional economy, a regional economy that included both monopolized and open markets.

How did Chūemon fare after his success in the late 1860s? It seems that he was hit hard by a number of events. The 1870 to 1871 crash of silkworm egg prices, triggered by the Franco-Prussian War and the defeat of French forces in Sedan (because France was the high-end consumer of silk goods) severely hurt Chūemon.[72] More importantly, however, despite his diversification—or perhaps because of his overdiversification—nothing could compensate for his losses in his core business when the silkworm egg business declined in the 1870s. In September 1873 Chūemon sold his land and buildings to pay off his debts and closed his business. By 1874 he departed from Yokohama, moved to Hachiōji, and at the advanced age of sixty-nine bought about fifty acres of ruined land for reclamation and cultivation. Before Chūemon died in 1890 at the age of eighty-two, he succeeded in creating a new community, bequeathed its operations to his second son, Naotarō, and finally retired to his home village at the age of eighty-one.[73]

Kōshūya Chūemon's business in Yokohama fell victim to a long-term trend, but he remained energetic to the end. The favorable conditions that welcomed silk merchants at Yokohama were temporary. By the 1870s they began to dissipate. Louis Pasteur discovered the solution to the pebrine crisis in Europe around 1870. The Taiping Rebellion had finally ended in 1864 and Chinese silk production could resume without fear of war. By 1872 Chinese exports surpassed their prewar peak.[74] Thus, opportunities for profit diminished with the recoveries of the Chinese export industry and of the European silk industry. These developments destroyed Chūemon's business.

THE DOMAINS OF EASTERN JAPAN

If Kōshūya Chūemon folded his business in 1873, what happened to Yoshimuraya Kōbei? Kōbei succeeded by becoming one of the six merchants certified by Maebashi domain to handle its raw silk exports in May 1862. But in 1866 domain authorities created Shikishimaya, disguised as a merchant enterprise, to act as the main seller of Maebashi domain's raw silk. After three years of preparation, in 1869, Maebashi domain officially established its own proprietary shop, shutting out the former domain monopoly merchants. Following Maebashi's lead, neighboring Takasaki domain and Nagano's Ueda, Matsushiro, and Suwa domains decided to follow suit.[75] These domains in the silk-producing regions sought to cut out the middleman and retain the merchants' profits for themselves. As such, Yoshimuraya, dependent on Gunma, particularly Maebashi silk, was faced with a sudden drop in handling fees and returned to the riskier raw silk speculation business. Moreover, the early 1870s proved to be a more volatile period than usual for the silk business.[76] Until the demise of the domains in 1871 and until Yoshimuraya could rebuild his network of producers, business would remain precarious for this once great merchant house.

Which leads us to the question: why did the domains of eastern Japan suddenly turn on the merchants? The answer is doubly ironic. First, the domains had finally gained enough wealth and experience from foreign trade to be independent of the merchants. Thus when the domain authorities were able to conduct the trade directly, they cut out the merchants, who were no longer needed. These domains safeguarded the interests of their samurai and then of its peasant producers. The merchants were expendable. Second, the Meiji Restoration destroyed the ties that bound the vassal (*fudai*) domains to the shogunate, and the vassal domains had to act as independent domains rather than as samurai serving the shogun. As such it became more important to gain the benefits of trade rather than maintaining the fiction that samurai should not be interested in profit and leaving profitable businesses to the merchants.

Let us examine the second answer first. If the shogunate had a dual role, as the government representing Japan and as the government of the Tokugawa clan, the vassal domains also had a dual role. The lords of the vassal domains started out as vassals of the Tokugawa shoguns. Their initial loyalty lay with the shogun. But they were also lords of their own domain. A few vassal lords, such as Ii clan of Hikone domain (in existence in the same place from 1600 to 1871), stayed in one location long enough to form strong ties with the locals and began to see themselves more as lords with responsibilities to their lands than as vassals of the shogun. Thus Hikone domain, which produced the last regent, Ii Naosuke, betrayed the shogunate at the last hour and actively supported Satsuma and Chōshū domains in their war against the shogun.[77]

Recognizing this possibility, the shogunate frequently moved many vassal lords from one location to another, preventing many of them from forging strong ties with the local people they governed. This policy kept the vassal lords more reliant on shogunal will than on the people they governed. Also, because most vassal lords had relatively small domains scattered across a wide geographic area, it was hard for many of them to envision the land they governed as a coherent unit, and they primarily saw it as a source of revenue.[78] These systematic efforts to keep the vassal lords more loyal to the shogun than to the land and people they governed disappeared when Satsuma and Chōshū destroyed the Tokugawa shogunate. As such, the vassal lords of eastern Japan could no longer rely on the shogun for any help. It was up to them to maintain their domains, and all sources of revenue would now be sought.

Let us now take the story back to Maebashi domain and the first answer.[79] Maebashi domain, whose headquarters was located in Kawagoe since 1767, began the reconstruction of Maebashi castle in 1863. In 1867, after a hundred-year absence, the domain finally moved back to Maebashi. This reconstruction and relocation was costly. Even without the Meiji Restoration, the domain probably would have moved to control the raw silk market to pay for these costs. After the relocation, many of the samurai families also began to engage in sericulture. In time, Maebashi domain declared that a new company called Shikishimaya would now control the raw silk produced in the domain. This Shikishimaya was a samurai-run domain monopoly company, and to increase production, Fukazawa Yūzō and Hayami Kensō, together with the help of the Swiss consul, bought twelve Italian-made silk reeling machines in 1870. Thus, Han'ei Maebashi Seishijo (domain-operated Maebashi raw silk producer)[80] became the first raw silk reeling machine operator in Japan. Led by Swiss engineer C. Müller, the twenty-four female employees produced high-quality raw silk in Maebashi for the Maebashi domain.[81]

Takasaki domain was similar in many ways to Maebashi.[82] Both domains had many ruling families during the first half of the early modern period until one family settled down. Before the Ōkōchi clan arrived in 1717, six other clans had ruled the domain. Takasaki domain had a size of around 80,000 *koku*. The two domains controlled roughly a third of the 500,000 *koku* in the province. Both ruling families were also close allies of the Tokugawa clan, since Gunma was seen as the northwestern gate to Kantō. But Takasaki differed in one crucial respect; it was terribly mismanaged, more so than Maebashi, which was a disaster as seen earlier. Takasaki domain had one of the highest rural taxes in the surrounding region and a correspondingly desperate peasant population. These led to poor domain finances and impoverished samurai, despite the high taxes. Ironically the castle town of Takasaki became an extremely prosperous castle town because unlike Maebashi it was located on one of the main highways of the realm, the Nakasendō, and it became the local center of the silk trade. Most troubling were the mounting debts. Debts to the House of Mitsui in 1767 had amounted to 6,100 *ryō*, plus the accumulated interest of 1,800 *ryō*, combining for a total of 7,900 *ryō*; the strained domain finances could only repay 200 *ryō* of the principal and 79 *ryō* of the interest. Toward the end of the period, the domain borrowed from one merchant to repay another, snowballing into 214,582 *ryō* in debts.

Even the peasants used to say, "don't send your daughter off to marry in Takasaki, it would be like making her carry thorns on her bare back." Statistical analyses of local tax records by historians have indicated that the *daimyō* took almost 80 percent of the rice as taxes in certain parts of the domain. The failure of the domain to help the rural economy or at least to ameliorate taxation resulted in massive population decline when coupled with serious natural disasters like Mount Asama's eruption in 1783 or the Tenmei famine of 1780s. Even before the famine, one village declined from a population of around 710 people from 1772 and 1776 to 539 in 1835. The core of Takasaki domain, the 50,000 *koku* of land surrounding the castle town with forty-five villages, lost more than 4,300 people between the 1750s and 1790s. The same region lost an additional 1,890 people between the 1790s and 1870s.[83] The Tempō famine of the 1830s compounded the problem with little relief in sight.[84] The massive population loss in northern Kantō was partly caused by natural disasters but also seriously compounded by domain mismanagement.

A possible solution to the domain's problems was to tax the merchants in the castle town. The town of Takasaki was one of the largest markets in Gunma because of its location on one of the main highways of the realm, the Nakasendō. With trading in sake, silk, and tobacco, among other goods, the merchant population of the castle town's three core streets climbed from 1,411 in 1784 to 1,610 in 1813 and then to 2,001 in 1862. Linked to the national economy through the highway and with the samurai population of approximately 3,000 living and consuming in the city (though they were increasingly impoverished), the city of Takasaki was transformed from a castle town into a specialized market. Unwilling or not knowing how to tap into the increasingly commercialized economy except to extract forcible "loans" from the merchants, the domain staggered through the later Tokugawa period. With peasants fleeing from the devastated rural areas to Takasaki, the mercantile section of the town prospered while the samurai living in the city grew poor.

Simply put, domains had to readjust their taxes. Itakura Kiyonobu, through an analysis of Sōma domain (60,000 *koku*) in present-day Fukushima prefecture, discovered the Laffer curve[85] for the domain. Itakura compared the annual rice tax yields with the population census that Sōma domain conducted since the mid-seventeenth century. As a result, he found that per capita tax of more than 0.576 *koku* or more than 1.8 bales of rice led to a decline in income and population. Thus in the seventeenth century when taxes were lower than 1.8 bales per person, population had increased. Starting around 1700, taxes began to rise above 1.8 bales per person, perhaps as costs of running the domain crept up.[86] As population and tax receipts slowly dwindled, the domain mismanaged and taxed at an even higher rate at 1.9 and sometimes 2.0 bales per person until the 1760s. The increasingly harsh taxes caused a significant decline in population, from 89,505 people in 1702 to 58,300 people in 1766, and the rate of decline accelerated as tax rates climbed. The Tenmei famine of 1783 to 1785 devastated the population of Sōma domain, lowering it to 35,785 people.[87] Still maintaining a high tax rate of between 1.8 and 1.9 bales per person, Sōma domain managed to retain the 35,000 people but did not increase its population despite a number of programs, such as bribing peasants to bear more children or policing to prevent infanticides. After borrowing all the money it could from the shogunate and various merchants, Sōma domain finally initiated a new program in 1817 to lower taxes. To compensate, domain expenditures were cut by a quarter, and in the short run debts decreased. When the Tempō famine struck, the new philosophy to protect the peasants met its severest test. From 1833 to 1838 the domain suffered a string of bad harvests. This time the domain abandoned all income, provided emergency food, borrowed money, and managed to prevent starvation deaths entirely. As a result, peasants from other domains fled to Sōma, and the population started to increase when the authorities lowered the tax rate to less than 1.8 bales per person. By the time domains were abolished in 1873, the population had recovered to the 58,000 level, equivalent to the era before the Tenmei famine a century ago.[88]

Many domains faced serious structural problems. They were chronically in the red and this fact tended to lead to mismanagement. Domains, particularly of those whose lords could trace their lineage back to the Warring States era, faced the problem of overstaffing. Designed to conquer and defend more territory, hiring too many vassals in an age of expansion had not been a problem. But in an age of peace, having too many samurai was a clear burden on domain expenses. In addition, because the economic base of most domains was agriculture, the production of grain and other crops was dependent on the weather and difficult to stabilize. These two issues by themselves should have been ameliorated by the massive increase in agricultural output in the years between 1550 and 1700. And yet their budget deficits remained.

One problem was overspending after the expansion phase. In an age of high growth, excess spending may not be a problem, especially if past debts could be repaid by larger future income. But once the output ceased to grow, it was difficult to reduce spending and return to a lower standard of living, especially since *daimyō* status was intricately linked to the amount of spending. Lords typically boasted about their expenditures on luxuries to each other and to the commoners, but more importantly a lord of 100,000 *koku* status had to maintain a certain level of ostentation, set above those of a 50,000 *koku* lord. And if the standard levels had risen over the years of increasing agricultural yields, as they had, then for any one lord to break rank and lower his standard of living would have been difficult.[89]

Many domains in eastern Japan raised their taxes over the point of diminishing returns during the early eighteenth century and subsequently lost population. The long-term population decline in eastern Japan was not an accident nor the simple result of natural disasters.[90] That urbane world of excess during the late seventeenth and early eighteenth centuries known as the cultural flowering of the Genroku era derived its material base from money formerly earmarked for capital investments, like the building of levees and canals. Such investments had benefited the rural economy and brought cash to the countryside. But in the Genroku era that money was sent to the cities. Moreover, as temporary tax breaks from opening new fields ended around the early eighteenth century, effective tax rates rose. In short, the peasants were deprived of a source of income and the lords spent the money that used to be spent on peasants on themselves. Lords and merchants living in cities naturally benefitted during the Genroku period.

Here is another way to think of this problem. During the Edo period, the population of the samurai was roughly 7 percent. The population of the other urban dwellers, mainly merchants and artisans, was roughly 9 percent. Thus the total urban population was roughly 16 percent and the rural population was roughly 84 percent.[91] According to Satō Tsuneo, the *bakufu* and domains originally collected 50 to 60 percent of the rural income as taxes, but by the early eighteenth century, the shogunate was only collecting around 33 percent in *koku* from the peasants.[92] The only reason why the early tax rates were tenable was because the shogunate and domains hired the peasants to engage in various construction projects. This meant that the taxes immediately went back to the peasants as payment for working on land reclamation or riparian projects. But once those projects ended, the actual tax rates needed to fall. The urban 16 percent consuming 50 percent of the agricultural income and the rural 84 percent consuming only 50 percent of the agricultural income was untenable. As long as the samurai did not collect taxes from the newly opened fields, the actual tax rates fell. By Hakuseki's time, the *bakufu* left 70 percent of the agricultural income to the countryside, where 84 percent of the people resided. And the urban population of 16 percent lived off 30 percent of the agricultural income. This meant that life in the cities was still better than life in the countryside. By the nineteenth century, in locations where rural production continued to improve, villages were paying roughly between 10 and 20 percent of their actual production in taxes.[93] Consequently, the urban population of 16 percent received 10 to 20 percent of the agricultural income, a more balanced amount. And with more wealth in the countryside, there was less need to migrate to the cities. From the perspective of the samurai, this was a relative decline in income. However, if certain domains insisted on collecting 50 percent of the income of the peasants, as they did in the seventeenth century, without compensating the peasants, then that would crush the lives of the peasantry.

By the 1720s, peasants in eastern Japan who lived in those domains had had enough. They began to stop having children or ran away to Edo and other cities. Consequently, those domains collected less in taxes. Should they have raised taxes in response? The answer is no. In this case the response should have been to lower tax rates. Instead many *daimyō* chose to combine borrowing money with raising taxes and sometimes cutting costs. If the taxes were close to or beyond the Laffer curve, as it was in many eastern domains, then both the returns and population would only diminish as taxes rose. Even if tax rates were not raised, they were sufficiently high enough that any severe weather would seriously disrupt the peasants' ability to pay taxes and feed themselves. In general, peasants in eastern Japan must have been living at the boundary of maximum taxation, with intermittent famines slowly reducing the population of Kantō from 1720 to 1846. Only the advent of widespread rural by-employment in Kantō, itself a long and painful process of acclimatization to the commercial economy, ensured the overall well-being of the peasants in the mid-nineteenth century (because the authorities did not tax manufacturing heavily) to allow for the population to increase.[94]

Gross mismanagement occurred when those domains not only did not recognize the problem, but actually raised taxes further. In Sōma domain, taxes remained higher than the Laffer curve for one hundred years, right through the Tenmei famine. Since the samurai population cannot flee to another domain and essentially cannot be laid off, the desire to maintain a stable tax yield is understandable, but the continued decline in revenue was inexorable. Caught between relatively inelastic costs and a diminishing income, more and more domains had to rely on loans, even forcible loans, that they could not pay. The result was terrible.

The population of northern Kantō (modern-day prefectures of Gunma, Tochigi, and Ibaraki) dropped by an astonishing 27.9 percent. Southern Kantō (Saitama, Tokyo, Kanagawa, and Chiba prefectures) managed to limit the decline to 5.2 percent. The neighboring Mutsu province to the north (currently divided into Aomori, Morioka, Miyagi, and Fukushima prefectures) lost 18.1 percent of its population. This was the disaster that was befalling eastern Japan. Population actually fell in eastern Japan during the period from 1721 to 1846. This is in marked contrast to the populations of Chūgoku, Shikoku, and southern Kyūshū regions (a total of twelve western Japanese prefectures), where population actually rose more than 20 percent during the same time period. In the west, the people were able to recover from the famines and natural disasters, but in the east they were not.[95] Thus the supposed stability of the population of Japan from 1721 to 1846, in which shogunal records show the commoner population increasing from 26.05 million to 26.84 million during this time period, understates the dramatic changes in conditions inside Japan.

This chapter devoted extra space to this topic of domain mismanagement because of its importance to economic development. Many domains in eastern Japan eventually realized their mistake in not caring for their people. The demographic and anecdotal evidence demonstrate that domains in western Japan had adjusted to a commercialized economy sooner and were not as poorly managed compared to those in eastern Japan.[96] Even in eastern Japan, most domains such as Sōma, Maebashi, even Takasaki learned their lesson by the time of the Meiji Restoration: domain governments must care for the people.

"Caring for the people" cannot remain empty rhetoric. When natural disasters strike, the government must be seen to do everything in its power to help the people. In those places where there was a combination of popular desire for a better life (backed up by folk morality and an "industrious revolution")[97] with samurai governance based on the philosophy of "benevolent rule" (derived from Confucianism), material prosperity for ordinary people increased. Both of these things—popular will and benevolent rule—would be critical for the future development of the Japanese economy. People would not want to work hard if they felt that their efforts would be in vain. And in turn people would work harder if they knew that their efforts would be rewarded materially. By the early nineteenth century, things were improving throughout the archipelago and population began to increase.

In the mid-nineteenth century, the mounting foreign presence pressured domains to modernize their weapons and send military personnel to guard the coast, adding further costs to an already distressed fiscal situation. Thus even in Shinano province, where population increased throughout the Edo period, domain finances became ever tighter, dooming the province to a prolonged period of fiscal troubles.[98] Thus, regardless of the economic situation that domains were in, a new solution was called for, and many domains adopted domain monopolies as one way to tap into the newly available resources. This successful tactic employed by western domains for more than a century began to be set up in domains connected to Yokohama and the new international trade as well.

YOSHIMURAYA KŌBEI: SURVIVAL STRATEGIES

In 1869 at least five domains in eastern Japan—Maebashi, Takasaki, Ueda, Matsushiro, and Suwa—created domain monopolies over raw silk.[99] For Yoshimuraya Kōbei, who was reliant on Maebashi domain patronage, this was a major crisis. The domains had earlier cut out the small-scale merchants from the raw silk business mercilessly, which benefitted Kōbei. But now the domains were going to cut out the large-scale merchants and engage in trade directly. The samurai-centric nature of domain governments showed itself.

In a letter dated Meiji 2/2/27 (8 April 1869) Kōbei wrote of the news of the creation of Shikishimaya, the new and official Maebashi domain monopoly. He mentioned that there was no need to panic, since he had enough raw silk on hand and because he could buy raw silk directly from Sawakichi in Kiryū outside the domain.[100] Unfortunately, 1869 did not start out or end well. Initially raw silk did not sell well in Yokohama[101]; by the time prices went up, he did not have adequate supplies to sell the raw silk,[102] or the price of raw silk rose inside Japan, so there was little opportunity for arbitrage.[103] The situation was so bad that Kōbei could not return home to Ōmama for *obon* (festival of the dead) during the year that the main family's patriarch had died.[104] By 1869/8 and 1869/9, he sold most of his merchandise, despite the low prices, and began to actively seek new sources of raw silk outside Maebashi domain to sell. Interestingly, the raw silk he could not sell to Western merchants in Yokohama (either because their prices were too low or because the quality of the raw silk was too low), he sent to Kyoto and Osaka and made a reasonable profit.[105]

Thus Kōbei began sending agents to Fukushima, where he and his friends once went to gather raw silk when he started his business, though a *noriai* (a "riding together" in which merchants pooled their resources to buy products). He also sent agents to Nishi-Hachiōji and other parts of Gunma prefecture not controlled by Maebashi domain.[106] Kōshūya Chūemon had expanded his business by contacting producers that lay between his hometown and Yokohama, essentially cultivating the expansion of his business by foot. In contrast, Yoshimuraya, who was forced out of Maebashi domain, used his business contacts formed over the years as a monopoly merchant for Maebashi domain to land in spots with known producers and buyers of raw silk. But not maintaining close contact with local sellers between 1860 and 1869 prevented his agents from buying as much quality raw silk as he had hoped.[107]

Thus 1869 was a dangerous year for Yoshimuraya Kōbei. He was forced to enter the direct buying of raw silk from local Japanese producers and the direct sale of raw silk to Western merchants. If this had happened during the early 1860s, when the price of raw silk almost always went up, it was not as dangerous. But as noted earlier, by 1869 raw silk prices were not guaranteed to go up because of the return of Chinese exports to the European market. By the 1870s, the Europeans reentered the market by conquering pebrine disease, further increasing volatility. If the severed ties with the domain hurt Yoshimuraya, what saved him was his previous connection to the shogunate. At the beginning of 1869, the new Meiji government ordered Yoshimuraya to exchange 10,000 *ryō* with Mexican silver dollars. This later expanded to exchanging a million *ryō* for Mexican silver dollars, and in the process, the government granted Yoshimuraya a 2 percent commission fee for the exchanges. The Meiji government also ordered Yoshimuraya to buy the paper currency it was issuing (*dajōkanfuda*). Both of these measures provided emergency income to Yoshimuraya through commission fees and direct funding.[108]

In other words, Yoshimuraya was stripped of his status as a domain monopoly merchant, and he first tried to create its own network independent of other domains. When this plan did not work as well as hoped, Yoshimuraya began to transition to become a merchant connected with the new central government of Japan.

The following year, 1870, would become a roller coaster year. In the first half of the year, raw silk prices had risen and Yoshimuraya Kōbei sold raw silk collected at the end of 1869 at a high margin.[109] However, with the outbreak of the Franco-Prussian War in July 1870, raw silk prices began to decline. By 1870/7/9 (5 August 1870), raw silk prices collapsed in Yokohama. Eleven days later, when news of war reached Yokohama, Western merchants stopped buying raw silk.[110] Even news that Napoleon III surrendered on 2 September 1870 did not restart purchases. The defeat of France had put a damper on the desire of Western merchants to buy raw silk for the French silk industry. When trade resumed in late 1870/9 (October 1870), prices remained depressed. And even these low-priced purchases stopped once again at the end of the year.[111]

To break out of this rut, Kōbei tried to sell silkworm eggs.[112] He was desperate, as his father and his brother were about to leave Ōmama and its pawnshop, to come and live in Yokohama.[113] If 1869 was a dangerous year that was saved only by his connection with the Meiji government, 1870 was a critical year for Yoshimuraya. This year there was no support from the Meiji government, and with losses of more than 3,500 *ryō*,[114] it was crushing. Many smaller businesses went under, with one merchant, Nagataya Seigorō, committing *seppuku* (disembowelment) because he could not pay his debts.[115] By the end of the year, the situation became so dire that Yoshimuraya's workers feared next year's New Years' celebration may have to be canceled.[116] The only reason Yoshimuraya did not perish then was because

Yoshimuraya built up a cash buffer during his years as the monopoly merchant of Maebashi domain.

One piece of good news kept spirits high, however. The new Meiji government's ministry of treasury chose Yoshimuraya Kōbei (along with three other merchants from Yokohama, three from Osaka, and four from Tokyo) to go to the United States and report on the American financial and banking system. Since Kōbei went to America from 1870/11/2 to 1871/4 as part of an all-expenses-paid mission from the treasury ministry, many Yokohama merchants envied him.[117] Unfortunately, his letter from America, which included photographs, was not available.[118] These letters sent between Yokohama and Ōmama continued until 1872/2, when all family members would relocate to Yokohama. So let us follow his letters for one more year.

After the loss of domain monopoly in 1869, business was bad for Yoshimuraya. But the Meiji government saved the business in 1869 by helping Yoshimuraya intervene in the silver and paper money markets. And 1870 continued to be a brutal year for business and there was no direct help from the Meiji government. Yoshimuraya's business survived because he had a cash cushion to absorb the losses. Would 1871 be a turnaround year?

Things began to improve at the end of 1870, when Western merchants started to buy raw silk, even if still at low prices.[119] By 1871/1/19 (9 March 1871), a month after Paris fell, raw silk from northeastern Japan began to sell at reasonable prices in Yokohama.[120] Interestingly Yoshimuraya Kōbei's agent claims that Maebashi silk and Ōmama silk were selling at terrible prices, essentially at a loss. Since Maebashi domain silk was under the monopoly of Shikishimaya and Maebashi domain was improving its raw silk quality, it seems that Yoshimuraya was buying low-quality raw silk that Shikishimaya did not want to handle.[121] His agent wrote that raw silk without the seal from Maebashi domain was selling at low prices[122] but that raw silk from Ōmama without bumps in the thread (and therefore of high quality)[123] was selling briskly.[124]

When Kōbei returned from his trip to the United States, business was still slow. In fact his return coincided with a case in which a foreign merchant cheated Yokohama merchants, causing a huge commotion.[125] Apparently this merchant took raw silk worth around 60,000 *ryō* and sailed back to Europe without payment, a rare occurrence according to Kōbei. Two merchants took the bulk of this loss; Dairoku lost around 23,000 *ryō* and Kobashiya lost 26,000 *ryō*.[126] There is little mention of Kōbei's return from America in the available letters. We know only that he must have returned from America sometime in 1871/4 based on the letter dated 1871/4/29 that mentioned him returning from Tokyo to file a report to the treasury ministry of his trip.[127] Returning to this scandal in Yokohama and being informed by his agent on 1871/5/9 that the Italian silkworm egg industry had recovered and that Chinese producers were expecting a bountiful year,[128] Kōbei must have expected continuing bad news for 1871.

Indeed, the bad news continued. Kōbei was able to buy some Maebashi raw silk, but he had to sell it to Shikishimaya, for the prices that he could get from the Western merchants were low.[129] The domain jealously guarded its monopoly rights. The mounting losses eventually forced Yoshimuraya Kōbei to fire many of his workers on 1871/5/19.[130] However, as the saying goes, it is always darkest before dawn. Just five days later, on 1871/5/24 Western merchants suddenly began showing interest in buying raw silk in bulk, even if it was at low prices.[131] Expecting a possible bulk sale, even though prices were low, Yoshimuraya began buying raw silk from Maebashi and Ōmama.[132] Then ten days after sales picked up on 1871/6/4, the price of raw silk jumped and Yoshimuraya sought to buy more raw silk from Maebashi, Ōmama, and Hachiōji.[133] By 1871/7/9 the raw silk that Yoshimuraya could buy from northeastern Japan and Nagano prefectures were selling at a good price; even the mid-quality and low-quality Maebashi and Ōmama raw silks sold, albeit at lower prices.

What is interesting is that while his business was recovering in 1871, there seems to have been a secret order from the government-run Tomioka Silk Mill. Yoshimuraya began to purchase silkworm cocoons in bulk starting on 1871/5/29 and planned to spend tens of thousands of *ryō* on the cocoons in Numata.[134] Soon he had bought enough cocoons that in 1871/10 and 1871/11 he was selling the cocoons to the Tomioka Silk Mill.[135] There was zero risk that the Tomioka Silk Mill would not pay him, thus the more cocoons he could sell, the greater his profits. In the end, 1871 brought Yoshimuraya Kōbei's business back to its feet.

The source of Kōbei's success was clearly good information. His agent reported earlier in the year that Italy had recovered from the silkworm egg industry collapse and that China was about to return to the raw silk market.[136] From this information one could predict that silkworm egg prices would be in trouble, and as suspected, 1871 was a catastrophic year for silkworm egg merchants in Japan. By 1871/7/29 it was clear to all in Yokohama that there were way too many silkworm egg cards. Around 1.5 million cards were in Yokohama, and only 600,000 to 700,000 cards could be sold.[137] Although there were plans to sell the cards directly to Europe (this event would mark the start of Japanese merchants' desire to sell their products abroad directly), in the end the oversupply of eggs ruined many. The merchants at Yokohama tried to prevent the price of silkworm eggs from collapsing by agreeing not to export a third of their supply, or 500,000 cards,[138] but the boon in Italy coupled with an oversupply in Japan lead to a crash in silkworm egg price.

Yoshimuraya had wisely stayed away from silkworm eggs that year, and this crisis did not affect him. Instead he began to buy silkworm cocoons in tens of thousands of *ryō*, something that Yoshimuraya had not specialized in before. He probably did this because he received orders from the Meiji government to supply the Tomioka Silk Mill. Although he was no longer a domain monopoly merchant, he had cultivated new contacts with Meiji government officials. His contact was probably Itō Hirobumi. Itō, the future prime minister, was at the time an official in the treasury ministry. Yoshimuraya and other merchants would go to the United States to learn about banking in 1870 with Itō and Yoshikawa Akimasa of the treasury ministry's paper money office.[139] The day before departure, Itō and around thirty officials held a large bon voyage party with these merchants at Yokohama.[140]

After Kōbei's return in 1871/4, he learned that his business was in trouble and that he had to fire employees on 1871/5/19. Just ten days later on 1871/5/29, Kōbei received a major government contract worth tens of thousands of *ryō* after Itō returned from America sometime in 1871/5.[141] When a business opportunity that surprised him emerged, he immediately tried to take advantage of it. He probably expected the Chinese to export a fair amount and that may be why he shifted his capital toward buying cocoons and speculating in silver dollars. Thus he may not have had as much capital as he wanted to engage in the raw silk trade. But he immediately reacted and bought as much raw silk as he could from Maebashi, Ōmama, Hachiōji, Nagano, and northeastern Japan once he realized that raw silk would sell. Clearly he spent everything he had. His father even ordered his family to borrow 25 *ryō* from the Ōtsuka family to get through *obon*, presumably because all available capital was spent buying cocoons and raw silk.[142] Finally Yoshimuraya made 4,000 to 5,000 *ryō* in profits from speculating in the Mexican silver dollar price.[143] The successful silver speculation and the information about Italy and China were probably the result of his or his agent's hard work. Nevertheless, some of the sources of Yoshimuraya Kōbei's success from 1869 to 1871 seems to lie with the major support he had from the Meiji government.

Whether success resulted from luck, personal effort, astute employees, or government connections, the point is that Yoshimuraya's business survived after it lost its domain monopoly status in 1869. The tough times did not last too long. His big break came on 1871/7/14 (29 August 1871), when the Meiji government abolished the domains. With the abolition of the domains, Shikishimaya had to fold. The abolition of Maebashi domain and Shikishimaya was his great opportunity. Yoshimuraya Kōbei could now return to Maebashi to take control of the raw silk produced in the former domain, but the letters from 1871/7 to 1872/2 do not show a major effort to recapture the raw silk market that he dominated from 1862 to 1869. In fact, the newspaper records of 1873 and 1874 show that Kameya, House of Mitsui, and Nozawaya dominated the raw silk market of Gunma with 83,787, 82,787, and 78,532 *kin* each. Yoshimuraya bought only 35,184 *kin* from Gunma prefecture. In fact, of the six Maebashi domain monopoly merchants in 1869, Yoshimuraya and Nozawaya were the only major buyers left in Gunma.

In 1876, Yoshimuraya boosted his share to be at the top with 139,350 *kin* bought in Gunma, but by 1879, Yoshimuraya was down to third place at 91,683 *kin*. In turn, Kameya and Nozawaya were back at number one and two, controlling 187,927 and 176,394 *kin* respectively. Hara Zenzaburō from northern Saitama prefecture on the border with Gunma prefecture ran Kameya, and Mogi Sōbei from Takasaki, Gunma, ran Nozawaya. By 1879 Yoshimuraya Kōbei had lost the battle to control the raw silk from Gunma to two rivals from nearby cities. Kōbei covered this loss by acquiring raw silk from other parts of Japan, such as the northeastern and Nagano prefectures, so that in total he sold 302,839 *kin* in 1879. This was not far off from Kameya's 310,207 *kin*. However, Yoshimuraya lost another more important battle over machine-reeled raw silk. Out of the 302,839 *kin* bought in 1879, only 28,572 *kin* were classified as machine-reeled raw silk. This would prove fatal. By the end of 1879, when demand for machine-reeled raw silk was rising, Kōbei would decide to retire. After twenty years in business, Yoshimuraya folded as an enterprise and Kōbei went into quiet retirement in Tokyo.[144] On 4 October 1907, Yoshimuraya Kōbei died of a lung disease.

CONCLUSION

One could argue that market forces brought the major Japanese and European silk markets such as Yokohama, London, and Lyon closer and that market forces brought Yokohama and the numerous small markets of eastern Japan together. And this argument would not necessarily be wrong. But this abstracts the people involved and the important noneconomic means used to create this new market in eastern Japan. Hopefully this chapter has demonstrated how merchants and domains created a new hinterland for Yokohama.

The major raw silk–producing domains used both economic and noneconomic means to collect the raw silk produced inside their domains and then to ship them to Yokohama. Maebashi domain first created a domain monopoly controlled by six merchants then later adopted an inspection system that allowed them to control all high-quality raw silk. These moves encouraged more production of raw silk. This pattern could be seen in other domains such as Nihonmatsu, Matsushiro, and Yonezawa and was not unique to Maebashi.

In 1873 former Nihonmatsu domain samurai created a private silk-reeling factory, the Nihonmatsu silk factory, in the remains of Fukushima castle in northeastern Japan. The Nihonmatsu samurai worked together with the Ono-gumi, an old Kyoto silk house, which provided the capital, and Hayami Kensō, who provided technical advice.[145] Matsushiro domain's monopoly

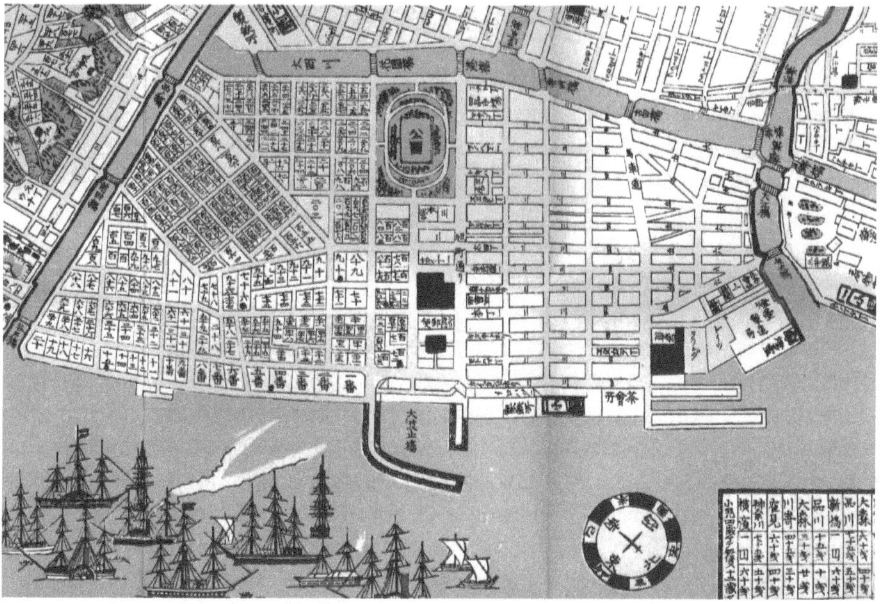

Figure 5.1. A Map of Yokohama in 1877. Notice that the foreign quarters are fully developed, the rice paddy fields have been reclaimed with the central part turned into a park, and a canal has been dug to turn the peninsula into an artificial island. *Source*: A segment from the map *Ozaki Tomigorō, Kaisei Yokohama bunken chizu* (Yokohama: Kinseidō, 1877).

silk dealer would become famous for being the first direct seller of silkworm eggs overseas in 1870. And in 1874, after the domain was dismantled, former Matsushiro samurai would establish a private raw silk–reeling factory, the Rokkōsha. Wada Ei, a daughter of a Matsushiro samurai, and a former employee at Tomioka Silk Mill would be central members in Rokkōsha's founding and operation. Yonezawa domain in Yamagata prefecture, northeastern Japan, followed a similar path, with its samurai creating the Yonezawa silk factory.[146]

In areas where domains were weak or nonexistent, individual merchants bound towns and villages with Yokohama through their personal connections and commercial activities. Once some villagers realized the profits to be had from foreign trade, their neighbors became producers and entered the trade. If these rural producers did not have the capital to start raising silkworms or to reel raw silk, the merchants would lend them whatever money that they needed. These activities spread sericulture widely, from older established sericulture "points" in Maebashi, Takasaki, Ashikaga, Kiryū, Matsushiro, Ueda, Nihonmatsu, Yonezawa, and so on to create sericulture "regions" covering areas such as northern Kantō, Nagano and Yamanashi prefectures, and Fukushima and Yamagata prefectures. Eventually machine reeling would spread as it increased production. In Tsukiji, Tokyo, the Onogumi would establish its own silk-reeling factory in 1871. In 1874 a farmer named Itō Kozaemon, who used to produce tea in Mie prefecture, built the Muroyama silk factory. This small factory initially tried to model itself on Onogumi's factories in Suwa, Nagano prefecture, but eventually managed to learn Tomioka Silk Mill's state-of-the-art methods by sending his nephew, his nephew's wife and daughter to Tomioka. By 1877 Muroyama silk factory produced high-quality raw silk on par with Tomioka's silk.[147] These local stories flesh out a broader regional story of how Yokohama expanded its hinterland.

Therefore, the domains and the individual merchants operating in the "free" markets created a flow of goods to and from Japan during the last ten years of the Tokugawa *bakufu*. Peasants in northern Kantō and in Shinano and Kai provinces along with peasants near Yokohama produced raw silk for export. They shipped the raw silk to Yokohama through domains and Japanese merchants with license to trade with foreigners. The domains and Japanese merchants in turn sold the raw silk to Western merchants, who then shipped the raw silk to Europe, mostly to France. In the mid-nineteenth century, France was the center of the European silk weaving industry, but the silkworm disease pebrine destroyed European raw silk production.

A similar story can be told for the other major product, namely tea. The peasants in Kansai and in Suruga province (later eastern Shizuoka prefecture) had been producing tea for the domestic market before the opening of Japan. In the case of tea, initially Western merchants hired Japanese agents to buy this tea. Peasants near Yokohama also made some tea and sent it to Yokohama. Eventually, Japanese tea producers caught on, just like with raw silk, and began to ship their tea to Yokohama for export. In Yokohama, Chinese supervisors and Japanese workers then "fired" the tea to prevent it from spoiling during the long voyage to Europe, mainly Britain. Once fired, the Western merchants shipped the tea to Europe. Japanese tea, like Japanese silk, replaced the Chinese tea that the Europeans could no longer import because of war and rebellion inside China.[148]

In terms of imports, the two major items were cottons and woolens. British manufacturers mass produced both items and shipped them throughout the world, including Japan. During the last ten years of the shogunate, Japan actually imported more woolens than cotton cloth (if one includes cotton yarn, then Japan imported more cotton products). Most of these products first came to Yokohama; the rest went mostly to Nagasaki. Then the Japanese merchants who bought the woolens probably sent them along to Edo and other domains that were westernizing their troops. Satsuma domain had been trying to modernize since the rule of Shimazu Nariakira (1851–1858) and Chōshū began to modernize in earnest after its defeat in

1864. In 1862, the shogun began assembling a Western-style military, with a navy and a model infantry, cavalry, and artillery.[149] British woolens and cottons were necessary to make Western-style uniforms.

The threads of commerce tied Japan with the West. To be blunt and specific, desperation and greed tied eastern Japan's raw silk with France, and western and central Japan's tea with Britain. British textiles in turn linked mostly with Edo but also a few domains in southwestern Japan. Thus as explained at the end of chapter 2, a large majority of the goods that came to and left from Japan went through Yokohama. Yokohama became the network node that connected Japan with Europe, and this trade immediately overtook the more traditional China trade.

Chapter 2 examined the political negotiations to open Yokohama between the Tokugawa shogunate, domains, the imperial court, and Western powers, chiefly the United States. The resulting unequal treaties deprived Japan of tariff autonomy, but they also prevented Westerners from entering the Japanese interior and indirectly promoted the growth of Japanese merchants, connecting the interior with Yokohama. Chapter 3 then examined the actual opening of the port city and the roles of its first merchant, the domains, and the shogunate in starting the trade. Careful shogunal efforts to cultivate the new port and to control the massive flow of goods both out of and into Japan guaranteed that Yokohama would not fail. In fact, Yokohama grew to become a major city that would demand not only trade goods, but also ordinary goods for survival. Hotta Masayoshi and Iwase Tadanari would have been pleased, but by 1861 Iwase had died of illness, and Hotta died three years later. No one in the *bakufu* could harness this rising trade enough to save it from collapse.

Instead Satsuma domain and Chōshū domain overthrew the shogunate and established a new government: Meiji *ishin* or the Meiji Restoration. A travel diary from 1875, sixteen years after the start of economic transformation and seven years after the political revolution, provides testimony for these changes. The author toured Tokyo, Kanagawa, and Yamanashi prefectures. The town of Kawasaki, between Tokyo and Yokohama, produced nori (dried seaweed) for the residents of Tokyo, but it also grew fruits and vegetables for customers in Yokohama and specialized in straw hats and other crafts for the foreigners in Yokohama. In the villages next to Yokohama, eight or nine out of ten villagers produced fruits for sale as well as rice. A little further away, near the hills of Nōkendō, villagers focused on potatoes and charcoal. Beyond, in southern Kanagawa, people were busy raising silkworms and growing mulberry trees. Even the port of Uraga, where Perry landed, was beginning to turn from its traditional fishing and maritime activities toward farming.[150] Inland Yamanashi villages grew mulberry and raised silkworms and competed to flatten the peaks and fill the valleys to make the famously inaccessible roads easier to travel. Near the capital of the prefecture, just about where Chūemon used to collect his eggs, a Western-style factory had been set up with two hundred female workers to reel the silk.[151]

These changes took place because merchants and farmers engaged in all types of trade. Chapter 5 continued to focus on the silk trade because of its dominant position in foreign trade, but other trades sprang up along this path. In fact, for a silk trader such as Kōshūya Chūemon, dabbling in all sorts of other trades was typical.

In light of the struggles of the merchants described so far, the importance of the Meiji Restoration can be seen clearly. It was revolutionary not just for destroying the shogunate, but also because it dismantled the domains. The domains clearly influenced the Japanese economy heavily, but after the abolition of domains on 29 August 1871, the only major political actor in the economy would be the national government. Local prefectural governments could intervene, but ultimately bureaucrats at the national level made the decisions. Also this national government would be committed to resolving all cases that came before its courts. Fraud and cheating would be prosecuted fully, and the government claimed to represent the interests of not just the samurai, but of all the citizens of Japan. The people living at the time recognized these revolutionary changes to the character of the government and colloquially called this *Meiji no goisshin*, literally "Meiji's Honorable Start from One."[152]

The next chapter focuses on a Japan without domains. This transition would have two contradictory effects. In the 1870s, the silkworm egg industry would be placed under more regulation inside Japan, while the raw silk exporting industry would evade regulation inside Japan. If a capitalist society can be defined as a society basing its fundamental principles on profit and designing society according to the laws of commerce, as the shogun's treasury officials put it,[153] then with the Meiji revolution, Japan would become capitalist as the government unreservedly supported moneymaking ventures.

NOTES

1. For more details on Yoshimuraya, see Nishikawa's introduction in Yokohama kaikō shiryōkan (ed.), *Yoshimuraya Kōbei kankei shokan* (Yokohama: Yokohama kaikō shiryō fukyū kyōkai, 1989), his *Bakumatsu Meiji no kokusai shijō to Nihon: Kiito bōeki to Yokohama*, (Tokyo: Yūzankaku, 1997), 73–155, and Yokohama kaikō shiryōkan (ed.), *Yokohama shōnin to sono jidai* (Yokohama: Yūrindō, 1994), 82–106.

2. Yokohama kaikō shiryōkan (ed.), *Yoshimuraya Kōbei kankei shokan*, iii, also see note 1 on xiv. Henceforth cited as YKKS.

3. In total he would borrow 1,300 *ryō* from his friends and neighbors between 1859 and 1862. His grandfather's family would also send more than 1,100 *ryō* to Kōbei between 1861 and 1864. Finally between 1860 and 1864 Kōbei borrowed from his father 1,175 *ryō* and repaid 1,045 *ryō* by 1863. YKKS, xv, iv.

4. Between 1860 and 1862 his father spent 1,866 *ryō* to buy raw silk and received 3,159 *ryō* as payment, a profit of 1,293 *ryō* or 69 percent. YKKS, iv.

5. YKKS, iv.

6. "Yokohama shōninroku" in Yokohama kyōdo kenkyūkai (ed.), *Yokoreki sōsho* vol. 12: *Kurofune raikō to Yokohama* (Yokohama: Yokohama kyōdo kenkyūkai, 1993), 136, 138. Directory of merchants, copied by Kōshūya Chūemon in 1862.

7. YKKS, iv.

8. I have relied upon Yamada Takemaro, et al., *Jōshū no shohan*, 2 vols. (Maebashi: Jōge shimbunsha, 1981, 1982), vol. II, 2–58, for Maebashi domain.

9. Kitō Hiroshi, *Jinkō kara yomu Nihon no rekishi* (Tokyo: Kōdansha, 2000), 99.

10. Before focusing on improving the situation, Matsudaira Naritsune plotted to leave Maebashi and Kawagoe in 1840 in the famous three-way swap, where his clan would move to Shōnai domain, the lord of Shōnai to Nagaoka, and the lord of Nagaoka to Maebashi/Kawagoe. This plan was aborted at the last minute in 1841.

11. As noted in chapter 3, this is the edict that Nakaiya Jūbei protested against and that would ultimately lead to his downfall.

12. Nishikawa, *Bakumatsu Meiji kokusai shijō to Nihon*, 46.

13. In 1862/7 Enshūya was ejected and replaced by Matsuzakaya in 1862/8.

14. Gunma kenshi hensan iinkai (eds.), *Gunma kenshi: Shiryōhen* XIII, *Kinsei* V, (Maebashi: Gunma ken, 1970s), 466. Henceforth cited as GK: S. Nishikawa, *Bakumatsu Meiji kokusai shijō to Nihon*, 45–48; Hagiwara Susumu, *Hono'o no kiitoshō Nakaiya Jūbei* (Yokohama: Yūrindō, 1978), 174–78.

15. The editors of YKKS believe that money lent by other merchants to Yoshimuraya was the key to its success. YKKS, iii–iv, xv, note 3. Nishikawa, *Bakumatsu Meiji kokusai shijō to Nihon*, 73–78.

16. Hagiwara, *Hono'o no kiitoshō Nakaiya Jūbei*, 179.

17. Nishikawa, *Bakumatsu Meiji kokusai shijō to Nihon*, 47.

18. YKKS, iv–vi.

19. Nishikawa, *Bakumatsu Meiji kokusai shijō to Nihon*, 87–89.

20. Nishikawa, *Bakumatsu Meiji kokusai shijō to Nihon*, 50–51.

21. After Mogi Sōbei's death, Nozawaya became Mogi shōkai (or Mogi commercial association) and rapidly expanded to become a *zaibatsu* (conglomerate) until its collapse during the post–World War I depression.

22. Yokohama-shi (ed.), *Yokohama shishi*, vol. 2 (Yokohama: Yūrindō, 1959), 690–94. Henceforth abbreviated as YS, II. Yokohama kaikō shiryōkan (ed.), *Yokohama shōnin to sono jidai* (Yokohama: Yūrindō, 1994), 54.

23. Nishikawa, *Bakumatsu Meiji kokusai shijō to Nihon*, 88–91; Yokohama kaikō shiryōkan (ed.), *Yokohama shōnin to sono jidai*, 89–93; YKKS, iv.

24. A term coined by Fukuchi Gen'ichirō, the translator for the Tokugawa shogunate and later a biographer and playwright in Meiji Japan. Ishii Takashi (ed.), *Yokohama urikomishō, Kōshūya monjo* (Yokohama: Yūrindō, 1984), 5. Henceforth cited as KM.

25. The directory records a store 45 *tsubo* large, but the oral history remembers a store at least 50 *tsubo* large.

26. Nishikawa has his take on shogunal officials storming into Nakaiya's store. Ostensibly, the authorities wanted to punish him for building a mansion above his station. This arrest may also have been a warning to other merchants, for Nakaiya by then had worked with Satsuma domain officials to smuggle raw silk out of the country when the *bakufu* tried to ban its export. Nishikawa, *Bakumatsu Meiji kokusai shijō to Nihon*, 58–59.

27. It is doubtful that Tezuka could have made that amount purely through commissions. I suspect that he himself entered the silk trade and thus gathered the differential in silk prices between Yokohama and its hinterland as suggested by the narrator's following story.

28. Ishii Mitsutarō and Tōkairin Shizuo, eds, *Yokohama dontaku*. 2 vols. (Yokohama: Yūrindō, 1973), 167–70.

29. YS, II, 579–82, KM, #22.

30. This was the same rainy day that Nakaiya Jūbei received his lease in Yokohama, so perhaps the two met at foreign magistrate Mizuno Tadanori's office. Considering that Nakaiya, Tezuka, and Kōshūya all claim to have received a directive to build a store that would not shame the country, it seems very likely that Mizuno gave a speech to a group of merchants gathered in one room that rainy day.

31. KM, #1, #3, #31.
32. Kōshūya Chūemon's store is on the second block of Ōdori's south side. "Yokohama shōninroku" in *Kurofune raikō to Yokohama*, 97–99.
33. KM, #13.
34. "Yokohama shōninroku" in *Kurofune raikō to Yokohama*, 85–165.
35. KM, #24, #27, #29.
36. KM, #18, #28.
37. KM, #51.
38. KM, #111.
39. This is the type of business that Nakaiya Jūbei and Yoshimuraya Kōbei operated.
40. Hayashi Reiko and Ōishi Shinzaburō, *Ryūtsū rettō no tanjō: shinsho Edojidai*, vol. 5 (Tokyo: Kōdansha, 1995), 133–42.
41. One can also see Okazaki's argument in English in Okazaki Tetsuji, "The Role of Merchant Coalitions in Pre-Modern Japanese Economic Development: An Historical Institutional Analysis," *Explorations in Economic History* 42 (2005): 184–201.
42. I am assuming that this Baruberu is the same Baruberu as in Tezuka's case, for there is record of only one J. S. Barber in Yokohama at this time. This is not to single out Barber as a scoundrel. We do not have Barber's account of what happened in these transactions.
43. KM, #20, #21.
44. KM, #53, #54, #57, #61.
45. KM, #33.
46. KM, #62.
47. KM, #64, #66, #67.1, #67.2, #68, #70, #75.
48. One *hiki* tailors two kimonos.
49. GK: S IX, *Kinsei* I (Maebashi: Gunma ken, 1970s), no. 283.
50. GK: S IX, *Kinsei* I, no. 283.
51. GK: S IX, *Kinsei* I, no. 274, 278, 279; GK: S X, *Kinsei* II, no. 162.
52. Itō Yoshiichi, *Kinsei zaikataichi no kōzō* (Tokyo: Rinjinsha, 1967), 120–54.
53. Hayashi Reiko, *Edo tonya nakama no kenkyū* (Tokyo: Ochanomizu shobō, 1967), 241–44.
54. Itō, *Kinsei zaikataichi no kōzō*, 120–54.
55. KM, #34, #35.
56. KM, #69.
57. KM, #84, #107.
58. KM, #23.
59. KM, #23, #32, #39, #43.
60. KM, #52, #74, #75.
61. Mitsui at this point specialized in foreign currency exchange. KM, #95.
62. KM, #112.
63. KM, #146, #148.
64. KM, #134, #137.2.
65. KM, #132, #210, #211.
66. KM, #162, #169, #166.
67. KM, #188.
68. KM, #228.1 and map attached to the back of KM.
69. KM, #256, #264, #270, #271.
70. KM, #234, #256, #264, #270, #271, #295.
71. He is complaining about this office a year after its operation. KM, #228.1.
72. KM, #338, #340, #343.2.
73. KM, 11.
74. Giovanni Federico, *An Economic History of the Silk Industry, 1830–1930* (Cambridge: Cambridge University Press, 1997), 197, Table AII. The records compiled by Federico and Yokohama city history do not match because Federico is probably adding raw silk numbers with thrown silk numbers. Thus I use only the Chinese data from Federico.
75. YKKS, #125.
76. YKKS, #120, #125, #153, #181, 7.

77. After Ii Naosuke's assassination, shogunal authorities blamed the regent's tactics for the unrest, and relations between the shogunate and Hikone domain soured. Even so, the domain sent troops to help defend Kyoto from Chōshū's attack in 1864 and participated in the second attack against Chōshū domain in 1866. However, Chōshū had modernized its army and dealt a crushing defeat on Hikone domain's forces. Afterward, Hikone domain leaders began to side with Satsuma and Chōshū forces. Other vassal domains that sided with Satsuma and Chōshū include Yodo domain (Lord Inaba Masakuni, patron of Nakaiya's father, was in Edo when domain elders decided to switch sides), Ueda domain (Lord Matsudaira Tadanari), Maebashi domain (Lord Matsudaira Naokatsu), and others.

78. The outer lords (*tozama*) had no dual nature. They existed before the Tokugawa shogunate, rarely moved, and knew that their existence was based on the samurai retainers, the land, and the people they governed. These lords did not hesitate to betray the shogunate when it was opportune.

79. Yamada, *Jōshū no shohan*, vol. II, 2–58.

80. Later known as Ōwatari seishijo.

81. Yomiuri shimbunsha Maebashi shikyoku (ed.), *Kinu no saihakken* (Maebashi: Kankodō, 1969), 46–47.

82. Yamada, *Jōshū no shohan*, vol. I, 2–68.

83. Sources do not indicate the number of people residing in the villages prior to the 1750s, but a typical early modern village numbered anywhere from 100 to 400 people each. The statistical average for a village in the 1720s was 350 to 380 people: divide the total population (approximately 26,000,000 commoners—townsmen) with the total number of villages (approximately 63,000). Using the smaller estimate, there may have been more than 15,000 villages. Thus a decline of 6,200 may represent a 41 percent drop. Another way to examine this is from the perspective of each individual village. In Takasaki, the decline was 6,200 people over 120 years from 45 villages, therefore each village during those 120 years declined by 138 people (if the villages declined uniformly). This calculation indicates that some villages could have been abandoned altogether.

84. Yamada, *Jōshū no shohan*, vol. I, 2–68.

85. Today the Laffer curve is derided in advanced economies, but that's because the tax rates in advanced capitalist economies are nowhere near 80 percent of total income. The historical experience of eastern Japan during the Edo period seems to indicate that somewhere near 70 percent is the maximum amount a government can tax its population before the people lose enthusiasm for work or simply leave.

86. And in all nine domains of Gunma, domain policies shifted to try to increase tax rates around 1700 as well, although the reasons for attempting to raise taxes differed with each domain. Some conscientiously tried to cut costs before raising taxes, as in Maebashi under an earlier *daimyō* family. Others, such as the Oda in Obata domain or Sanada in Numata domain, raised taxes to present an outward appearance of luxury, even though some of the administrators must have known that their domains were not as productive as asserted.

87. The population figures for Sōma domain include samurai as well as townsmen and peasants. At the start of the famine in 1783, there were still 53,276 people, so during the famine, the domain lost 17,491 people, a staggering loss of 32.8 percent in three years. This was after declining by 36,229 people between 1702 and 1783, a 40 percent drop in population during those eighty years. Thus from 1702 to 1786, the domain declined by 53,730 people, a 60 percent drop from its peak population of 89,505 people. Because Mutsu province as a whole declined in population from 1721 to 1846—but not by 60 percent—one must conclude that a large number of people fled the badly mismanaged Sōma domain in the eighteenth century.

88. Itakura Kiyonobu, *Nihonshi saihakken: Rikei no shiten kara* (Tokyo: Asahi shobō, 1993), 166–244.

89. However, many domains seemed to have no compunction about slashing the salaries of their samurai.

90. Kitō, *Jinkō kara yomu Nihon no rekishi*, 96–104.

91. The 7 percent number is derived from the early population surveys of the Meiji states. According to the 1872 census (Jinshin koseki), the samurai population totaled 5.9 percent (*shizoku* 3.9 percent; *sotsuzoku* 2 percent). *Shizoku* were the upper ranking samurai and *sotsu-*

zoku were the lower ranking samurai. Adding the samurai in eastern Japan, who were counted as commoners (because their side lost the Boshin War), demographers have agreed on roughly 7 percent as a good figure for the number of samurai in Edo-period Japan. According to the 1870 survey the number of aristocrats, priests, monks, and nuns was roughly 1.3 percent. The number of "untouchables" was roughly 1.5 percent. The commoners were 91 percent, with the ratio between the farmers and the merchants and artisans being 8:1 and the ratio between merchants and artisans being 2:1. In this survey the number of samurai was 6.4 percent. The shogunate tried to limit the number of townspeople, but the Meiji state did not and allowed people to migrate to cities. Sekiyama Naotarō, *Kinsei Nihon no jinkō kōzō* (Tokyo: Yoshikawa kōbunkan, 1958).

92. Satō Tsuneo and Ōishi Shinzaburō, *Hinnō shikan wo minaosu* (Tokyo: Kōdansha, 1995), 111–15. Arai Hakuseki in his biography claims that the *bakufu* was collecting only 28.9 percent in taxes, but he blamed this on corruption by various officials who stole the rice before it reached the shogun's coffers and did not believe the official tax rate had gone down. By creating the *okanjō ginmiyaku* (treasury inspectors), he claimed that the corruption was reduced and consequently the burden on the peasants was lessened. Arai Hakuseki, *Oritaku shiba no ki* (Tokyo: Iwanami, 1999), 254.

93. Satō and Ōishi, *Hinnō shikan wo minaosu*, 116–18.

94. Whether the population increased first and thus allowed for rural by-employment to take hold or rural by-employments became widespread and thus population increased cannot be determined for certain. But considering the nature of heavy *daimyō* taxation and population stagnation or decline, I am more inclined to believe that an increase in prosperity trigged the population to increase.

95. Kitō, *Jinkō kara yomu Nihon no rekishi*, 99.

96. Robert Bellah, *Tokugawa Religion: The Values of Preindustrial Japan* (New York: Free Press, 1957) makes this argument and specifically focuses on Ishida Baigan and his Shingaku movement in western Japan.

97. Yasumaru Yoshio focused on eastern Japan and coined the term *tsūzoku dōtoku*, or folk morality. Yasumaru Yoshio, *Nihon no kindaika to minshū shisō* (Tokyo: Heibonsha, 1999, reprint of 1974 edition). Hayami Akira coined the phrase "industrious revolution" in English, and his argument is in *Rekishi jinkōgaku de mita Nihon* (Tokyo: Bungei shunjū, 2001), 96–100. In English, aside from Robert Bellah, Thomas Smith's *Agrarian Origins of Modern Japan* (Stanford: Stanford University Press, 1959) also makes these arguments. This was a way to incorporate Max Weber's famous idea about the Protestant work ethic for non-Protestants.

98. Unless, of course, they could somehow raise taxes from the merchants and lower taxes on peasants, but only a few took such a radical move in eastern Japan.

99. YKKS, #125.

100. YKKS, #120.

101. YKKS, #122, #129, #133, #154, #158, #173.

102. YKKS, #184, #185.

103. YKKS, #187.

104. YKKS, #169.

105. YKKS, #174, #181.

106. YKKS, #181, #182, #187.

107. YKKS, #185.

108. YKKS, #89, #90, #97, #126.

109. YKKS, #216, #220.

110. YKKS, #291, #301.

111. YKKS, #331, #363.

112. YKKS, #333, #334.

113. YKKS, #353.

114. YKKS, #341.

115. YKKS, #340.

116. YKKS, #354.

117. YKKS, #357, #358, #360, #363, #368.

118. YKKS, #387.

119. YKKS, #383, #384.
120. YKKS, #388.
121. Plus, there was contact between Shikishimaya and Yoshimuraya, so there was not a total break between the two. YKKS #388.
122. YKKS, #409, #415.
123. When reeling raw silk, sometimes the thread broke. When the thread broke, the reeler tied the thread together again. These knots created bumps. The fewer bumps, the better the quality of the raw silk.
124. YKKS, #412.
125. Nishikawa thinks the merchant was a Prussian named E. Seyd from the 1870 *Japan Herald Directory*.
126. YKKS, #407, #408.
127. YKKS, #410.
128. YKKS, #416.
129. YKKS, #419, #420, #422.
130. YKKS, #425.
131. YKKS, #427.
132. YKKS, #431.
133. YKKS, #434.
134. YKKS, #430, #433, #438.
135. YKKS, #462, #489, #499, #506.
136. YKKS, #416.
137. YKKS, #450.
138. YKKS, #454, #484.
139. One of them would be Fukuchi Gen'ichirō.
140. YKKS, #360, #368.
141. YKKS, #425, #430.
142. YKKS, #431, #433, #434, #438.
143. YKKS, #470.
144. YKKS, 11–14.
145. The Maebashi domain silk-reeling factory fell under the control of Gunma prefecture after the domain was abolished, and two years later in 1873 the facilities were sold to the Onogumi. Hayami Kensō was in charge of the Maebashi domain silk-reeling factory from its founding until 1873.
146. Ishii Kanji, *Nihon sanshigyōshi bunseki* (Tokyo: Tokyo University Press, 1972), 62–66.
147. Ishii, *Nihon sanshigyōshi bunseki*, 49, 66–67.
148. A good summary of the tea industry from 1859 to 1941 can be found in Teramoto Yasuhide, *Senzenki Nihon chagyōshi kenkyū* (Tokyo: Yūhikaku, 1999). In English, see Robert Hellyer, "1874: Tea and Japan's New Trading Regime," in *Asia Inside Out: Trading Empires of the South China Coast, South Asia, and the Gulf Region*, vol. 1: *Critical Times*, ed. Helen Siu, Peter Perdue, and Eric Tagliacozzo (Cambridge, MA: Harvard University Press, 2015), 186–206.
149. Imports being used for military purposes explains why Nagasaki held a relatively large share of imports (an average of 30 percent of imports; Hakodate had a miniscule 1 percent, and Yokohama held the rest at 69 percent of imports) compared to exports (Yokohama dominated exports with 83 percent of the share, Hakodate also exported a tiny 3 percent, so Nagasaki's share of exports was 14 percent, a much smaller figure than its imports). Satsuma and Chōshū domains relied on Nagasaki for their imports. These numbers are calculated from the numbers in tables 2.1 and 2.4 in chapter 2. Yokohama-shi (ed.), *Yokohama shishi*: vol. 2 (Yokohama: Yūrindō, 1959), 388, 391–393, 527, 530, 534, 537, 558.
150. Oda Kanshi, "Bukōsōshū kaireki nisshi," in *Nihon shomin seikatsu shiryōshūsei*, vol. 12: *sesō* 1. (Tokyo: Sanyōsha, 1971), 325–29.
151. Oda, "Bukōsōshū kaireki nisshi," 337–38.
152. The phrase *Meiji ishin* is essentially the same as *Meiji no goisshin*, meaning the Meiji "revolution." However, another phrase was often used at the time, which was the Monarchical

Restoration (*Ōsei fukko*). In English these two phrases were combined to form the phrase "Meiji Restoration."

153. Tokyo daigaku shiryō hensanjo (ed.), *Dainihon komonjo: Bakumatsu gaikoku kankei monjo* (Tokyo: Tokyo University Press, 1930) 15, no. 158.

Chapter Six

The Producers of Eastern Japan

Bombyx mori, usually known as the silkworm moth, goes through a series of transformations: it is born as an egg, then hatches to become a larva that feeds on mulberry leaves, then it forms a cocoon to become a pupa inside, and then finally emerges from the cocoon as an adult moth. Because this moth does not feed as an adult and dies in around ten days, mating early to lay eggs is essential to continue the cycle.[1]

For humans, it is of course the silk that the silkworm spins that is valuable. When the silkworm creates its cocoon, it spins a single thread of silk, roughly one kilometer in length, glued together into a white oval cocoon. When the moth emerges from the cocoon, it gnaws its way through the cocoon, breaking the single thread of silk that was used to make the cocoon in the first place. Since commercial-quality raw silk has few knots that tie the thread together (making the silkworm its supreme artisan, spinning out a single strand), a cocoon with a hole in it only can be reeled as silk floss or silk waste. Thus the sericulturalist must make a decision. The silk farmer can wait for the cocoon to hatch and sell the eggs that the female moths lay, or he can boil the cocoon, killing the silkworm inside, and reel the thread. It is a mutually exclusive choice.

For Japanese sericulturalists in the 1860s and 1870s, both the eggs and the raw silk were highly profitable export commodities and producers of both types proliferated. Even cocoons that had been "dried," which also killed the pupae inside, sold well overseas. By the 1880s, however, the primary export was raw silk. This transition was neither expected nor inevitable, and it reflected a major shift in the conditions of the international silk industry.

These two decades witnessed a historic change, which can be traced to show how local and individual decisions contributed to the formation of a new global division of labor in the silk industry. If the previous chapters examined the emergence of a new domestic economic region in the 1860s—built upon the foundation of an early modern Kantō regional economy, the political decision to open Yokohama as its international gate, and the busy activities of local economic agents—this chapter focuses on the international dimensions of the Japanese silk trade. This focus is important because eastern Japan's silk-producing region retreated from the European market while gaining in the U. S. market during the 1870s. This was a painful decade for many producers, particularly for those who reared silkworms for their eggs. Many of them fought tooth and nail to retain their market share in Europe. In contrast, the American market seemed at first to be a minor market with only a few pioneering producers and merchants looking to sell their products there. But in the end, this transition from Europe to America helped to transform the Japanese economy by rerouting the flow of goods and money.

NEW INFRASTRUCTURES 1: A NATIONAL MARKET AND THE TELEGRAPH

The Meiji Restoration brought revolutionary change not only to the Japanese polity, but also to its silk industry. Four major positive changes to the infrastructure that were critical to the silk industry were telegraph lines, railroads, shipping, and banking. Another major change, which was actually the elimination of an obstacle, was the dismantling of the domains. For anyone operating comfortably within the *bakumatsu* (1853–1868) system of domain monopolies, the dismantling of domains brought the most radical of changes.

In the formation of Yokohama's regional economy, the domains had played a critical role by either embracing or rejecting foreign trade. In embracing trade, many domains had also created or nurtured the great merchant houses that relied upon domain monopolies to maintain their grip over the producers. With their abolition, two changes ensued. First, the disappearance of the various political boundaries of the domains unified the domestic market. Combined with the Meiji state's policy of aggressively adopting new technology, such as the telegraph, the railroad, and the steamship, the domestic and foreign markets integrated rapidly. Second, the great merchant houses either became "capitalists" who used capital instead of domain monopolies to maintain their decade-old "traditional" role or else they collapsed. These new merchant-capitalists concentrated their power through the banks they controlled, by sitting on the board of directors, and by granting their other businesses low-interest loans in order for them to lend to the producers in the provinces. The technological innovations and the banks formed a new infrastructure that unified the domestic market, tightened its connection with the international market, and reduced the opportunity for speculators. These changes meant that the producers of the silk products now fully accepted the risks but also the profits of the industry.

In most people's imagination, the first telegraph, the first (model) railroad, and the first steamship all came to Japan with Commodore Matthew Perry.[2] As part of his effort to impress the Japanese reception committee, Perry established temporary telegraph stations between Yokohama and a location one mile away, out of sight. He also brought with him a working quarter model of a steam locomotive with passenger cars and tracks, and of course he commanded a fleet that included steamships. In his attempt to impress the Japanese, Perry succeeded. The *bakufu* noticed that all three were technologies that could radically alter the military, political, and economic balance. Before its collapse, the *bakufu* issued ordinances to construct telegraph stations between Edo and Yokohama. It also granted permission to an American diplomat to build a railroad between Edo and Yokohama. And, it bought steamships and began constructing a naval yard at Yokosuka, south of Yokohama.[3] Domains, with the permission of the shogunate, also began constructing steamships. Satsuma domain constructed the first Japanese steam engine and placed it onboard a ship in 1855. In 1863 Saga domain constructed the first working steamship in Japan.

The Meiji state inherited the *bakufu*'s legacy and also the *bakufu*'s and the daimyō's debts. It too recognized the strategic and economic value of these technologies and aggressively pursued them. On 7 January 1870 the government laid the first telegraph in Japan between Tokyo (formerly Edo) and Yokohama. After approving a Danish company's proposal to connect Nagasaki with both Shanghai and Vladivostok, the government then began construction of a telegraph line between Yokohama and Nagasaki. On 30 August 1871 the Danes connected Nagasaki and Shanghai with an undersea cable, and five months later they laid the Nagasaki-Vladivostok cable. Within Japan, the telegraph line that connected Tokyo, Yokohama, Kyoto, Osaka, Kobe, and Nagasaki became operational in February 1873. With this telegraph, it became possible to transmit information between London and Tokyo in two, or at most three, days. Soon afterward, telegraph wires spread throughout Japan. Between 1874 and 1879 many lines went up in rapid succession, connecting Tokyo with 113 cities, almost every major city in Japan. With more than 70,000 telegrams domestically and approximately 7,000 internationally sent from Yokohama in 1877,[4] this technology transformed business.[5]

Merchants who had speculated on the prices between markets in the hinterland and Yokohama could no longer do so profitably. Shimomura Zentarō, the first mayor of the city of Maebashi during the Meiji period, built his fortune on this price differential. He started from scratch but by 1863 had amassed more than 10,000 *ryō*. By 1876 his fortune consisted of several hundred thousand *ryō* and it was all thanks to his information network consisting of Yokohama geisha house owners and other informants in Yokohama. This network was efficient enough to bring him information a day before his competitors.

On one occasion, when he was in Yokohama and heard that all the exporters were out of raw silk, he did not go back to Maebashi immediately. He feared that if he moved too quickly others might deduce the situation, for he had built quite a reputation for knowing the market. Instead, he held a massive banquet at Yokohama for his colleagues. After his competitors were all drunk, he returned to Maebashi posthaste and bought all the raw silk and cocoons in northern Kantō. With the Tokyo-Maebashi telegraph line opening in 1877, this sort of trick became impossible. Continuing to speculate, he lost a significant amount in 1886 when raw silk prices suddenly collapsed.[6]

The benefit of the telegraph was that no matter how the physical network was connected, because the information by wire moved at the speed of electrons, there was very little time differential in propagating the information. Naturally, prices converged internationally as well as nationally.[7] Because arbitrage opportunities shrank over time, merchants became less interested in speculation and became either bankers, who earned a steady income through loans to the producers, or carriers, who charged a handling fee for transporting goods. Under these circumstances, the producers retained more of the profits but were also exposed to the risk from the fluctuations in prices.

NEW INFRASTRUCTURES 2: RAILROADS AND SHIPPING

The railroad did not directly affect the silk industry until late in the nineteenth century. As stated earlier, the *bakufu* granted the first commission to build a railroad between Edo and Yokohama to an American diplomat. However, with the overthrow of the regime, the new Meiji government rescinded permission with an eye toward building one itself. A group of Yokohama merchants also proposed to build a railroad in 1869, but in the end, the Meiji state constructed the first railroad in Japan, between Tokyo and Yokohama, in 1872.[8]

The railroads, like the telegraph, spread rapidly throughout the country, with both the government and private enterprises building railroads (unlike the telegraph, which the government monopolized). The railroads also proved to be crucial in uniting eastern Japan with Tokyo as its center, more so than the telegraph. The major lines completed by the early twentieth century traced the old highway network: the Tōkaidō line (extending the Shimbashi-Yokohama line out west along the old Tōkaidō highway), the Chūō line (extending from Shinjuku to Hachiōji along the old Kōshū kaidō highway), the Takasaki line (extending from Ueno to Ōmiya and then to Takasaki following the old Nakasendō highway), the Tōhoku line (also extending from Ueno to Ōmiya and then veering toward Utsunomiya to trace the old Nikkō kaidō/Ōshū kaidō highways), even the Nikkō reiheishi kaidō had a railroad that ran parallel to its route, which connected Takasaki with Maebashi, Tochigi, and Oyama, which then extended to Mito.

For the silk trade, the creation of this railroad network meant that Yokohama could extend its reach deeper into the interior of Japan. Railroads were, in effect, an artificial waterway that altered Johann von Thünen's economic geography. In his *Isolated State*, von Thünen had imagined a flat world with a city in the middle. In such a world, without barriers or expressways, he postulated that land prices would fall as one moved away from the city center, and as a consequence, the city would be ringed by bands of products, with the more expensive products nearer the center. Geography merely altered this idealized economic order. Thus rivers brought areas adjacent to the

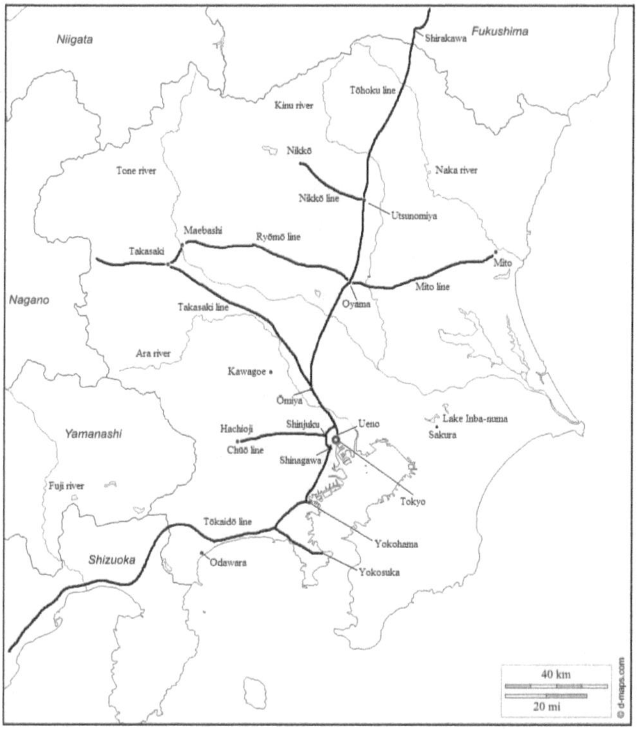

Figure 6.1. Map of Kantō Railroads in 1891. Notice that the Chūō line has been built only from Shinjuku to Hachiōji and that the Takasaki line extends only partway into the former Nakasendō highway. *Source*: http://d-maps.com/carte.php?num_car=115415&lang=en. Modified by the author to include railway lines and the names of cities.

river closer to the city, while mountains and rough terrain pushed producers in that region farther away economically from the city than mere physical distance.[9] In mountainous areas of central Japan where the rivers were often very treacherous and difficult to navigate, the railroads radically altered the economic geography, connecting previously difficult-to-reach areas to major markets.

Tokyo was a major domestic market, but Yokohama was legally one of only five treaty ports connected to the outside world until 1899. This meant that silk products along the Takasaki and Tōhoku lines (Gunma, Fukushima, and other northeastern prefectures) and along the Chūō line (Yamanashi and Nagano prefectures) could be sent by rail to Tokyo and then transshipped to Yokohama. From there, the silk products were shipped by Japanese and Western merchants to Europe and America.

The railroad lines constructed in 1884 and 1885 strengthened existing ties between Gunma and Yokohama. In May 1884, Nippon Tetsudō, a private railroad company, connected Ueno in Tokyo with Takasaki. Then in August the company linked Takasaki with Maebashi; the two centers of raw silk production now had easy access to Ueno. In 1885 the company created Ōmiya station (between Tokyo and Takasaki), and from Ōmiya, the railroad extended to the northeast, linking Maebashi and Takasaki with northeastern Japan. Once Ueno and Tokyo were connected by rail that same year (1885), cargo could seamlessly move from Maebashi and Takasaki to Ueno to Tokyo to Yokohama. In contrast to the three or four days it took to carry the cargo on horseback and then on boats down the river at a cost of ¥2.8 per horse load, after the construction of the railroad, it took only one day to reach Yokohama at a cost of ¥0.5 per load.[10]

The Chūō line, which started out as the Kōbu Tetsudō, connected Shinjuku in Tokyo with Hachiōji in 1889, and then extended the line into Yamanashi and Nagano prefectures. Although it took until 1911 for completion, by cutting through mountainous terrain, the railroad expanded what once was a minor overland connection that depended on the transport of goods on horseback.[11] This railroad allowed for the transport of goods from the mountains of Nagano and Yamanashi to Hachiōji, then from Hachiōji to Tokyo, and finally from Tokyo to Yokohama.

However, the Chūō line had one problem. Ever since 1859, Yokohama merchants such as Nakaiya Jūbei, Yoshimuraya Kōbei, and Kōshūya Chūemon had travelled directly between Yokohama and Hachiōji. For them the railroads rerouted an existing path along a major detour. Thus Yokohama merchant-capitalists worked together to create a new railroad line to challenge this Tokyo-centric pattern. In 1908 they built the Yokohama line, a line dedicated to the silk trade, transporting silk goods directly from Hachiōji to Yokohama. Unfortunately, by 1917 the railroad had failed as a commercial venture and was subsequently nationalized. Since the transportation cost of silk was small compared to its price in terms of weight, capital-intensive attempts to reduce transportation costs were not cost effective. Instead raw silk merchants sent their cargo of raw silk with bulkier and heavier items to Tokyo first and then transshipped them to Yokohama.[12]

The transfer of the three Tama counties from Kanagawa prefecture to the Tokyo metropolitan district (Tokyo-*fu*) demonstrates the transformative power of the railroads.[13] Originally the city of Edo was part of the province of Musashi and its four southwestern counties comprised the Tama region (counties of North Tama, South Tama, East Tama, and West Tama). At the extreme south of Musashi province were the cities of Kanagawa and Yokohama. When the new Meiji government decided to devise new administrative entities called prefectures (*ken*), they mostly followed the old province and domain boundaries. However, in the case of Edo and Yokohama, they took special measures. They detached Edo from Musashi province and called it Tokyo-*fu*, an area under special administration. Later Tokyo gained East Tama county.[14] The areas north of Tokyo, the bulk of Musashi province, became Saitama prefecture. Kanagawa and Yokohama were also detached from Musashi province and initially became its own administrative district. When the domains were abolished in 1871, the domains in the western portion of Sagami province were merged into its own Ashigara prefecture while Yokohama remained Kanagawa prefecture. Many parts of the three Tama counties fell within the forty kilometer (twenty-five mile) radius of Yokohama, areas where foreigners had unfettered access under the treaties, and as such, in 1871 they also became part of Kanagawa prefecture. In other words, Yokohama and its zone of foreign access was its own special prefecture for five years. It is only in 1876 that Ashigara prefecture merged with Kanagawa prefecture; Odawara, the former first city of Sagami province and the birthplace of Ninomiya Sontoku, now played second fiddle to Yokohama.

For many in the three Tama counties of North Tama, South Tama, and West Tama, being part of Kanagawa prefecture made sense. In the early nineteenth century, Hachiōji, the principal city of the four counties, had developed into a rural market for Edo, specializing in raw silk. However, with the advent of foreign trade in 1859, Hachiōji's focus turned from Edo to Yokohama and it functioned as a satellite city for Yokohama, collecting silk products from the nearby rural areas and beyond, such as Yamanashi and Nagano. The narrow, mountainous road between Hachiōji and Yokohama, traversed by silk-bearing horses, eventually became known as Japan's "silk road."[15] The creation of Kanagawa prefecture and the inclusion of the Tama counties within the new prefecture was thus welcomed.

Consequently, when the Jiyūtō (the Liberal Party) passed a law in Parliament to transfer the three Tama counties from Kanagawa to Tokyo in 1893, there was strong opposition from not only the various political factions, but also from the residents. Fifty years later, however, in forming a new Tokyo

Metropolitan District (Tokyo-*to*) in 1943, the residents organized a movement to incorporate the three Tama counties as part of the new metropolis. If the initial transfer had been opposed by a large segment of the population, by 1943 the vast majority of the residents had clearly viewed their interests to lie with Tokyo and no longer with Yokohama.

A combination of several factors resulted in the two transition proposals. From urban Tokyo's perspective, controlling the Tama counties was a perennial issue. This was because the Tama counties were a source of water for the city, and controlling it was seen as essential. Also in 1893 the Jiyūtō leadership schemed to dominate the Tokyo district assembly by incorporating Tama counties' Jiyūtō representatives. On Kanagawa's side, Jiyūtō, the prefecture's dominant political party, had split between the more business-oriented wing and the more populist wing, with the business wing supporting the shift from Kanagawa to Tokyo in 1893. Kanagawa's executive branch, which at this time was headed by a governor appointed by the central government, was more than willing to divest itself of the consistently uncooperative Tama deputies. However, by 1943 this constellation of forces was no more. Over the long term, the 1889 completion of the Kōbu railroad line (later part of the Chūō line), connecting Tokyo and Hachiōji and then continuing into Yamanashi prefecture, proved to be the factor that reoriented Hachiōji back to Edo/Tokyo. If for a brief moment Hachiōji was within Yokohama's orbit on account of the lure of foreign trade, the railroad reversed the situation.

The Chūō line first replaced small local businesses that transported goods between Hachiōji and Yokohama. Later, despite the creation of the Yokohama line, which connected Yokohama directly with Hachiōji, it was the Chūō line and the Tōkaidō line, as the main trunk lines operated by the government, that dominated the economic scene. With a much larger population, Tokyo always had a higher demand for bulk goods such as rice and coal. Silk, because of its high price relative to its transport cost, could not by itself keep afloat a line that connected Hachiōji directly with Yokohama. Despite the roundabout route, it made more economic sense to send silk along with other goods to Tokyo and then from Tokyo to Yokohama because of the cheaper overall transport cost. Eventually the Yokohama line had to be auctioned to the government. The railroads built in the Meiji era effectively endorsed Hotta Masayoshi and Iwase Tadanari's vision. Yokohama served as the main port to connect with the outside world, but inside Japan, Yokohama would serve the interests of Edo/Tokyo.

In shipping—the last of the technologies that altered the patterns of Yokohama trade—the greatest change occurred in 1870. In that year, the Pacific Mail company opened a periodic shipping lane that connected San Francisco with Yokohama, eventually extending it to Kobe, Nagasaki, and finally Shanghai. This shipping lane transformed the relative position of Yokohama. Hitherto, Yokohama was on the eastern edge of a global shipping network centered on Europe (with the western coast of the United States on the western edge). In other words, at least in commercial terms, the world saw little commerce across the Pacific. With the establishment of this new shipping lane combined with the transcontinental railroad across the United States (completed in 1869), the commercial world became more global. Moreover, competition between American, British, and Japanese companies over these shipping lanes—particularly by government-subsidized companies such as Mitsubishi and later Japan Mail—multiplied the Pacific and East Asian routes.[16]

For the international silk trade, opening the Pacific to commercial traffic halved the distance travelled between Japan and the United States. Previously Japanese raw silk left Yokohama, crossed the Indian Ocean to round the Cape of Good Hope and arrived in New York for a total distance of 15,020 nautical miles. Or the raw silk left Yokohama, crossed the southern Pacific Ocean to round the Straits of Magellan to reach New York for a total distance of 16,205 nautical miles. Taking the shortcut through the Suez Canal (completed in 1869) did not shorten the distance too much—it was still a daunting 13,040 nautical miles. The raw silk arrived in New York because the center of the U.S. silk industry was in Paterson, New Jersey. By shipping to San Francisco and then to New York, only 7,439 nautical miles must be traversed, roughly half the distance. Other routes existed from Yokohama to New York, but Yokohama to San Francisco to New York became the most important route for Japanese (and Chinese) sericulturalists. Of course, for Italian and French producers of silk products, the transatlantic route remained the most important. In the nineteenth century, New York and San Francisco were the only two ports of significance to import raw silk.[17]

This Pacific route effectively halved the distance travelled between Yokohama and New York. Moreover, for Japanese producers, New York became closer to Yokohama than London to Yokohama by more than 3,000 nautical miles.[18] An added benefit for the silk trade was that on the Pacific route, the products reached the end markets more predictably, as 37 percent of the transpacific route was on land (3,191 land miles or 2,773 nautical miles between New York and San Francisco). For American producers of silk fabrics, which were typically short on cash and without a large stock of raw silk, an idle factory was something to be avoided if at all possible, so a more predictable shipment was always welcome.

NEW INFRASTRUCTURE 3: BANKING

Among the infrastructural changes underway in the 1870s, the emergence of banks occupies a unique position. Banks are not technological creations, but institutional inventions that empowered the great merchants. After the Meiji

Restoration, one of the pillars of support for these great merchants had vanished, namely the domains. The other pillar, the system of loans binding the merchants and the producers, continued but became more competitive. As described in the previous chapter, the relationship between the two pillars during the *bakumatsu* period was complementary. The great merchants, sanctioned and protected within a partnering domain's boundary, provided loans to encourage more producers. The merchants themselves borrowed from more established merchants within the domains to expand their operations. Nine of these great silk merchants, including the House of Mitsui, Hara Zenzaburō, Mogi Sōbei, and Yoshimuraya Kōbei, eventually formed an association in 1867 to borrow large sums from the *bakufu*. With the demise of the *bakufu* and the domains, however, the merchants had only capital to offer to the local producers. Early Meiji Japan was not a perfectly rational world. However, producers flocked to the merchant providing the lowest interest rate. As this competition among the former domain-backed merchants intensified, a few succeeded but many dropped out. Even formerly giant merchants folded their businesses. With this competition, it became crucial to have a large and stable supply of capital.

Some of the great merchant houses of Yokohama responded to this challenge through cooperation. In fact, immediately after the fall of the *bakufu* and before the demise of the domains, they convinced the Meiji state to continue the *bakufu* practice of providing loans to the great merchants and to create an agency to provide a number of services, including the inspection of export goods and monetary exchange. Eventually with bankruptcies among the merchants and Western objections to the "silk inspection centers" (which they perceived to be a monopoly guild),[19] the government stopped helping the mercantile community directly.[20]

In 1871 Itō Hirobumi and Yoshimuraya Kōbei returned from their trip to the United States to learn about the American banking system. The result was the National Bank Law of 1872, modeled after the American system without a central bank. In 1874, the great merchant houses that survived major price fluctuations and the dismantlement of the domains established Second National Bank headquartered in Yokohama. Second National Bank took the form of a Western-style bank with approximately 2,500 shares at ¥100 each. Of these shares, the two largest Yokohama merchants, Hara Zenzaburō of Kameya and Mogi Sōbei of Nozawaya, together controlled 800 shares. The older established merchants such as the House of Mitsui controlled only 400 shares among them. Aside from Hara's and Mogi's shares, other Yokohama merchants such as Yoshimuraya Kōbei controlled another 1,200 shares. With 2,000 of the 2,500 shares under the control of Yokohama merchants, Second National Bank acted to benefit them. Its two initial branches in Takasaki, Gunma prefecture, and Ueda, Nagano prefecture, demonstrated that this bank was interested in the silk trade and offered loans to the members of the silk industry at competitive interest rates. Other banks of this type, as part of government policy, emerged throughout the country in the 1870s, and by 1879 there were 153 of these national banks.[21]

Ultimately, however, these national banks failed because of a fiduciary crisis. Without an expanding client base yet continuing to issue credit, the banks eroded the value of their notes. Aside from the government's initial capital infusion and the capital from the shareholders themselves, few people created accounts at the banks. This lack of outside capital was not perceived as a problem initially, since the banks were to issue their own notes backed by the shareholders' and the government's hard currency. The problem was that the customers were also the owners. Thus, the banks were unable to refrain from printing extra banknotes to provide cheap capital. With no corresponding increase in the banks' hard currency, eventually the public lost confidence in the expanding supply of banknotes. The decline in the value of the banknotes in turn pushed the owner-customers of the banks to issue more notes that the public rated to be below their face value. As a consequence, inflationary pressures began to afflict the economy.

To resolve the crisis, Matsukata Masayoshi, who had studied finance under Léon Say (France's minister of finance and grandson of economist Jean-Baptiste Say) from 1877 to 1878, became the finance minister in 1881.[22] He created the Bank of Japan, which monopolized the issuance of currency in 1884. The former national banks became commercial banks, which had to maintain strict reserve requirements and could not issue their own notes. In recalling these banknotes and replacing them with Bank of Japan's yen notes, monetary stability was reestablished. In the end, Japan moved from the nineteenth-century American system without a central bank to a European system with a powerful central bank modeled after the Central Bank of Belgium.

When the dust settled, three major banks survived in Yokohama: Second National Bank, Seventy-Fourth National Bank, and Yokohama Specie Bank. Hara owned the principal share of Second National, which had ¥0.5 million as its capital, and Mogi tried to dominate with the Seventy-Fourth National, which had ¥0.4 million. As a group the Yokohama merchants owned these two banks. In particular, silk money dominated the Second National, with approximately 75 percent of the capital provided by Yokohama-based silk merchants, and additional capital provided by provincial shareholders engaged in the silk trade. This transition of the great raw silk merchants into bankers gave them control over the silk trade, since now they could provide loans to producers.[23] Seventy-Fourth National was also a bank for Yokohama's elite, but it was not dominated by silk merchants nor was it patronized by the government like Second National. It was owned by a variety of business interests, such as the major tea merchants. Yokohama Specie Bank, with six to seven times the capital, at ¥3 million, was a semiofficial bank with the mandate to handle currency exchange to facilitate foreign trade.[24]

The case of Katsuno Kichibei of northern Gifu prefecture illustrates how the merchant-capitalists operated through their banks. In the Meiji period Katsuno established Katsuno store, later renamed Shinshōsha, one of the largest mechanical silk filature factories in Gifu prefecture. Before the opening of Yokohama in 1859, his family had bought raw silk from producers in what would become Gifu and Nagano prefectures. They were part of the network that sent the raw silk to Kyoto for final finishing. With the opening of Yokohama, Katsuno had hoped to sell the raw silk there, especially after witnessing merchants from neighboring Yamanashi sell raw silk at enormous profit. However, Nagoya domain, which controlled northern Gifu prefecture, banned foreign trade, and when Katsuno tried to sell the raw silk, the authorities sentenced him to house arrest for more than a month. This region had to await the demise of the domains before engaging in foreign trade. Katsuno first contacted the House of Mitsui, but by 1876 he relied on Mogi's Nozawaya to sell his raw silk abroad. The connection between Katsuno and Mogi strengthened over time. Although his own company, Shinshōsha,[25] never accepted direct capital investment from Mogi, Katsuno continually borrowed from Mogi and sold only to him. Katsuno's fourth son established Sanryūsha in Okazaki, Aichi prefecture, with capital provided by both his father and Mogi. In this manner, Mogi Sōbei used capital to gather his raw silk to be sold to foreign merchants.[26] Political coercion through the domains became a relic of the past. Money became the principal means to influence people, and with the cash he gathered, his descendants built a *zaibatsu* (conglomerate).[27]

Hara Zenzaburō, another great Yokohama silk merchant, took control through capital. With his bank, Second National, Hara had easy access to capital and founded a silk filature in his hometown and in 1902 bought the formerly state-run Tomioka Silk Mill factory from the House of Mitsui. The Tomioka Silk Mill, established in 1872, was not profitable while under state supervision and in 1893 was sold to Mitsui. Hara's Kameya therefore expanded from a mercantile enterprise to banking and eventually to industry. Hara Zenzaburō eventually became interested in politics and served as a city councillor and as a member of Parliament.[28] Zenzaburō's adopted son inherited the Hara *zaibatsu*, but he was uninterested in politics and more interested in culture. He preserved important cultural artifacts at Yokohama's Sankeien. Yoshimuraya Kōbei, as seen in the previous chapter, simply retired. The House of Mitsui amicably split in the early Meiji period. The main family kept the name Mitsui and in 1876 began Mitsui banking. By the end of the Meiji period it became the giant Mitsui *zaibatsu*. As a conglomerate it owned many factories, but in 1902 Mitsui decided to withdraw from the silk industry and sold all its silk filatures. A branch family broke off to form Mitsukoshi, and this family continued to engage in the silk trade. Inheriting the tradition of selling to retail customers since the Edo period, Mitsukoshi in 1905 declared itself to be Japan's first department store and adopted the format of Western department stores.[29]

Thus with ample backing from the banks (that they themselves controlled), the Yokohama merchant-capitalists invested in raw silk production. They were driven by a desire to secure high-quality raw silk, and in order to do so, they indirectly controlled the producers by providing cheap capital in exchange for exclusive purchasing rights and sometimes directly operating raw silk factories. With the profits accumulated, the descendants took many different paths: conglomerates, politics, cultural preservationist, department store, and retirement. For the Yokohama merchants, controlling the capital of the banks proved crucial to surviving the loss of access to cheap capital from the *bakufu* and domains, the loss of political backing from the domains, and the turbulence of price fluctuations. Although the power to coerce was no longer an option, with a larger and integrated economic playing field, access to capital enabled the largest of the Yokohama merchant-capitalists to expand and invest. The new Meiji government was not a samurai government; it encouraged making money, and with this attitude change, it was fully capitalistic. In fact, the close connections between the men of business and the men of politics formed what we today might call "crony capitalism."

The decade following the Meiji Restoration transformed the underlying conditions of the silk trade and opened new possibilities for Yokohama. The dismantling of the domains led to a truly unified national market and an environment in which local political authorities could no longer interfere in business (at least openly). The new innovations had some antecedents in *bakufu* policy, but time and commitment were needed to bring out their full potential. Once completed, however, telegraph cables ensured rapid and accurate transmission of information, reducing the profits of the speculators. The railroads deepened previous connections, even if it meant that silk producers had to send their cargo to Tokyo first. The Pacific shipping lanes and the American transcontinental railroad opened an untapped market on the other side of the world. And banking, though in its infancy, made capital more available than before for the myriad producers, while granting more power to the established merchants. Cumulatively, these innovations would help transform the Japanese economy.

REARING AND REELING

Between 8 and 18 June 1869, an Italian mission headed by Comte Vittorio Sallier de la Tour, the Italian minister to Japan, toured the silk-producing region of Gunma prefecture. Four days later, on 22 June, Francis Ottiwell Adams, secretary to the British legation in Japan, headed another mission and left for Gunma and Nagano prefectures. This group returned on 6 July 1869.[30] Traveling in the wake of a civil war, these European missions sought to establish direct ties between their merchants and the Japanese producers in the provinces. Irritatingly for them, the treaties that the first negotiators had signed prevented the merchants from traveling beyond a forty kilometer (twenty-five mile) radius from the treaty ports. Thus the diplomats, who had special sanction to travel in the interior, led their merchants on a tour of Yokohama's hinterland.

The Italians went to Gunma for a specific product, namely the silkworm eggs. Pebrine had almost destroyed a 250 million lira per annum industry at home. In Europe the Italians and French had begun to specialize in raw silk and silk cloth, respectively. Pebrine, which killed the silkworms, struck the Italians harder, for the French could look for other sources of raw silk. When the Italian merchants discovered that Japan produced disease-free eggs, the desperation in Italy led to large imports and even outright fraud, with some selling diseased Italian eggs in Japanese wrapping. To counter these schemes and to ensure a stable supply, the Italian mission had gone to Gunma to gain direct access to the silkworm eggs. The mission seems to have been successful. According to Tajima Yahei's travel diary, when he made his trip from Shimamura, in southern Gunma, to Yokohama in summer 1869, he sold some of his village's silkworm eggs to some Italian merchants, such as Pietro Savio, Ferdinando Meazza, and Ernesto Prato,[31] as well as to Japanese merchants. De la Tour's mission successfully fostered direct contact between the Japanese producers of eggs and Italian merchants.[32]

The Adams group, which included not only British, but also American and French merchants, toured the area to inspect the industry as a whole. From the growth of mulberry leaves, to the raising of silkworms, and finally to the reeling of raw silk, Adams reported in detail on the state of the Japanese silk industry at the time. His mission was a response to a complaint of the Yokohama General Chamber of Commerce (composed of Western merchants at Yokohama) that the quality of the Japanese raw silks had been severely compromised in recent years. After the tour, Adams concluded that the Japanese silk industry had to overcome two problems: the quality of the reeled silk and the quality of the silk itself. The quality of the reeled silk had suffered in recent years because Japanese producers had concentrated on increasing the volume at the expense of quality. The reelers were often inexperienced and under tremendous pressure to finish quickly rather than to take time and reel carefully. The only solution was to adopt mechanical reeling methods to reel consistently and at a higher quality. Since silk could be improved only by using better silkworm eggs, there was no real solution to the problem of the quality of the silk except by preventing the export of high quality silkworm eggs. And that, according to him, was unlikely as long as Western merchants outbid the Japanese for the best eggs.[33]

Some other Western merchants sent Japanese representatives to southern Gunma to purchase eggs rather than wait at Yokohama. Eventually this practice faded as trade patterns changed, but also because the major Japanese silk merchants formed mercantile associations in the old Tokugawa period tradition and due to Japanese government action.

In 1869, the cash-strapped Meiji government decided to ensure that it would collect all the exports tariffs that were its due. The Finance Ministry, over the objections of the Foreign Ministry, established silk inspection centers in every treaty port to inspect both the raw silk and silkworm eggs and to collect export tariffs on them. The Foreign Ministry could see that this might invite Western criticism as interfering in "free trade." In 1873, Japanese merchants created the Yokohama kiito aratame kaisha (Yokohama Raw Silk Inspection Company) and the local version called the chihō kiito aratame kaisha (Local Raw Silk Inspection Company) in 1873 with the support of the Meiji state.

Many Japanese historians believe these actions were part of a plan by the government to control the production and distribution of raw silk. In one case, the authorities harassed and arrested a Japanese representative of an Italian merchant who seemed to be carrying too much cash. The Italian minister to Japan in turn sent a letter demanding his release and noninterference in commercial transactions. The Japanese foreign ministry argued that the practice of foreign merchants sending their representatives into the interior violated the treaties, since the treaties limited foreign trade to the open ports. The Italian minister replied that there was no provision banning travel or trade by Japanese in the interior, even if hired by Westerners. In this particular case, the Italians were on firmer ground and the Japanese Foreign Ministry backed down.[34]

Were these companies part of a nationalistic attempt to retain or retake commercial sovereignty vis-à-vis the foreign merchants in Japan? As seen in earlier chapters, dealing with fraud and cheating was a major issue during the Tokugawa era, and mercantile associations were necessary to insure commercial transactions. I would make the argument that the Meiji state simply carried on the tradition of the recent past and merely wanted more revenue. The nationalistic element was a side issue. After all, this practice continued despite foreign criticism. By 1874 the companies officially were disbanded when many foreign merchants criticized them as "guilds" and foreign governments complained loudly to the Meiji state. However, as if to prove that the Japanese merchants themselves felt the need for some sort of mercantile association, even after the companies disbanded, the merchants continued to act through voluntary mercantile associations, and the great merchants such as Hara and Mogi firmly retained control of the raw silk business.[35]

These associations pledged not to deal with Japanese representatives of Western merchants and thus weakened the representatives' ability to buy silk products from the sericulturalists of Kantō. Later as the Yokohama merchants became bankers, controlling Second National and the Seventy-Fourth National banks, they firmly established their control through competitive loans. The dominance of the Japanese Yokohama silk merchants and their later transformation into bankers helped shape the future of Kantō's industrial development. For unlike central and southern China, eastern Japan's silk industry did not establish factories in the treaty ports; instead the merchant-bankers funded the creation of numerous small-scale factories in the rural hinterland.[36]

The government at the very top level of of the Meiji state was run by officials who understood the importance of economic policy. Now that Japan was unified under one government, instead of running a domain mercantilism as many domains in western Japan had done vis-à-vis the rest of the country, the Meiji government pursued mercantilism for the entire nation vis-à-vis the rest of the world. As such Ōkubo Toshimichi, the single most powerful man in the new government, argued in favor of native industry and the importance of exports.[37] The establishment of the government-run Tomioka Silk Mill in 1872 (planning for it had begun in 1870) and the Japanese exhibit at the 1873 Vienna exposition firmly established raw silk and silkworm eggs as Japan's main export industries. The question was which to promote, raw silk or eggs? For many, such as Inoue Kaoru, one of the leading voices in the Finance Ministry, eggs loomed as the more important product. He did not deny the importance of raw silk, ordering a report on the state of the silk industry in Japan for the exhibition, and advocated some questionable schemes, such as promoting "mountain silk," silk drawn from insects other than the domesticated silkworm.[38] Overall, he and the Meiji state seemed to prefer the silkworm egg industry over the raw silk industry when Western merchants began to criticize the declining quality of both the raw silk and the silkworm eggs.

Ironically, just as the Meiji government was actively supporting the development of the silkworm egg industry, the international environment for the silk industry as a whole began to change. The crisis in silk production, of which Japan had been the main beneficiary, was ending. By the early 1870s, Chinese exports recovered from the effects of the Taiping Rebellion, which had in the mid-1860s reduced Chinese exports to half of the pre-rebellion level. In Europe, Louis Pasteur developed a simple and elegant method to keep silkworms healthy in 1865. Mating the insects in cells, the producers could identify the diseased parents and the infected eggs, and thus avoid them. This cellular system spread in Italy from the late 1860s to the early 1870s, ending the pebrine crisis. Market crashes—such as that caused by the 1871 defeat of France in the Franco-Prussian War and the expected decline in French consumption—and price spikes—caused by the 1876 and 1877 silkworm crop failures in Italy—disrupted the price of the eggs, but the long-term trend was clear.[39] Because both China and Europe returned to the global market as suppliers, prices dropped.

Table 6.1, Japanese Exports of Silkworm Eggs, reveals a number of interesting points. The first is the annual volatility in price. The variation in volume between 1867 and 1868 is due primarily to Japan's civil war, which disrupted the export but not the production of eggs. The unsold stock from 1867 was sold the next year. The market for eggs crashed in the early 1870s, which some scholars attribute to France's defeat in the Franco-Prussian War. Many merchants at the time had expected the primary global customer of raw silk, French weavers of fine silk, to produce less because of the defeat. To counter this problem of overly cheap egg prices, the producers burned ap-

Table 6.1. Japanese Exports of Silkworm Eggs

	Volume (in cards)	*Value (in $ or ¥)*	*Price per Card*
1865	1,321,521	$660,160	$0.50
1867	738,156	$2,214,468	$3.00
1868	2,106,171	$4,199,138	$2.00
1869	1,367,143	$2,728,500	$2.00
1870	1,392,665	$3,473,150	$2.50
1871	1,453,755	$2,184,688	$1.50
1872	1,315,835	$1,963,159	$1.50
1873	1,410,555	$3,032,459	$2.15
1874	1,334,625	$731,275	$0.55
1875	727,463	$474,921	$0.65
1876	1,018,525	$1,902,271	$1.87
1877	1,176,142	$346,998	$0.30
1878	887,767	$682,606	$0.77
1879	813,949	$582,623	$0.72
1880	530,452	$991,021	$1.87
1881	374,494	$311,140	$0.83
1882	177,240	$122,486	$0.69
1883	75,091	$55,287	$0.73
1884	59,785	$40,708	$0.68
1885	41,653	¥33,330	¥0.80

Source: After 1873, the Mexican dollar and the yen are more or less equivalent. YS, II, 512, 519; YS: S, II, 5.

proximately 450,000 cards of overstock in 1874.[40] Nevertheless, silkworm egg prices followed the general global trend of the last five hundred years—the price decline of primary goods. In this case, the cause was most likely increased global production. After the next crisis in 1877, which seems to have stemmed from overcompensation due to the Italian crop failures of 1876 and 1877,[41] Japan's egg exports declined steadily, ceasing completely in 1898.

Historians normally attribute this decline to the drop in the quality of Japanese silkworm eggs or simply ignore it. However, one must ask the question, why did Japanese eggs fail to maintain their share in the European market? If shoddy products could not sell, then why did producers of quality Japanese silkworm eggs, such as the Shimamura villagers, fail in their export attempts? After all, when the Italian mission and the Adams mission toured the silk-producing region, which included Shimamura, Tajima Yahei, a prominent producer from Shimamura, made contacts with Western merchants and sold what he and others considered to be high-quality eggs. In fact, the villagers of Shimamura were convinced that if they could directly ship their high-quality eggs to Italy, bypassing the Yokohama merchants (both Japanese and Western) and their fees, their products would sell. Thus, we now turn to the journals and letters of Shimamura producers who directly sold their eggs in Italy. These sources may explain why Japanese silkworm eggs failed to maintain their market share, or even a foothold, in Europe.

SHIMAMURA: "WE ARE THE EGGMEN"

Shimamura village is on the southern edge of Gunma prefecture. More importantly, it is on the edge of the river Tone. Traditionally the river separated the provinces of Kōzuke and Musashi; Shimamura was on the northern side of this border. However, after a major river control project in the early twentieth century, the river now runs through what was once the center of the village. Until then, floods periodically devastated the village. For example, between 1846 and 1863 the river flooded six times.[42] With such frequent floods, rice cultivation was unthinkable. Even the less productive dry fields were always at the mercy of the river, which, when changing course, could not only inundate the fields, but also destroy the villagers' homes. It was only in the early nineteenth century, after the Kantō regional economy began to commercialize, that the river became a source of income rather than sorrow. The villagers, rather than relying solely on agriculture, began to engage in the riparian transport business and sericulture.[43]

The periodic floods proved beneficial when growing mulberry, because the trees could withstand minor floods and the waters brought nutrition. As an added benefit, the floodwaters washed away the eggs of a parasitic fly that harmed silkworms. Sericulture was a new business in which only a dozen or more households engaged before the start of foreign trade. It was not an easy business. A household needed to hire laborers for the sericulture season, which required capital, and it was intensive work. For Shimamura the season ran from April to July. Extra labor was needed to cut the mulberry branches, chop the leaves into smaller portions, feed the worms, distinguish the male and female moths, and then mate the moths to get the eggs. Around the middle of April, the villagers prepared for their busiest season by washing their equipment and hiring laborers, typically women from nearby villages and men from further away. By May, the busiest month, they dedicated all of their time to harvesting the mulberry leaves and raising the silkworms. They woke at four in the morning and worked until eleven at night. Even at night, they took shifts to feed the worms and ensure healthy living conditions for the silkworms. During this one month, the worms would molt four times, and grow ten thousand–fold to approximately four grams each. Fully grown, the worms spun their cocoons in two to three days, and ten days later, they gnawed their way out as adult moths. The villagers would then mate the male with the female moths; each female moth could lay about six hundred eggs. With each female enclosed inside a small cardboard circle, the moth would lay its eggs in a circle. These cardboard circles were densely packed onto a card and removed once the egg laying was complete. This single card could hold approximately fifteen to twenty thousand eggs. Their reproductive cycle completed, the moths died over the next few days. But in their wake, they left their legacy. The villagers kept some eggs for the next year, for a new generation. The vast majority were now a commodity destined to be sold to someone who would raise the silkworm eggs for the raw silk from the cocoons.[44]

According to Tajima Yahei, in 1863, a year before the shogunal ban on the sale of silkworm eggs was lifted, a Shimamura villager illegally sold the first silkworm eggs to an Italian merchant named Enrico Andreossi[45] at Yokohama. Hearing of this, a few other foreign merchants came to this unnamed villager, providing him with a boon.[46] In the few short years after the government legalized the trade, Shimamura villagers concentrated on silkworm rearing. Of the approximately 350 households, by 1872, 180 people engaged in silkworm rearing, and by 1877, 250 villagers were involved in this global business.[47]

Recognizing the importance of sericulture to their livelihood, 205 villagers formed a company called the Shimamura kangyō kaisha with ¥6,000 borrowed from the newly formed Tokyo Mitsui Bank in 1872, a year after the price of eggs crashed. This company performed a number of roles. It set standards by organizing their products according to quality. It reassured foreign merchants at a time when Japanese merchants and producers often tricked foreign merchants into buying low-quality or even fraudulent products. It actively tried to cultivate a brand name to be able to sell their eggs for a better price. The company also provided capital to its members to encourage production. At first, everything seemed to go well. Foreign merchants, trusting in the quality of Shimamura eggs, bought the cards at ¥5 each, providing the company with enough cash to repay the bank and leave them with profits. After another price crash in 1877 and the subsequent destruction of 310,000 cards at Yokohama, the company decided not to go through Japanese Yokohama merchants, whom the villagers thought were unfairly lumping their quality products with lower-quality eggs. Thus in 1878 the company set up a Tokyo office from which it sold all 72,672 cards in one day to foreign Yokohama merchants.

The villagers' efforts in forming a company, standardizing quality, creating a brand, increasing output, and directly selling to foreign merchants had paid off. Not only did they sell all their eggs, they did this when the industry as a whole suffered again, leading to the destruction of more silkworm eggs at Yokohama that same year. During the 1870s, Shimamura villagers increased output and sales despite the decreasing volume of total Japanese exports.

Their crisis came in 1879, when only a portion of the 89,288 cards were sold at their office in Tokyo. The company members, who now felt cheated by the foreign merchants as well, voted to export 50,000 or so of the remaining cards to Italy themselves without going through any merchant, Japanese or foreign, at Yokohama. After gaining support from the Mitsui Trading Company[48] in this venture, on 1 December 1879, the 239 members elected Tajima Shin with 228 votes to head a three-man delegation to Italy. Shin was

Table 6.2. Sales of Silkworm Egg Cards from Shimamura

	Silkworm Egg Cards
1871	36,868
1872	44,078
1873	43,266
1874	50,449
1875	32,179
1876	31,061
1877	63,617
1878	72,672
1879	89,288

Source: Tajima Yahei, "Bakumatsu yori Meiji shoki santane yushutsu kiroku," SSYN, 4–5. The numbers listed here are from his text, which claim that the output matched sales every year.

thirty-three years old and the head of the largest landlord family in Shimamura.[49] As Tajima Yasaburō, a member of the delegation (not related to Shin), noted however, Mitsui Trading Company was primarily responsible for the itinerary of the three-man delegation and the sale of the eggs. Tajima's mission on this trip was to inspect the Italian silk industry and to give advice on the sale of eggs.[50]

Thus after consultation with Mitsui officials, including the president of Mitsui Trading Company, Tajima Shin, Tajima Yasaburō, and Tajima Yahei[51] decided to circumnavigate the globe by first going from Shimamura to Yokohama then to San Francisco. From San Francisco they would travel onward to New York, London, Paris, and finally to Milan. The return trip would be from Milan, through the Italian peninsula, and then to the Suez Canal, Singapore, Hong Kong, Yokohama, and finally to Shimamura. This route was similar to that taken by the Iwakura mission several years earlier but with some tourist stops in between, such as Niagara Falls. Interestingly two Italian silkworm egg merchants, Pompeo Mazzocchi and Pietro Bertone,[52] traveled along with them. They were together throughout the trip from Yokohama (leaving on 12 December 1879) to Chicago (6 January 1880). At Chicago they parted ways, and the trio went to Niagara Falls, while the Italians went to Philadelphia. When the trio arrived at New York, on 8 January 1880, the three men met with a Mitsui official during the day and the Italian merchants in the evening. During their weeklong stay in New York, they met with Japanese consular officials and were introduced to other Japanese merchants working there.[53]

Once the trio left New York and arrived in Europe, the business aspect of the trip became apparent. They were unable to sightsee in London and hurried on to Paris. As soon as they arrived there on 27 January 1880, a Mitsui official greeted them and informed the Shimamura merchants that he had contracted Marco Arese, who was based in Milan, for help.[54] This Mitsui official had already gone to Lyon and talked with a major silk merchant there to find a contact for them in Milan. The day after they arrived in Milan, on 3 February 1880, they visited their Italian branch office that Mitsui had set up for them and paid a visit to Arese. They stayed in Milan until 22 May 1880 and worked to sell as much of their merchandise as they could. They met some merchants that they had encountered already, such as Mazzocchi and Savio,[55] but they also expanded their contacts as much as possible. The three Tajimas rotated their duties so that only one of them was present at the office at any one time. They also hired an assistant to be there every day and thus were able to fulfill their mission to inspect the Italian silk industry and to oversee sales. They traveled the area, mingled with the local merchants, saw how the locals raised silkworms (21 March, 21 April, 17 May), toured a silk factory (20 March), and of course haggled over the price of their eggs.[56]

Initially things seemed to go smoothly as Tajima Yahei's letter, sent on 20 February 1880, attests:

> Of the silkworm eggs, every day customers buy a few of Shimamura's cards, but none of the other eggs that we brought on behalf of Mitsui sell. Of the over 6,000 of these cards, we have so far sold 30, at five francs each. If things continue in this manner, the eggs, aside from the Shimamura eggs, will rot.
>
> Among Japanese silkworm eggs, Akita and Shimamura are famous, but the rest are merely known as Japanese eggs so that the peasants do not know where nor who has made them. Since the buyers know that the Akita and Shimamura eggs are quality eggs and feel that the rest cannot be trusted, if we bring our Shimamura eggs produced this year [in summer 1880] here [to Italy] rather than sell them in Japan, then they will assuredly be bought.[57]

The price of the eggs reflected this, as they sold the eggs from anywhere between seven and eleven francs.[58] Some of the Italian buyers were quite optimistic, because when Tajima Shin visited Enrico Andreossi and Giovanni Butta on 13 February, they agreed that approximately fifty thousand cards from Shimamura could be sold in Italy annually (although the Italians did not forget to caution them that a surplus of eggs would cause a collapse in price).[59]

Even the declining trend of Japanese exports seemed reversible:

> When I [Tajima Yahei] asked Walesu [Marco Arese], why Italy which used to import a massive amount of Japanese eggs recently began to import less, and if there was future profit to be made, he replied that there are a number of theories to explain the phenomenon, but I [Arese] think it is because currently Italy prefers the yellow cocoon silkworm, the "jaruloto."[60] Although he does not know how tough these silkworm are, since he has never experimented with them, because the Italian people and the government would prefer not to import silkworm eggs and rely on their own domestic eggs, there are only a few that truly prefer Japanese eggs. It is only because the current Italian eggs are inferior to Japanese eggs that the people are forced to buy Japanese. I considered this carefully; their yellow strain is weak and has potential to fail as it grows, thus the Italians do not like it. But [despite the flaws] if this yellow cocoon strain proves to be more profitable, they would no longer buy Japanese silkworm eggs. Now I believe that, if we could test them thoroughly, we could prove that the Japanese eggs are more profitable, and therefore they may want to import more Japanese eggs again.[61]

Perhaps this optimism coupled with their belief in their product prevented them from lowering prices. After all, lowering the price drastically would wound the Shimamura brand, a mistake Yahei wanted to avoid in the company's first trip to Italy.

Yet inevitably as the year progressed and the season neared its end in Italy, prices came down. They fluctuated between a low of two francs and a high of eight francs. Moreover, there seemed no set pattern to how they sold their products, for they would sell a single card or one hundred, five hundred, or even a thousand cards at a time.[62] In the middle of May, nature terminated their efforts, for the eggs, patiently waiting and kept cool in caves, finally could wait no longer. When they inspected one batch on 15 May 1880, thousands of silkworms had hatched, rendering that batch useless; eventually 22,369 cards had to be destroyed.[63]

Ultimately, on their first trip from 1879 to 1880, they sold 29,851 cards in Italy, far less than their early optimistic estimate, but still generating a profit of ¥0.53 per card after all expenses were accounted for.[64] Considering that this was a new venture for them, it was a success. As the trio left Italy via the Suez, their fellow villagers were in the middle of the 1880 silkworm egg season. By the time they returned to Japan, on 12 July 1880, most of the production had been completed for their second attempt to export directly.

SHIMAMURA: THE ITALIAN CONNECTION

The second trip took the same format, with Mitsui in charge of sales. This time, however, there was dissent. Once Tajima Takebei and Tajima Yasaburō, the two representatives for this trip, reached Yokohama on 11 November 1880, some members balked. These men preferred to sell their products in Yokohama rather than await the return of the two from Europe before collecting their profits. The next day Takebei drafted a compromise. The *Belgic*, an American ship, was scheduled to sail out of Yokohama on 24 or 25 November, so if they could find a buyer who would buy all 56,000 cards at a fair price before its departure, they would sell, if not they would leave and seek to sell abroad. With a fair price decided by averaging the proposed prices of all who were present at the meeting, the day came to a close.[65]

The problem was, as stated earlier, the export of silkworm eggs had suddenly boomed and was now just as suddenly crashing. In Shimamura before the exports began in the 1860s, only a dozen or more households engaged in silkworm rearing for the domestic market. By 1868, of the 360 or 370 households, some 250 households had entered the business. By the time exports were crashing in 1877, the majority of these new producers, who depended primarily on the export market, was forced to take on more risk. In contrast, the large landholders of Shimamura, who had produced 25 percent of the total silkworm egg production in 1877, were relatively safe. They sold mostly to a domestic market and contributed only 10 percent of Shimamura's exports. And yet, Tajima Shin, the thirty-three-year-old head of the largest landowner family in Shimamura, led the first delegation to sell their eggs directly to Italy. I prefer to take the charitable view that the wealthiest families in Shimamura wanted to encourage exports so that all families in the village could benefit. From the wealthiest family to the poorer families, more than 74 percent of the villagers engaged in the first of the five-year (four-trip) attempt to export directly.[66]

The villagers' commitment to foreign trade, however, would be tested on the second trip. On the first trip, some of the cards had been sold in Yokohama, and it was the unsold cards that went abroad. This masked a critical difference between the wealthier and poorer producers. The more established wealthier producers could afford to take the risk, since foreign exports were only part of their income. Perhaps more importantly, they could wait for the return of their representatives from Italy for their profits. The poorer producers, however, who probably had to borrow to produce in the first place, were unable to wait for their representatives to return. Every day they waited meant that they had to pay interests on the money they borrowed. Thus even if their representatives returned from Italy with profits, the delay meant that their profits would be less compared to those who did not have to borrow.

When foreign merchants proposed to buy half the eggs on 19 November 1880, the villagers split into two groups. The Yokohama faction strongly favored selling, while the export faction insisted on going abroad with "arguments raging all day without end." The squabbling factions even split their lodging, with the exporters sleeping on the second floor and Yokohama sellers on the ground floor of an inn in Yokohama, frustrating Tajima Takebei no end. It is clear from his diary that he wanted to sell and travel abroad. Takebei expected the Yokohama market to be depressed that year (approximately 40,000 cards to be sold instead of 80,000 to 100,000 in past years) and consequently tried to quash the persistent rumors that Shimamura villagers were going to sell in Yokohama this year. On 28 November 1880, after traveling back and forth between Yokohama and Tokyo on the railroad to talk to Mitsui officials, government officials, other merchants, and even the Italian minister to Japan and after letters and telegrams sent to and received from Shimamura, Tajima Takebei and Tajima Yasaburō finally left Yokohama on the French ship *Volga*.[67]

The two factions had compromised. Those who wanted to sell in Yokohama would sell their share—18,000 cards—to those who still wanted to sell in Italy for ¥5.50 per card. Those who wanted to export would pay them ¥1 per card, the difference to be paid with interest upon the return of Takebei and Yasaburō from Italy. The problem, of course, was that the exporters needed capital to buy the cards now, and Mitsui, who was in charge of the export venture, had not heard of this change in plans. Nevertheless, Takebei and Yasaburō managed to continue their mission.[68]

This time they sailed through Asia, stopping at Hong Kong (5–8 December), where they changed ships, and continued to Saigon (11–12 December), Singapore (14–15 December), Colombo (20–21 December), Aden (27–28

December), and the Suez Canal (1–3 January) to finally reach Naples (7–8 January). At Naples they boarded a train bound for Rome and then transferred trains to arrive at Milan on 8 January 1881 with no sightseeing except for their views from the train windows. The return trip was also without any frills as they reversed their itinerary.[69]

Their stay in Milan was like the trip, all business. Immediately upon arrival, they inspected their cargo and met silkworm egg merchants of Italy and the Japanese consul of Milan. By 12 January they began their tour of the countryside, first at Turin, to sell their eggs. On 17 January 1881, upon hearing local rumors that they were not selling their eggs, they decided that rather than haggling for the price of each card, they would sell with a price chart in plain view: 1 to 50 cards at 16 francs each, 51 to 200 cards at 14.5 francs, 201 to 1,000 cards at 13.5 francs each, 1,001 to 3,000 cards at 12.5 francs. Coincidentally that day, they sold 3,000 cards to their first customer. Italian merchants from the previous trip such as Savio, Arese, Andreossi, Dell'oro and Antongini again bought large invoices.[70] Unfortunately Takebei suffered health problems (a number of stomach problems and headaches) during the course of the trip and his early stay in Milan. Their trip to the Alps to store the eggs in a cool climate made his health even worse. Nevertheless, they were selling so well that when they met Japan's consul at Milan,[71] they were bullish about their prospects and promised to come back every year to sell their eggs.[72]

As the months progressed, the same problem as the previous year occurred. Under pressure to sell the eggs before they hatched, Takebei and Yasaburō debated whether to lower prices. Initially Takebei was opposed according to Yasaburō. Takebei, in his own diary, agreed to lower prices, first for wholesale, on 6 March 1881, then for retail on 14 March 1881 to 11 francs per card. Yasaburō in his diary mentions that they were still arguing about the issue at that time, and he does not mention a settlement. In theory they were supposed to rotate their duties at the shop and thus their agreement on any issue was critical. But because Takebei became bedridden by April, Yasaburō won any argument by virtue of being the only active manager. As April passed, the buyers knew that Yasaburō had to sell and waited for the price to drop. By 25 April, since only small batches were sold before that month, Yasaburō decided to lower the price to sell as much as he could before the eggs hatched. Yet he still had pride in their eggs and felt that lowering the price too drastically would wound the brand name of Shimamura. This awareness of the importance of brand names was an important positive legacy of the Tokugawa economy. When a buyer asked if he would sell for 5 francs, Yasaburō refused, arguing that the lowest he could go was for 6 francs wholesale. On 7 May 1881, he finally gave up on selling the eggs and began the process of comparing their books with Mitsui officials.[73]

Takebei, for his part, felt guilty that he could not help his partner in this endeavor, especially after 15 April, when he had to go to Cassano for treatment. Even in his dreams, he worried about the market for eggs. Takebei eventually recovered from surgery and wrote letters to Milan. Yasaburō's replies were not encouraging, and he worried even more what would happen when they returned to Japan. By the time Takebei returned to Milan on 4 May 1881, Yasaburō was ready to close shop and an Italian national exhibition was about to open in Milan. After the two closed their shop, they visited the exhibition. Later the two visited the consul's mansion to inspect the Italian method in rearing silkworms and for a farewell party. Yasaburō's diary ends on 12 May, two days before they left Milan, while Takebei chronicles the return voyage.[74] They returned to Yokohama on 24 June 1881.

The third and fourth sales proved to be very different from the first or the second trip. Mitsui, which was reeling from overexpansion and the Matsukata deflation, had begun its retrenchment, including Milan, requiring more commitment from Shimamura villagers.[75] Moreover, as Tajima Yasaburō, and presumably Takebei, learned on 4 April 1881, the Shimamura company had dissolved, and the export faction had to re-form into another company with only 118 members as of February 1881.[76] Under these circumstances, the young Tajima Keitarō, the twenty-six-year-old son of Yasaburō, went to Milan in November 1881 and stayed until July 1883 to handle the business of Shimamura kangyō kaisha. Unfortunately, his journal for the third trip is lost (since his journal, titled "Ōkō kiji, 2," for the fourth direct sales attempt exists, presumably he must have written "Ōkō kiji, 1"), but his letters are available for the three years that he was in Milan.

Keitarō's letters, dated 15 April, 22 April, 27 May, and 3 June 1882, demonstrate that he too experienced similar problems faced by his father and his colleagues.[77] However, he also tried new solutions. Though it is fascinating to read how he developed his strategy through trial and error, his conclusions were to learn Italian, to target retail sales rather than larger scale merchants who bought in bulk (even though the latter seems to have been the preferred sales in the first two trips), and to sell only the best quality eggs. Would things have succeeded if others had followed his suggestions?

Learning Italian is more or less self-explanatory. Any business, if it is to have long-term prospects, must learn the local language. This suggestion could only help if followed. So let us consider the issue of retail versus bulk sales. Following in the footsteps of the second direct sales attempt, in January Keitarō publicized the prices for the eggs: for Shimamura eggs, 10 francs per card for retail, and 7.5 francs per card for bulk sales or for any sale greater than 1,000 cards; for other Japanese eggs, 7.5 francs for retail and 5 francs for bulk sales. He claimed that he was the first among dealers of eggs to publicly declare the price of eggs, forgetting what his predecessors had done. He set these prices according to the advice of an Italian merchant.

However, compared to the previous year, these prices were considerably lower, and for those who had preordered from the previous winter, he even discounted another franc from the retail price. These lower prices at bulk eventually hurt his profit margin and this may be the reason why he preferred retail sales.

He did try to maintain the image of Shimamura eggs as higher in quality by separating them from other Japanese eggs in terms of price and by using a specific brand logo (the rising sun). The problem was that Shimamura eggs could be bought in Yokohama, and thus he was in competition with his fellow villagers who chose not to export through the company. And these villagers were also selling the same Shimamura brand eggs. Thus, the larger scale Italian merchants tried to lower the price of bulk purchases down to 5 francs, regardless of their transactional history. Although Keitarō resisted, ultimately he acceded to their demands since two orders sold 8,000 cards and then another 4,000 cards.

The problem with selling retail, however, was that it was highly volatile, perhaps more so than the normal volatility associated with silkworm eggs. As he discovered during his first year, bulk sales primarily occurred in January, making February and March relatively quiet. Retail sales only picked up in April, close to the season of rearing silkworms, perhaps because retail sales was dominated by small local producers and merchants who could not gauge ahead of time whether they would engage in sericulture this year or not. Structurally this made for a game of chicken. Keitarō and his customers were so close to the time the eggs hatched that obstinacy by one or both parties could spell disaster for both. Even if prices did not drop as low as bulk sales, a total loss was far worse. Moreover, with marginal customers, if anything went wrong—for example, what happened in April 1882, a freak cold front and a frost that destroyed the mulberry crop—sales could and did suddenly end. To counter this, as mentioned earlier, he tried to cultivate long-term customers by selling at a discount to those who had promised to buy eggs from the previous year.

The issue of quality arose due to the matter of taste. By 1881 Italian strains of silkworms were gaining popularity. The Italian raw silk industry, which had survived the devastation of pebrine by importing Japanese silkworm eggs, was returning to its normal pattern. Ironically, the "returning" Italian strain were crossbreeds, part Italian, part Japanese. If the traditional Italian strains were known for their yellowish color and fatness, the Japanese ones were bluish but healthier. The crossbreeds were still yellow, but fatter than Japanese strains and more resistant to disease than the old Italian strains. The combination understandably drew popularity, for it had a familiar color and shape and was healthier than before. Despite their popularity in Italy, however, Keitarō believed that the best of the Japanese silkworms was still better than the new Italian strains. He reckoned that as a group they produced more raw silk because they were healthier, with fewer failed cocoons. Thus he believed that at reasonable prices—the best Japanese eggs, such as those produced at Shimamura—would be able to gain the favor of the consumers and continue to be sold. In the best case scenario, he hoped that Italian merchants would stop going to Yokohama to buy regular Japanese eggs and instead that two or three Japanese merchants would come to Italy to sell only the best of their eggs. For this to happen, he believed it was critical for the Shimamura company to maintain favor among its customers.[78]

His suggestions and strategy would be tested in the last of the four attempts to sell the Shimamura eggs in Italy. In his letters dated 15 July and 5 August 1882, Tajima Keitarō wrote of his overall strategy. He sought to brand Shimamura eggs by specializing in higher quality eggs and by settling on prices independently of Yokohama prices. Unfortunately, there were rumors that Shimamura's eggs were not good this year, and he feared that unless he lowered the price of Shimamura's eggs to half the price of Akita's eggs—the more popular Japanese eggs—he would not be able to sell all of them. Lowering the price would ruin any attempts to brand Shimamura village as a provider of quality silkworm eggs. But not selling any eggs would financially ruin the producers. Caught between strategy and reality, he hoped for a price of 12.5 francs for the best quality eggs, chosen through microscopes, and 7.5 francs as the regular retail price but feared that he may have to lower the regular price to 4 francs.[79]

From Japan, Tajima Yahei addressed to Keitarō a letter dated 25 October 1882 and agreed with him on most points. The Shimamura company assented to lowering the price to 4 francs if necessary and agreed with Keitarō's earlier suggestion that domestic sales would have to take precedence over foreign sales. Assuming that Japanese exports would be a maximum of 200,000 cards, the cooperative sent him 20,000 cards that autumn. Unfortunately Keitarō's fears came true. Shimamura eggs were not selling well, and he had to lower prices to 4 francs for bulk sales and 5 francs for retail sales to the Italian buyers. In his letter dated 3 March 1883, Keitarō complained of three things. First, the peasants and the merchants did not have the money to buy the eggs, for the local economy was so bad that no one was lending money. Second, the raw silk was so cheap that people no longer wanted to raise silkworms. And finally, the weather had suddenly turned warm, invoking fears of last year's disastrous crop. These were all bad signs, for the eggs would hatch in less than two months. Even after he lowered prices to 3.5 francs, sales were still minimal. From 22 March to 10 May, only 2,714 cards were sold at 7,746.05 francs (averaging 2.85 francs per card).[80] This was an unmitigated disaster that could not be recouped elsewhere.

On 20 May 1883, the company held a general meeting. It decided to more or less retreat from direct exports and to recall Tajima Keitarō from Italy. The company would continue to try to export, at 5,000 cards a year through the acting consul for the Japanese government. Following Keitarō's suggestions, only the best eggs would be exported. Interestingly, though, they also suspected that because the consul was an Italian aristocrat, he would not be a particularly good merchant in selling their eggs. In any case, next year's crop would be set at about 19,000 to 20,000 cards, of which only 5,000 would go to the Italian market.

When Keitarō heard of this decision, understandably he was upset. He continued to believe that Japanese eggs could sell well in Italy, for the Italians did not care if the eggs were imported or not. He believed that they only cared if they made money. Thus, the eggs and the worms needed to be healthy. The differences in color did not matter as much as imagined. And finally, a minor adjustment was necessary, since the Italians sold their eggs by the ounce (27 grams) and Shimamura sold by the card (typically 22 to 23 grams).[81] Nevertheless, on 7 July 1883, Keitarō left Milan for Japan, ending his twenty-month-long stay in Italy.

SHIMAMURA'S LEGACY

According to Ushiki Yukio's analysis of the records, which includes the various journals kept by these men traveling to Italy, the first three attempts successfully generated profits and the last and final one incurred losses. On the first trip, 54,204 cards were shipped out, and 29,851 cards were sold in Italy, generating a profit of ¥0.53 per card shipped. On the second trip, 56,400 cards were shipped out, and 35,180 cards were sold in Italy, generating a profit of ¥1.53 per card shipped. On the third trip, 28,000 cards were shipped out, and 22,922 cards were sold in Italy, generating a profit of ¥0.91 per card shipped. On the fourth and final trip, 20,000 cards were shipped out, but only 7,327 cards were sold in Italy, thus incurring a loss of ¥0.35 per card shipped. In that same year as the fourth trip, 1883, the company sold 9,200 cards domestically at a profit of ¥0.5 per card. It was clear that the experiment to sell directly to foreigners should come to an end. The company had tried to match demand with their supply, matching one year's exports to the amount that was actually sold in Italy the previous year. Unfortunately, however, this meant that overall production and participation declined at the company. In terms of participation, at the beginning of the attempt to export, there were 236 individuals who tried again. By the third trip, participation was reduced to 128 individuals from 1881 to 1882 and then to 124 from 1882 and 1883. Production as a whole fell as well: from 89,288 cards in 1879 to 29,200 cards in 1883 and then even lower during the three following years (11,088 cards, 15,385 cards, and 10,435 cards, respectively). By 1885, only forty households engaged in silkworm egg rearing in Shimamura. The small-scale producers who had experienced the boom until 1882 took the brunt of the effects of the decline and dropped out, while the larger producers, who still had domestic buyers and could afford to weather a bad turn, maintained their production.[82]

The cost of this failure to maintain a share in the European market was clear. It devastated the economy of Shimamura and many other producers of eggs. The reasons its failure, however, remain unclear. Most historians cite the recovery of the European industry as the reason. But if quality Japanese silkworm eggs such as Shimamura's were being sold at ever-cheaper prices (the price increased from 6.2 francs per card to 11.5 francs per card then dropped radically to 4.8 francs per card and 3.7 francs per card), then should there not have been some opportunity to maintain their presence?[83]

If the first decade following the opening of Yokohama (1859–1868) established the pattern for Japan's first phase of international trade, the second decade (1868–1879) began with a revolution and finished with a virtual end of that first phase of international trade. The Meiji Restoration promised to alter the domestic political setting and definitively did so when the new regime abolished the feudal domains in 1871. While production of silkworm eggs and raw silk soared, the global political and economic situation changed, throwing the future of these goods into doubt. When the Chinese and European silk industries recovered, the 1870s proved to be a difficult decade for Japanese producers, as French and Italian peasants ceased to purchase Japanese silkworm eggs, and the manufacturers, preferring European or Chinese raw silk, bought less raw silk from Japan. The international silk industry needed a bigger market to absorb the increased global production.

It is in this context that Shimamura's experience must be analyzed. Although the company was able to expand exports for a while, eventually it too lost its foothold in the European market. There are a number of reasons for this failure. As Tajima Keitarō noticed, once the French and Italian silkworm eggs returned, there was an undeniable preference for these eggs. Japanese eggs, particularly when bought by the large wholesale merchants, sold at cheaper prices, prices that may have been lower than the cost to produce the eggs toward the end of this experience. In order to avoid this, Tajima Keitarō considered the possibility of selling retail.

However, when selling at the retail price to the Italian peasants, three problems quickly emerged. First was the scale. By definition, the peasants were paying retail, but Shimamura was sending at least 20,000 cards. Even if each retail buyer bought fifty cards, to clear 20,000 cards of inventory meant selling to at least 400 buyers. Since a retail buyer was not likely to buy more than ten cards, in reality the company probably needed 2,000 retail buyers.[84] Second was the need to maintain the loyalty of these buyers. Maintaining ties with a small number of merchants was much easier than maintaining ties with a large number of small buyers. Finally, the retail customers often did not have enough cash to buy the eggs at the beginning of the season. This was in fact the same problem faced by Japanese merchants in the hinterlands of Yokohama. There, the larger merchants lent money to the peasants to buy the eggs (and the top merchants eventually became bankers), but here in Italy, it would be extremely difficult for a company of Japanese villagers producing silkworm eggs to gather enough cash to lend to Italian buyers to make raw silk.

Beyond these problems in selling silkworm eggs, there was an ironic structural problem as well. As more raw silk flooded the global market, the price of raw silk declined to such an extent that some Italian peasants began to stop producing raw silk. In France peasants had already stopped making raw silk and were concentrating on rearing high-quality French silkworm eggs or manufacturing of high-quality artisanal silk cloth. The Italians also moved toward making high-quality raw silk, slowly phasing out the production of lower quality raw silk. Thus to survive in the Italian silkworm egg market, high-quality eggs, the basis for high-quality raw silk, was absolutely necessary. And in this, Shimamura and other Japanese silkworm egg producers failed to convince the Italians that they could produce high-quality eggs. The Italian buyers thought of the best Japanese silkworm eggs as two, sometimes even three, ranks lower than what the French could offer.

The possibility of a Japanese silkworm egg export sector disappeared in the 1880s. Shimamura returned to its traditional role as a supplier for the Japanese market. This transition was a wrenching one, for it entailed the loss of a major industry at a time of major depression within Japan. The villagers who believed in the rising tide lifting all boats were betrayed. For a while it may have been true, but by 1885 only forty people made 10,435 cards, of which 9,600 cards were for the domestic market. A few people had succeeded in the boom and managed to hold on or even prosper after this boom, but most people rose and fell with it. A few unlucky ones who were wealthy even before the boom also lost out in the 1880s, returning the village to the old pattern of haves and have-nots.[85] Despite the best efforts of the Shimamura villagers, including its wealthiest, they failed. Despite the support the Meiji government gave to the silkworm egg industry, as a foreign export industry it perished.

The hinterland of Yokohama was diverse enough. The silk industry produced silkworm eggs, cocoons, raw silk, and silk cloths for the domestic market. Among these silk products, raw silk remained a major export product. Now we turn to the export of raw silk in the 1870s and 1880s.

THE BROTHERS HOSHINO

This study now turns to the opening days of the American trade. In the end it was the American market and its voracious appetite for Japanese raw silk that rescued the Kantō economic region's silk export industry. In the late 1870s the silk industry in Japan was in crisis. Stronger global competition meant not only declining sales of the silkworm eggs, but also stagnant raw silk sales.[86] Importing negligible amounts of Japanese silk in the 1870s, America by 1881 was the second-largest importer after France, and became the primary importer of Japanese silk in 1883, a distinction the United States held until World War II. In the 1890s the Americans would import at minimum 1.5 million *kin* (¥11 million) and, at their most, 3.9 million *kin* (¥32 million) of Japanese raw silk. This massive boom picked up any slack left from the loss of the silkworm egg export industry.[87]

It cannot be emphasized strongly enough that Japan's success in the American market was not preordained. Therefore an explanation for this development is necessary. There was no inherent reason why the American buyers would prefer Japanese raw silk over, say, Italian raw silk or Chinese raw silk. Nevertheless the Americans chose to import the bulk of their raw silk through Japan.[88] Thus we examine the roles played by a pioneering family in silk production and sales, Japanese government officials in New York, the U.S. silk industry, and global economic developments.

The Hoshino family was the leading family of Mizunuma, a mountainous village in Gunma prefecture. It was not a wealthy village, but it was a village that had engaged in sericulture since the early Edo period. Despite the general poverty surrounding the area, the family had done well through most of the early modern period. The fact that the *bakufu* administered the village also helped, as it did not suffer from the abusive tax policies of many domains in eastern Japan. Toward the end of the Edo period, however, the family fell into dire financial problems. The chief causes were the inability of their lord to pay the loans the family had provided and a sudden boom and bust of their sake brewing business. To supplement their income, they had already begun to shift toward producing mulberry leaves for sale, but it was not enough to save them from their financial problems. The civil war imposed further hardship as Hoshino Yahei sided with the shogunate and was jailed for it. Yahei was eventually released but he was not happy with his treatment. The eldest son, Hoshino Chōtarō was born in 1845 and was already a young man when the civil war ended. Hoshino Ryōsuke (later Arai Rioichiro[89]; he was adopted into the Arai family at age twelve) was born as the sixth son in 1855.

In this section the spotlight is on this pioneering family, the Hoshino brothers. In a draft resume that Hoshino Chōtarō wrote in 1883, he proclaims that

> when I returned to my village and agriculture on the side of the Akagi mountain range, after being drafted by the Iwabana prefecture in 1869[90] to work in its accounting office for a few months, I realized that it was impossible to rescue our fortune solely by farming since we were surrounded by mountains with few rice paddies to speak of. Thus I decided that expansion of raw silk must be the path to our economic well-being, for silk is an age-old specialty of our land, and because our land is suited for the mulberry tree, even if it not suited for agriculture. My decision to fully devote our work to raising silkworms and spinning raw silk came in September of Meiji 5 (1872).[91]

No doubt he was influenced by the silk markets of Takasaki and Maebashi, the transformation taking place in Yokohama, and the region it was creating at the time. What made the family unique, however, was that they decided to radically improve their product and to sell abroad directly. The older brother would build a factory in the Western style and the younger brother would go to New York to sell to the foreigners directly.

These were both bold moves. The factory that Hoshino Chōtarō opened on 20 February 1874 in Mizunuma became the first privately operated silk-reeling factory in Japan. He learned from Swiss engineer Caspar Müller and Hayami Kensō at the Maebashi domain raw silk factory. He sent his wife and others to Maebashi to learn how to operate the machines. He tried to cut costs by using water power instead of steam, by not hiring foreign engineers (who were expensive), and by keeping the number of buildings at a bare minimum. This was a risky venture. The first batch of raw silk that his factory made was sold to a Japanese merchant who then sold the raw silk to a Western merchant. The result was terrible, despite the high praise for the quality of the raw silk; apparently the quantity was too small and he suffered a loss. Chōtarō decided to take the raw silk to Yokohama himself and sell to a Western merchant there. This time he made a profit but it was small. Commissions, tariffs, transportation costs, and all the miscellaneous fees added up. Yet he did not give up. Chōtarō, while suffering from the lack of capital, continued to produce quality raw silk. He tried to cover the rough spots by asking for infusions of cash from the government and by loans using family land as collateral. Although the factory would continually struggle, Chōtarō's efforts to organize the small producers of raw silk in Gunma into the Watarase group and to raise the quality of raw silk yielded good results. Now, he had the products to sell and he resolved to sell without intermediaries, Japanese or Western.[92] The only question was how.

Arai Rioichiro in his draft resume written in 1907 recalls that he had decided with his brother that sericulture and silk reeling was crucial to the nation and began studying English at the prefectural school in 1873. He was being modest. Rioichiro had decided to study English after visiting Tokyo in 1869. In 1871 he began his studies in English at Takasaki Domain English School, but the school was abolished in 1872. At this point Rioichiro decided to follow the best teacher at the school to his teacher's new school and continue his studies.[93] From 1873 to 1874 Rioichiro was at Yamada, near Ise, learning from this teacher. Finally in 1874 he returned to Tokyo and entered Kaisei Gakkō, a school that would later be a part of Tokyo University, to further study English. In 1875, Chōtarō met Rioichiro at Tokyo on his way back from selling raw silk in Yokohama. They agreed that Rioichiro should continue his studies in English but that he should also study Western commercial practices. Accordingly in October 1875 he entered the Institute for Commercial Law (Shōhō kōshūjo, today's Hitotsubashi University).[94]

After studying English for five years and commercial law for five months, in March 1876 Rioichiro met Satō Momotarō, a man who had just returned from an eight-year-long stay in the United States. This was a fateful encounter. Satō Momotarō, born in 1854, came from an impeccable background. He was the grandson of Satō Taizen, the personal doctor to Lord Hotta Masayoshi of Sakura domain,[95] and the son of Satō Shōchū, the founder of Juntendō hospital and medical school (today's Juntendō University). Momotarō's uncle was Matsumoto Ryōjun, the personal doctor to Shogun Tokugawa Iemochi, and first surgeon general of Japan. However, unlike his relatives who were all doctors, Momotarō received a business education in the United States. At the age of thirteen he had gone to San Francisco to study. When the Iwakura Mission came to the United States in 1872, he served as one of its translators. After the Iwakura Mission left for Europe, Momotarō opened a small business in New York. By 1875 he planned to expand his tea exporting business and returned to Japan to collect tea from Sayama, Saitama. He was also looking for business partners.[96]

After Satō Momotarō met Hayami Kensō and asked about a suitable business partner, Hayami arranged a meeting with Hoshino Chōtarō. A year earlier, in 1874, Hoshino had opened his own factory modeled after Hayami's Maebashi domain raw silk factory. Hayami must have thought that Hoshino would be a good fit for Satō. At Kumagaya, Saitama, the three met and it was decided there and then that Arai Rioichiro, age twenty, would go with Satō Momotarō, age twenty-one, to New York City. When Rioichiro read his brother's letter informing him of this decision, he responded enthusiastically. Satō, with his family background and connections with Fukuzawa Yukichi, among others, was able to recruit four other men to help him in his venture. These six young men would cross the Pacific Ocean on steerage and travel by rail to New York City on coach (the lowest class for both). Without government aid, they had to cut as much cost as possible. They were "the first Japanese group to travel in this lowest class."[97]

COMING TO NEW YORK

In New York, Arai Rioichiro found a cheap place to stay in Brooklyn. From Brooklyn to Satō Momotarō's store in Manhattan, he used a ferry and then walked. He could have used a streetcar but chose to save the nickel it cost. With some samples of raw silk from his brother's factory and Japanese consul Tomita Tetsunosuke's letter of introduction to American merchants, Rioichiro began his side of the family business: to sell raw silk to the Americans.[98]

The initial reception was discouraging.

> His first visit to one William Skinner turned out to be an unhappy experience, though instructive. It was Skinner's first encounter with a Japanese, although he had imported Japanese silk via London in the past, and he looked at Arai with skepticism. Taking him to the back of his office and pointing to a bundle of silk, which on examination revealed pieces of metal and other extraneous materials mixed in to increase its weight, he shouted angrily, "See here, I don't want this kind of stuff. You man, you get out!"[99]

The rampant fraud that occurred in Yokohama in 1859 and the 1860s had consequences in New York even in 1876.

> Our product was rejected everywhere and I had almost lost complete hope. Only 400 *kin* of raw silk was sold, but once I was able to inform how to make the raw silk back home, because our prices in New York were so much better than the price to be had in Yokohama, we started to produce them according to their specifications. . . . Later when we were finally ready to ship the raw silk in September (1876), the price of raw silk skyrocketed to 1,200, 1,300 yen per 100 *kin*. Under the circumstances many relatives and friends advised that we sell at the inflated price at Yokohama, rather than risk the long overseas shipment and fulfill the promise at a cheap price. . . . But my brother and I strenuously disagreed for we knew that breaking a contract with foreigners was not easily forgiven, and instead shipped the products at the promised price in September. With that we gained a good reputation and immediately gained the deep trust of the Americans. From that moment onward, I was able to sell all the raw silk that our family produced.[100]

In operating in a world without adequate international courts, Rioichiro quickly learned that trust was crucial. In his 7 May 1876 letter to his brother, Rioichiro explained that in all of New York City there were fewer than twenty silk merchants and only thirty or so factories that produced silk cloth in all of the United States. In such a small community, any news of trust-worthiness would spread fast and make his job much easier.[101] Therefore, when Rioichiro received the shipment of raw silk from Chōtarō on 21 September 1876, he honored B. Richardson & Son's order at the price he had quoted and sold at a loss. Upon Richardson's receipt, below is the letter Rioichiro received on 26 September 1876:

> Mr. R. Arai
> Dear Sir
> I have your note of the 21st. I am glad you have filled the order we gave you altho prices advanced on your hand. You have acted like an honest merchant and you will not hereafter be sorry that you did so. After your doing as you have done I beg to assure you that I will do my best to improve the price for you.
>
> Yours faithfully,
> B. Richardson[102]

That the Hoshino brothers had to convince fewer than thirty silk merchants[103] that they were trustworthy must have helped. The American silk industry was small enough that it effectively was like an Edo period guild. When the aforementioned William Skinner became Rioichiro's good friend, his path to success became more likely. By coincidence Rioichiro had arrived just when the U.S. silk industry was about to blossom, and so he came to know the people who would play central roles in the future of a blossoming silk industry in America. However, at the time he saw it pessimistically as a nonexistent market where quality products did not sell well and Chinese silk dominated.

When Rioichiro managed to start selling raw silk in 1876, all of the physical infrastructures were completed for the direct sale of raw silk in America. Regular transpacific shipping had commenced in 1870. Telegraph lines connected Japan with the world in 1873. Hoshino Chōtarō had opened a Western-style factory to reel raw silk in 1874. And direct mail connected Japan with the United States in 1875. With these in place, Rioichiro could sell Japanese raw silk to B. Richardson & Son. Ironically the problem was now how to send the money back to Japan.

The non-physical infrastructure, banking, was the last infrastructure to be set up for direct foreign trade. Without the semiofficial Yokohama Specie Bank established in 1879, it was extremely difficult to move money back and forth between the United States and Japan. In his first transaction, Rioichiro had to entrust a returning Japanese man with silver coins so that his brother, Chōtarō, could get payment for the raw silk. Rioichiro must have realized that his business might succeed, thus in 1877 he decided to open a bank account with an American bank. He would have to wait a couple more years for easier money transfers, but for now he had an account in New York and remained loyal to the bank until 1939, the year he died.[104]

The year Rioichiro arrived in America had been the one hundredth anniversary of the United States, and that summer Philadelphia hosted an international exhibition. Arriving on 1 August, Rioichiro saw the inside of a light air balloon. He also saw that the Japanese section had sold its products well.[105] Japanese officials had tried to sell samples of their country's products at these fairs, whether in Vienna in 1873 or in Philadelphia in 1876.[106] The Home Ministry's Commercial Development Agency had been sending officials to various cities in the United States to report on possible commercial ventures.[107] In particular, the Foreign Ministry's Tomita Tetsunosuke, the Japanese consul in New York and the man who had written letters of recommendation for Rioichiro, had tried to promote Japanese raw silk and had a major impact on the development of commercial ties between the United States and Japan.

Three years earlier in 1873 the Silk Association of America was formed to promote the manufacture of silk in America. By the next year, the members and subscribers numbered eighty-two, with almost everyone located in New York, New Jersey, Pennsylvania, Connecticut, or Massachusetts.[108] In increasing its members, this association was not a guild that tried to limit participation (as in the Edo period), nor was it a mercantile association (like in Japan) that tried to enforce certain behavior on behalf of its members. In the United States, commercial law and functional courts existed to deal with cases of fraud and cheating. Nevertheless, it is intriguing that both in the United States and Japan, people saw the need to organize to protect and expand their businesses.

The Silk Association of America also had two newly elected honorary members. One was Robert Hamil, the president of the Silk Industry Association of Paterson, New Jersey, the center of silk manufacturing at the time, and the other person was "T. Tomita, Vice-Consul of the Empire of Japan."[109] The election of Robert Hamil was unsurprising as he represented the American silk industry. The election of Tomita was surprising because in 1873, Japan only exported ¥48,000 worth of raw silk to America. Considering that Japan exported a total of ¥7.2 million worth of raw silk to the world and the United States imported a total of $6.5 million worth of raw silk from the world that same year, the Japan-U.S. trade in raw silk was a minor trade indeed. Thus Tomita's surprise election seemed like a symbolic action. However, as the Japanese vice-consul in New York, the city in which twenty-six of the twenty-seven American importers of raw silk were located, Tomita seized this opportunity.[110] And the vice-consul joined at a truly opportune moment.So it is surprising that Tomita tried to push for silk exports from Japan to the United States. The consul joined at an opportune moment. In 1874 when Hoshino Chōtarō had set up his factory in Japan to reel quality raw silk, the Silk Association of America's Seth Low bemoaned the low quality of raw silk coming in from China and hoped that the standards of Japanese raw silk would rise with the active help of a vice-consul. Tomita's short remarks at the second anniversary dinner observed "that there was no clashing of interests between the producers in Japan and in America. Their interests were identical, their commerce was the same, and they were united in questions affecting their commercial and general relations."[111] True to his word, Tomita would do his best to inform the producers in Japan of American desires and boost Japanese products to American purchasers.

This is not to imply that the Chinese idly sat by. Silk Association complaints about the low quality of Chinese raw silk were relayed to the American consul-general in China, who in turn informed the Chinese officials. Official letters were then sent out by the governors of Chinese silk regions, relaying the American complaint, and copies of the official letters were then translated and sent back to the Silk Association. But plainly Tomita's detailed letter to the Silk Association, and his eighty-two samples of raw silk brought back from Japan in 1875 made a bigger impression. In the letter Tomita blamed the deterioration of the quality of raw silk to the rise of the silkworm egg export business, an analysis shared by the Adams reports (but also conflicting with some official government plans to promote the sales of silkworm eggs). He then explained the various different types of silk reeled in Japan at the time, matching the season and location to some of the samples, and finally requested that:

> I now desire the co-operation of your society, with its vast and numerous interests represented, to give such clear and concise directions to my countrymen, that no unnecessary delay occur in bringing the raw silk trade to perfection. With this end in view, carefully examine each and all the samples herewith submitted and give an unqualified expression as to their
>
> 1st. Quality, compared with silk from other countries in regard to color, strength, smoothness, twisting and reeling.
>
> 2nd. Adaptation to this market, stating for what purpose each may be used.
>
> 3rd. If any kinds are used not represented by these samples, please designate them by description or sample.
>
> Annexed is list of samples herewith submitted, showing name of maker, province, season, color, and by process reeled.[112]

The Silk Association of America enthusiastically welcomed this letter and samples.

A major obstacle in international trade was the inability to match the various products in distant lands. Yokohama merchants could travel the interior and create an economic region by linking the various producers. New York merchants could travel to New Jersey and elicit what the factories in Paterson wanted. The biggest problem was in connecting the two. Once the reputation of Japanese silks were ruined in the late 1860s, it was extremely difficult to regain the trust of American buyers. But now Tomita had opened a structural possibility to link what the factories in Paterson, New Jersey wanted with what the reelers in eastern Japan could provide. He even started a tradition where Japanese consuls enrolled as members of the Silk Association of America. The arrival of Arai Rioichiro in New York in 1876 with samples from his brother, Hoshino Chōtarō, meant that a trusted commercial link directly tying the producers with the consumers could be achieved for the first time. Rioichiro and other Japanese silk merchants in New York, such as N. Adachi, M. Fukui, and K. Yamao, also joined the Silk Association of America.[113] Over the next few years, praise from individual merchants, factories, and the Silk Association of America on the quality of Japanese raw silk helped to reverse the earlier negative reputation of Japanese raw silk. Arai Rioichiro convinced many merchants, as represented by the aforementioned letter dated 26 September 1876 from B. Richardson & Son praising his honesty.[114] Then the factories began to accept the quality of Japanese raw silk. On 16 May 1877, a factory in Paterson, New Jersey, Pergram & Meyer, wrote to Satō Momotarō:

> In regard to the lot of Japanese silk purchased from you in February of this year, we would say that we have been extremely well pleased with the same, it being of very uniform sizes, clean thread, good winding, and free from impurities.[115]

Finally, the Silk Association of America as the representative organ of the silk industry in America had this to say in its annual report of 1878:

> Much of the singular increase of exports to this country during the past year must be attributed to the intelligent efforts of Mr. Tomita, who showed a profound interest in the subject when Vice-Consul of Japan at this port, and has, since his return to his native country, taken pains to spread information as to the best methods of preparing silk for this market. The silks of Japan have, as a rule, won high esteem during the past year, and, in several instances, have been preferred to the European product.[116]

The efforts of these men proved worthwhile. The American silk industry now sought to buy Japanese raw silk.

The huge explosion in the export of Japanese raw silk to the United States is attributable to the expansion of the U.S. silk industry. Although the growth of the U.S. silk industry is outside of the scope of this book, some background is necessary. As late as 1859, Paterson, New Jersey, the center of U.S. silk industry, employed only 900 workers in the larger industrial mills. The U.S. industry still had many small-scale operators in Paterson and also scattered across the northeast. At this time the two dominant nations that produced silk cloth were France and Britain. France had the skilled laborers who could change production design on a dime, and its industry was known to produce the best designed products. It commanded the highest reputation. Britain on the other hand had pushed toward mechanical production for the mass market. Employing more than 130,000 people in 1851, it competed with the French behind a tariff barrier in Britain. However, the Cobden free trade treaty of 1860 effectively destroyed the British industry in Cheshire County. In contrast, the U.S. government during the Civil War erected high tariff barriers, partly to protect its infant industry but also to raise revenue, and maintained them after the war. The silk industry, protected behind this wall, took root and a large number of skilled silk workers migrated from Britain to the United States, particularly Paterson.[117] Until 1883, the tariff rates in the United States on silk products were set at 60 percent, payable in gold (effectively raising the rates even further). With British immigrants, some of whom were now mill owners in America, demanding high tariffs on Capitol Hill, the rate remained at 50 percent even after 1883. Combined with the phenomenal growth of the American economy in the late nineteenth century, the so-called Gilded Age, the American silk industry primarily catered to the domestic market. With a native sericulture industry missing, the Americans were forced to import raw silk. Thus when Japanese raw silk eventually triumphed to capture 50 percent of the American market by being responsive to American tastes and maintaining quality,[118] that alone almost ensured a massive long-term boon to the Kantō region.

RIOICHIRO AND CHŌTARŌ'S LEGACY

So what happened to the first Japanese silk merchant in New York? Haru Reischauer's biography of Arai Rioichiro tells a story happier than that of Nakaiya Jūbei. By 1879, his business had grown so much that he needed help. When he returned to Japan in 1880 to hire help, he was welcomed as a hero. When he did so, he found out that Chōtarō's Watarase group had expanded to become Seishi gensha (Original Raw Silk Company), that his brother's factory had replaced the waterwheel with a steam engine, and that many of his relatives had converted to Christianity. Since high-quality raw silk production from Seishi gensha and the Mizunuma raw silk factory had reached sufficient quantities, Hayami Kensō and Hoshino Chōtarō formed a company called Yokohama dōshin kaisha to export the raw silk directly. Arai Rioichiro, back in New York City, sold this raw silk sent by Hayami and his brother. With the Yokohama Specie Bank in operation and the entire infrastructure necessary for direct foreign sales in place, this business succeeded in selling large quantities of raw silk. In 1884 he returned to Japan once again to marry Ushiba Tazu at the age of twenty-nine. Together they would have a son and a daughter.

Two years after his marriage, the Silk Association of America wrote a special article on Arai Rioichiro. He was recognized as the merchant responsible for raising the profile and quality of Japanese raw silk in America. He was the merchant who handled 50 percent of the raw silk imports to the

United States. In 1890 Chōtarō travelled to the United States and Europe to see the world. In his journey he stayed in New York for one hundred days where his brother Rioichiro was. Of course, he took a short trip to Paterson with his brother and visited many of the silk factories weaving silk cloths. During this trip to the United States, Chōtarō saw how much of the work was mechanized. The factories thus required high-quality raw silk that would not break from being put through powerful machines. These years may have been the best years for the brothers as their respective businesses provided tangible success.[119] These years may have been the best years for the brothers as their respective businesses provided tangible success.

The year 1893 was an important year for the brothers, for that year Chōtarō and Rioichiro parted ways. Since Yokohama dōshin kaisha wanted Rioichiro's pay to switch from a commission to a salary, Rioichiro decided to leave and form Yokohama kiito gōmei kaisha with Mogi Sōbei and Hara Zenzaburō. By handling even more raw silk, he became a millionaire. Also in 1893, Rioichiro built a three-story mansion at Riverside in Old Greenwich, Conneticut, for his wife and two children. He was likely the first Japanese man to play golf, and he came to love the game and became a member of an exclusive golf club in Connecticut. Amazingly, it was hard to convince other Japanese to play golf with him back then. In 1901 he was elected to the board of governors of the Silk Association of America.

While Arai Rioichiro continued to focus on his business, his brother, Hoshino Chōtarō shifted his focus to politics. As exports of raw silk expanded, Chōtarō wanted to work with the Meiji government to encourage more direct exports. Specifically he was hoping the government would establish branch offices of the Yokohama Specie Bank in New York and Lyon so that it could lend freely to his company, Yokohama dōshin kaisha. He also wanted the government to disseminate information about the major markets of the world, encourage the creation of brands and brand logos, and help people produce higher quality raw silk.[120] Many of these ideas are the result of his experience in direct trade. Transmitting money was a major issue that the brothers faced, and it continued to be an issue. Funding was always an issue for almost all businesses, and creating brands was something the Japanese economy understood to be important by the early nineteenth century.

After one of the boom-bust cycles severely weakened the silk market in 1890, Chōtarō and others lobbied more intensely but received little support. Later, his efforts were seen in a more favorable light because European governments began to protect their silk industry while the Chinese factories began to produce higher quality raw silk. Nevertheless, when the topic of government support for the raw silk industry was first debated in 1892 in the Japanese Parliament, there was much opposition to giving the industry special treatment. When a law was finally passed in 1898, foreign pressure forced the government to repeal it in three months.[121] It is not surprising that Chōtarō decided to become a member of parliament himself.

In 1904, Chōtarō was elected to Japanese Parliament, but this required money for his election campaigns. As his own funds dwindled, Chōtarō requested that money from Rioichiro. This led to a rift between the two, and Chōtarō died estranged from Rioichiro in 1908. The Hoshino and Arai families would not reconcile until 1935. In happier news, in 1907, Arai became a founding board member of the Japan Society in New York to increase social contact between Americans and Japanese. By 1919 Rioichiro had converted to Christianity, like many of his relatives. And in 1927 Rioichiro gave control of his company to Mitsubishi Trading Company, even though he never truly retired. This was opportune, for the Great Depression hurt the company severely. He remained an honest businessman, an avid golfer, a loving family man, and worked his utmost for friendly and mutually beneficial American-Japanese relations. Arai Rioichiro died in 1939, aged eighty-four, and is buried at Woodlawn Cemetery in the Bronx.[122]

CONCLUSION

The 1880s proved to be the decisive decade in determining the character of the Kantō economic region. The early nineteenth century witnessed the emergence of a commercial economic zone centered around Edo. The shogunate's decision to open Yokohama in 1859 allowed feudal domains and individual merchants to build upon that Edo-centered commerce to create a new type of economic region. This new economic region would base itself on international trade with Yokohama as its center. The rise of the new Meiji state in 1868 only furthered this process by eliminating old feudal barriers within the Kantō region and by placing new infrastructure to unite it as never before with telegraphs, railroads, steamship connections, and modern banking. The Meiji state clearly succeeded in strengthening this economic region. Yet Yokohama's Kantō hinterland, tied to Europe in the 1860s and 1870s, could not continue as it did, despite the wishes of merchants and the Meiji state. In the 1880s, as part of a global restructuring of the silk industry—the revival of sericulture in Europe (and the end to the Japanese silkworm egg exporting industry), the return of Chinese silk exports, the demise of the British silk manufacture industry, and the subsequent rise of the American silk industry—the Japanese silk industry shifted its export of raw silk to the United States.

This was not an inevitable result. The Japanese silkworm egg exporting industry did not necessarily have to die, even if the odds of success were against it. The United States could have chosen to remain with Chinese raw silk coupled with high-quality European raw silk if Japanese silk did not measure up to its standards. In the end, individuals who were able to set up a structural framework to sample and create a feedback system for Japanese products set the stage for triumph. In doing these things on a day-to-day basis, the merchants and producers adapted to and led the change; it was not the Meiji state. In this manner, the Japanese economy in the silk industry changed from being dominated by politically connected merchants (a pseudo-capitalist or a crony capitalist model) to a more fully capitalist model, wherein the state provided the infrastructure so that the producers and merchants could make money without political interference.

One of the unforeseen consequences of redirecting Yokohama and its hinterland to the United States was the flow of American wealth into eastern Japan. To supply its domestic market, the Americans needed raw silk. Moreover, the imbalance in trade between the United States and Japan never became a major issue (perhaps because the Americans had a high tariff barrier whereas Japan had none, or, rather, could not have one under the unequal treaties). For a decade in the 1880s, Japan experienced a positive balance of trade to revert to parity afterward. And Yokohama was almost consistently in the black until World War II. Here we have a major clue to the question of Japanese economic development: a national positive balance of trade that disappears and a regional positive balance of trade that persists.

NOTES

1. Humans have domesticated this insect for so long that today they cannot survive in the wild. Many books have been written on sericulture. The ones I perused are in Japanese: Zenkoku yōsan nōgyō kyōdō kumiai rengōkai shidōseisanbu sanshi no hikari (ed.), *Zukai yōsan: gijutsu, shikumi ga yoku wakaru* (Tokyo: Zenkoku yōsan nōgyō kyōdō kumiai rengōkai shidōseisanbu sanshi no hikari, 1995), and Koizumi Katsuo, *Sanshi no chishiki to katsuyō* (Tokyo, 1998).

2. The latter two are correct but in the case of telegraphs, by 1851 Sakuma Shōzan of Matsushiro domain in Shinano province (Nagano prefecture) had created batteries and the telegraph machine in Japan. Sakuma was an interesting man who was both a Confucian scholar and a *rangaku* (Dutch learning) scholar. He eventually taught Katsu Kaishū and Yoshida Shōin among others but was assassinated for his Western-leaning views. In 2007 I visited Sanada Hōmotsukan (Sanada Treasure Museum), which also houses Zōzan kinenkan and saw his devices on display.

3. Yokohama-shi (ed.), *Yokohama shishi* 3, no. 1 (Yokohama: Yūrindō, 1961), 227–31. Henceforth cited as YS III.I.

4. In 1877, 72,753 out of 853,000 cables sent nationally within Japan originated in Yokohama, and 6,922 out of 16,351 cables sent internationally from Japan came out of Yokohama. YS III.I, 266; Nihon denshin denwa kōsha (ed.), *Denshin denwa jigyōshi, bekkan* (Tokyo: Denki denshin kyōkai, 1960), 592, 635, henceforth cited as DDJ. In other Western countries, the telegraph was far better established. By 1875 there were 75,000 stations in the United States, 5,375 stations in Britain, 4,406 stations in France, 1,860 in Italy, and even colonial India had 956 stations, compared to the 133 stations in Japan in 1879. DDJ, 632. Interestingly, however, although cable traffic was high in Western countries—the U.S. leading with more than 21 million cables in 1875 and Britain following with more than 19 million cables—Indian traffic was low. In Japan users sent 678,000 cables in 1875, whereas India, with far more stations, recorded sending only 981,000 cables in the same year. In 1876, 61 Britons and 54

Americans utilized the cable in 1876, while only 23 Frenchmen and 17 Italians, and 1.9 Japanese and 0.4 Indians used the cable per 100 persons. DDJ, 635, 640.

5. DDJ, 2–38; YS III.I, 257–66.

6. Yomiuri shimbunsha Maebashi shikyoku (ed.), *Kinu no saihakken* (Maebashi: Kankodō, 1969), 55–58; Ishii Kanji, *Nihon sanshigyōshi bunseki* (Tokyo: University of Tokyo Press, 1972), 100–101. Shimomura continued to speculate. In 1903 at the age of sixty-seven, he went to Yokohama to trade and died en route at a Tokyo hospital.

7. Giovanni Federico, *An Economic History of the Silk Industry, 1830–1930* (Cambridge, UK: Cambridge University Press, 1997), 41.

8. YS III.I, 293–325.

9. Kondō Yasuo, *Chiunen koritsukoku no kenkyū* (Tokyo: Nōson gyoson bunka kyōkai, 1974); William Cronon, *Nature's Metropolis: Chicago and the Great West* (New York: W. W. Norton, 1991), 48–52. William Cronon tracing the movement of many goods to and through Chicago was one major inspiration for this book. I realized that tracing the flow of goods can lead to important economic insights as well as provide a great narrative.

10. Noda Masaho et al., *Kanagawa no tetsudō, 1872–1996* (Tokyo: Nippon Keizai hyōronsha, 1996), 14–23; Yomiuri shimbunsha Maebashi shikyoku, *Kinu no saihakken*, 164–67.

11. Steven J. Ericson, *The Sound of the Whistle: Railroads and the State in Meiji Japan* (Cambridge, MA: Harvard University Press, 1996), 42–53.

12. For example, it cost nearly £300,000 to lay the eighteen-mile track from Yokohama to Tokyo. In the long run, however, the failure of the Yokohama-Hachiōji line proved crucial in transforming Yokohama from a purely mercantile city into an industrial city. The harbor and railroad provided access to raw materials imported by ships and rail into northern Yokohama. The manufactured goods were sold in the markets of Tokyo, Yokohama, and beyond. The Yokohama line carried pebbles, lumber, coal, and other industrial materials from the interior to fuel heavy industry. Noda, *Kanagawa no tetsudō*, 6–8, 102–3; Ericson, *The Sound of the Whistle*, 10.

13. This section about the three Tama counties is mainly drawn from Umeda Sadahiro, *Naze Tama wa Tokyo-to to nattaka* (Tachikawa, Tokyo: Keyaki shuppan, 1993), 3–25.

14. East Tama county is now Nakano-ku and Suginami-ku. Ku are often translated as "wards." Today Tokyo has twenty-three wards.

15. Sataki Yoshihiro, *Nihon no shirukurōdo: Tomioka seishijō to kinusangyō isangun* (Tokyo: Chūōkōronshinsha, 2007). Sataki also uses the term but he does not specify which route the silk travelled on its way from Gunma to Yokohama, whether it took the Tokyo route or the Hachiōji route. I would like to emphasize here that the path between Hachiōji and Yokohama was the first major "silk road" for Japan. The shogunate tried to control the flow of silk products by mandating these goods first gather at Edo before being shipped to Yokohama. The domains mostly complied but the Yokohama merchants who wanted to ignore these controls established the alternate Hachiōji-Yokohama path.

16. Nihon yūsen kabushiki kaisha (ed.), *Nihon yūsen kabushiki kaisha 50nenshi* (Tokyo: 1935).

17. William C. Wyckoff, "Report on the Silk Manufacturing Industry of the United States," in *Report on the Manufactures of the United States at the Tenth Census (June 1 1880)*, (Washington, DC: Government Printing Office, 1883), 19 (923).

18. The direct surface distance difference between New York to Gibraltar (3,154) and London to Gibraltar (948) is 2,206 miles. Since the direct surface distance between London and Gibraltar is shorter than the shipping distance (ships being unable to cross the Pyrenees), and since the direct surface distance between New York and Gibraltar and the shipping distance between New York and Gibraltar is probably not that different, the shipping distance difference between New York to Gibraltar and London to Gibraltar is probably smaller. This means that, Yokohama to London must be at least 10,834 miles (Yokohama to Suez to New York being 13,040 minus 2,206 miles). Thus, the shipping distance difference between the underestimated Yokohama-to-London route (10,834) and the new Yokohama-to-San Francisco-to-New York route (7,439) is at least 3,395 miles. All distances are in nautical miles for this discussion.

19. The Meiji government was not of a single mind regarding the creation of this agency. As early as 1869, the finance ministry with its development agency pushed for a program of domestic industrial and commercial development, while the foreign ministry, citing international law, was far less convinced about interfering in the market. Ōkurashō (ed.), *Meiji zenki zaisei keizaishiryō shūsei*, vol. 3: *Ōkurashō enkakushi* no. 2 (Tokyo: Kaizōsha, 1934), 361–63.

20. YS III.I, 166–217.

21. YS III.I, 218–26.

22. Haru Matsukata Reischauer, *Samurai and Silk: A Japanese and American Heritage* (Cambridge, MA: Harvard University Press, 1986), 81–84, 95–96. This book is a biography of two men, Matsukata Masayoshi and Arai Rioichiro, written by their granddaughter and wife of the American scholar and diplomat Edwin O. Reischauer. The book has no footnotes but is a good source of oral history.

23. Ishii Kanji, *Nihon sanshigyōshi bunseki* (Tokyo: Tokyo University Press, 1972), 442–51. Yamaguchi Kazuo, an economic historian of late Edo and Meiji Japan, in *Meiji zenki Keizai no bunseki* (Tokyo: Tokyo University Press, 1956) and Yamaguchi Kazuo (ed.), *Nihon sangyō kin'yūshi kenkyū: Seishi kin'yūhen* (Tokyo: Tokyo University Press, 1966), pointed this out earlier.

24. YS III.II, 411–520.

25. Named partly to confuse the Western buyers with "Shinshiu," aka Nagano prefecture, the center of mechanized silk reeling and reputed to produce the best quality raw silks.

26. Hirano Masahiro, "Mogikei seishi—Shinshōsha no bunseki," *Yokohama kaikō shiryōkan kiyō*, vol. 15 (1997): 72–91; Hirano Masahiro, "Kiito urikomishō no seishigyō he no shinshutsu," 1, 2 in *Kaikō no hiroba*, vol. 54, 55 (1996, 1997).

27. Mogi gōmei kaisha, or the Mogi conglomerate, folded in 1920 during the post–World War I economic crisis in Japan. Yokohama kaikō shiryōkan (ed.), *Yokohama shōnin to sono jidai* (Yokohama: Yūrindō, 1994), 77–80.

28. By 1898, Hara Zenzaburō was the twentieth in annual income. Of the top twenty, ten were former lords such as Shimazu Tadashige and Mōri Motoakira. Number one was Mitsubishi's owner Iwasaki Yatarō, number two was Mitsui Hachirōemon, number four was Sumitomo Kichizaemon of Sumitomo, and number six was Yasuda Zenjirō. Mogi Sōbei was twenty-third in annual income. Yokohama kaikō shiryōkan (ed.), *Yokohama shōnin to sono jidai*, 21, 35–44.

29. Mitsui public relations committee homepage. Mitsui kōhō iinkai: Mitsui no rekishi: Meiji ki.

30. Hattori Kazuma, "Meiji shoki ni okeru seiōjin no sanshigyōchitai shisatsu to sono eikyō," Kantō gakuen Matsudaira kinen keizai bunka kenkyūjo (eds.), *Tonegawa suikei chiiki no shakai to rōdō: Kantō gakuen Matsudaira kinen keizai bunka kenkyūjo sōsho*, vol. 2 (Ōtashi, Gunma: Kantō gakuen Matsudaira kinen keizai bunka kenkyūjo, 1991), 1–32, examines these trips in detail. His source for the Italian mission comes from Japanese observations, but for the British mission he uses British Parliamentary records. See also YS III.I, 71–77.

31. Many Italian names were originally rendered in Japanese and it was impossible for me to decipher who they were. Professor Claudio Zanier has kindly helped me connect the Japanese names with the Italian names in this chapter through correspondences and his book. Claudio Zanier, *Semai: Setaioli Italiani in Giappone (1861–1880) "interpretare e comunicare senza tradurre"* (Padova: Coop. Libraria Editrice Università di Padova, 2006), #128, 383; #98, 357; #116, 373.

32. Presumably the Japanese merchants who bought Tajima Yahei's eggs sold them to foreign buyers. Hattori, "Meiji shoki ni okeru seiōjin no sanshigyōchitai shisatsu to sono eikyō," *Tonegawa suikei chiiki no shakai to rōdō*, vol. 2, 2–18.

33. Adams also reported his finding to the Japanese government. YS III.I, 73–74; Adams report in *Parliamentary Papers* in Hattori, "Meiji shoki ni okeru seiōjin no sanshigyōchitai shisatsu to sono eikyō," *Tonegawa suikei chiiki no shakai to rōdō*, vol. 2, 1–32.

34. YS III.I, 92–124.

35. Yokohama kaikō shiryōkan, *Yokohama shōnin to sono jidai*, 22–25.

36. YS III.I, 71–123; Ōuchi Hyōe and Tsuchiya Takao (eds.), *Meiji zenki zaisei keizai shiryō shūsei*, vol. 2 (Tokyo: Kaizōsha, 1932), 248–49; Ōuchi Hyōe and Tsuchiya Takao (eds.), *Meiji zenki zaisei keizai shiryō shūsei*, vol. 3 (Tokyo: Kaizōsha, 1934), 361–62.

37. "Shokusan kōgyō ni kansuru kengisho" (Proposal for Industrial Development), May or June 1874. Nihon shiseki kyōkai (eds.), *Nihon shiseki kyōkai sōsho*, vol. 32: *Ōkubo Toshimichi monjo*, no. 5 (Tokyo: Tokyo University Press, 1933, 1968), #900, 561–66.

38. Sakatani Yoshio et al. (eds.), *Segai Inoue-kō den*, vol. 2 (Tokyo: Naigai shoseki, 1933), 453–67.

39. Federico, *An Economic History of the Silk Industry*, 40.

40. YS III.I, 145.

41. The government destroyed another 310,000 cards in 1877 and 110,000 cards in 1878. Ushiki Yukio (ed.). *Kaiko no mura no yōkō nikki: Jōshū santane gyōsha, Meiji shonen no Yōroppa taiken* (Tokyo: Heibonsha, 1995), 62.

42. Yomiuri shimbunsha Maebashi shikyoku, *Kinu no saihakken*, 21.

43. Ushiki Yukio, *Kaiko no mura no yōkō nikki*, 56–59.

44. Yomiuri shimbunsha Maebashi shikyoku, *Kinu no saihakken*, 21–25, 41–43, 62.

45. In the Japanese text the name is rendered "Andaraosshi." Zanier, *Semai*, #006, 271.

46. Tajima Yahei, "Bakumatsu yori Meiji shoki santane yushutsu kiroku" in *Shimamura santane gyōsha no yōkō nikki: Sakai-machishi shiryōshū*, ed. Yuasa Masahiko, vol. 4 *(Rekishi-hen)* (Sakai-machi, Gunma: Sakai-machi, 1988), 1. Henceforth cited as SSYN.

47. Ushiki Yukio, introduction and "Kaisetsu," SSYN, vii, 315; Yomiuri shimbunsha Maebashi shikyoku, *Kinu no saihakken*, 23.

48. If Mitsui banking was the main branch of the House of Mitsui from Tokugawa times, then Mitsui *bussan* (Mitsui Trading Company) traces its origin to the Senshū gaisha, a company with government support to trade various goods. Mitsui bought Senshū geisha in 1876. Together these two companies formed the core of the Mitsui *zaibatsu* as the bank financed its industrial factories and the trading company bought the raw materials necessary for the factories and sold the products made in the factories.

49. Tajima Yahei, "Bakumatsu yori Meiji shoki santane yushutsu kiroku," SSYN, 3–5; Tajima Shin, "Ōbei ryokō nisshi," SSYN, 20–21.

50. Tajima Yasaburō, "Italī koku kōkō nisshi," SSYN, 93.

51. The man who had made contact with Italian merchants in 1869, also unrelated to the other two. Tajima happens to be a common last name in this village.

52. The names are rendered as "Matsuwoki" and "Worutonī" in the original text. Zanier, *Semai*, #96, 352; #22, 286.

53. Perhaps including Arai Rioichiro, the younger brother of Hoshino Chōtarō. Tajima Shin, "Ōbei ryokō nisshi," SSYN, 20–26.

54. Originally rendered "Walesu." Marco Arese's family was one of the richest families in Milan, Lombardy, and he had a major interest in silk production and the silk trade. As such, Arese was appointed secretary to the Italian embassy in Japan. Zanier, personal correspondence.

55. Likely the same Savio that Tajima Yahei met in Yokohama in 1869.

56. Tajima Shin, "Ōbei ryokō nisshi," SSYN, 26–45; Tajima Yasaburō, "Italī koku kōkō nisshi," SSYN, 108–9, 112–13, 118.

57. Tajima Yahei, "Letter," SSYN, 138–39.

58. The merchants and the Italian peasants used francs.

59. Tajima Shin, "Ōbei ryokō nisshi," SSYN, 29; Tajima Yasaburō, "Italī koku kōkō nisshi," SSYN, 102; Zanier, *Semai*, #34, 299.

60. This may refer to the Diyarbakir variety, which spins yellow cocoons. An alternate spelling for Diyarbakir was "Diarbekr," and it was used until the early twentieth century. Department of Commerce, Bureau of Foreign and Domestic Commerce, *Daily Consular and Trade Reports* vol. 1, nos 1–75 (Washington DC: January, February, and March 1914), February 10, issue 34, 532.

61. Tajima Yahei "Italī koku Mirano zairyū santane uriharai nisshi," SSYN, 133.

62. Tajima Shin, "Ōbei ryokō nisshi," SSYN, 68–74.

63. Tajima Shin, "Ōbei ryokō nisshi," SSYN, 44; Tajima Yasaburō, "Italī koku kōkō nisshi," SSYN, 117–18.

64. Ushiki, *Kaiko no mura no yōkō nikki*, 99.

65. Tajima Takebei, "Yōkō ryochū kenbun nisshi," SSYN, 168; Tajima Yasaburō, "Yōkō nisshi," SSYN, 234.

66. Yomiuri shimbunsha Maebashi shikyoku, *Kinu no saihakken*, 23; Ushiki, *Kaiko no mura no yōkō nikki*, 65–80.

67. Presumably, they missed the *Belgic* because of the squabbling.

68. Tajima Takebei, "Yōkō ryochū kenbun nisshi," SSYN, 168–78; Tajima Yasaburō, "Yōkō nisshi," SSYN, 234–36.

69. Map, "Dai nikai jika yushutsu kōteizu," SSYN, 160–61.

70. The names are rendered as "Savio," "Walesu," "Andarahosshi," "Derooro," and "Antonshinī." Derooro is Isidoro or Giuseppe Dell'oro and Antonshinī is Carlo Antongini. Zanier, *Semai*, #50, 313; #9, 276. From July to August 1868, Arese and Antongini had gone to Niigata to buy silkworm eggs and were familiar with Japanese eggs.

71. The Japanese government appointed an Italian silkworm egg merchant named Locaderī (presumably Pietro Locatelli) as its consul in Milan. Zanier, *Semai*, #80, 345.

72. Tajima Takebei, "Yōkō ryochū kenbun nisshi," SSYN, 191–95, 198; Tajima Yasaburō, "Yōkō nisshi," SSYN, 242–44. Interestingly Japan's consul at Venice, Berushī, also dabbled in silkworms.

73. Tajima Yasaburō, "Yōkō nisshi," SSYN, 246–47; Tajima Takebei, "Yōkō ryochū kenbun nisshi," SSYN, 201–2 .

74. Tajima Takebei, "Yōkō ryochū kenbun nisshi," SSYN, 208–13; Tajima Yasaburō, "Yōkō nisshi," SSYN, 252–53.

75. *Mitsui bussan kaisha kessan setsumeisho*, 253–54, in Ushiki, "Kaisetsu," SSYN.

76. Tajima Takebei, "Yōkō ryochū kenbun nisshi," SSYN, 206; Tajima Yasaburō, "Yōkō nisshi," SSYN, 249.

77. The following discussion is based on his letters. Tajima Keitarō, "Letters," SSYN, 255–62.

78. Tajima Keitarō, "Letters," SSYN, 255–62.

79. Tajima Keitarō, "Letters," SSYN, 265–67.

80. Tajima Keitarō, "Letters," SSYN, 272–79; Tajima Yahei, "Letter, 25 October 1882," SSYN, 285–87.

81. Tajima Keitarō, "Letters," SSYN, 283–84; Tajima Yahei, "Letter, 22 May 1883," SSYN, 290–92.

82. Ushiki, *Kaiko no mura no yōkō nikki*, 98–103; Ushiki, "Kaisetsu," SSYN, 315, 340–41.

83. Of course there is always the possibility that the prices were driven so low that the Japanese producers could no longer compete.

84. Each card has approximately 600 eggs, so if all the eggs hatched that would mean 6,000 silkworms. One would need a fairly large farm with enough mulberry trees to feed that many silkworms. One tree is not enough to feed just 100 silkworms!

85. Ushiki, "Kaisetsu," SSYN, 315, 320–22.

86. The price of raw silk fluctuated such that in value it swung from year to year, but in terms of volume, exports remained consistent if not declining. After the bumper crop year in 1876, 1.8 million *kin* (¥13.2 million), production remained flat or slightly below rather than increasing as in the previous years. 1875 1.2 million *kin* (¥5.4 million); 1877, 1.7 (9.6); 1878, 1.5 (8.3); 1879, 1.6 (9.7); 1880, 1.5 (8.6); 1881, 1.8 (10.6); 1882, 2.9 (16.2); 1883, 3.1 (16.2); 1884, 2.1 (11); 1885, 2.5 (13); 1886, 2.6 (17); 1887, 3.1 (19). YS: S II, 6, 16.

87. YS: S II, 180–81.

88. At its peak the silkworm egg exports were at $4 million (see the table 6.1). At this time, $1 was anywhere between ¥1 and ¥2. The pattern was set by the early 1880s; imports from Europe typically accounted for 25 percent, 40 to 50 percent from Japan, and the rest from China. *Annual Report of the Silk Association of America* XIII–XIV (1886). Henceforth, AR-SAA (1886).

89. In standard Romanization, the name would be rendered "Ryōichirō," but he himself used "Rioichiro" when writing his name in English.

90. It was actually 1868.

91. Katō Ryū, Sakata Yasuo, Akiya Norio, eds., *Nichi-Bei kiito bōeki shiryō*, vol. 1: *Shiryōhen* 1 (Tokyo: Kondō shuppansha, 1987), I, 1. Henceforth NKBS.

92. NKBS, I, 34–50; Reischauer, *Samurai and Silk*, 185.

93. First Takasaki domain was abolished in 1871, but the school continued. However, when the capital of Gunma prefecture moved to Maebashi in 1872, the school, which the prefecture now ran, closed.

94. Reischauer, *Samurai and Silk*, 177–80, 184–87.

95. The same Dutch-crazy Hotta Masayoshi from chapter 2.

96. Reischauer, *Samurai and Silk*, 190–91.

97. Reischauer, *Samurai and Silk*, 192–93, 195–200.

98. Reischauer, *Samurai and Silk*, 202–7.

99. Reischauer, *Samurai and Silk*, 207.

100. This recollection actually masks the fact that Hoshino Chōtarō suggested renegotiating prices. Reischauer, *Samurai and Silk*, 209; NKBS, I, 4.

101. NKBS, IV, 1. Reischauer, *Samurai and Silk*, 208. Reischauer has the date as 6 May 1876 instead of 7 May 1876.

102. Reischauer, *Samurai and Silk*, 210. NKBS, IV,13 has the same letter.

103. Rioichiro underestimated the numbers of raw silk merchants.

104. Reischauer, *Samurai and Silk*, 211–13.

105. Steven J. Ericson, "Japonica, Indica: Rice and Foreign Trade in Meiji Japan," *Journal of Japanese Studies* 41, no. 2 (2015): 332–33.

106. NKBS, IV, 9.

107. NKBS, IV, 48.

108. Two of the eighty-two were located outside America. One merchant resided in Shanghai and another company had addresses in Hong Kong and Shanghai.

109. ARSAA (1874), 11–13, 21, 33.

110. 1 Yen was roughly equivalent to 1 US dollar and 1 Mexican dollar in 1873. YS: S II, 180; William C. Wyckoff, "Report on the Silk Manufacturing Industry of the United States," in Report on the Manufactures of the United States at the Tenth Census (June 1 1880), (Washington, DC: Government Printing Office, 1883), 19 (923).

111. ARSAA (1874), 60.

112. ARSAA (1875), 20–23.

113. ARSAA (1879), 5–8. All but Ryōichirō would be gone by 1884. However, "T. Takaki" is listed as a member in 1884. ARSAA (1884), 5–8. The silk trade remained a volatile business.

114. NKBS, IV, 13.

115. NKBS, IV, 45.

116. ARSAA (1878), 10.

117. For more on the migration of artisans from Britain to the United States, see Richard Dobson Margrave, "The Emigration of Silk Workers from England to the United State in the Nineteenth Century" (PhD diss., London School of Economics and Political Science, 1981).

118. A task that was made considerably easier with a Japanese consul and merchants in the Silk Association.

119. Tomizawa Kazuhiro, *Kita Kantō chihōshi kenkyū: Kiito to hitobito no kurashi* (Tokyo: Nihon keizai hyōronsha, 2010), 91–97.

120. Tomizawa, *Kita Kantō chihōshi kenkyū*, 42.

121. Tomizawa, *Kita Kantō chihōshi kenkyū*, 3–22.

122. Reischauer, *Samurai and Silk*, 203–59.

Conclusion

This book has employed an explicitly regional focus to trace the flow of silk products from the interior of Japan to Yokohama and from Yokohama to the West. This alone is an important and worthy subject of study. After all, there are many scholarly and popular works that explain the various trades in the history of world. Perhaps the most famous and most studied large-scale trade in the West is the Atlantic triangular trade.[1] Following the flow of any product also follows the flow of money, albeit in a reverse direction. This in turn can explain why certain countries have gotten richer of the years. In other words, tracing the flow of major products, such as silk, can help answer one of the oldest questions in economic history: how did some countries become wealthy?

The previous six chapters have asked how Japan changed between the years 1843 and 1893. In the process, this book has demonstrated that nothing was certain; there was no guarantee that trade with the West would be successful or that the transition from an agricultural economy to an industrial economy would be smooth and easy. In fact, I am tempted to use the word "miraculous" to describe Japan's successful transition.

Before discussing success, however, let's review how things could have gone wrong. The following are major potential political pitfalls after the signing of the Treaty of Kanagawa in 1854 and opening diplomatic relations between Japan and the United States. If the leading minister (*rōjū*) and temperamental conservative, Abe Masahiro, had not died at the relatively young age of thirty-seven in 1857, xenophobic lords such as Tokugawa Nariaki may have blocked a new set of treaties that opened trade between Japan and the West in 1859. If the new chief minister had not been the "Dutch-crazy" Hotta Masayoshi, the suggestion by the treasury officials to open Uraga (a port much farther away from Edo and the main highway), may have been adopted, and Yokohama could have remained a small fishing village. Furthermore, the shogunate could have decided to follow through on the xenophobes' wish to keep Japan closed and engaged in full-scale war when Satsuma and Chōshū domains fired on Western naval vessels in 1863 and 1864. In such a scenario, Western powers could have defeated Japan and forced upon Japan more onerous terms in subsequent treaties, such as allowing the import of opium or possibly even colonizing the country.

Even after trade with the West commenced, economic circumstances could have blocked the development of Japan's trade. If the Chinese were not preoccupied with a Western invasion and engaged in a massive civil war until 1864, the West would have continued to focus their trade on China and the Japan trade would have remained small. If Western countries were not suffering from a silkworm disease from the 1850s until the 1870s, Japan's silk trade would not have boomed. Even when these opportunities presented themselves internationally, many tried to block the expansion of trade domestically. Shogunal officials tried to limit the export of raw silk to protect the domestic silk cloth industry. A few domains outright banned their merchants from engaging in trade with the West. Xenophobic samurai carried out terrorist acts in and near the treaty ports. Unscrupulous merchants defrauded and cheated their customers, reducing the all-important trust necessary in the absence of a functional commercial court.

Yet, despite it all, trade with the West did succeed. Realistic leadership under Hotta coupled with competent officials such as Iwase Tadanari ensured the opening of Yokohama to Western trade in 1859. Cooler heads ensured that a wider war would not break out. The economic crisis of eastern Japan in the eighteenth century ensured that many domains were serious about the welfare of their people in the nineteenth century. And the cultural and economic transformation of eastern Japan in the eighteenth and nineteenth ensured that when Japanese merchants recognized the Western merchants' desire to buy silk products in large quantities, the producers in eastern Japan could respond by producing high-quality raw silk and silkworm eggs.

This is why silk merchants such as Nakaiya Jūbei and Yoshimuraya Kōbei could take full advantage of their position as domain monopoly merchants and sell massive quantities of raw silk to Western merchants. After the revolution in 1868, the Meiji government finally abolished feudal domains in 1871. All merchants and producers now had the opportunity to prosper under a government that did not prioritize the welfare of the samurai. Ironically the 1870s would coincide with the death of the European market for Japanese silk products, since the pebrine crisis was finally abating, and even heroic efforts by the egg producers of Shimamura could not change the tide. However, Arai Rioichiro, Hoshino Chōtarō, and successive Japanese consuls in New York would diligently and faithfully restore trust in the quality of raw silk from Japan and capture the American market by 1886.

None could have known that the United States market would become the largest consumer of silk products in the world by the end of the nineteenth century, nor that Kantō would effectively provide half of the raw silk for the American producers of silk cloth, chiefly in Paterson, New Jersey. Yet, in the mid-1870s, a close and important link was formed with the nucleus of the U.S. industry, and together they forged a pipeline durable and reliable enough to send eastern Japan's raw silk to the eastern United States in massive quantities.

This transition, from an agricultural economy to the early phase of industrialization, provides insights and helps us better understand the broader picture of nineteenth-century Japan. It may seem obvious, but it is worth emphasizing that the first non-Western nation to industrialize did so through light industry. In particular, the rural light industry in eastern Japan, namely silk reeling, led the way. Later, toward the end of the century, Kansai began to industrialize in cities based on cotton. The Meiji government helped in providing the infrastructural support, particularly the strategically important railroads, but not through direct subsidies or management. In light industry, the famous state-owned Tomioka Silk Mill remained a model and a center of educating potential private entrepreneurs from 1872. However, after its sale in 1893 to the House of Mitsui, the government ended its direct support. In other words, the story of early industrialization in Japan is primarily a story of private industry. Public support mattered, but the government took a supporting role. Heavy industrialization, starting with the publicly operated Yawata Steel Works, came later after the first Sino-Japanese War (1894–1895). Now that we have reviewed the historical contingencies, let's examine the proposed model for Japan's economic development in the nineteenth century.

THE MODEL

To construct this model, a number of things must be explained. First, as most economic historians have pointed out, Meiji Japan did not accumulate trade surpluses or trade deficits. Japan's trade with the outside world was in balance. This fact has led many to conclude that Japan exported raw silk to import necessary products for development.[2] This model expands on this idea and explains how silk exports created two light industrial centers inside Japan. Second, when tracing the flow of goods, one must realize that the reverse of that flow must be money if different products of similar value do not balance it. Third, these insights must be combined with a regional view, a national view, and a global view. In this manner, we can find a cycle of the flow of goods.

When the divided *bakufu* opened Yokohama in 1859 as its main port for foreign trade, the merchants were ready to connect the port city with the rural countryside, and its rural communities were ready to shift production depending on possible profits. Some domains were also ready for the onset of foreign trade. And the world economy proved to be ready, and even eager, for Japan to enter international trade. The double disaster of pebrine in Europe and the Taiping Rebellion in China disrupted global silk production, and Japan appeared at just the right moment to fill in the gap.

This initial trade, however, meant that Japan would be drawn into the Chinese and Indian pattern of global trade. Japan would be exporting raw materials, such as silkworm eggs and raw silk to Europe, and importing manufactured goods, such as cotton cloth, but also guns and ships from Britain and other European countries. Therefore from 1859 to the 1870s, the economy of Japan had no major reason to industrialize. Overall, neither side amassed a large imbalance in trade. This balance proved fortunate, for if Japan had sustained a massive positive balance of trade, Britain may have tried to sell opium to Japan to cover its losses, as they had in China earlier. Also in this period, the domestic suppliers of silk products forged their links to Yokohama in order to export abroad.

Starting in the 1880s, this pattern shifted. Japan no longer exported to Europe, but instead exported to the United States. The hard work of Arai Rioichiro, Hoshino Chōtarō, and the consuls in New York was paying off. American silk factories began to buy Japanese raw silk in huge quantities, resulting a positive balance of trade for Japan until 1893.

Even when the country lost its positive balance of payments, the port of Yokohama continued to experience a positive balance until the 1930s. Exports to the United States produced a positive balance because the United States had little to export to Japan and because the U.S. government did not politically pressure Japan to accept American exports.

The above description means that during the first period, from 1859 to the early 1870s, Japan participated in a standard colonial trade. It was the next period, from the late 1870s to the 1880s, that launched Japan's industrial takeoff. Starting in the 1880s, eastern Japan managed to find a new, even more voracious, customer in the United States, despite a transition that destroyed the silkworm egg export industry. So now let's follow the flow of money.

The immense American demand for raw silk eclipsed anything the Europeans had demanded earlier,[3] increasing production and turning some egg producers who survived the transition from exporters into domestic suppliers. This single industry—exporting to a single country, which sometimes accounted for more than 20 percent of total exports[4]—was concentrated in eastern Japan. Maintaining this regional focus is important. As a result of American money flowing in, the rural producers in eastern Japan began to

Table C.1. Exports and Imports from Japan and Yokohama, in Yen, 1880–1893

	Exports from Japan	*Exports from Yokohama*	*Imports to Japan*	*Imports to Yokohama*
1880	28,395,386	18,984,217	36,626,601	26,324,650
1881	31,058,887	21,481,187	31,191,246	21,584,318
1882	37,721,750	26,925,513	29,446,593	20,352,427
1883	36,268,019	26,073,654	28,444,841	19,223,443
1884	33,871,465	21,838,466	29,672,647	19,461,496
1885	36,108,886	23,850,368	29,345,379	19,007,525
1886	47,997,956	31,537,775	32,099,748	20,130,818
1887	51,547,407	33,428,248	44,276,327	27,163,149
1888	64,891,682	40,254,587	65,416,234	36,623,610
1889	69,306,893	41,507,835	66,041,584	34,286,456
1890	55,791,846	31,952,217	81,670,354	40,603,545
1891	78,738,053	49,102,396	62,880,670	28,967,839
1892	90,404,735	61,175,382	71,276,942	31,310,091
1893	88,950,014	54,878,778	88,187,628	36,284,425

Source: From 1894 until the mid-twentieth century, the balance of trade turned against Japan. The initial cause may have been the Sino-Japanese War, but the surge in imports was a long-term trend that continued and was barely balanced by an increase in exports. The port of Yokohama, however, maintained a positive balance of trade until the 1930s. Yokohama-shi (ed.), *Yokohama shishi: Shiryōhen 2* (Yokohama: Yūrindō, 1980), 8, 33, 48, 68, 76, 104, 118, 145. Henceforth cited as YS: S II.

consume more. Most conspicuous were the new houses that these producers built in the late nineteenth century, with rooms designed specifically for feeding silkworms. These were the big ticket items that changed the landscape of areas engaged in sericulture.[5]

Yanagita Kunio's stories of the increased consumption of sugar also provide us with hints about what the money coming into eastern Japan was spent on. Sugar was a product previously associated more with medicine than food.[6] Examining the import data proves that Yanagita's observations were correct. There was a massive increase in the import of sugar, and initially its import was concentrated in Yokohama. In 1880, ¥3.5 million worth of sugar was imported, of which ¥2.7 million worth of sugar (77 percent) came in through Yokohama. In 1885 imports to Japan climbed to ¥4.7 million, and in 1890 it was at ¥8.4 million. Even the Sino-Japanese War did not stop the imports, with ¥11.7 million worth of sugar imported in 1895.[7] However, in contrast to the increased amount of imports, Yokohama's share of imports declined. In 1885 Yokohama handled ¥3.2 million (68 percent) worth of sugar. In 1890 it was ¥5.3 million (63 percent), and in 1895, ¥6.8 million worth of sugar flowed into Yokohama, but it accounted for only 58 percent of total sugar imports.[8] Imported sugar changed from a rarity to a common product, and it was the people of eastern Japan who consumed the bulk of the imported sugar first. Later on, as other ports began to handle sugar more, people from the rest of the archipelago also bought it.

Cotton consumption also rose. More specifically, consumption of cotton products made in the factories of western Japan rose, while imports of foreign-made cotton shirting and other cotton cloths did not increase.[9] Because the native cotton-growing industry was destroyed by British imports in the 1860s and 1870s, raw cotton now had to be imported to make cotton products. Accordingly, imports of raw cotton exploded after the 1890s and the flood of imports lasted. This explosion in the imports of raw cotton, more than anything else, explains the balance of payment shortfall in Japanese trade from the late 1890s onward.

In 1905 imports of ginned cotton were at ¥109 million, 22 percent of total imports. In 1910 raw cotton imports hit 34 percent of all imports, and in 1915 raw cotton imports accounted for 41 percent of all imports to Japan. This imported raw cotton did not come through Yokohama. In fact, the portion that passed through Yokohama declined over time. If in 1885, 33.3 percent of raw cotton imports passed through Yokohama, by 1895 it was down to 13.6 percent, and by 1905 only 13.1 percent passed through Yokohama. By 1915, only ¥24 million worth of raw cotton went through Yokohama, only 11.1 percent of cotton imports to Japan.[10]

Table C.2. Cotton Imports to Japan and Yokohama and Total Imports and Total Exports in Yen

	Cotton Imports to Japan	*Cotton Imports to Yokohama*	*Total Imports*	*Total Exports*
1885	0.6 million	0.2 million	29.3 million	36.1 million
1890	4.1 million	1.3 million	81.7 million	55.8 million
1895	24.3 million	3.3 million	129.1 million	135 million
1900	58.5 million	5.7 million	286.6 million	200.2 million
1905	109.3 million	14.3 million	487.7 million	318.3 million
1910	157.8 million	24.0 million	463.5 million	455.1 million
1915	216.5 million	23.8 million	529.7 million	699.9 million
1930	361.7 million	25.5 million	1,542.1 million	1,434.6 million

Source: YS: S II, 33, 57, 68, 130.

These numbers clearly demonstrate that after the 1890s, someone inside Japan but outside Yokohama's economic orbit was buying raw cotton and turning it into cotton cloth. The port importing the raw cotton was Kobe, Yokohama's rival port city in western Japan. This massive import of raw cotton counterbalanced the massive export of raw silk from eastern Japan. Thus two regional patterns emerged: eastern Japan had a positive balance of trade from exporting raw silk, while western Japan had a negative balance of trade from importing raw cotton. The overall positive balance of trade from 1882 to 1893 was temporary, and international trade for all of Japan balanced out after 1893.[11] In the process, the manufacturers of the cotton cloth in western Japan displaced foreign cotton yarns and cotton cloths and succeeded in import substitution.[12]

This story is similar to the story of historical demography during the Edo period covered in chapter 1. For a long time, many people thought that the Japanese population simply stagnated in the eighteenth and early nineteenth centuries. However, historical demographers discovered that this national overall balance masked a huge regional divide; eastern Japan's population was shrinking while western Japan's population was increasing. Similarly, the Meiji period's overall balance in trade is masked by a large trade surplus in eastern Japan and a large trade deficit in western Japan. What seemed to be static in a national framework is revealed to be a dynamic system from a regional framework.

Let's now put the above information together to see the start of Japan's industrialization in the 1880s. Once again, we shall trace the flow of money. Money flowed from eastern America to eastern Japan in exchange for raw silk. The demand for raw silk in America pushed industrialization in the rural hinterland of eastern Japan, because the American factories demanded raw silk that was uniform and could withstand the silk cloth–making machines in the United States. The money from America paid for the new factories and increased future raw silk production. Also with this money, the people of eastern Japan consumed much more sugar and began to buy cotton cloth. As sugar consumption rose, some money flowed from eastern Japan to places like Taiwan. As cotton cloth consumption rose, money flowed from eastern Japan to western Japan and in exchange cotton cloth flowed eastward. Western Japan, particularly the area centered on Osaka, began to produce cotton yarn with the imported raw cotton. Businesses built new factories with this money from eastern Japan to cope with the rising demand. To feed the factories producing ever more cotton products, Kobe began importing massive amounts of raw cotton from British India.[13] Eventually western Japan produced enough cotton cloth to export and effectively eliminated foreign imports of cotton cloth by World War I. My preliminary research indicates that the consumers in eastern Japan also bought cotton cloth made in Aichi prefecture and that Aichi cloth makers bought their cotton yarn from Osaka factories.

Going from the regional, to a national, to an international view completes the model. We can now hypothesize a global loop that moved money and products in the late nineteenth century. Money flowed from eastern United States to Yokohama and eastern Japan in exchange for raw silk. Money then flowed from eastern Japan to western Japan centered on Osaka and Kobe in exchange for cotton products. From the port of Kobe, money flowed to India in exchange for raw cotton. India, being a colony of Britain, remitted money to London (£25 million per year by 1900),[14] and from there the capitalists of London invested the money back in the United States. And thus the global loop is complete. The continual flow of money and the increasing demand for silk and cotton in two economic regions in Japan pushed people to build factories in both regions and to produce ever more. This is what transformed Japan from an agricultural economy into a light industrial economy.

No one created this loop intentionally. There was no master plan for Japan's light industrialization. Japan's case was a haphazard, organic evolution that had many potential pitfalls. In hindsight, it becomes clear that this was possible because after the 1870s, Japan was no longer tied to European economic trade, which insisted that Asians not have a large positive balance in trade. The second key factor enabling the evolution was the U.S. market. In order to satisfy its own internal demand for silk cloth after the 1880s, the Americans bought immense quantities of Japanese raw silk, while ignoring the large imbalance in trade.[15] This demand led to an increasing cycle of accumulation that took place in the rural countryside of eastern Japan where factories eventually emerged to exploit the availability of both the raw materials (mulberry leaves, silkworm eggs, and cocoons) and labor nearby. The wealth was, to be sure, partly concentrated in the great merchant houses, partly consumed in imported consumables such as sugar, but it was also directed to the consumption of cotton cloth. In the 1880s, as the traditionally "advanced" region in western Japan near Osaka recovered from the loss of its cotton growing industry, Osaka began to industrialize by importing raw cotton from India and manufacturing cotton cloth to meet the demand in eastern Japan. Eventually, the cotton manufacturers in western Japan won the battle against imported cotton yarn and further industrialized the region.

Japan exported raw silk and practiced import substitution of cotton cloth on its path to industrialization in the late nineteenth century. This path to industrialization was similar to British or American industrialization in that it was led first and foremost by light industry. British industrialization with cotton goods started because Britain had a mercantilist policy to replace Indian cotton cloths in the eighteenth century. American industrialization took off with high tariffs in the mid-nineteenth century to counter British factory-made cotton cloth and replace it with its own domestic textiles. Import substitution led to successes in the past. Looking back through Japanese history, Japan practiced its own form of import substitution starting in the eighteenth century under Ogiwara Shigehide and Arai Hakuseki. Under their policies, Japan created vibrant domestic silk and cotton industries by the early nineteenth century. In the late nineteenth century, the legacy of these two industries led to eastern Japan specializing in silk and western Japan specializing in cotton, complementing each other and propelling Japanese industrialization.

This is a point worth emphasizing: east and west complemented each other. The virtuous cycle in eastern Japan was enough to transform the lives of the people of the Yokohama region and perhaps even eastern Japan, but the raw silk exports did not impact the lives of the people in western Japan as much. If cotton cloth continued to be imported from overseas, Japan could have turned into a country with two radically different economic regions like northern and southern Italy. But that did not happen. Raw cotton was imported to Kobe and Osaka, where it was spun and turned into cotton yarn, then factories in Osaka and Aichi prefectures took the cotton yarn to produce cotton cloth and sold it in eastern Japan.

To complicate matters further, after the first Sino-Japanese War (1894–1895), the Meiji government decided to industrialize northern Kyushu by building Yawata Steel Works. With this an industrial belt that linked Tokyo, Yokohama, Nagoya, Osaka, Kobe, and northern Kyushu would form. This is the core of what would eventually become the Pacific Belt, or the Pacific Industrial Zone. The price to be paid for this radical restructuring of the economic geography of Japan was that what once were prosperous regions on the Japan Sea side of the archipelago were now reduced to the periphery of a new Japanese economic order as providers of labor, energy, and materials.[16] People on the Japan Sea side of the archipelago would have to wait until Prime Minister Tanaka Kakuei proposed the Japanese Archipelago Restructuring Plan in 1972 to extend the bullet trains and build other infrastructures to connect all of Japan.[17]

This book's hypothesis argues that an analysis that captures within its scope the regional, national, international, and global connections must be used to properly understand the economic development of Japan. Japan's story is important because it can serve as another example for other countries. Many countries have followed Britain's first industrialization. Their many paths show that seeking the causes of the initial industrialization is perhaps less important than seeking the causes of the various other successes and failures. Examining the *how* of development to illuminate particular historical experiences should be emphasized more when asking the question first asked by Adam Smith: "why are some countries wealthy?"

This study examined how silk transformed eastern Japan during the second half of the nineteenth century. Its stated purpose in the introduction, to examine the creation of this network, has been fulfilled through the six main chapters. Chapters 1 and 2 examined the economic geography of early modern Japan and documented how some members of the shogunate actually wanted to open trade with the West to strengthen the power of the shogun and to reorient foreign trade around Edo. Their grand design was to strengthen the economic position of eastern Japan. Chapters 3, 4, and 5 demonstrate how merchants linked various parts of eastern Japan with Yokohama, the newly opened port. Hampered by fraud and cheating, some relied on domains for this process and others relied on no political authorities to create this new commercial network in eastern Japan. Chapter 6 described how the producers in the countryside then began to connect with their buyers in the West. Through luck, hard work, and the support of Japanese consuls, the merchants and producers of eastern Japan won the American raw silk market in the 1880s. Eastern Japan would continue to export raw silk as its most valuable export item until World War II and help the Japanese economy grow.

In analyzing the impact of the silk industry, this study proposes a model of economic and industrial development that focuses on the flow of goods and money. This is not a standard neoclassical approach to economic analysis. It is closer to economic geography and provides explanations about how and why the economic ties formed. This approach invites further research into the rural industries of eastern Japan, the development of the Kansai economic region, the links between Kantō and Kansai regions, the links between Japan and the world, and more comparative studies about events in Europe, America, China, and India. The threads of commerce weave the globe together.

NOTES

1. This trade is the start of capitalism. Like socialism, capitalism is a broad term that encompasses many forms. Mercantilism, slavery in the antebellum South, crony capitalism, and free market capitalism are all different forms of capitalism. What they share is the simple idea that "greed is good." Making this idea the central tenet in a society is a radical departure from the norm in most parts of the world, including the West. Before the advent of Atlantic triangular trade and the acceptance of the use of slaves to make money, the West was a Christian world. In this Christian society, or Christendom, slaves captured by Muslim raiders were freed. Life was not about making money, but rather about living according to the Beatitudes in the New Testament. In this worldview the poor and weak were supposed to inherit the Kingdom of Heaven, not the rich and powerful. Trade also existed in the Middle East and throughout the Indian Ocean, stretching to Southeast Asia. This trade was dominated by Muslim traders. But these traders could not change their society to make greed the most important value. In these Muslim societies, living according to the principles outlined in the Koran was the most important thing in life, and the Koran warns against greed. East Asia also had a robust trading culture, but greed did not become the principal factor for society. Instead Confucian and Buddhist values held the central positions in society. These two religious traditions also do not condone greed. The idea that "greed is good" is a truly radical idea.

2. One economic historian has downplayed the importance of silk exports. "Though the effect on foreign exchange earnings was undoubtedly great, because silk was a luxury consu-

mer good, its scale of production remained small. Furthermore, since production of silk relied in part on traditional technology, its ability to induce the development of other industries or to generate a surge of modern economic growth was limited." This book argues that the impact of the silk industry comes not only through the building of raw silk factories, but in a more widespread manner through the consumption of various goods. And in this, the high price that this luxury item commanded was helpful. Ippei Yamazawa, "Raw-Silk Exports and Japanese Economic Development," in *The Textile Industry and the Rise of the Japanese Economy*, ed. Michael Smitka (New York: Garland, 1998), 302–3.

3. The largest European demand for raw silk occurred in 1876, totaling approximately ¥11.8 million, and declined from then on. American demand in 1876 was ¥76,000 yen but in 1886 was ¥9.8 million. In 1896 it was ¥14 million (1896 was a bad year, in 1895 Japan exported ¥27.8 million, and in 1897 exported ¥32.3 million), and in 1906 the Americans bought ¥78.4 million worth of raw silk. YS: S II, 180–81.

4. In 1885, raw silk exports to the United States amounted to approximately ¥7.3 million, with total exports of approximately ¥36.1 million; raw silk exports to the United States accounted for 20.2 percent of total exports. In 1886, raw silk exports to the United States was ¥9.8 million as mentioned in note 3. Total Japanese exports amounted to ¥48 million, resulting in a share of 20.4 percent of total exports. In 1892 raw silk export to the United States was 25.1 percent of total exports. Even in1896, a bad year, it still amounted to 12.1 percent of total exports. YS: S II, 32, 181

5. Yomiuri shimbunsha Maebashi shikyoku (ed.), *Kinu no saihakken* (Maebashi: Kankodō, 1969), 7.

6. Yanagita Kunio, *Meiji Taishōshi: Sesou hen* (Tokyo: Heibonsha, 1967), 57.

7. YS: S II, 36, 52, 246–47.

8. YS: S II, 106, 122.

9. In fact, the ¥3.6 million import of gray shirting (the largest category in cotton cloth imports) in 1874 was not surpassed until the ¥4.1 million import of 1896. Total imports of cotton tissues increased in the first decade of the twentieth century, but it was temporary. YS: S II, 40, 58, 273.

10. YS: S II, 57, 68, 130. The raw cotton came from India, the United States, and China. YS: S II, 263–65.

11. If anything, Japan would have a slight negative balance of trade until World War I. YS: S II, 33, 68.

12. Cotton yarn imports declined after 1889. Except for 1896, Japan would not import more than ¥6 million worth of cotton yarn after 1889. Total cotton cloth (labeled cotton tissues) imports would hit their peak in 1905 at ¥9.1 million and would decline thereafter. Since cotton cloth exports did not become a major factor until after 1917, the years from 1889 to 1917 were the period when the domestic cotton industry saturated the domestic market. YS: S II, 21, 130, 132.

13. India was the largest exporter of raw cotton to Japan. The second largest source of raw cotton was America. So there was also a smaller loop of money flow between the United States and Japan. YS: S II, 263–66.

14. Inflation has made this number seem small, but this is roughly equivalent to £2.77 trillion, or more than $4 trillion in today's money. Dietmar Rothermund, *An Economic History of India* (London: Routledge, 1988), 37. Historical inflation calculator from www.thisismoney.co.uk.

15. The United States had no choice. There was no domestic raw silk industry in America.

16. Furumaya Tadao, *Uranihon* (Tokyo: Iwanami, 1997).

17. The Tōhoku bullet train completed its project in 2010, the Kyushu bullet train completed its project in 2011, the Hokuriku bullet train completed its project in 2015, and the Hokkaido bullet train finally made its connecting service to Sapporo in 2016.

Appendix A

Japan's Exports and Imports since 1860

Year	*Total Exports*	*Total Imports*	*Exports-Imports*
1860	3,954,299	945,714	3,008,585
1861	2,682,952	1,494,315	1,188,637
1862	6,305,128	3,074,231	3,230,897
1863	10,554,022	3,701,089	6,852,933
1864	8,997,484	5,553,594	3,443,890
1865	17,467,728	13,153,024	4,314,704
1866	8,537,850		
1867	9,708,907	14,908,785	-5,199,878
1868	20,435,333	15,000,871	5,434,462
1869	11,485,645	17,356,932	-5,871,287
1870	15,143,246	31,120,641	-15,977,395
1871	19,184,805	17,745,605	1,439,200
1872	24,294,532	26,188,441	-1,893,909
1873	20,660,994	27,443,368	-6,782,374
1874	20,164,585	24,226,629	-4,062,044
1875	17,917,845	28,174,194	-10,256,349
1876	27,578,851	23,969,004	3,609,847
1877	22,866,708	25,900,541	-3,033,833
1878	26,259,419	33,334,392	-7,074,973
1879	27,372,976	32,603,838	-5,230,862
1880	27,419,629	36,622,243	-9,202,614
1881	30,326,607	31,032,742	-706,135
1882	37,235,775	29,168,041	8,067,734
1883	35,709,066	27,848,992	7,860,074
1884	33,076,839	29,381,678	3,695,161
1885	36,108,886	29,345,379	6,763,507
1886	47,997,956	32,099,748	15,898,208
1887	51,547,407	44,276,327	7,271,080
1888	64,891,682	65,416,234	-524,552
1889	69,306,893	66,041,584	3,265,309
1890	55,791,846	81,670,354	-25,878,508
1891	78,738,053	62,880,670	15,857,383
1892	90,404,735	71,276,942	19,127,793
1893	88,950,014	88,187,628	762,386

Year	Total Exports	Total Imports	Exports-Imports
1894	112,171,175	117,371,361	-5,200,186
1895	134,991,029	129,083,297	5,907,732
1896	116,575,578	171,459,555	-54,883,977
1897	161,459,311	219,155,356	-57,696,045
1898	162,903,212	277,270,728	-114,367,516
1899	212,952,136	220,050,983	-7,098,847
1900	200,178,993	286,588,420	-86,409,427
1910	455,091,860	463,482,735	-8,390,875
1920	1,915,959,341	2,326,585,702	-410,626,361
1930	1,434,644,634	1,542,094,095	-107,449,461
1940	3,639,064,479	3,438,470,035	200,594,444

Records for 1866 are partial. Mexican dollars until 1884. Yen from 1885. After 1873 Mexican dollars and yen are effectively equivalent.
Source: For exports between 1860 and 1967: Yokohama-shi (ed.), *Yokohama shishi*, vol. 2 (Yokohama: Yūrindō, 1959), 370–75, 505, 512, 516, 519. Henceforth abbreviated as YS, II. *Yokohama shishi: Shiryōhen*, vol. 2 will be abbreviated as YS: S, II. For exports between 1868 and 1940: YS: S, II, 3, 5, 7, 9, 10, 16–21, 33. For imports between 1860 and 1867: YS, II, 388–93, 527, 530, 534, 537. For imports between 1868 and 1940: YS: S, II, 49, 68.

Appendix B

Exports in Silk Goods and Tea, with Total Exports

Year	*Total Exports*	*Raw Silk*	*Silk Tissues*	*Cocoon*	*Silkworm Eggs*	*Tea*
1860	3,954,299	2,594,563				308,452
1861	2,682,952	1,831,935				448,437
1862	6,305,128	5,422,372				567,080
1863	10,554,022	8,824,050				541,176
1864	8,997,484	6,162,240		24,100	200,000	465,324
1865	17,467,728	14,611,500		178,160	660,160	1,777,440
1866	8,537,850	7,035,750				1,502,100
1867	9,708,907	5,214,750			2,214,468	1,618,230
1868	20,435,333	9,948,800		123,040	4,199,138	3,084,580
1869	11,485,645	4,414,900		177,805	2,728,500	2,019,130
1870	15,143,246	4,580,800		111,310	3,473,150	3,848,231
1871	19,184,805	7,687,680		41,127	2,184,688	4,651,292
1872	24,294,532	7,178,500		150,280	1,963,159	5,445,438
1873	20,660,994	7,050,656		253,998	3,032,459	4,401,160
1874	20,164,585	5,301,755		247,252	731,275	7,796,536
1875	17,917,845	5,424,916	23,646	254,222	474,921	6,915,692
1876	27,578,851	13,197,891	15,869	530,946	1,902,271	5,468,658
1877	22,866,708	9,626,931	10,015	260,270	346,998	4,409,320
1878	26,259,419	8,283,918	12,657	228,534	682,606	4,412,457
1879	27,372,976	9,734,534	3,294	460,294	582,623	7,445,489
1880	27,419,629	8,606,867		107,439	991,021	7,497,923

Year	*Total Exports*	*Raw Silk*	*Silk Tissues*	*Cocoon*	*Silkworm Eggs*	*Tea*
1881	30,326,607	10,647,310	9,749	447,093	311,140	7,020,859
1882	37,235,775	16,232,150	24,355	499,893	122,486	7,029,716
1883	35,709,066	16,183,540	22,638	219,232	55,287	6,106,427
1884	33,076,839	11,005,672	12,418	255,592	40,708	5,817,736
1885	36,108,886	13,033,871	57,711	160,617	33,330	6,854,120
1886	47,997,956	17,321,361	74,598	421,657	3,950	7,723,320
1887	51,547,407	19,280,002	149,233	279,067	2,955	7,603,341
1888	64,891,682	25,916,860	267,617	242,610	649	6,124,816
1889	69,306,893	26,616,541	628,528	260,360	8,627	6,156,728
1890	55,791,846	13,859,338	1,181,344	148,007	8,436	6,326,680
1891	78,738,053	29,356,338	1,771,355	208,021	3,361	7,033,049
1892	90,404,735	36,269,743	4,459,697	320,803	3,790	7,525,315
1893	88,950,014	28,167,411	4,146,585	402,255	4,244	7,702,088
1894	112,171,175	39,353,155	8,489,033	227,572	1,515	7,930,286
1895	134,991,029	47,866,256	10,060,838	178,571	1,226	8,879,241
1896	116,575,578	28,830,601	7,438,673	50,771	406	6,372,328
1897	161,459,311	55,630,460	9,852,908	17,644	20	7,860,460
1898	162,903,212	42,047,411	12,786,657	32,079		8,215,664
1899	212,952,136	62,627,721	17,447,459			8,498,782
1900	200,178,993	44,657,028	18,603,654			9,035,819
1910	455,091,860	130,182,138	32,796,679	524,151		14,542,334

Year	*Total Exports*	*Raw Silk*	*Silk Tissues*	*Cocoon*	*Silkworm Eggs*	*Tea*
1920	1,915,959,341	382,221,798	158,416,012	2,373,953		19,828,296
1930	1,434,644,634	416,646,814	65,775,306	393,271		14,479,618
1940	3,639,064,479	446,060,422	37,698,509	134,871		57,977,630

Records for 1866 are partial. Mexican dollars until 1884. Yen from 1885. After 1873 Mexican dollars and yen are effectively equivalent. Silk piece goods until 1884; silk tissues after 1885.

Source: For exports between 1860 and 1967: Yokohama-shi (ed.), *Yokohama shishi*: vol. 2 (Yokohama: Yūrindō, 1959), 370–75, 505, 512, 516, 519. Henceforth abbreviated as YS, II. *Yokohama shishi: Shiryōhen*, vol. 2 will be abbreviated as YS: S, II. For exports between 1868 and 1940: YS: S, II, 3, 5, 7, 9, 10, 16–21, 33. For imports between 1860 and 1867: YS, II, 388–93, 527, 530, 534, 537. For imports between 1868 and 1940: YS: S, II, 49, 68.

Appendix C

Exports in Cotton Goods, Copper, and Rice, with Total Exports

Year	Raw Cotton	Cotton Yarn	Cotton Tissues	Copper	Rice	Total Exports
1860				209,248		3,954,299
1861				95,815		2,682,952
1862				77,588		6,305,128
1863	933,940					10,554,022
1864	1,792,000					8,997,484
1865	58,180					17,467,728
1866						8,537,850
1867						9,708,907
1868				608		20,435,333
1869				95,635		11,485,645
1870				461,093		15,143,246
1871				416,630		19,184,805
1872				1,353,545	1,610,937	24,294,532
1873			1,331	646,499	521,609	20,660,994
1874			5,191	554,863	833,590	20,164,585
1875	5,402		22,025	423,985	17,091	17,917,845
1876			8,814	289,708	810,760	27,578,851
1877			9,072	822,855	2,236,936	22,866,708
1878			10,307	862,897	4,117,486	26,259,419
1879			6,065	836,687	375,943	27,372,976
1880			2,384	473,860	210,405	27,419,629

Year	Raw Cotton	Cotton Yarn	Cotton Tissues	Copper	Rice	Total Exports
1881	31		175	605,849	261,735	30,326,607
1882			5,043	848,669	1,648,857	37,235,775
1883	35,841		48,676	735,502	1,000,940	35,709,066
1884			101,203	1,413,433	2,072,784	33,076,839
1885			177,998	1,859,738	766,759	36,108,886
1886			231,498	2,204,355	3,301,169	47,997,956
1887			170,639	2,069,393	2,255,113	51,547,407
1888			153,593	3,537,176	7,421,238	64,891,682
1889			147,035	2,901,777	7,434,653	69,306,893
1890			173,842	5,377,620	1,321,635	55,791,846
1891		7,872	243,358	4,909,497	6,213,331	78,738,053
1892		7,719	544,022	4,902,182	4,162,451	90,404,735
1893		59,175	1,109,543	4,600,878	5,001,157	88,950,014
1894		955,529	1,861,202	4,929,596	5,593,152	112,171,175
1895		1,034,478	2,315,940	5,188,844	7,207,345	134,991,029
1896		4,029,424	2,224,403	5,512,431	7,951,087	116,575,578
1897		13,490,196	2,512,375	5,823,723	6,141,217	161,459,311
1898		20,116,585	2,597,979	7,314,073	5,920,185	162,903,212
1899		28,521,438	3,910,483	11,523,017	10,282,011	212,952,136
1900		20,589,262	5,723,668	12,922,416	3,576,569	200,178,993
1910		45,346,964	20,462,535	21,176,194	5,900,477	455,091,860

Year	*Raw Cotton*	*Cotton Yarn*	*Cotton Tissues*	*Copper*	*Rice*	*Total Exports*
1920		152,393,931	334,966,026	12,721,336	5,902,514	1,915,959,341
1930		15,032,819	272,116,781	21,280,644	6,570,718	1,434,644,634
1940		57,975,942	399,137,536	11,182,565	7,026,480	3,639,064,479

Records for 1866 are partial. Mexican dollars until 1884. Yen from 1885. After 1873 Mexican dollars and yen are effectively equivalent. Cotton piece goods until 1884; cotton tissues after 1885.

Source: For exports between 1860 and 1967: Yokohama-shi (ed.), *Yokohama shishi*: vol. 2 (Yokohama: Yūrindō, 1959), 370–75, 505, 512, 516, 519. Henceforth abbreviated as YS, II. *Yokohama shishi: Shiryōhen*, vol. 2 will be abbreviated as YS: S, II. For exports between 1868 and 1940: YS: S, II, 3, 5, 7, 9, 10, 16–21, 33. For imports between 1860 and 1867: YS, II, 388–93, 527, 530, 534, 537. For imports between 1868 and 1940: YS: S, II, 49, 68.

Appendix D

Each Export Good As a Percentage of Total Exports

Year	*Raw Silk*	*Silk Tissues*	*Tea*	*Cotton Yarn*	*Cotton Tissues*	*Sum of These Five Goods*
1860	66%		8%			74%
1861	68%		17%			85%
1862	86%		9%			95%
1863	84%		5%			89%
1864	68%		5%			73%
1865	84%		10%			94%
1866	82%		18%			100%
1867	54%		17%			71%
1868	49%		15%			64%
1869	38%		18%			56%
1870	30%		25%			55%
1871	40%		24%			64%
1872	30%		22%			52%
1873	34%		21%		0%	55%
1874	26%		39%		0%	65%
1875	30%	0%	39%		0%	69%
1876	48%	0%	20%		0%	68%
1877	42%	0%	19%		0%	61%
1878	32%	0%	17%		0%	51%
1879	36%	0%	27%		0%	63%
1880	31%		27%		0%	58%
1881	35%	0%	23%		0%	58%
1882	44%	0%	19%		0%	63%
1883	45%	0%	17%		0%	62%
1884	33%	0%	18%		0%	51%
1885	36%	0%	19%		0%	55%
1886	36%	0%	16%		0%	52%
1887	37%	0%	15%		0%	52%
1888	40%	0%	9%		0%	49%
1889	38%	1%	9%		0%	48%
1890	25%	2%	11%		0%	38%

Year	*Raw Silk*	*Silk Tissues*	*Tea*	*Cotton Yarn*	*Cotton Tissues*	*Sum of These Five Goods*
1891	37%	2%	9%	0%	0%	48%
1892	40%	5%	8%	0%	1%	54%
1893	32%	5%	9%	0%	1%	47%
1894	35%	8%	7%	1%	2%	53%
1895	35%	7%	7%	1%	2%	52%
1896	25%	6%	5%	3%	2%	41%
1897	34%	6%	5%	8%	2%	55%
1898	26%	8%	5%	12%	2%	53%
1899	29%	8%	4%	13%	2%	56%
1900	22%	9%	5%	10%	3%	49%
1910	29%	7%	3%	10%	4%	53%
1920	20%	8%	1%	8%	17%	54%
1930	29%	5%	1%	1%	19%	55%
1940	12%	1%	2%	2%	11%	28%

Records for 1866 are partial. Silk piece goods until 1884; silk tissues after 1885. Cotton piece goods until 1884; cotton tissues after 1885.

Source: For exports between 1860 and 1967: Yokohama-shi (ed.), *Yokohama shishi*: vol. 2 (Yokohama: Yūrindō, 1959), 370–75, 505, 512, 516, 519. Henceforth abbreviated as YS, II. *Yokohama shishi: Shiryōhen*, vol. 2 will be abbreviated as YS: S, II. For exports between 1868 and 1940: YS: S, II, 3, 5, 7, 9, 10, 16–21, 33. For imports between 1860 and 1867: YS, II, 388–93, 527, 530, 534, 537. For imports between 1868 and 1940: YS: S, II, 49, 68.

Selected Bibliography

This bibliography is not a complete record of all the materials I have read over the years. However, it is a list that includes the works consulted in the making of this book. Japanese names are given in their traditional order with family names first and given names second, therefore they do not have commas between the names in the Japanese language section of the bibliography. Western names are given in their traditional order with given names first and family names last, and therefore they have commas between the names in the Western languages section of the bibliography.

JAPANESE LANGUAGE PRIMARY MATERIALS INCLUDING *SHIRYŌSHŪ* (COLLECTED DOCUMENTS)

Arai Hakuseki. *Oritaku shiba no ki*. Tokyo: Iwanami, 1999.

Fukuchi Gen'ichirō. *Bakumatsu seijika*. Tokyo: Heibonsha, 1989.

Fukuzawa Yukichi. *Bunmeiron no gairyaku*. 1875.

Gunma kenshi hensan iinkai, eds. *Gunma kenshi: Shiryōhen* XIII, *Kinsei* V; IX, *Kinsei* I; X, *Kinsei* II. Maebashi: Gunma ken, 1970s.

Hashimoto Gountei Gyokuransai Sadahide. *Yokohama kaikō kenbunshi*. Tokyo: Meicho kankōkai, 1967.

Ishii Mitsutarō and Tōkairin Shizuo, eds. *Yokohama dontaku*. 2 vols. Yokohama: Yūrindō, 1973. This book is a republication of *Yokohama bōeki shimpō*'s (*Yokohama Trade Newspaper*) fifty-year retrospective column titled "Kaikō sokumenshi" (Side Stories of the Open Port).

Ishii Takashi, ed. *Yokohama urikomishō Kōshūya monjo*. Yokohama: Yūrindō, 1984.

Kanagawa-ken toshokankyōkai kyōdoshiryō shūsei hensan iinkai, ed. *Mikan Yokohama kaikō shiryō*. Yokohama: Kanagawa-ken toshokankyōkai, 1960.

Katō Ryū, Sakata Yasuo, and Akiya Norio, eds. *Nichi-Bei kiito bōeki shiryō*, vol. 1: *Shiryōhen* 1. Tokyo: Kondō shuppansha, 1987.

Nihon shiseki kyōkai, eds. *Nihon shiseki kyōkai sōsho*, vol. 32: *Ōkubo Toshimichi monjo*, no. 5. Tokyo: Tokyo University Press, 1933, 1968.

Oda Kanshi. "Bukōsōshū kaireki nisshi." In *Nihon shomin seikatsu shiryōshūsei*, vol. 12: *sesō* 1. Tokyo: Sanyōsha, 1971.

Ōkurashō, ed. *Dainihon gaikoku bōeki nenpyō, Meiji 33*. Tokyo: Ōkurashō, 1990.
———, ed. *Meiji zenki zaisei keizaishiryō shūsei*, vol. 3: *Ōkurashō enkakushi*, no. 2. Tokyo: Kaizōsha, 1934.
Osaka-shi, ed. *Osaka shishi*, vol. 1, 2, 5. Osaka: Seibundō, 1979.
Shinji Yoshimoto, ed. *Kyūji shimonroku: Edo bakufu yakunin no shōgen*. 2 vols. Tokyo: Iwanami, 1986.
Tokyo daigaku shiryō hensanjo, ed. *Dainihon komonjo: Bakumatsu gaikoku kankei monjo*, vols. 14, 15, 16, 17, 18, 19, 20, 21. Tokyo: Tokyo University Press, 1930.
Tokyo-to, ed. *Tokyo shishikō: Shigaihen*, vol. 50. Tokyo: Tokyo-to, 1961.
Ueda-shi, ed. *Ueda shishi*. 2 vols. Tokyo: Shinano mainichi shimbunsha, 1975.
Wada Ei. *Tomioka nikki*. Tokyo: Chikuma shobō, 2014. First published in 1905.
Yokohama kaikō shiryōkan, ed. *Yoshimuraya K ō bei kankei shokan*. Yokohama: Yokohama kaikō shiryō fukyū kyōkai, 1989.
Yokohama kyōdo kenkyūkai, ed. *Yokoreki sōsho*, vol. 12: *Kurofune raikō to Yokohama*. Yokohama: Yokohama kyōdo kenkyūkai, 1993.
Yokohama-shi, ed. *Yokohama shishi*, vol. 2, 3.1. Yokohama: Yūrindō, 1959, 1961.
———. *Yokohama shishi: Shiryōhen 2 Nihon bōeki tōkei (zōteiban) 1868–1945 Tōkei hen*. Yokohama: Yūrindō, 1980.
Yoshimoto Tadasu. *A Peasant Sage of Japan: The Life and Work of Sontoku Ninomiya*. New York: Longmans, 1912. This is a translation of Tomita Kōkei's *Hōtokuki*.
Yuasa Masahiko, ed. *Shimamura santane gyōsha no yōkō nikki: Sakai-machishi shiryōshū*, vol. 4 *(Rekishihen)*. Sakai-machi, Gunma: Sakai-machi, 1988.

ENGLISH LANGUAGE PRIMARY MATERIALS

Alcock, Rutherford. *Capital of the Tycoon*. 2 vols. New York: Harper, 1863.
Annual Report of the Silk Association of America XIII–XXV. 1874, 1875, 1878, 1879, 1884, 1886.
Black, John R. *Young Japan: Yokohama and Yedo*. 2 vols. London: Trubner, 1881.
Department of Commerce, Bureau of Foreign and Domestic Commerce. *Daily Consular and Trade Reports*, vol. 1, nos. 1–75 (Washington DC: January, February, and March 1914), February 10, issue 34.
Hall, Francis. *Japan through American Eyes: The Journal of Francis Hall Kanagawa and Yokohama 1859–1866*, ed. F. G. Notehelfer. Princeton, NJ: Princeton University Press, 1992.
Hansard, Thomas. *Parliamentary Debates*, third series, vol. CLXXII, from 1 July 1863 to 28 July 1863. London: Cornelius Buck, 1863. Earl Grey on 10 July 1863.
Satow, Ernest M. *A Diplomat in Japan*. Philadelphia: J. B. Lippincott, 1921.
Wyckoff, William C. Report on the Silk Manufacturing Industry of the United States. In *Report on the Manufactures of the United States at the Tenth Census (June 1 1880)*. Washington, DC: Government Printing Office, 1883.

JAPANESE LANGUAGE SECONDARY WORKS

Araki Mikio. *Nihon sanshigyō hattatsu to sono kiban: Yōsan nōka keiei*. Kyoto: Mineruva shobō, 1996.
Chiba-ken naimubu. *Hotta Masayoshi*. Tokyo: Shōbundo, 1921.
Fujita Gorō. *Nihon kindai sangyō no seisei*. Tokyo: Nihon hyōronsha, 1948.
Fujita Satoru. *Mizuno Tadakuni: Seijikaikaku ni kaketa kinken rōjū*. Tokyo: Tōyō Keizai shimpōsha, 1994.
———. *Tempō no kaikaku*. Tokyo: Yoshikawa kōbunkan, 1989.
Furumaya Tadao. *Uranihon*. Tokyo: Iwanami, 1997.
Hagiwara Susumu. *Hono'o no kiitoshō: Nakaiya Jūbei*. Yokohama: Yūrindō, 1988.

Hamano Kiyoshi. *Kinsei Kyoto no rekishi jinkōgaku teki kenkyū*. Tokyo: Keio University Press, 2007.
Hattori Kazuma. "Meiji shoki ni okeru seiōjin no sanshigyōchitai shisatsu to sono eikyō." In Kantō gakuen Matsudaira kinen keizai bunka kenkyūjo, eds. *Tonegawa suikei chiiki no shakai to rōdō: Kantō gakuen Matsudaira kinen keizai bunka kenkyūjo sōsho*, vol. 2. Ōtashi, Gunma: Kantō gakuen Matsudaira kinen keizai bunka kenkyūjo, 1991.
Hattori Shisō. "Ishinshi hōhōjō no shomondai." *Rekishi kagaku* 2, no. 3 (1933).
Hayakawa Naose. *Honpō sanshigyō to Beikoku kengyō*. Tokyo: Meibundō, 1917.
———. *Kiito to sono bōeki*. Tokyo: Dōbunkan, 1922.
———. *Seishi keizaigaku*. Tokyo: Meibundō, 1927.
———. *Yōsan rōdō keizairon*. Tokyo: Dōbunkan, 1923.
Hayami Akira. *Rekishi jinkōgaku de mita Nihon*. Tokyo: Bungei shunjū, 2001.
Hayashi Reiko. *Edo tonya nakama no kenkyū*. Tokyo: Ochanomizu shobō, 1967.
Hayashi Reiko and Ōishi Shinzaburō. *Ryūtsū rettō no tanjō*. Tokyo: Kōdansha, 1995.
Hirano Masahiro. "Kiito urikomishō no seishigyō he no shinshutsu." Parts 1, 2. *Kaikō no hiroba* vol. 54, 55 (1996, 1997).
———. "Mogikei seishi—Shinshōsha no bunseki." *Yokohama kaikō shiryōkan kiyō* 15 (1997): 72–91.
Hirano Yasushi. *Kindai yōsangyō no hatten to kumiai seishi*. Tokyo: University of Tokyo Press, 1990.
Hosoi Wakizō. *Jokō aishi*. Tokyo: Kaizō, 1925.
Igawa Katsuhiko. *Kindai Nihon seishigyō to mayu seisan*. Tokyo: Tokyo keizai jōhō shuppan, 1998.
Iijima Chiaki. *Edo bakufu zaisei no kenkyū*. Tokyo: Yoshikawa Kōbunkan, 2004.
Ishii Kanji. *Nihon sanshigyōshi bunseki*. Tokyo: University of Tokyo Press, 1972.
Ishii Takashi. *Bakumatsu kaikōki keizaishi kenkyū*. Yokohama: Yūrindō, 1987.
Isoda Michifumi. *Bushi no kakeibo: "Kagahan gosanyōmono" no bakumatsu ishin*. Tokyo: Shinchōsha, 2003.
Itakura Kiyonobu. *Nihonshi saihakken: rikei no shiten kara*. Tokyo: Asahi shimbunsha, 1993.
Itō Yoshiichi. *Kinsei zaikataichi no kōzō*. Tokyo: Rinjinsha, 1967.
Katō Yūzō. *Bakumatsu gaikō to kaikoku*. Tokyo: Chikuma shobō, 2004.
———. *Igirisu to ajia: Kindaishi no genga*. Tokyo: Iwanami, 1980.
———. *Kurofune zengo no sekai*. Tokyo: Chikuma shobō, 1994.
Kimura Motoi. *Kinsei no mura*. Tokyo: Kyōikusha, 1980.
Kitō Hiroshi. *Jinkō kara yomu Nihon no rekishi*. Tokyo: Kōdansha, 2000.
Koizumi Katsuo. *Sanshi no chishiki to katsuyō*. Tokyo, 1998.
Kojima Keizō. *Edo no sangyō runessansu*. Tokyo: Chūkō shinsho, 1989.
Komatsu Shigeo. *Hatamoto no keizaigaku: Oniwaban Kawamura Nagatomi no todomeshū*. Tokyo: Shinchōsha, 1991.
Kondō Yasuo. *Chiunen koritsukoku no kenkyū*. Tokyo: Nōson gyoson bunka kyōkai, 1974.
Matsuoka Hideo. *Iwase Tadanari*. Tokyo: Chūkō shinsho, 1981.
Miyanaga Takashi. *Bakumatsu ijin sasshōroku*. Tokyo: Kadokawa, 1996.
Murai Atsushi. *Kanjō bugyō Ogiwara Shigehide no shōgai*. Tokyo: Shūeisha, 2007.
Nihon denshin denwa kōsha, ed. *Denshin denwa jigyōshi, bekkan*. Tokyo: Denki denshin kyōkai, 1960.
Nihon yūsen kabushiki kaisha, ed. *Nihon yūsen kabushiki kaisha 50nenshi*. Tokyo: 1935.
Nishikawa Takeomi. *Bakumatsu Meiji no kokusai shijō to Nihon: Kiito bōeki to Yokohama*. Tokyo: Yūzankaku, 1997.
———. *Edo naiwan no minato to ryūtsū*. Tokyo: Iwata shoten, 1993.
Noda Masaho et al. *Kanagawa no tetsudō, 1872–1996*. Tokyo: Nippon Keizai hyōronsha, 1996.
Ōishi Shinzaburō. *Edo jidai*. Tokyo: Chūōkōronsha, 1977.
———. *Shogun to sobayōnin no seiji*. Tokyo: Kōdansha, 1995.
Okazaki Tetsuji. *Edo no shijōkeizai*. Tokyo: Kōdansha, 1999.
Ono Takeo, ed. *Edo bukka jiten*. Tokyo: Tenbōsha, 1998.

Ootsuka Hideki. "Edo jidai ni okeru kaichū no rekishi to sono hyōka." Nihon ginko kinyū kenkyūjo, *Kinyū kenkyū* 18, no. 4 (September 1999): 81.
Ōuchi Hyōe, Tsuchiya Takao, eds. *Meiji zenki zaisei keizai shiryō shūsei*, vols. 2, 3. Tokyo: Kaizōsha, 1932, 1934.
Saitō Seiji. "Edo jidai no toshi jinkō." *Chiiki kaihatsu* 240 (September 1984): 48–63.
Saitō Yoshiyuki. *Utsumibune to bakuhansei shijō no kaitai*. Tokyo: Kashiwa shobō, 1994.
Sakatani Yoshio et al., eds. *Segai Inoue-kō den*, vol. 2. Tokyo: Naigai shoseki, 1933.
Sataki Yoshihiro. *Nihon no shirukurōdo: Tomioka seishijō to kinusangyō isangun*. Tokyo: Chūōkōronshinsha, 2007.
Satō Tsuneo and Ōishi Shinzaburō. *Hinnō shikan wo minaosu*. Tokyo: Kōdansha, 1995.
Sekiyama Naotarō. *Kinsei Nihon no jinkō kōzō*. Tokyo: Yoshikawa kōbunkan, 1958.
Shimada Saburō. *Kaikoku shimatsu: Bakumatsu ishin shiryō sōsho*. Tokyo: Jinbutsu ōraisha, 1968. Reprint of 1888 edition.
Shimazaki Tōson. *Yoakemae*. 4 vols. Tokyo: Shinchōsha, 1932, 1935.
Shiratori Kouji. *Inbanuma monogatari* (*Story of Lake Inba-numa*). Chiba: Committee for Lake Inba-numa Watershed Management and Chiba prefecture, 2014.
Takasaki keizai daigaku fuzoku sangyō kenkyūjo, ed. *Kindai Gunma no sanshigyō: Sangyō to seikatsu kara no shōsha*. Tokyo: Nihon Keizai hyōronsha, 1999.
Takizawa Takeo. *Nihon no kahei no rekishi*. Tokyo: Yoshikawa kōbunkan, 1996.
Teramoto Yasuhide. *Senzenki Nihon chagyōshi kenkyū*. Tokyo: Yūhikaku, 1999.
Tokutomi Iichiro. *Kinsei Nihon kokuminshi*, vol. 28; *Tempō kaikakuhen;* vol. 29; *Bakufu jitsuryoku shittsui jidai*, vol. 30; *Perī raikō izen no keisei*, vol. 31; *Perī raikō oyobi sono tōji*, vol. 32; *Kanagawa jōyaku teiketsu hen*, vol. 34; *Kōmei tennō shoki sesōhen*. Tokyo: Minyūsha, 1928, 1935.
Tomizawa Kazuhiro. *Kita Kantō chihōshi kenkyū: Kiito to hitobito no kurashi*. Tokyo: Nihon keizai hyōronsha, 2010.
Tsunoyama Sakae. *Cha no sekaishi*. Tokyo: Chūōkōronsha, 1980.
Tsurumi Yoshiyuki. *Namako no me*. Tokyo: Chikuma shobō, 1993.
Umeda Sadahiro. *Naze Tama wa Tokyo-to to nattaka*. Tachikawa, Tokyo: Keyaki shuppan, 1993.
Ushiki Yukio, ed. *Kaiko no mura no yōkō nikki: Jōshū santane gyōsha, Meiji shonen no Yōroppa taiken*. Tokyo: Heibonsha, 1995.
Usui Ryūichirō. *Kōhī ga mawari, sekai ga mawaru*. Tokyo: Chūōkōronsha, 1992.
Yagi Akio. *Nihon kindai seishigyō no seiritsu*. Tokyo: Ochanomizu shobō, 1960.
Yamada Moritarō. *Nihon shihonshugi bunseki*. Tokyo: Iwanami, 1934.
Yamada Takemaro et al. *Jōshū no shohan*. 2 vols. Maebashi: Jōge shimbunsha, 1981, 1982.
Yamaguchi Kazuo. "Meiji jidai no seishi kin'yū." *Keizaigaku ronshū* 28, no. 2 (1962): 1–45.
———. *Meiji zenki Keizai no bunseki*. Tokyo: Tokyo University Press, 1956.
———, ed. *Nihon sangyō kin'yūshi kenkyū: Seishi kin'yūhen*. Tokyo: Tokyo University Press, 1966.
Yamakawa Kikue. *Oboegaki, Bakumatsu no Mitohan*. Tokyo: Iwanami, 1991 reprint edition.
Yanagita Kunio. *Meiji Taishōshi: Sesou hen*. Tokyo: Heibonsha, 1967.
Yasumaru Yoshio. *Nihon no kindaika to minshū shisō*. Tokyo: Heibonsha, 1999. Originally published in 1974.
Yokohama kaikō shiryōkan, ed. *Yokohama gaikokujin kyoryūchi, zusetsu*. Yokohama: Yūrindō, 1998.
———, ed. *Yokohama jinbutsuden: Rekishi of irodotta 50 nin*. Yokohama: Kanagawa shimbun, 1995.
———, ed. *Yokohama shōnin to sono jidai*. Yokohama: Yūrindō, 1994.
Yokohama kaikō shiryōkan: Yokohama kyoryūchi kenkyūkai, ed. *Yokohama kyoryūchi to ibunka kōryū: 19seiki kōhan no kokusai toshi wo yomu*. Tokyo: Yamakawa, 1996.
Yomiuri shimbunsha Maebashi shikyoku, ed. *Kinu no saihakken*. Maebashi: Kankodō, 1969.
Zenkoku yōsan nōgyō kyōdō kumiai rengōkai shidōseisanbu sanshi no hikari, ed. *Zukai yōsan: gijutsu, shikumi ga yoku wakaru*. Tokyo: Zenkoku yōsan nōgyō kyōdō kumiai rengōkai shidōseisanbu sanshi no hikari, 1995.

WESTERN LANGUAGE SECONDARY WORKS

Amin, Abdul Amir. *British Interests in the Persian Gulf.* Leiden: E. J. Brill, 1967.

Auslin, Michael. *Negotiating with Imperialism: The Unequal Treaties and the Culture of Japanese Diplomacy*. Cambridge, MA: Harvard University Press, 2004.

Beasley, W. G. *Great Britain and the Opening of Japan, 1834–1858*. Sandgate, Folkestone, Kent: Japan Library, 1951.

Bellah, Robert. *Tokugawa Religion: The Values of Preindustrial Japan*. New York: Free Press, 1957.

Chamberlain, Basil Hall. *Japanese Things: Being Notes on Various Subjects Connected with Japan*. Rutland, VT: Charles E. Tuttle, 1971.

Chang, Richard T. *Justice of the Western Consular Courts in Nineteenth-Century Japan*. Westport, CT: Greenwood Press, 1984.

Cronon, William. *Nature's Metropolis: Chicago and the Great West*. New York: W. W. Norton, 1991.

Drixler, Fabian. *Mabiki: Infanticide and Population Growth in Eastern Japan, 1660–1950*. Berkeley: University of California Press, 2012.

Ericson, Steven J. "Japonica, Indica: Rice and Foreign Trade in Meiji Japan." *Journal of Japanese Studies* 41, no. 2 (2015): 332–33.

———. *The Sound of the Whistle: Railroads and the State in Meiji Japan*. Cambridge, MA: Harvard University Press, 1996.

Federico, Giovanni. *An Economic History of the Silk Industry, 1830–1930*. Cambridge: Cambridge University Press, 1997.

Frank, Andre G. *ReOrient: Global Economy in the Asian Age*. Berkeley: University of California Press, 1998.

Frost, Peter. *The Bakumatsu Currency Crisis*. Cambridge, MA: Harvard University Press, 1970.

Greif, Avner. "Contract Enforceability and Economic Institutions in Early Trade: The Maghribi Traders' Coalition." *American Economic Review* 83, no. 3 (June 1993): 525–48.

Griffis, William Elliot. *Townsend Harris: First American Envoy in Japan*. Boston: Houghton, Mifflin, 1895.

Hall, John Whitney. *Tanuma Okitsugu, 1719–1788: Forerunner of Modern Japan*. Cambridge, MA: Harvard University Press, 1955.

Hanley, Susan. "A High Standard of Living in Nineteenth-Century Japan: Fact or Fantasy?" *Journal of Economic History* 43 (March 1983): 183–92.

Harootunian, H. D. *Toward Restoration: The Growth of Political Consciousness in Tokugawa Japan*. Berkeley: University of California Press, 1991.

Hayami, Akira. "A Great Transformation: Social and Economic Change in Sixteenth and Seventeenth Century Japan." *Bonner Zeitschrift für Japanologie* 8 (1986).

Hayashi, Reiko. "Provisioning Edo in the Early Eighteenth Century: The Pricing Policies of the Shogunate and the Crisis of 1733." In *Edo and Paris: Urban Life and the State in the Early Modern Era*, ed. James McClain, John Merriman, and Ugawa Kaoru. Ithaca, NY: Cornell University Press, 1994.

Hellyer, Robert. "1874: Tea and Japan's New Trading Regime." In *Asia Inside Out: Trading Empires of the South China Coast, South Asia, and the Gulf Region*, vol. 1: *Critical Times*, ed. Helen Siu, Peter Perdue, and Eric Tagliacozzo. Cambridge, MA: Harvard University Press, 2015.

Hoare, James E. *Japan's Treaty Ports and Foreign Settlements: The Uninvited Guests, 1859–1899*. Folkestone, Kent: Japan Library, 1994.

Howell, David. *Capitalism from Within: Economy, Society, and the State in a Japanese Fishery*. Berkeley: University of California Press, 1995.

Hunter, Janet. *Women and the Labour Market in Japan's Industrializing Economy: The Textile Industry before the Pacific War*. London: Routledge, 2003.

Koschmann, J. Victor. *The Mito Ideology: Discourse, Reform and Insurrection in Late Tokugawa Japan, 1790–1864*. Berkeley: University of California Press, 1987.

Kurlansky, Mark. *Cod: A Biography of a Fish That Changed the World*. New York: Walker, 1997.

Lane-Poole, Stanley. *Life of Sir Harry Parkes*. Vol. 1, *Consul in China*. London: MacMillan, 1894.

Lockwood, William. *The Economic Development of Japan: Growth and Structural Change 1868–1938*. Princeton, NJ: Princeton University Press, 1954.

Margrave, Richard Dobson. "The Emigration of Silk Workers from England to the United States in the Nineteenth Century." PhD diss., London School of Economics and Political Science, 1981.

McCallion, Stephen W. "Trial and Error: The Model Filature at Tomioka." In *Managing Industrial Enterprise: Cases from Japan's Prewar Experience*, ed. William D. Wray. Cambridge, MA: Council on East Asian Studies, Harvard University, 1989.

McMaster, John. "Alcock and Harris: Foreign Diplomacy in Bakumatsu Japan." *Monumenta Nipponica* 22, no. 3 (1967): 321–29.

Nakai, Kate Wildman. *Shogunal Politics: Arai Hakuseki and the Premises of Tokugawa Rule*. Cambridge, MA: Harvard University Press, 1988.

Nakamura, Takafusa. *Economic Growth in Prewar Japan*. Translated by Robert A Feldman. New Haven, CT: Yale University Press, 1983.

Nakane, Chie, and Ōishi, Shinzaburō, eds. *Tokugawa Japan: The Social and Economic Antecedents of Modern Japan*. Translated by Conrad Totman. Tokyo: University of Tokyo Press, 1990.

Ohkura, Takehiko, and Shimbo, Hiroshi. "Tokugawa Monetary Policy in the Eighteenth and Nineteenth Centuries." *Explorations in Economic History* 15, no. 1 (January 1978): 101–24. The same essay is also available in Michael Smitka, ed., *Japanese Economic History 1600–1960: The Japanese Economy in the Tokugawa Era, 1600–1868* (New York: Routledge, 1998).

Okazaki, Tetsuji. "The Role of Merchant Coalitions in Pre-Modern Japanese Economic Development: An Historical Institutional Analysis." *Explorations in Economic History* 42 (2005): 184–201.

Ooms, Herman. *Charismatic Bureaucrat: A Political Biography of Matsudaira Sadanobu, 1758–1829*. Chicago: University of Chicago Press, 1975.

Parry, Clive, ed. "Treaty of Amity and Commerce between Japan and the United States." *The Consolidated Treaty Series*, vol. 119. London: Oceana, 1969.

Parthasarathi, Prasannan. *Why Europe Grew Rich and Asia Did Not: Global Economic Divergence, 1600–1850*. Cambridge: Cambridge University Press, 2011.

Pratt, Edward. *Japan's Protoindustrial Elite: The Economic Foundations of the Gono*. Cambridge, MA: Harvard University Press, 1999.

Reischauer, Haru Matsukata. *Samurai and Silk: A Japanese and American Heritage*. Cambridge, MA: Harvard University Press, 1986.

Rothermund, Dietmar. *An Economic History of India*. London: Routledge, 1988.

Singh, Abhay Kumar. *Modern World-System and Indian Proto-Industrialization: Bengal 1650–1800*, vol. 1. New Delhi: Northern Book Centre, 2006.

Smith, Thomas. *Agrarian Origins of Modern Japan*. Stanford, CA: Stanford University Press, 1959.

———. *Native Sources of Japanese Industrialization, 1750–1920*. Berkeley: University of California Press, 1988.

Statler, Oliver. *Shimoda Story*. Honolulu: University of Hawaii Press, 1969.

Toby, Ronald. *State and Diplomacy in Early Modern Japan: Asia in the Development of the Tokugawa Bakufu*. Stanford, CA: Stanford University Press, 1984.

Totman, Conrad. *Early Modern Japan*. Berkeley: University of California Press, 1993.

Tsurumi, E. Patricia. *Factory Girls: Women in the Thread Mills of Meiji Japan*. Princeton, NJ: Princeton University Press, 1990.

Vlastos, Stephen. *Peasant Protests and Uprisings in Tokugawa Japan*. Berkeley: University of California Press, 1986.

Wakabayashi, Bob Tadashi. *Anti-Foreignism and Western Learning in Early-Modern Japan: The* New Theses *of 1825*. London: Harvard University Press, 1991.

Wigen, Kären. *The Making of a Japanese Periphery, 1750–1920*. Berkeley: University of California Press, 1995.

Yamamura, Kozo. "Returns on Unification: Economic Growth in Japan, 1550–1650." In *Japan before Tokugawa: Political Consolidation and Economic Growth, 1500–1650*, ed. John W. Hall, Nagahara Keiji, and Kozo Yamamura. Princeton, NJ: Princeton University Press, 1981.

Yamazawa, Ippei. "Raw-Silk Exports and Japanese Economic Development." In *The Textile Industry and the Rise of the Japanese Economy*, ed. Michael Smitka. New York: Garland Publishing, 1998.

Zanier, Claudio. *Semai: Setaioli Italiani in Giappone (1861–1880) "interpretare e comunicare senza tradurre."* Padova: Coop. Libraria Editrice Università di Padova, 2006.

Index

About the Author

Yasuhiro Makimura is a historian. Born in Kitakyushu, Japan in 1971, he has lived in Japan, the United States, and the United Kingdom. He received his PhD from Columbia University. He has also received the Yokohama Association for International Communications and Exchanges Fellowship, the Japan Foundation Fellowship, the Heyman Center Fellowship, and the Japan Society for the Promotion of Science Fellowship. He is currently an associate professor of history teaching Japanese history, East Asian history, global history, and economic history at Iona College. He lives in New York.

www.ingramcontent.com/pod-product-compliance
Lightning Source LLC
Chambersburg PA
CBHW051219230926
51612CB00007B/31